From Virile Woman to WomanChrist

University of Pennsylvania Press
MIDDLE AGES SERIES
Edited by
Edward Peters
Henry Charles Lea Professor
of Medieval History
University of Pennsylvania

A listing of the available books
in the series appears at the
back of this volume

From Virile Woman to WomanChrist

Studies in Medieval Religion and Literature

Barbara Newman

University of Pennsylvania Press

Philadelphia

In Memoriam

JOHN BOSWELL

Non enim habemus hic manentem civitatem.

Chapters of this book have appeared in an earlier form in the following publications:
"Flaws in the Golden Bowl: Gender and Spiritual Formation in the Twelfth Century." *Traditio* 45. Copyright © 1990 by Fordham University Press. Reprinted with permission.
"Authority, Authenticity, and the Repression of Heloise." *Journal of Medieval and Renaissance Studies* 22.2. Copyright © 1992 by Duke University Press. Reprinted with permission.
"Renaissance Feminism and Esoteric Theology: The Case of Cornelius Agrippa." *Viator* 24. Copyright © 1993 by University of California Press. Reprinted with permission.

Cover: Eric Gill, "Nuptials of God." Wood engraving designed as an ordination card, 1922. Courtesy of the Board of Trustees, Victoria and Albert Museum, London.

Library of Congress Cataloging-in-Publication Data
Newman, Barbara, 1953–
   From virile woman to womanChrist : studies in medieval religion and literature / Barbara Newman.
      p.   cm. — (Middle Ages series)
   Includes bibliographical references and index.
   ISBN 0-8122-3273-9. — ISBN 0-8122-1545-1 (pbk.)
   1. Women in Christianity—History.   2. Women in literature—History.   3. Literature, Medieval—History and criticism.
4. Church history—Middle Ages, 600–1500.   5. Middle Ages—History.
I. Title.   II. Series.
BV639.W7N48   1995
274'.05–dc20   94-37704
                                                                        CIP

Contents

Illustrations

Introduction

The crowds of women standing by answered Jeremiah, "We will not listen to what you tell us in the name of the Lord. We intend to fulfill all the promises by which we have bound ourselves: we will burn sacrifices to the Queen of Heaven and pour drink-offerings to her as we used to do, we and our fathers, our kings and our princes, in the cities of Judah and in the streets of Jerusalem. We then had food in plenty and were content; no calamity touched us."—Jeremiah 44:15–17 (New English Bible)

On Sundays, in particular, she used to pay homage to Mary, Queen of Heaven. . . . She one time requested Our Lady herself to grant her a vision of her. And this she obtained. . . . she beheld her in a golden garment, having on her head a crown of twelve stars, and the moon beneath her feet, and a tablet in her hand, on which was written: "Daughters, be obedient to the law of the Mother."—*Life of the Blessed Aldobrandesca of Siena*[1]

The women were Mary of Magdala, Joanna, and Mary the mother of James, and they, with the other women, told the apostles [that Christ had risen]. But the story appeared to them to be nonsense, and they would not believe them.—Luke 24:10–11

Plus ça change, plus c'est la même chose. From the earliest years of Christianity, the Church has had a problem with women. Yet, age after age, women have flocked to the Church—not only as nominal or compulsory members, but as uncommonly fervent ones; not only as docile followers of their male teachers and directors, but as leaders, initiating movements of piety and charity that have all in due time been co-opted, formalized, and regulated by men. Despite the overwhelmingly masculine face that the Church presents to the world and to "her" own adherents, there has never been a time when women were absent, hence never a time when gender was not an issue. As for the Queen of Heaven, triumphant despite Jeremiah's rage, we might as well paraphrase St. Athanasius and admit that "there never was when She was not."

The essays in this volume look from various angles at some highly committed Christians who were women. They were nuns, beguines, recluses, tertiaries, "irregulars"; they were virgins, mothers, widows, and women who had lovers; their origins were noble or peasant or bourgeoise; they were highly learned or illiterate or anywhere in between; they were eulogized, canonized, persecuted, burnt. Some chose their lifeways with sovereign freedom or superb defiance; others, forced into roles they abhorred, did the best they could with the hands life dealt them. But none of them were ordinary, for all these women won the power of the word: they either wrote themselves—letters, memoirs, visions, poems—or inspired men to write for or about them. The essays that follow scrutinize these texts for the clues they hold about women's gender-specific dilemmas, choices, and ways of being Christian during the period from approximately 1100 through 1500.

All the essays take misogyny more or less for granted, noting its repercussions in women's lives without attempting to trace either its historical origins or its psychological roots. The complex of beliefs and practices surrounding female subordination, though infinitely variable, seems to constitute one of the few melancholy universals to be observed across the immense range of human cultures. Patriarchy did not originate with either the Greeks or the Hebrews, much less with their Christian heirs, even if its classical and biblical forms happen to be those best known to the inheritors of European civilization. The strength of misogynist taboos and patriarchal strictures should never be underestimated; their power to constrict human lives and psyches could be enormous. But for the student of medieval religion, the endless iteration of these clichés quickly fades into a kind of ground bass—always present, sometimes annoyingly loud, but easy to tune out if one is intent on the more interesting harmonies and discords that are woven above and around it.[2] Without the persistence of misogyny, there would of course be no "gender problem." Acknowledging the problem, this book concentrates on attempted solutions: the strategies that religious women, and some of their male advisers and admirers, crafted to avert their perennial fate of inferiority, insignificance, and silence. I use the word "strategy" with caution. It may, but need not always, imply conscious subversion or manipulation of gender roles. Individual women were capable of such action, then as now, but in a pre-feminist culture their adaptations were far more often improvised or oblique than deliberate and direct.

Although each of these essays is complete in itself, together they trace a gradual and ambiguous transition from an older gender strategy, already found in Platonic and Stoic thought, toward a newer one that evolved within Christendom and shows signs of outlasting it. In contemporary parlance we might call these the unisex ideal and the Goddess ideal. The ancient unisex ideal, given new vigor by the Enlightenment and the politics of classic liberalism, still provides a foundation—albeit an increasingly eroded one—for feminist thought and polity. Its byword is "equality"— the equality of souls before God or, in a secular framework, of rights before the law. The Goddess ideal, with its strong tinge of romanticism, is a religious version of so-called "difference feminism" and remains alive and well among Wiccans and ecofeminists. It claims for women not mere equality, much less identity, with the problematic male norm, but a set of alternative and ostensibly superior values. These two models are theoretically opposed, though often practically combined. Both continue to provide options for women, Christian or post-Christian, who seek to follow a spiritual vocation without falling afoul of biblical stumbling blocks like 1 Timothy 2:12: "I permit no woman to teach or to have authority over men; she is to keep silent."[3]

For medieval women, living in a world where such authoritative teachings could not be opposed head-on, these gender strategies furnished alternatives to mainstream femininity, that is, to silence. Both strategies were deeply though differently rooted in the structure of Christian thought, yet oblique enough to avoid direct and obvious threats to male dominance. The first, preferred by men of the patristic era and lingering throughout the middle ages, can take its name from the sources: it is the model of the *femina virilis* or virago. The second, which has many variants but no proper name, is the model chiefly explored in this book. It is not a succinct ideology so much as an experimental praxis, diversely and sporadically theorized: the possibility that women, qua women, could practice some form of the *imitatio Christi* with specifically feminine inflections and thereby attain a particularly exalted status in the realm of the spirit. For want of a better term, I will call this the womanChrist model.[4]

The virago ideal originates in the most radical, egalitarian strain to be found within New Testament Christianity—the idea that baptism abrogates all barriers of gender, class, and race, so that "there is neither Jew nor Greek, there is neither slave nor free, there is neither male nor female; for you are all one in Christ Jesus" (Galatians 3:28). Egalitarian rhetoric did not, of course, empty these categories of significance: they were far too heavily laden with psychic and social meaning to wither away. Egalitarian praxis barely survived beyond the immediate circle of Jesus and his friends, except in a few fiercely repressed and marginalized groups. Nevertheless, Paul's ringing liberationist manifesto did profoundly change the way Christians, if they so chose, could understand the most basic social categories. In the apostle's own churches, the baptismal declaration made possible a genuine transvaluation of values, a reciprocal and at least inwardly dramatic exchange of roles. Jewish Christians (including Paul himself) became "Greek" by renouncing ethnic "chosenness" and observance of the Law; Greek Christians became "Jewish" by agreeing to worship the Jewish God and accept the Jewish Scriptures as their sacred books. Christian slaves became "freedmen of Christ," while freeborn Christians became "Christ's slaves." Baptized women fleetingly gained—and fought tenaciously to retain—the rights of honorary men, while baptized men fleetingly submitted to the loss of status entailed by membership in a cult that many pagans saw as effeminate.

As is well known, this novel outlook issued in no widespread emancipation of slaves, Jews, or women. But despite the chasm between theory and practice, the theory had been perpetually inscribed in Holy Writ, where it lay in a state of dormancy and could be reactivated at any time. It should, perhaps, be more astonishing that revivals of such a radical and dangerous ideal occurred at all than that they occurred only rarely and partially. For women, the most important of these "revivals" took place in the monastic movement of the fourth century, a movement whose vast literary and institutional legacy outlasted its creators' expectations for the life of the world itself. Underlying the anthropology of the desert, in its varying forms, was a persistent angelism. The monk or nun, purified by fasting and illumined by prayer, learned to live as an "angel in the body," transcending both the defilement of sex and the limitations of gender to become a passionless, Spirit-filled, miracle-working source of life and holiness for Christians still mired in the flesh. The "virile woman" is a subset of the class "embodied angel": since female is to male as body is to spirit, the achievement of the sexless, angelic state is tantamount for her to becoming male.[5] Jerome states the position clearly: "As long as a woman is for birth and children, she is different from man as body is from soul. But when she wishes to serve Christ more than the world, then she will cease to be a woman, and will be called man."[6] Through chastity, the upward pull of grace could neutralize the earthbound gravity of the feminine.[7]

Hammered out by "the fathers"—the ascetic monks of the desert and the platonizing bishop-theologians of the fourth century—this ideology maintained its hold on clerics, and through them on religious women, until the Reformation. The intense religiosity of the late middle ages, in all its exuberance and grotesquerie, nearly overwhelmed this late antique stratum with layer upon layer of new devotions, but the overlay only obscured without effacing the original deposit. Indeed, the desert fathers enjoyed a new surge of popularity among such influential orders as the Cistercians and Carthusians, even as these monks promulgated their own very different brands of spirituality. In the super-saturated religious atmosphere of the thirteenth through fifteenth centuries, beliefs and practices that had developed in the most divergent milieux coalesced: the new often transmogrified the old, but little or nothing disappeared. As a result, traces of the virile woman ideal may surface even in texts where the predominant ideas of gender seem wholly incompatible with it, just as the most rapturous stigmatic or bridal mystic may appear in the stern garb of the earthly angel.

Even in the fourth century, however, the virago was not the only model of the holy woman. Despite its coherence within the largely Platonic and Stoic anthropology of monasticism, the model posed difficulties for both sexes. The emergence of a few "virile women" in no way undermined the entrenched belief in female inferiority. At best, it only lifted that stigma from an elite group of consecrated, usually wealthy, virgins and widows. Even for these women, given the stubborn persistence of female bodies and male libidos, gender only seemed to vanish. Their actual status, as witnessed by countless synodal canons, monastic rules, and exemplary tales, veered uneasily between "angelic" and "dangerously female, all the same." Clerical obsession with such topics as the veiling of virgins, cosmetics, claustration, transvestite nuns, and the peril of double monasteries serves warning that the "virile woman" topos, whatever its rhetorical value, functioned best in hagiography where the subject was safely dead. Living women, however savage their self-denial or forbidding their dress, forgot their sex at their peril.

If equality was a tenuous hope for even celibate women, the monastic construction of gender did offer a second option: a fragile, limited, paradoxical, yet real superiority. The consecrated woman was potentially *virago* but ideally, and often factually, *virgo* as well. Although didactic writers liked to pun on these labels as if they were functionally equivalent, their affective connotations diverged widely. The virago was an honorary male, aspiring to the unisex ideal, while the virgin aspired to a highly gendered ideal embodied in the Virgin Mary. Though more than female, she was neither less nor other. But the meaning of virginity in her own eyes was not necessarily the same as its meaning for her male directors. The "virgin" symbol in the psychology of celibate men has been exhaustively analyzed.[8] In the dichotomy of Eve and Mary, demonized *femina* and idealized *virgo*, it is easy to discern the mechanisms of projection and splitting. Medieval writers themselves often remarked that the Virgin's Ave was but Eva inverted. But the same symbol held a more complex meaning for women themselves.

Whatever else virginity may have meant, it conferred both status and freedom. A young girl did not need a pathological fear of sex to yearn for escape from the successive entrapments of womanhood: arranged marriage at puberty, a husband sometimes old enough to be her father, the likelihood of physical and verbal abuse, the legal and economic constraints of wifehood, the long series of inescapable, often life-threatening pregnancies. As an alternative to matrimony under such conditions, the rigors of poverty, chastity, and obedience in a convent might easily be preferred, especially by women with intellectual, spiritual, or administrative gifts. Materially, the nun might be no less comfortable than a married woman of her class and station; and since obedience was in any case her destiny as a female, she might choose the fairly predictable demands of an abbess and a rule over the whims of a husband. Moreover, women with a talent for sublimation need not even give up their eroticism. Beginning in the twelfth century and increasingly thereafter, the brides of Christ were not only allowed but encouraged to engage in a rich, imaginative playing-out of their privileged relationship with God. This bridal status, in turn, gave them an added cachet in the male imagination. As Abelard wrote to Heloise, she began to outrank him on the day she became the bride of his lord while he remained a mere servant.

Virginity, then, was the first and most consistent means by which a religious woman might not only equal but surpass her brethren. But it was not the only means. In my work on Hildegard of Bingen, I argued that although some of her correspondents explained her charismatic leadership through the "virile woman" topos, Hildegard herself ignored this model. Instead of seeing herself as masculine, she developed a paradoxical self-image combining two different versions of the feminine: the "weak woman" (whom God had chosen to shame strong men) and the exalted virgin. Hildegard's ideal of feminine chastity united *virginitas* with *viriditas*, the gracious fertility that bloomed in both flesh and spirit. Far from remaining abstract and bloodless, this ideal was embodied in the Virgin Mary and each individual virgin, but also in diverse instantiations of the "queen of heaven"—the cosmic Ecclesia, the feminine Virtues, the divine figures of Wisdom and Charity. Such a powerfully articulated theology of the feminine furnished her nuns with a religious ideal that did away with female inferiority while retaining the structure of an impeccably orthodox piety. At the same time, the model of the "weak woman" as a vessel of prophecy enabled the abbess to perform such quintessentially masculine acts as preaching, teaching, and writing without overtly threatening the ideology of male dominance.[9]

Few religious women were able to match Hildegard's versatility and success. Not only did she possess uncommon gifts of mind and spirit; she was also the beneficiary of unusually favorable circumstances, including the support of such powerful men as Bernard of Clairvaux and his protégé, Pope Eugene III. During Hildegard's lifetime, long-standing alliances and family ties between the German nobility and the clerical hierarchy made life difficult for reformers in Rome. But these ties also eased the path to authority and respectability for abbesses like Hildegard, who were themselves noble and usually had brothers, cousins, and nephews in high places, in both secular and ecclesiastical office. Most of the women treated in this book were less fortunate. Unlike Hildegard, many encountered opposition from their families or found themselves thwarted by obstacles ranging from motherhood to suspicions of heresy. Nevertheless, they forged their own paths to holiness, seldom accepting either the misogynist denigration of their sex or the prospect of honorary maleness at face value. Instead, turning acknowledged weakness into a sometimes terrifying strength, they invented new ways of being women precisely because they tried to be Christians first.

The first and last chapters in this volume deal with men's attitudes toward the virgin, the virile woman, and the womanChrist ideal, beginning with Abelard in the twelfth century and ending with Cornelius Agrippa in the sixteenth. These two men would hardly have seen eye to eye, and my reasons for pairing them may be less than obvious. Yet both thinkers could be characterized as progressives or even radicals in their day; both pioneered new and intensely controversial methods of theologizing; and both had stormy careers fraught with unhappiness and scandal. Each embodied the contradictory trends of an age in his own person: Abelard was both disputatious *magister* and fervent (if unsuccessful) Benedictine abbot, while Agrippa was at once Catholic and evangelical, occultist and skeptic. Not surprisingly, then, when these intellectual firebrands addressed the "woman problem" in Christianity, both created new paradigms that still have power to startle, for they show us the furthest bounds attainable by proto-feminist thought in their respective eras.

Yet each thinker, true to his times, holds conflicting elements in solution without resolution. Abelard, in his corpus of writings for Heloise, denies the significance of gender and affirms the virile woman ideal; yet at the same time he manages to assert both the superiority of religious women (qua brides of Christ) and their need for subordination to a male superior. Agrippa, in his playful but astonishing treatise "On the Nobility and Superiority of the Female Sex," spices a refurbished virago ideal with an esoteric case for the superiority of women per se, including the outrageous theory that Christ was incarnate as a man because, in humility, he chose to assume the inferior masculine sex instead of the nobler feminine. These two pieces, spanning the distance between the virile woman of 1130 and the hypothetical womanChrist of 1530, bracket five chapters on the experience of religious women themselves.

"Flaws in the Golden Bowl" uses that Jamesian artifact as a trope for the twelfth-century religious woman's precarious status. Golden in her chastity, a pure vessel of heavenly grace, she was nonetheless suspect. For beneath the gilt was there not a fragile feminine body, a glass deeply flawed with the fissures of her sex? This chapter places Abelard's monastic writings in the context of a wide range of formative literature for monks, nuns, and solitaries. Seldom read nowadays but deeply influential in their time, these texts usually represent the angelic life as a gender-neutral ideal, but in their concentration on virginity, the writings for women betray an emphasis that remains gender-specific. In particular, their accent on chastity as the essence of women's consecration leads the writers to promote a form of piety that is self-contained rather than social, static rather than dynamic. These tendencies contrast sharply with twelfth-century formative writing for monks, which deals extensively with friendship, community, and the stages of spiritual progress.

Religious women not only provided a captive audience for such texts but actively solicited them, if the writers' protestations are to be believed. Nevertheless, the life women lived was not necessarily the life their male associates wished or imagined for them. In spite of warnings about imperiled chastity, devout women formed intimate friendships with people of both sexes, and they developed their own (frequently nonlinear) theories of spiritual growth and development. For many nuns, virginity remained a central value and defilement a haunting fear. But as women who were not virgins were increasingly drawn to the religious life, they needed to forge a Christian identity that did not depend on the almost magical status ascribed to the inviolate female body. While the virginal Queen of Heaven was honored as bride and mother of God, the ordinary non-virgin wife and mother ranked among "the least of these" in the kingdom of heaven— if the arbiters of grace deigned to admit her at all. "Bride" and "mother" were potent symbols of spiritual experience as long as they remained metaphorical, but women who had enacted these roles in the flesh had to find tortuous routes indeed if they wished to seek holiness.

"Authority, Authenticity, and the Repression of Heloise" looks at an abbess whose chief claim to fame was not chastity but erotic passion. The young Heloise notoriously rejected the conventional feminine roles of virgin and wife, embracing the masculine ideal of the Philosopher—a version of the earthly angel—for herself as well as for Abelard. But neither did she wish to become a virile woman. Despite her objections to marriage, it was not chastity that she preferred to it: she defiantly and tragically hoped to sustain both the ascetic life of learning and the intensity of her love affair. The mature Heloise, abbess in spite of herself, was too keenly aware of her sex and gender to accept the standard model of neutrality, even when it was proposed to her by Abelard. Unwilling or unable to adopt his poetics of castration, she persevered in her own discourse of desire—but with a difference. My reading of Heloise interprets her as a mystic manquée: the first in a long series of religious women who expressed their love in the language of disinterested passion and absolute self-surrender. Like the beguines and *beatae* of a later generation, Heloise perfected an erotic style that was at once abject and proudly, artfully self-assured. Her difference, of course, lay in the fact that her desire was directed not to Christ but to an earthly man, a crime that made it unacceptable even to him.

Ironically, this woman who virtually defined femininity for a long line of sentimental and romantic writers has been misread, in these latter days, as a bizarre parody of the *femina virilis*. Although there is no convincing evidence that Heloise's letters are anything other than genuine, there persists a stubborn suspicion that they were forged, the chief suspect being Abelard himself—the godly ventriloquist behind the seductive feminine mask. I present both historical and textual evidence to refute this hypothesis, arguing that it is founded in a priori and largely unexamined assumptions about what a religious woman could or could not have written. Heloise's concerns about spiritual authority and sexual repression, I maintain, are crucial to understanding not only her life and letters, but also the debate about their authenticity. The same concerns that troubled Heloise herself have queered both the medieval poetic appropriation and the modern critical reception of her texts.

Casual readers of the correspondence may barely recall that the famous lovers had a son, Astralabe, who was raised by Abelard's sister in Brittany. Among the numerous roles that Heloise played, "mother" is scarcely the first that comes to mind. Yet her very silence about this abandoned child, who had so little to do with either of his parents, bears eloquent witness to her dilemma. Motherhood in the middle ages mixed as uneasily with monastic profession as it mixes with women's professions to this day. In "Crueel Corage," I examine a group of saints' lives in which mothers, normally young widows, win praise for abandoning small children or even acquiescing in the children's deaths in order to take religious vows. As a particularly chilling form of renunciation, the theme of child sacrifice was inherited from classical and biblical antiquity. In the thirteenth and fourteenth centuries, however, we see a shift toward emphasis on the mother, rather than the father, as the sacrificing parent. Whereas patristic writers like Jerome had exalted the "maternal martyr" as a virile woman, medieval vitae more often represent her as a "mother of tears" whose renunciation of her children becomes a form of holy poverty, enabling her to identify with the grief of Mary at the Cross. Since neither childbearing nor childrearing was valued in the religious realm, it was the glamorized act of child sacrifice that enabled the holy mother to compensate for her lost virginity. In this oblation she followed a paradigm jointly established by the eternal Father and the virgin Mother, who sacrificed their Son for the common good.

My essay compares the maternal martyr of hagiography with her sister in romance—the Griselda-type heroine who sacrifices her children not for God, but for her husband. The child-sacrifice plot, surprisingly familiar in romance, idealizes the "cruel mother" as the perfectly submissive wife whose sacrifice no longer undermines the patriarchal family, as it does in saints' lives, but reinforces its values. In the distance between sacred and secular versions of the maternal martyr, we see on the plane of motherhood the same tension that Heloise manifested on the plane of erotic desire. It is the tension between two contrasting yet hauntingly similar forms of sacrifice—to give all for one's husband, or all for God? In either case, feminine holiness or virtue bears the mark of abjection, the appropriate status for those who had fallen from virginity and fallen short of virility. Yet through abjection itself, the holy woman could achieve a mystical identification with the abject Christ, the crucified God. In her weakness lay her only strength.

Composed in the early third century, *The Passion of St. Perpetua* is a woman's first-person prison diary ending with a third-person account of her martyrdom.[10] Like *The Diary of Anne Frank*, which it poignantly resembles, it bears witness to an earlier if far more circumscribed holocaust. Perpetua's narrative is also a paradigmatic showcase of the convergent themes in women's piety. Affluent, well-educated, recently married, Perpetua had ample resources and a resilient capacity to love; yet she bent her energies toward the martyr's crown as an Olympic athlete contends for the gold. A few days before her combat in the arena, she dreamed of her bout with wild beasts as a wrestling match in which she would physically become a man and only then win victory over the devil. But this virile woman was also a nursing mother whose greatest affliction was not fear of her own death, but grief for the infant she must leave behind. After prematurely weaning her child and rejecting her father's pleas to recant for the baby's sake, Perpetua gained a boon from God. Through prayers, tears, and visions she was allowed to ransom her little brother, who had died in childhood, from a place of torment and win his entrance to Paradise. In this way the maternal martyr, compelled to renounce her care for the living, found a new outlet for compassion and *pietas* by becoming an apostle to the dead.

In my chapter "On the Threshold of the Dead," I argue for this apostolate as a distinctive feature of medieval women's piety. The burgeoning interest in purgatory, from the mid-twelfth century onward, has been studied in such contexts as social stratification, popular beliefs about the afterlife, new ways of mapping the cosmos, and developments in the theology of penance. But it has seldom been viewed as a new sphere of influence for the ministerial gifts of women, as well as the legions of praying monks and chantry priests. Long before scholastic theologians finished systematizing the doctrine of purgatory, it caught the imagination of devout women, who found in their apostolate to the suffering dead a continuation of their traditional role as mourners and a channel for their gifts of visionary outreach and vicarious suffering. Through purgatorial piety, women could offer their prayers, tears, illnesses, and ascetic feats for the salvation of those they loved: daughter for parent, widow for husband, sister for religious sister. Such offerings were invisible but potent: they furnished women with yet another way to transform the pain of their lives, self-inflicted or otherwise, into free and constructive acts of love. The holy woman who mastered this alchemy of pain became a co-redeemer with Christ. Sharing his passion, she also shared in its redemptive sequel, the descent into hell.

This version of the womanChrist role inspired a remarkable motif in the theology of a few mystical women, namely a view of hell radically at odds with the orthodox stance on divine justice and eternal punishment. Defining herself through love as an "annihilated soul," a naught in the infinitude of God, the mystic measured her stature by her unbounded willingness to suffer, and she named the extreme bound of this boundlessness Hell. It was possible to desire God so purely that one could will, for God's sake, to abide forever in the darkness of his absence. To such a disinterested lover it seemed natural, as the beguine Hadewijch put it, "that hell should be the highest name of love." In a paradoxical *demande d'amour*, the mystic challenged God to damn her, and her alone, if he could thereby free the rest of the human race from hell. But since the creature's imperfect love could not surpass the Creator's infinite charity, God was expected to respond in kind by foregoing his acknowledged right to punish. In this way, the abjection of the female mystic could issue in a new charter of compassion for the most abject of the dead—damned souls themselves. While avoiding a direct affirmation of universalism, a number of women expressed doubts or palpable discomfort with the idea that God would condemn anyone to eternal fire.

Divine Love personified as a goddess—Caritas, Fine Amour, or Frau Minne—is an important figure in twelfth- and thirteenth-century mystical texts, especially those of women. The presence of this figure, a woman-Christ in the strict sense, should significantly alter the familiar construction of "bridal mysticism" as an erotic relation between the masculine God and a feminized soul. In *"La mystique courtoise,"* I explore the complicated dynamics of the mystical love affair as it was pursued by three literary beguines: Hadewijch, Mechthild of Magdeburg, and Marguerite Porete. Such women, threatening to churchmen because of their ambiguous position on the boundary between religious and secular, learned and lay, created their own sovereign state along the border. These *trobairitz* of God fused the monastic discourse of bridal mysticism with the dominant secular discourse of love—the *fine amour* of the troubadours and romance poets—to disclose new possibilities for the soul in its pursuit of divine *aventure*. In the *mystique courtoise* that is the hallmark of beguine literature, God could be either female or male, and so could God's lover. To name only a few possibilities, the beloved might be envisaged as the human Christ, as Lady

Love, as the Trinity, or as "abysmal fruition"; and the self could be exultant bride but also questing knight, suffering servant, or "annihilated soul."

Male and female, self and other, abjection and exaltation are in this language the multiple mirrors of an unbounded oneness, the reciprocal terms in a game of identity. Yet the game is not without rules. In its representation of the couples and communities that love defines, *la mystique courtoise* fruitfully if sometimes disturbingly transposes the social dynamics of *amour courtois*. But it does so in a realm of experience founded on the very qualities shut out of Love's secular garden—chastity, poverty, and self-denial pursued to the point of self-abnegation. Both the troubadour and the beguine take joy in the boundlessness of desire, the endless deferral of consummation. But if her language is haunted by echoes of his, her social experience is deliberately opposed: instead of acceptance and prestige she seeks humiliation and exile, and usually finds them.

In this quest, which is her version of the *apostolica vita* so prized in medieval piety, the beguine mystic both replicates and reverses the elitism inherent in courtly literature. "We few, we happy few"—the *edele herzen* who alone have refinement and taste sufficient for the purest love—are transmogrified into "we poor, abject, humiliated friends of God." But this elite fellowship of *fins amans* has not lost one iota of its specialness. The true lovers are still surrounded by a hostile, uncomprehending public of false lovers and spiritual peasants who will be forever excluded from their inner circle. In this construction of the divine love affair, the beguines make a sharp break with the older bridal mysticism cultivated by the Benedictines and Cistercians. However they might emphasize their own privileged status, the monks had always taken the loving soul as an emblem or microcosm of the real Bride of God, the community at large. For the mystical beguines, the community at large ("Holy Mother Church") is reduced to the status of a beggar maid, a retarded little sister who must have the constant support of God's true beloved in order to survive at all. This adversarial stance was a likely cause as well as an effect of the persecution beguines actually faced.

At the turn of the fourteenth century, heresy was indeed a burning matter. But when mysticism and its notoriously difficult language were at stake, neither the alleged heretics nor the orthodox faithful, much less modern historians and theologians, found it easy to determine what "orthodoxy" was. Even inquisitors couldn't always be sure. In 1310 Marguerite Porete was burnt at Paris for her book, *The Mirror of Simple Souls*—which nonetheless continued to be read anonymously, in four languages, in the most impeccable monastic houses. Ten years earlier, a woman named Guglielma had been exhumed from her grave in Milan and also burnt—although she had been venerated, since her death in 1281, as a perfectly orthodox miracle-working saint. Her cult had been promoted by Cistercian monks until, in 1300, an inquisitorial process turned up several dozen sectarians, both men and women, who confessed to worshiping Guglielma as the Holy Spirit incarnate. Members of the sect awaited their foundress's second coming to establish a new, purified Church in which the Pope and cardinals would be female, and in the meantime their current leader, Sister Maifreda, had already celebrated Mass and consecrated hosts over Guglielma's grave.

The Guglielmites have previously been studied as an example of thirteenth-century "enthusiasm." Like other heretical movements of their day, they looked forward to a new dispensation, an *ecclesia spiritualis* such as Joachim of Fiore had prophesied, in which the pristine life of Christ would be recapitulated and the age of apostolic purity renewed. In "WomanSpirit, Woman Pope," I examine the Guglielmites from a different perspective, showing that these sectarians were not only responding to the immediate political and ecclesiastical turmoil of their age, but also enacting an ancient form of "alternative Christianity," periodically revived and as often suppressed, that can be traced back to Jewish-Christian, Gnostic, and Montanist circles in the first centuries of the Common Era. This tradition linked millennial dreams and criticism of the established Church directly with female charismatic leadership and a feminine Holy Spirit. Considering the zeal with which it has been repressed, it has proved remarkably persistent.

Only twenty-eight years after the trial of the Guglielmites, a Franciscan tertiary called Na Prous Boneta was burnt in Carcassonne for similar testimony. She too believed herself to be the embodiment of the Holy Spirit, a modern analogue of the Virgin Mary, and the harbinger of a new, uncorrupted Church. By the sixteenth century the dissident longing for a womanChrist (or womanSpirit) had lost none of its urgency. The eccentric humanist Guillaume Postel once again renewed the grandiose claims of the Guglielmites, this time on behalf of his own spiritual mother, an Italian holy woman called "Mother Johanna," who—like Guglielma herself—may or may not have sown the seeds of her posthumous greatness. My chapter investigates the peculiar and recurrent linkage of apocalyptic designs with the notion of deity incarnate in a female body and served by feminine priests (with or without male colleagues). With the veneration of womanSpirit, we seem at last to have reached a version of female deity that, unlike the allegorical Wisdom of the twelfth century or the mystical Minne of the thirteenth, usually meant to contemporaries what it suggests today: a self-consciously subversive, even revolutionary stance.

Not all subversion, of course, deserves the name "revolution." The most outrageously subversive remarks may be offered, like some of the dicier propositions in Chaucer, "bitwixen game and ernest." In the case of Cornelius Agrippa's youthful *jeu d'esprit*, "On the Nobility and Superiority of the Female Sex," game and earnest are decidedly mixed. I have chosen to end with this text because it embodies a perfect equipoise—if not a flagrant contradiction—between the opposing ideals of gender equality ("virile woman") and female superiority ("womanChrist"). Agrippa's brief, scandalously popular tract shows the two gender strategies in a moment of convergence or amalgamation, on the way to forming a composite that we could recognizably call "feminist." Original though he was, the author took much of his ammunition from the medieval *querelle des femmes*, which was in the process of becoming the Renaissance *querelle des femmes*. This was a literary parlor game that seems to have been taken more seriously by its rare female participants (Christine de Pizan, "Jane Anger") than by the male rhetoricians who, like college debaters, could score points with equal facility on both sides. But Agrippa is a special case. In "Renaissance Feminism and Esoteric Theology," I argue that his most distinctive material comes from his unique and unstable blend of occultism with evangelical humanism. By using the ever-contested "woman question" as a showcase for his theological daring, the wily magus almost inadvertently came closer to making a serious feminist case than any of his precursors or successors in the genre.

Religion may be profitably studied by the theologian, the psychologist, or the cultural historian, and I have drawn on insights from all these disciplines. But this volume is subtitled "Studies in Medieval Religion and Literature" because my primary interest is in religious texts as such: verbal artifacts created by authors with specific if sometimes discordant intentions, within or between the boundaries of specific genres, for the needs of specific audiences. I have tried to attend, with varying emphases, to all these parameters of literary composition. When discussing the most accomplished and original writers, such as Heloise, Hadewijch, and Agrippa, I have focused on individual rhetorical strategies. Elsewhere the accent falls more on convention and audience, as in the case of highly conservative genres like formative literature and hagiography. As a way of highlighting the "literariness" of religious texts, I have also explored the constant interchange between religious and secular writing: the reception of Heloise by Jean de Meun and Chaucer, the appropriation of courtly lyric by the mystical beguines, the interplay of romance plots and saints' lives.

One further methodological assumption requires some comment. Against the grain of much contemporary writing, I persist in the belief that religious texts bear witness to religious experience, and I will make three assertions about that experience. None is in itself uncommon, but in these tendentious times, to maintain all three at once is a feat rarely attempted. First, I believe that religious experience is the experience of individual human subjects with a developed interiority—that is, with conscious and unconscious wishes, anxieties, projects, and beliefs regarding such perennial human concerns as birth and death, sexuality and gender— and that these profound layers of the psyche are powerfully affected by and expressed through religion. I must therefore oppose all forms of the currently fashionable constructivism that would reduce the private self to a blank page on which society inscribes its endless fascination with power.[11]

Second, I believe that religious experience occurs within complex and dynamic cultures that, no matter how static their prevailing ideologies, are always sites of struggle wherein competing forces—whether defined by class, gender, occupation, language, or other social markers—contend for their interests. If the self is not passively determined by society, neither is it isolated from society or from the many particular subgroups to which everyone, even the recluse sealed in her anchorhold, must inevitably belong. This proposition needs little defense, since it passes for self-evident among contemporary historians. But it entails the rejection of a naive, now happily rare psychohistory that would pathologize certain religious beliefs and behaviors—the experience of visions or trances, for example—even when they express dominant values of a historical society. I should add that I do not interpret gender or class struggle in any mechanistic way: the fact that competing subgroups often clashed does not mean they clashed always and everywhere. Knights and merchants, stewards and minstrels, scholastic theologians and beguines might substantially agree about vast areas of belief and practice; and where they differed, no individual's allegiance can be determined a priori without particular, relevant evidence.

Finally and most controversially, I believe that religious experience reveals the traces, however opaquely filtered, of a real and transcendent object. This is not to exclude the possibilities of self-deception and deliberate fraud, both common in medieval Christendom as in all societies where religion is a hegemonic force. Nor is it to deny what I have just asserted:

the presence of innumerable and rarely translucent filters, both psychologi-cal and social, that serve to veil the transcendent object. In fact, my essays deal explicitly with these "filters" and not with what lies beyond them. I write as a historian and literary critic, not as a theologian. Nevertheless, I assert this conviction to clarify my theoretical stance and to overthrow the last bastion of reductionism. To leave a space for transcendence means to allow for the possibility that, when historical subjects assert religious belief or experience as the motive of their actions, they may at times be telling the truth. It also means to accept the irreducibility of the phenomena, and thereby to reject all totalizing explanations. The complexity of human ex-perience, but especially experience of the divine, is such that no historical reconstruction can be more than partial and provisional. Where no trace of uncertainty remains, there bias and illusion hold triumphant sway.

These essays are offered as a contribution to the study of medieval Christianity, and more specifically of women's experience within that faith. As the foregoing remarks suggest, readers who are looking for "theory" in the sense of global interpretations of gender, culture, power, or reli-gion, will need to look elsewhere—although my book puts forth numerous theories, all of them partial, provisional, and subject to revision. In trac-ing a progress "from virile woman to womanChrist," I wish to emphasize that I am not presenting a new master narrative of the history of Chris-tianity, but highlighting one iridescent strand in a dense and intricate web. I have investigated phenomena like maternal martyrdom, doubts about hell, and the cultivation of female deity not because these represent a consen-sus piety of medieval women, but because they are anomalous enough to challenge more familiar perceptions, thus contributing to a more nuanced understanding of an extremely (if unwillingly) pluralistic Church.

I would like to dedicate this volume to John Boswell, teacher and scholar extraordinaire, whose learning, humane intelligence, and gener-osity have ever been an inspiration. It was his monumental work on aban-doned children that set the third chapter of this book in motion. My debts to two other great medievalists are too profound to be rehearsed. They are Caroline Walker Bynum, whose richly textured work inaugurated a para-digm shift in the study of religious women, and Peter Dronke, whose wide-ranging research and sophisticated readings have immeasurably enhanced the canon of medieval literature. For help with particular problems I thank Sharon Achinstein, Nicole Bériou, Alan Bernstein, Elizabeth A. R. Brown, Louisa Burnham, Madeline Caviness, Ray Clemens, Marcia Colish, David D'Avray, Rosemary Hale, Jeffrey Hamburger, Menachem Kellner, Robert

Lerner, Mary Martin McLaughlin, Jo Ann McNamara, Catherine Mooney, William Paden Jr., and James Poag. I am especially indebted to Nicholas Watson for a generous and stimulating exchange of texts and ideas. The Humanities Center of Northwestern University deserves thanks for the research grant that gave me leisure to complete this project. As always I am grateful to my best and friendliest critic, Richard Kieckhefer, for help and support of innumerable kinds. Last but never least, I thank MagnifiCat and Persephone, who suggest an appealing alternative to the often savage asceticism of my historical subjects.

1. Flaws in the Golden Bowl: Gender and Spiritual Formation in the Twelfth Century

In the early 1130s Peter Abelard received three letters from Heloise, once his mistress and wife, now his sister and daughter in religion. The first two made such painful reading that he must have thought twice before scanning the third, in which Heloise resolutely turned from the subject of tragic love to the minutiae of monastic observance. For romantic readers, the correspondence lapses from titillation into tedium with this epistle. But Abelard was no doubt immensely relieved. Laying aside her griefs, Heloise now wrote to him as abbess to abbot, asking for only two things: a treatise explaining "how the order of nuns began," and a rule for her daughters at the Paraclete. Although they were already observing the Benedictine Rule, she complained that as it "was clearly written for men alone, it can only be fully obeyed by men," because it is not fair to lay "the same yoke of monastic ordinance on the weaker sex as on the stronger."[1] Heloise went on to specify several concrete areas of concern, such as the use of meat and wine, the dangers of hospitality, the practice of manual labor, and the liturgical role assigned to the abbot. To underline her point, she even observed that the regulation underwear prescribed in the Benedictine Rule is not suitable for women because "the monthly purging of their superfluous humours must avoid such things."

Abelard responded with alacrity to Heloise's plea. But although he produced the desired rule, he began with an almost brusque dismissal of her chief concern. For his rule states at the outset that there is virtually no difference between monks and nuns: "as in name and profession of continence you are one with us, so nearly all our institutions are suitable for you."[2] And in reply to her conventional remarks about "the weaker sex," he wrote in his letter on the dignity of nuns that if "the female sex is weaker, their virtue is more perfect and more pleasing to God."[3] Moreover, most of this long epistle is devoted to proving that throughout the Bible and Christian history, women emerge as equal or superior to men. This exchange is the culmination of a debate that runs throughout the correspondence, in which Heloise appears repeatedly as a denigrator of her sex and Abelard as an almost courtly champion.[4] But the question raised by Heloise has a significance beyond the tangled web of her relations with Abelard. Reduced to essentials, that question is whether arrangements for men and women in the religious life were to be separate but equal, separate but unequal, or identical. Here if anywhere, one might expect to find "neither male nor female," as St. Paul had proclaimed (Gal. 3:28), for it was universally agreed that monks and nuns had embarked on that transcendent life in which they neither marry nor are given in marriage, but are like angels in heaven (Matt. 22:30).

Studies of monastic legislation have shown that in fact, whatever the theory might be, medieval women were far more restricted than men in their institutional practice of religion.[5] Their creativity, at least in the later middle ages, lay more in the realm of spirituality than in experiments with new structural forms,[6] and the one undeniable innovation they did make—the beguine movement—was notorious in its early days for a radical resistance to structure. But the saints, the mystical writers, and the religious gadflies—those who attracted the greatest acclaim and the most ferocious harassment—were by definition exceptional. These rare beings still receive a disproportionate share of attention, as they will continue to do in this book, for the simple reason that exceptions pique our curiosity more than the norms they challenge. But without a firm grasp of the norms, it is impossible to understand those who contest them. Either the extraordinary comes to seem ordinary for want of context, or else it arises as if from some deep reservoir of feminine Otherness, and not in response to concrete historical conditions. In this chapter, therefore, I will consider the ordinary religious woman—or rather, the religious woman as she emerges, alongside her male counterpart, from the pages of a vast and highly conventional literature written for her instruction. Heloise's question—is the nun's life gendered or gender-neutral?—can be addressed to a body of neglected texts that occupy a middle ground between monastic rules and mystical writings. To answer the question fairly, we must compare texts intended specifically for women with those addressed to male religious.

I will refer to these texts collectively as "the literature of formation." This term can be applied to a large and diffuse body of writing concerned with training professed religious in the spiritual life, the practice of virtues, and communal and private discipline. It includes a number of overlapping genres: instruction for novices; commentaries on religious rules; works of guidance for solitaries; letters of direction to individual monks, nuns, and recluses; and treatises dealing with aspects of spirituality and the common life.[7] I have examined forty-five texts in these genres composed between 1075 and 1225.[8] Of these works, all but two are male-authored. Eighteen were written by Benedictines, thirteen by Cistercians, eight by canons regular, five by secular clerks, and one by a Carthusian. Twenty-seven of them are addressed to men, fourteen to women, and four to a mixed audience. The texts come from England, Germany, and France; they span a period of a century and a half; and they range in length from two-page letters to lengthy volumes. Some were written for men or women living in community, others for hermits or anchoresses. Together, they reflect the striking variety of medieval religious life as well as the individual spirituality of their authors. At the same time, however, they testify to the inherently conservative character of religious tradition, appealing constantly as they do to the Scriptures and their commentaries, the desert fathers, and such authors as Jerome and Gregory the Great.

Of all the variables involved in representation of the spiritual life, gender is by no means the most significant. To a perhaps surprising extent, the texts do present a gender-neutral ideal, as befits the angelic life that chastity was meant to confer. The essential monastic virtues of humility, poverty, obedience, abstinence, discretion, and charity are the same for both sexes, and men and women alike are to practice fasting, vigils, liturgical and private prayer, confession, meditation, reading, and silence. Men as well as women are to perceive themselves as Christ's brides; women as well as men are to fight in Christ's army. For both sexes, the ascetic life undertaken in the fear of God is to culminate in the contemplative love of him, and for both, this enterprise is continually threatened by the world, the flesh, and the devil.

Insofar as the religious ideal transcended gender, works addressed to men or to women could be read and used freely by religious of both sexes. For example, the writings for monks attributed to St. Bernard had an avid female readership.[9] Conversely, men were no less willing to benefit from works of advice for nuns or anchoresses. Aelred of Rievaulx's *Rule for Recluses*, written for his virgin sister, was frequently abridged, translated, and incorporated into other rules; manuscripts of the text found their way into Augustinian, Benedictine, Carthusian, Cistercian, and Franciscan houses. Aelred influenced not only the author of the *Ancrene Wisse*, another guidebook for women, but also the Carthusian Ludolf of Saxony and, through him, Ignatius Loyola.[10] Copies of the *Speculum virginum*, intended for nuns, were procured by numerous houses of monks and canons. In fact, all but two of the thirty-five extant manuscripts of the Latin text belonged to male monasteries; nuns of the later middle ages read the book in German translation.[11] A systematic study of the manuscript diffusion of this literature would probably reveal similar patterns.[12]

Yet within this background of consensus and common readership, I believe we can also discern a pattern of gender-based difference cutting across the differences that arise from institutional contexts. Almost all the available texts from our period were written by men. Only two monastic women of the twelfth century, Heloise and Hildegard of Bingen, wrote significant works bearing on religious formation, and they both adopted certain traditional androcentric views even while criticizing others.[13] The texts under study, then, are primarily those of male writers voicing their views of a life they regarded in principle as gender-free, yet without divesting themselves of androcentric perceptions and stereotypes. I would like to focus on three areas where such perceptions emerge most clearly: first, gender as an explicit theme; second, the differential treatment of chastity; and third, gender as an implicit theme affecting the presentation of communal life and spiritual growth.

I. "Weak Women, Strong Men"

Where gender is treated explicitly, we find direct misogyny in abundance alongside another current that can be termed inverted misogyny. In the first place, there is the casual antifeminism derived from Greco-Roman culture and perpetuated by patristic authors, who used the female as a sign for all that is weak, carnal, and sensual. Spiritual writers drew on this tradition off-handedly as a source of metaphors, regardless of the gender of their audience. Thus the abbot Peter of Celle, writing for regular canons, lambasts worldly religious who cannot bear discipline: "They call themselves men, but their behavior places them with the effeminate."[14] William of St.-Thierry, a Cistercian, explains to the Carthusians that in the process of spiritual growth, the feminine soul (*anima*) is gradually transformed into the masculine mind or spirit (*animus*). "When [the soul] begins to be not only capable but also in possession of perfect reason, it immediately renounces the feminine gender. . . . For as long as it is *anima* it is quick to slip effeminately into the carnal; but the *animus* or spirit thinks only on what is virile and spiritual."[15] This is not a subtle doctrine of androgyny, but an image of progress from the lower to the higher.

The *Speculum virginum*, a widely read dialogue for nuns composed by a Benedictine around 1140, employs the same symbolism. The priest in this colloquy warns his virgin disciple that "delicacies render the masculine spirit (*animum*) female." Inveighing against pride, he says that vainglory is bad enough in men, who at least have something to boast about, "but an arrogant woman is like a monster, for there is nothing more fragile than her sex." The virgin in the dialogue is almost reduced to despair by the biblical text, "Better is the iniquity of a man than a woman doing good" (Ecclus. 42:14). But the priest consoles her by pointing out that this text is not to be taken literally. By "man" the inspired author meant the virile soul or rational mind, which may offend God through excessive zeal; while the "woman" is an "idle soul given over to wretched softness," who offends even more by her laziness in spite of her good intentions.[16] As we shall see, these remarks were intended not to disparage the female reader but to encourage her in pursuing a "virile" spirituality whereby she could rise above her sex.

Osbert of Clare, prior of Westminster Abbey, followed the same strategy in several letters of direction to nuns. To Ida of Barking he wrote, "Do not let lascivious mirth reduce you to your sex. Conquer the woman; conquer the flesh; conquer desire."[17] And to the abbess Alice, for whom he professed high esteem, he explained, "The pure meditation of a human being is mystically described under the name of 'man,' but weak thinking is noted by the title of 'woman.' We refer good works to the male, but we represent harmful acts by the character of the inferior sex."[18] Idung of Prüfening, a contentious monk who converted from the Cluniacs to the Cistercians in mid-century, agreed with Heloise that the Benedictine Rule was not suitable for women. In a diatribe calling for stricter female claustration, he wrote, "It is not expedient for that sex to enjoy the freedom of having its own governance—because of its natural fickleness and also because of outside temptations which womanly weakness is not strong enough to resist."[19] (By "outside temptations" he meant rapists.) Osbert was a friend of religious women, while Idung was overtly hostile to them, but both could draw on the same repertoire of stock antifeminist motifs.

Aside from carnality in general, the vice most frequently assigned to women was loquacity. Because the discipline of silence played such a large part in monastic life, exhortations to avoid wicked or idle speech occur frequently in the literature.[20] These are not aimed particularly at women or at men; both sexes are instructed in the virtue of silence and the vice of an unbridled tongue. In a beautifully ironic example, the canon Philip of Harvengt, author of a three-volume work *On the institution of clerics*, devoted ten chapters to learning, seventeen to poverty, forty-four to obedience, and one hundred and seventeen to silence.[21] But while idle words were considered a peril for all religious, the proverbial chatterbox was always female. Odo of St.-Victor, a regular canon, reminded a brother of St. James's dictum, "He who does not offend with his tongue is a perfect man" (Jas. 3:2). He explains that the word "man" (*vir*) is used because a strong, silent type is not swayed by that slippery member, the tongue, but stands his ground manfully. The chatterer, on the other hand, proves to be "frail and effeminate," carried away helplessly on the waves of his words.[22] Aelred of Rievaulx cites the same passage in the rule for his sister. Reviewing monastic prescriptions on silence, he sums up: "If this pertains to any decent man, how much more to a woman, how much more to a virgin, how much more to a recluse?"[23] Abelard suggests that women's supposed loquacity has a physiological basis: "The more sensitive [the tongue] is in you, and the more flexible from your softness of body, the more mobile and given to words it is."[24] He then cites the passage from 1 Tim. 2:11–12 in which the Apostle forbids women to teach—even though in a later epistle he warmly encouraged the nuns of the Paraclete to study Latin, Hebrew, and Greek because in Heloise they had a superlative teacher.[25]

Polemics against garrulous women can express such deep suspicion that, as R. Howard Bloch has argued, "the reproach against women [becomes] a form of reproach against language itself."[26] But women's supposed fluency of speech was not always interpreted in a negative sense, even among clerics; what was called "loquacity" *in malo* might be praised as "eloquence" *in bono*. A number of popular female saints were famed for their laudable speech: Mary Magdalene and Thecla, who engaged in apostolic preaching; Catherine of Alexandria, who confounded fifty pagan philosophers with her learning; Cecilia, who converted her pagan husband on their wedding night and persuaded him to embrace Christ instead of her in chaste union. From the early thirteenth century onward, a growing number of pious women imitated Cecilia's example; Marie of Oignies is only the best-known of these *mulieres sanctae*.[27] In his *Manual for Confessors* (circa 1215), Thomas of Chobham maintained that priests should actively encourage wives to "be preachers to their husbands" and sway them, through eloquence and feminine wiles, to be more just, merciful, and generous.[28] Thus the negative evaluation of female speech in the literature of formation is not a mark of antifeminism per se so much as a conservative topos that remained congenial because of the specifically monastic love of silence. Writers who viewed all speech with a professional suspicion employed misogynist rhetoric on this point even if they were not, in other respects, notably hostile to women.

Another recurrent topos is the denunciation of curiosity, with woman as its symbol. For Bernard, this trait was a dangerous vice, the first rung on the infernal ladder of pride, and its chief exemplars were Dinah and Eve. The exemplum of Dinah is particularly instructive, for it became a favorite in the literature of formation. Genesis 34 recounts the tragic story of Jacob's only daughter: Dinah "went out to visit the women of the land" and in consequence suffered rape. The biblical writer treats this experience only in passing and dwells on its aftermath: the perfidy of Dinah's brothers, the rift between Jacob and his sons, and the ensuing war between Israelites and Hivites. It was clear to medieval writers, however, that the chief villain in the piece was Dinah. Because of her "curious idleness or idle curiosity," Bernard states, she was to blame not only for her own rape, but for all the political disasters that followed.[29] Similar strictures are found in many other writings.[30] The *Ancrene Wisse* (circa 1215–1221) not only uses Dinah's story as a cautionary tale to reinforce the strict claustration of virgins, but goes so far as to blame hapless women for the desire they may arouse in men. A virgin who "causes" a man to rape her "is guilty before Our Lord of [his] death and must answer for his soul on the Day of Judgment, and make restitution for the loss . . . when she has no coin but herself."[31] In other words, having already surrendered her body to the rapist, she now forfeits her soul as well. While Dinah is negatively interpreted throughout the exegetical tradition, spiritual writers applied the exemplum differently to men and women. Bernard and Peter of Celle used it to warn their male readers against curiosity; but in writings directed to women, Dinah's story suggests a more concrete application and a graver warning. A virgin must never leave the confines of her nunnery or cell, and if she does, she is to blame for whatever may ensue.[32]

Examples of casual misogyny could be multiplied, but this particular dead horse has already been well beaten. The "weak woman" topos may have been such a familiar cliché that some users scarcely perceived it as misogynist, any more than some people today would perceive it as racist to speak of blackening a person's character. Even writers who generally exalted women, like Abelard and Hildegard of Bingen, made use of the topos. More significantly, however, both these authors also knew how to invert it. Women may be weak, but as Paul had observed, God's strength is made perfect in weakness (2 Cor. 12:9).[33] Thus, in exhortations to religious women as in lives of female saints, antifeminist clichés could easily modulate into praise for the woman strong-in-spite-of-herself. This commonplace provides a second context for the treatment of gender. We see an instance of inverted misogyny when St. Bernard commends the nun Sophia for renouncing the world: "If virtue is a rare bird upon earth among men, how much more in a weak and noble woman? Indeed, who shall find a valiant woman, much less a valiant noblewoman?"[34] Here both womanhood and privilege are seen as "weaknesses" that the nun has overcome, thus enhancing her virtue. Another nun is praised for rising above not only sex and class, but also youth and beauty.[35] Osbert of Clare, whose misogynist remarks I have already cited, urged the nun Ida to become a "splendid and radiant *virgo*, or rather a virile and incorrupt *virago*, through the virility of her husband Christ." Presenting the martyr Cecilia as a mirror of virginity, Osbert noted that because of her virile constancy and freedom, she was not "really" a woman. She even presumed to preach, thus earning the high honor of being buried among the popes—a privilege which "no woman before her had obtained, nor will any woman after her."[36]

As long as antifeminist topoi remained current, they could be countered with the claim that at least in religious life a woman is able to rise above her sex. Depending on the writer's ideology, she could be said to accomplish this feat either by becoming virile and therefore equal to men, or by virtue of an inverted hierarchy that leaves men behind. The two strategies are in fact antithetical. Osbert's praise of the virago or *femina virilis* relies on the straightforward androcentric notion that maleness is normative humanity and femaleness a defect, which may, however, be overcome if a woman is willing to give up her sexuality. This topos is well attested in patristic literature and especially in the letters of St. Jerome, whom Abelard consciously chose as his model.[37] Bernard's view of divine strength perfected in female weakness is more characteristic of the high middle ages. It depends on a distinctively Christian transvaluation of values by which social liabilities (such as humility, poverty, weakness, foolishness, and femaleness) become spiritual assets. This strategy was notably more congenial to women writers, such as Hrotswitha, Hildegard, and Elisabeth of Schönau, and it was increasingly adopted by the male biographers of female saints. In a transitional writer like Abelard, however, we see the two incompatible views jostling each other as he struggles to make sense of a contradiction.

No one went further in the ritual praise of women than Abelard. Describing Martha, Mary of Bethany, and Mary Magdalene as the first nuns, he pointed out that while the Holy Spirit had anointed the prophets, a woman anointed Christ, the Holy of Holies. Of all the disciples, only the women remained with Christ in his passion, and women were the first to see him risen. Therefore on Easter morning "these holy women were set as apostles (*apostolas*) above the Apostles themselves." In the early Church women took up the "Christian philosophy," or monasticism, with no less fervor than men. The nobility of nuns is shown by the fact that while monks can be consecrated on any day, priests only on fast days, and bishops on any Sunday, virgins can be consecrated only during the highest feasts, and then only by a bishop. A great many women, but very few men, have earned the double crown of martyrdom and virginity. Women even have certain extraordinary privileges: for instance, they are allowed to commit laudable suicide in order to preserve their chastity, and for the same reason they have permission to cross-dress. Some female monks, Abelard notes, have even served as abbots![38] His proto-feminist epistle was written to encourage the dispirited Heloise, and he goes much further than other writers were prepared to do. All the same, his arguments for female superiority fail to override the misogynist assumptions that emerge elsewhere in his writings for Heloise.

If there is anything novel about Abelard's deference to religious women, it lies in the odd institutional courtesy of his arrangements for the Paraclete (which Heloise, for all her protestations, apparently did not follow).[39] Abelard wanted an abbot to hold authority over both monks and nuns, but "in such a way that he regards . . . the brides of the Lord whose servant he is as his own mistresses, and so [he should] be glad to serve rather than rule them." In addition, all the brothers were supposed to make a formal profession of obedience to the abbess and "bind themselves by oath to the sisters not to consent to their oppression in any form."[40] These arrangements are strongly reminiscent of Fontevrault,[41] except that Abelard's insistence on mutual service left the lines of authority muddled, making his rule unworkable in practice. Its puzzling inconsistencies may be explained by the contradiction in ideology. On the one hand, women are the weaker sex and need to be under male authority; on the other, they are the privileged sex and men are responsible for serving them while they enjoy pure contemplative leisure. Thus Abelard's writings for the Paraclete constitute a veritable *Sic et non* on the question of gender. He seems to be groping toward a solution analogous to the one Chaucer's *Franklin's Tale* would propose for the disparity between male dominance in marriage and female dominance in love. Dorigen agrees to take Arveragus for her "servant in love and lord in mariage," but their novel arrangement undergoes serious testing in the course of the tale, and Dorigen's fate is ultimately determined by two men. The testing in a monastic community would no doubt have been equally severe, so it is no wonder if a bemused Heloise decided to lay the new rule aside and follow her own judgment, for once, instead of Abelard's.

II. "Holy Maidenhood"

In reviewing the explicit treatment of gender, we should be careful not to overlook the obvious. This issue rarely arises in treatises of formation for men, except in occasional metaphors. Monks, hermits, and canons are advised not as males but as religious who have professed a particular vocation. With few exceptions, however, male authors who wrote to edify women were deeply and self-consciously concerned with gender.[42] Male saints, by convention, were classified according to profession as bishops, monks, confessors, martyrs, evangelists, rulers, warriors, and the like, whereas holy women formed a class unto themselves.[43] The female saints most venerated in the middle ages were overwhelmingly virgins, with special preference for those who had earned what Abelard called the double crown: lilies for virginity and roses for martyrdom. The perception of virginity as the quintessence of female holiness had momentous consequences for the spiritual life, and advice on preserving this state dominates the women's literature of formation. Male chastity, while seen as an important virtue, never evoked either the same rapturous praise for its preservation or the same dire warnings about its loss.

Idung of Prüfening states the issue with irreproachable clarity. He notes that "a woman can lose her virginity by violence—a thing which in the masculine sex nature itself prevents." Therefore, because of the supreme value of this fragile possession, a virgin must be guarded with the utmost care:

> The more fragile the vessel, the more diligent the care it needs lest the vessel be broken . . . [or] carried off through theft or pillage, a protection which golden vessels require more than glass. A consecrated woman requires both kinds of protection for she can, metaphorically, be called a glass vessel because of her fragile sex and a golden vessel because of the ideal of the office of virgin.[44]

According to Aelred of Rievaulx, "a virgin's flesh is an earthen vessel in which gold is stored for testing."[45] If the vessel cracks in the fire, the gold is spilled and the vase can never be repaired. In the Middle English *Ancrene Wisse*, our "treasure in earthen vessels" is the precious balm of virginity, and "this frail vessel is as fragile as any glass, for once it is broken it may never be mended."[46] The recurrent image has an archetypal quality, which Henry James was to rediscover in his novel *The Golden Bowl*. An artifact of exquisite beauty and ineffable worth, given as a wedding gift to the heroine, the fabled bowl cracks in the end, for it proves to be only flawed crystal beneath its gilding. Such was the fear that medieval monastic writers expressed time and again about the virgins in their care.

Letters to religious women, as well as treatises on virginity, place the consecrated woman in a uniquely vulnerable position because of the eminence they ascribe to her. The novice monk is never perceived as sacrosanct in quite the same way: although his profession is holy, he is himself only a converted sinner who must struggle painfully to acquire virtues. The virgin, on the other hand, already *has* the exalted virtue that defines her state, and must apply herself only to preserving it. To impress the supreme value of virginity on its possessors, inspiring them to defend it with their lives, spiritual writers resort to the highest flattery; but then, fearing that their own praise may induce a kind of giddiness, they compensate with the warning that a humble widow or wife is better than a proud virgin.[47] Just as woman in general is the "weaker sex" in which divine strength is perfected, so the virgin in particular is the most exalted and therefore the most imperiled of all religious, and has the greatest need for humility.

In a typical opening gesture, the canonist Ivo of Chartres praises virginity to the nuns of St.-Avit and then warns, "The higher you rise, the harder you fall. The happier the supreme reward you may expect if you persevere, the more wretched and extreme the damnation you must fear if you fail."[48] Peter of Blois commends a nun for rejecting her noble suitor, but ends with a warning: "Although we may be healed of every sin through penance, the fall of virgins alone does not deserve the remedy of restoration."[49] The English work *Holy Maidenhood*, written around 1200, explains why maidens are in special danger:

> The higher you stand, the more sorely you should fear to fall; for the higher the degree, the worse the fall. The envious devil sees you risen so high toward heaven through maidenhood's might . . . and night and day he shoots his arrows dipped in venomous ointment at your heart, to wound you with weak will and make you fall.[50]

While an ex-virgin like Heloise might repent and enter the monastery as a "widow," her state would be markedly inferior in heaven. The thirty-, sixty-, and hundredfold fruits in the parable of the sower (Matt. 13:8) were routinely interpreted as types of marriage, widowhood, and virginity, so *Holy Maidenhood* tells the virgin that if she marries she will immediately "leap downward" seventy degrees.[51]

The dissimilar value placed on male virginity, even lost virginity, is reflected in Aelred's rule for his sister. Near the end of the work, when the abbot is teaching the virgin to count her blessings, he turns to autobiography and compares his own youthful debauchery with his sister's purity: God "has distinguished between you and me as between light and darkness, preserving you for himself and abandoning me to myself. . . . As wretched then as I am, having lost my chastity, so blessed are you whose virginity divine grace has protected." The monk is like a poor, naked refugee who has barely escaped shipwreck, the virgin like a ship richly laden with cargo, steering safely into port. But Aelred then tells his sister not to be jealous if God treats them equally: "You may think it a great embarrassment if, after so many offenses, I were to be found your equal in that life [to come]—although intervening vices may often diminish the glory of virginity, and changed habits and virtues supplanting vices may obliterate the disgrace of an old lifestyle."[52] Aelred's reverence for his sister's sheer status—her being, not her doing—emerges clearly, and so does his personal sense of shame. Nevertheless, he does not feel that he is irreparably broken, or that his lost chastity excludes him from present grace and future glory.[53]

In a study of the virgin ideal, Clarissa Atkinson has demonstrated the existence of two distinct but interwoven ideological strands.[54] A virgin could be defined either physically as one who had never had sexual contact, or spiritually as one "whose primary relationship is with God." The definitions are both ancient, the first being stressed by Jerome and the second by Augustine, and they coexisted throughout the medieval period. But from the twelfth century onward, the spiritual definition came increasingly to supplement and, little by little, to supplant the physical. By the fifteenth century, a mother of fourteen like Margery Kempe could be consoled by Christ's reassurance that she was "a maiden in [her] soul."[55] Now maidenhood of the soul, if shattered by sin, could easily be restored by penance, and it could be possessed in principle by chaste wives and widows—or, for that matter, men. Physical virginity, on the other hand, was not only a moral but a quasi-magical property; it conferred special powers, such as incorruption of the virgin's corpse or even (in the case of Joan of Arc) the charm of invincibility. This talismanic quality of the virgin—imaged in the precious balm, the golden bowl, and ubiquitous allusions to "the seal of maidenhood"—pertained only to the inviolate female body.[56] Whether or not they also "spiritualized" virginity, most male writers in our period felt the allure of the archetype (as did many women, like Hildegard and Christina of Markyate), and thus ascribed exaggerated importance to *virginitas intacta*.

As we have seen, virginity was often praised as the great equalizer that enabled a woman to rise above her sex, giving proof of a virile mind in a feminine body. Nevertheless, the literature of formation shows that the nun, "virile" or not, was still viewed very much as a woman—and not only woman but also desirable bride, obedient wife, and fruitful mother. Unlike monks, nuns were consistently imagined, and encouraged to imagine themselves, in gender-specific roles based on the sexuality they were renouncing. The monk was never allegorically described as a husband, although he might be portrayed cross-sexually as a bride, and he was never represented as a father unless he was an abbot or prior with spiritual sons. The nun or anchoress, on the other hand, was always portrayed as a bride of Christ and often as a mother of virtues, whether or not she was an abbess. Even physical beauty and elegant apparel, which she was constantly urged to renounce, were legitimate concerns if transferred to the spiritual plane, and monastic writers enjoyed meditating on the finery that these plain, dark-robed women would wear in heaven. St. Bernard told one nun not to envy the jewels of worldly women, for no queen's earrings ever equalled the blush on the face of a virgin; and what is more, those women would lose their beauty at death, while hers was inalienable, because internal and incorruptible.[57] Osbert of Clare helped his niece Cecilia prepare her trousseau: "In the celestial emperor's palace your bridesmaids will be the angels, the citizens of God, to lead you into the King's bedchamber. . . . Your virginity, which knows no loss of chastity in the sacred marriage, will be radiant in a golden diadem, and precious stones will be subtly sewn into your garment."[58]

More important than these allegorical frills is the notion, usually stated quite explicitly, that marriage to Christ surpasses earthly marriage in ways that might appeal to a nubile young maiden here and now. If she marries Christ the virgin will have a husband richer, nobler, more handsome, and more loving than any she could find on earth; as an added incentive, she will be spared the troubles of childbearing and the humiliations of patriarchy. The so-called bridal spirituality of the middle ages does not always evoke the refinements of mystical union; it could appeal to very earthly motives. Alan of Lille tells virgins:

> If you want to marry an earthly husband for riches, consider that earthly riches are deceptive and transitory, for they pass away either in the present life or at least in death. Therefore marry him whose treasures are incomparable, whose riches are immutable, where thief does not steal, nor moth corrupt. If you want to marry an earthly man for beauty, consider that either sickness mars beauty, or old age destroys it, or at the very least the moment of death annihilates it. Therefore marry him at whose beauty the sun and moon marvel.[59]

Recruited as virgins, defined as virgins, guarded as virgins, and ideally canonized as virgins, consecrated women were nevertheless seen as fulfilling to perfection their feminine roles of wife and mother. But in case such positive inducements would not suffice, a favorite motif in the virginity literature was the *molestiae nuptiarum* or "nuisances of marriage." This theme is a variant on the classical misogynist argument that a wise *man* should not marry, because it is impossible to combine the joys of philosophy with the trials of family life.[60] In this form, the commonplace occurs in Abelard's *Historia calamitatum* (where it is placed in Heloise's mouth) and in the *Speculum virginum*.[61] But the argument could be reversed: instead of persuading the philosopher to shun the malice and frivolity of wives, one might persuade the virgin to avoid the tyranny of husbands. Hildebert of Lavardin wrote in a much-imitated letter to the recluse Athalisa:

> Virgins do not know what a woman's weakness must endure in the licentiousness of marriage. They do not know the injuries to which a wife is subject— how much anxiety troubles a fertile wife, and how sorrow torments a barren one. If she is beautiful, it will be hard for her to avoid shame; if she is ugly, her husband spurns her. Never is the bed without quarreling; the wife must ever be ashamed or else weary of it.[62]

As for childbearing, says Peter of Blois, "the daughters of this world . . . conceive in sin, bear in sorrow, suckle in fear; they are constantly anxious about the living and inconsolably grieved for the dying." With a fine flourish he adds, "*Si vis parere, vis perire*. If you wish to bear, you wish to perish."[63] Osbert of Clare writes, "There is a great difference between heavenly marriage and earthly," and to prove it he paints a hideous portrait of the pregnant woman:

Her face becomes pale, and her bright eyes grow hollow with thick darkness; . . . the skin of her face grows taut with wrinkles, and her round fingers wither; the swollen belly is distended, and her vitals are torn apart within by the burden of pregnancy . . . nor does the wife laden with gold and jewels conceive or bear any differently in her palace than the poor and ragged woman in her hovel.[64]

Holy Maidenhood, the most celebrated work of this genre, not only quotes these writers, but adds its own crypto-feminist appeal. A virgin, says the English writer, is lady of all the world, and "so free of herself" that she need do nothing but sit and think of her beloved; but if she marries a "man of clay," she will lessen her ladyship to the degree that her second husband ranks below her first, and from freedom she sinks into bondage, "becomes a slave under man, and his thrall, to do and to suffer all that he pleases, though it suit her never so ill."[65] Most of the treatise is devoted to an attack on the despised institution of marriage, and it culminates in the ultimate tribute to harassed housewives: "What if I ask besides, though it seem ridiculous, how it stands with the wife who comes in and hears her child screaming, sees the cat at the flitch and the hound at the hide, her cake burning on the stone and her calf sucking the milk, the crock running into the fire, and the churl chiding?"[66] Such propaganda may indeed have been effective. If some women liked to escape from marriage into the fantasies of *fine amour*, at least in their light reading, others were happy to escape from it permanently in the cloister or the anchorhold.[67] *Holy Maidenhood* does not even insist on high-minded motives: "Even though it were never for love of God, nor hope of heaven, nor dread of hell, woman, you ought to shun this work [of marriage] above all things for the sake of your own flesh's integrity and your body's health."[68]

What we might call the "misandronist" motif in these treatises is not dominant, but the fact that it is present at all, in works written by men, is significant. It is also noteworthy that while tirades against wives occur mainly in works by secular clerics, not monks, the complementary warnings about husbands appear in the monastic literature on virginity. The common denominator is not misogyny but a widespread, if muted, perception that the institution of patriarchal marriage was itself problematic.[69] Worldly clerks (or proponents of the campaign for clerical celibacy) might inveigh against women because no husband could control them, while the propagandists of virginity told women how to escape control by avoiding husbands. Childbearing, too, was perceived as equally oppressive by the foes of women and by their self-styled friends. The satirist who feels aggrieved by the caprices of a pregnant wife and the monk who looks with pitying condescension on her sufferings are brothers under the skin. As Peter Brown has observed of late antiquity, the virginal life offered women an escape from the social control vested in marriage, procreation, and kinship networks,[70] and in the high middle ages its advocates were glad to highlight this appeal. Antifeminist satire and the panegyric of virginity express the same suspicion from different points of view: the first assumes that social control is desirable but laments that it is not effective, while the second denies that it is even desirable.

III. The Common Life

The consecrated woman, as we have seen, was addressed continually in her roles as virgin and bride; she was also represented frequently as a mother (of Christ or of the virtues) and as a widow. Other roles, however—those of "sister" and of questing individual—received less attention. These lacunae make a significant difference in the treatment of three crucial areas of religious formation: community, friendship, and spiritual growth. In effect, the fixation on virginity led the authors of formative literature for nuns to slight precisely those concerns that typify the renascence of male monastic life in the twelfth century. The result is a curiously static and anachronistic portrait of the religious woman, out of sync not only with her brothers, but with the evangelical ideals that were beginning to fire reform-minded women themselves.

Monks and canons of many orders felt that the common life was an essential part of their discipline and made it a subject for reflection. Black monks generally stressed the older ideals of obedience and humility, while the Cistercians preserved this Benedictine heritage but added a new concern with charity and affective development. Canons regular, though in some ways indistinguishable from monks, particularly emphasized the duty of mutual instruction and the power of example. And almost all the new religious movements of the twelfth century shared an interest in apostolic poverty.[71] When we look for treatises addressed to nuns on the common life, however, we find few from our period. There is no lack of edifying literature for individual women, whether anchoresses or nuns. But almost none of this writing deals specifically with relationships between sisters in a convent. "Brotherhood" was a major theme of twelfth-century religious writing, but "sisterhood" decidedly was not.

Reasons for this neglect are not hard to find. Much of the new empha-sis on community derives from either the Cistercians or the regular canons, and the latter, who were by definition clerics, had no "female branch."[72] In the case of the Cistercians, much of the significant literature of formation predates the order's extensive dealings with women. Not until the thir-teenth century, with the advent of beguines, third orders, and proliferating Cistercian nunneries, do we find comparable attention to women's commu-nal life.[73] Twelfth- and early thirteenth-century works for recluses appeal to an older tradition and, for obvious reasons, do not concern themselves with community. Another reason for the gap, however, lies in the way men characteristically defined religious women. Looking at themselves, they saw unity and diversity, brotherhood and discord; looking at women, they saw the virgin in relation to males—Christ, clerics, potential lovers—but seldom in relation to her sisters. The gender difference becomes obvious when we look at model homilies composed by preachers for cloistered men and women.

Alan of Lille's *Summa on the Art of Preaching*, written in the late twelfth century, includes a number of sample sermons tailored to different audi-ences. The one addressed to *claustrales*—monks or canons—takes as its text "Behold, how good and pleasant it is when brothers dwell together in unity" (Ps. 132:1). After dealing with unity in God and among the angels, Alan discusses the threefold unity that should exist among monks: in ob-servance, in common ownership, and in charity. The analogous sermon for nuns, on the other hand, is addressed "to virgins" and has for its text "I betrothed you to Christ to present you as a chaste virgin to one hus-band" (2 Cor. 11:2).[74] Not surprisingly, virginity is the theme. A comparable sermon collection by Peter of Blois reveals the same assumptions. Peter's sermon to *claustrales* deals with apostolic poverty, another aspect of the common life. But his two sermons for nuns both center on virginity, one emphasizing claustration and the other humility.[75] Since virginity was the essence of the consecrated woman's status, community naturally assumed less importance.

Neither Heloise nor Abelard was particularly concerned with relation-ships among sisters. Heloise worried about the dangers of hospitality, but took community for granted. Abelard, as we have seen, was preoccupied with the relation of nuns and monks in a double monastery, and he also made special provisions for the abbess: she should be a matron, well edu-cated, not too young, not chosen from the local nobility, and not dis-tinguished from her nuns by greater luxury or privacy.[76] Aside from this concern for solidarity, however, he mentions community only in a passing image. Abbess and abbot are like a queen and her steward, the other obedientiaries are "dukes or counts serving in their lord's army, while all the rest are the soldiers or infantry" in combat "against the evil one and his hordes."[77] The military image is a commonplace of monastic literature; it implies obedience and firm discipline without dwelling on the emotional or spiritual content of relationships within the cloister.

Nevertheless, the theme of community is not altogether ignored. St. Bernard, writing to a nun of Trier, discouraged her from becoming a recluse by offering a two-pronged argument. Either she is a holy nun and the community needs her good example, or else she is a sinner and needs the correction of her sisters. "If you are among the foolish virgins, you need the congregation; if among the wise, the congregation needs you. . . . Whether you are a sinner or a saint, do not separate yourself from the flock."[78] The *Speculum virginum* encourages solidarity by warning against snobbery: "Although a virgin of Christ may be the greatest among her sisters in learning or knowledge, in nobility, or in the grace of virtues, let her nevertheless be the least of all and the handmaid of all in her mind." The author speaks more explicitly against class prejudice:

> What, I ask, should I say of those who raise their eyebrows over lineage and overstep the bounds of courtesy among the other sisters, making distinctions on account of class (*conditionem dividentes*) and thereby detracting from the common nature while they glory in private [superiority]? . . . If you consider the flesh, it is a wonderful nobility, a wonderfully distinguished family, where worm is born from worm and corruption is praised by dust.[79]

In a series of letters to abbesses, Hildegard of Bingen deals only indirectly with the common life. She shows her respect for the cenobitic way by urging several reluctant superiors to persevere in their office and abandon dreams of an eremitic life, and with typical Benedictine discretion, she cautions against breaking the spirit of a convent through overly harsh discipline.[80] The one letter in which she deals overtly with the problems of community is her famous epistle to Tenxwind of Andernach. Tenxwind, *magistra* of the first nunnery to follow the Augustinian Rule, shared the evangelical ideals of her brother, the canonical reformer Richard of Springiersbach. She had attacked Hildegard for admitting only rich and noble girls to her convent in spite of Christ's well-known preference for the poor. "God is no respecter of persons," Tenxwind had reminded the visionary, for he chose a few poor fishermen to found his church. In her apologia Hildegard defended her policy on the ground that people of different classes must live in separate communities, just as beasts of different species are kept in separate stables, since they would otherwise "tear each other to shreds in hatred."[81] Class consciousness, so pronounced even in a maverick like Hildegard, must indeed have been a great obstacle to unity in many convents. The advice of the *Speculum virginum*, like Abelard's insistence that the abbess not be a noblewoman, flew in the face of contemporary practice.

Aside from gradations of status within the nobility, the class from which most nuns before 1200 were recruited, nunneries presented a fairly homogeneous social profile.[82] The only major social distinctions within the community set the virgins apart from widows on the one hand and *conversae* or lay sisters on the other. The latter enjoyed a semi-religious status but were properly servants rather than nuns; unlike their sisters in choir, they were not expected to be literate. Even anchoresses who were formally dead to the world often had servants; the *Ancrene Wisse* devotes several pages to the handmaids' rule and the relationship of mistress to servants. The anchoresses were expected to discipline their maids, but in a gentle spirit so that "there should always be more of love than of fear."[83]

Male monasteries, and sometimes nunneries as well, also had lay brothers as servants. But the distinction between choir monks and servants was far from the only significant difference between brothers. In general, the society of the male religious foundation was much more heterogeneous than that of the nunnery. The literature of formation reflects this diversity by claiming that the monastery is all things to all men. In his short tract *On the Cloistered Life*, Honorius describes it as a harbor for the prince shipwrecked in war; a shady haven for the tired man of affairs; a bed of rest for the oppressed laborer; an asylum for the fugitive knight; a school for children; a boot camp for adolescents; a prison for criminals; a purgatory for the penitent; a hell of torment for the wicked; and a paradise of delights for the wise.[84] For Hugh of Fouilloy, cloistered life is abundance for the poor, sufficiency for the middle class (*mediocres*), and a "tolerable yoke" for the rich. It is generous to the weak, full of compassion for the delicate, moderate to the strong, merciful to the penitent, severe with the perverse, and supremely good to the good.[85] Peter of Celle puts the images of social diversity to allegorical use, comparing the cloister in turn to the racetrack, the courtyard of the Temple, the treasury, the outer sanctuary, the royal bedchamber, the gibbet, and the marketplace.[86] Awareness of diversity in the social backgrounds and previous experience, as well as the spiritual development of members, undoubtedly contributed to monastic interest in the dynamics of community life. Allowances might have to be made; for instance, the canon Peter of Porto granted in his *Rule for clerics* (1116) that if lay scholars were admitted and, after a year or two of practice, proved hopeless at liturgical chant, they might be released "for higher things" more suited to their gifts and useful to the brethren.[87]

Twelfth-century men, unlike women, were keenly and sometimes distressingly aware of the many religious vocations available to them. An anonymous canon's *Treatise on the diverse orders and callings in the Church* sets out optimistically to show "how such servants of God differ and . . . that these differences among the callings please God."[88] But diversity was more often presented in a negative way, not only in polemics but also in warnings for the over-zealous novice. A mid-century treatise, *On instructing novices*, perhaps compiled by the Benedictine abbot Goswin of Anchin, quotes a cautionary passage from Cassian advising the new recruit to persevere in his chosen path without being dazzled by the virtues of alternative ways.[89] The same warning is repeated a century later in the Cistercian abbot Stephen of Sawley's *Mirror for Novices*:

> When fickle and ill-grounded minds hear others commended for their virtues and for their zeal, they are so set ablaze by the praise that they immediately wish to embrace their example and discipline; but in vain. Such change and divergence from their own way of life reaps them a loss and not a gain because he who follows after many things will not attain anything completely. Thus, it is expedient to each that, according to the path which he has chosen and the grace he has received, he strive with the greatest zeal and diligence to attain perfection in the task he has laid out for himself. He must praise, love, and admire the work and virtues of others; and once he has made his choice, he must never leave the place of his profession. God is reached by many paths.[90]

Despite such advice, transfers between orders were relatively frequent. Perhaps the most striking example of social as well as religious mobility is Adam of Perseigne (circa 1145–1221), born a serf of the count of Champagne, who rose to become court chaplain and poet of the Countess Marie and then embraced, in succession, the regular canons, the Benedictines, and the Cistercians, finally becoming an abbot and a prominent diplomat.[91] Adam would in turn write his own work of instruction for novices, praising stability as the rope by which we are "tied like pious beasts to the celestial stable."[92] Be that as it may, a trajectory like Adam's would have been impossible for a twelfth-century nun, given both the aristocratic flavor of women's monasticism and the much narrower range of options available to them. It is hardly surprising, then, that concerns about diversity find little place in spiritual writings for women.

Closely related to the theme of community is that of friendship. The twelfth century is well-known as a golden age of *amicitia*, as witnessed by the innumerable honeyed letters that passed between spiritual friends in different houses.[93] Aelred of Rievaulx's dialogue *On Spiritual Friendship*, a Christian adaptation of Cicero's *De amicitia*, won immediate popularity and later inspired a full-scale plagiarism by Peter of Blois.[94] Aelred discoursed on the origin and dignity of friendship, gave advice on choosing and testing one's friends, and analyzed problems that might arise in the course of friendship. So noble is friendship, he declared, that "in human affairs nothing more sacred may be striven for, nothing more useful sought after, . . . nothing more sweet experienced, and nothing more profitable possessed." He even advanced the proposition that "God is friendship."[95] Aelred also practiced what he preached, if we can believe the life written by the monk Walter Daniel. Walter reports that as the abbot lay on his sickbed in the infirmary, his monks would come to visit him "twenty or thirty at a time, to talk together of the spiritual delights of the Scriptures; . . . they walked and lay about his bed and talked with him as a little child prattles with its mother." With approval, Walter notes that Aelred was not suspicious even of physical contact between the monks. "He did not treat them with the pedantic imbecility habitual in some silly abbots who, if a monk takes a brother's hand in his own, . . . demand his cowl, strip and expel him. Not so Ailred, not so."[96] On the basis of such evidence, John Boswell has argued that Aelred must have lost his virginity in a homosexual encounter, and that he retained and spiritualized this orientation once he became a monk.[97]

Other monastic writers, however, worried that close friendships might lead to overtly homosexual acts and should therefore be avoided. In writings for men, the sternest warnings against friendship are to be found in Guibert of Nogent's grim little treatise *On Virginity*—the only one on the subject addressed to a person of his own sex. Guibert, who admits that he has himself lost the virtue he praises, is deeply troubled by the threat of erotic friendships between monks.[98] Any form of relaxation or banter is dangerous, he writes, because it can easily slip into baseness. Even friendships that begin with edifying conversation can become "harmful intimacies" and lead to amatory trifling, then to a "fatal love" that, in good Ovidian fashion, makes the lover more pale than any fever. Such lust is to be repressed with scourging, and the beloved should be rejected outright no matter how much offense it may give, for such "hatred" appeases God. The parting should be "so harsh and abrupt that no hope of repairing the love again may remain," and it should be reinforced by physical distance. But it is best to avoid friendship altogether.[99] Guibert was writing about eighty years before Aelred, and there is a great difference between the mores of 1080 and those of the 1160s. There is also a vast difference between Guibert, a misanthropic teenager apparently frightened by his homoerotic leanings, and the genial, elderly Cistercian abbot who had come to terms with his.

Where friendship is concerned, however, an author's interest in this virtue tended to be inversely proportional to his stress on chastity. Hence many of those who wrote for monks emphasized "safe" friendships in which modesty would not be endangered. In the first half of the eleventh century, the abbot John of Fruttuaria (called *Johannes Homo Dei*) prefaced his discussion of friendship with a lengthy discourse on *verecundia*, inveighing against sodomites and seemingly innocent merriment that might lead boys astray. He advised novices that while the companionship of their peers was sweeter, that of old monks was safer: "For nothing is more beautiful than to have [the seniors] as both teachers and witnesses of life. Therefore a beautiful bond is formed between old men and adolescents."[100] Adam of Perseigne's instruction for novices mentions chastity only in passing, but he too says that the young monk and the novice master should develop "a commendable kind of intimacy" that will "make the master bolder in reproving, the reproved novice more patient in discipline, and both more learned in understanding the Scriptures."[101] In contrast, Adam's Cistercian contemporary, Arnulf of Bohéries, wrote a short *Mirror of Monks* that shows no interest in spiritual friendship. The reader is told baldly that "[a monk] should have no intimate friend (*familiarem*)" and, a little later, that "if the friendship of men (*hominum*) is forbidden, how much more that of women?"[102] The reference to women again suggests that a concern for chastity is the chief obstacle to friendship.

Insofar as this concern looms larger in writings for virgins, the cultivation of personal ties receives less attention or is actively discouraged. Thus Aelred, the great apostle of friendship for monks, warns his sister in the strongest terms to avoid closeness of any kind. "I want no one to visit you too frequently, nor do I want you to have intimate privacy with anyone who visits you often. For a virgin's reputation is endangered by the frequent greeting of any person, and so is her conscience."[103] Gifts and letters should be neither sent nor received. Not only men are to be avoided, but also women and children. "Familiarity and contact with women and effeminate people" is listed among the sources of vice; old women are feared for their lascivious gossip; and even children may imperil a recluse's virtue. Aelred draws a caricature of the anchoress who keeps a school:

> She looks at each [child] and amid their girlish movements she is now angry, now smiling, now she threatens and now she coaxes, now she strikes and now she kisses, now she calls a girl who is weeping from the lash to come closer, touches her face, strokes her neck, and falling into an embrace, she calls her now daughter and now friend. What recollection of God can there be in all this . . . ?[104]

Aelred's rule for his sister was written circa 1160–1162, in a hiatus between the two portions of his work on friendship, so he had already begun to theologize on the role of human intimacy in the religious life. One might argue that his sister was a recluse, not a nun living in community, so that friendship was unsuitable for her. Nevertheless, it is clear that Aelred is concerned not only with her contemplative leisure, but also with the danger to her chastity posed by even the most seemingly innocuous human contact. Although he was not worried by monks taking one another's hands, the thought of his sister embracing a schoolgirl or listening to an old woman's chatter fills him with misgivings. Her affections are to be given wholly to Christ: human love is not a helpful stage in the way to God's love or even a way of sharing in it, as it is for monks, but a distraction at best and at worst a sin. Virginity, it seems, precludes not only sexual contact but all contact.

Warnings against female friendship were not necessarily reserved for recluses. Ivo of Chartres, writing to the nuns of St.-Avit (circa 1092), reminds the sisters that they have vowed to marry Christ, not clerics. Urging strict claustration, he tells the women not to worry about losing their friends by refusing to speak to them, because for every "carnal lover" they lose, God will give them a hundred spiritual lovers.[105] Ivo promises that God will not allow their property to be dispersed through the loss of lay patrons; it does not occur to him that the nuns' affection for friends outside their house can be anything other than carnal or mercenary. Nor does he deal with friendship among the sisters themselves. Thomas of Froidmont, a Cistercian writing a century later, follows in the tradition of Aelred. In a prolix book of advice to his sister—apparently a nun rather than a recluse—he praises friendship and "love of neighbor" in general terms without paying much attention to her actual circumstances. The word "friend," for example, appears only in the masculine gender. Platitudes about friendship are interspersed with exhortations to "love no one carnally" or immoderately.[106] These warnings are amplified in later chapters:

> Dearest sister, flee the company of secular women. . . . As a siren deceives mariners with her dulcet songs, so a secular woman deceives the servants of Christ with her treacherous speech. . . . If you avoid women so zealously, how much more should you flee men? . . . I warn you that no man, however holy, should have any companionship with you.[107]

There is nothing remarkable about this advice, which is a staple of the literature on virginity. But by the 1190s it has a distinctly archaic ring in comparison with analogous literature for men.

In other writings for women, we find a mixture of anxiety about friendship and recognition of its importance. The anonymous monk who wrote the *Speculum virginum* does not trust spiritual friendship between the sexes, no matter how holy: "Where a single wall encloses men and women alike, . . . even though the sanctity of both may move mountains by faith . . . yet unless the fear and love of God intervene, cohabitation will open the way for the slander of enemies."[108] Yet this author does not discourage friendships between women. In a rare discussion of this theme, he anticipates Aelred's advice to monks about choosing friends wisely:

> Seek holy friendships by which you can be helped if it happens that you are stricken by some adversity. She who devotes herself to friendship with someone whose character she does not know, without consideration, binds a fetter on her own feet. Therefore evaluate the life and character of a potential friend in advance, and admit her to friendship after she is thus tested. For she who is too quick to form friendships will be even quicker to make enemies.[109]

Osbert of Clare says nothing of sisterly love, but he positively encourages the abbess of Barking to "cultivate intimate and religious friendships with holy men," as St. Cecilia did with Pope Urban.[110] This advice is exceptional in the twelfth century and harks back to a more heroic era when close ties between male and female ascetics, such as St. Jerome and Paula, were regarded as a proof of Christian liberty rather than a danger to be shunned. Moreover, Barking was a large and wealthy abbey, and Osbert's admonitions probably have less to do with the new currents of spiritual friendship than with the hospitality that Anglo-Saxon abbesses, who were also great ladies, traditionally provided for churchmen. In general, the monastic cult of friendship found little place in the spiritual ideal proposed by twelfth-century men for women. Yet only a few decades later, a rich outpouring of female saints' lives and devotional works by women reveals that, regardless of the advice they received, pious women were busily cultivating friends of both sexes.[111]

Finally, one of the most distinctive features of twelfth-century literature of formation for monks is its dynamism. Alongside older currents of moral teaching centered on virtues and vices, a growing interest in psychology made itself felt in a fascination with the soul's progress from self-love to the love of God. The conception of spiritual life as a process of growth, rather than a simple turning from evil to good, is apparent in the very titles of works like Bernard's treatise *On the Steps of Humility and Pride* and Guigo the Carthusian's *Ladder of Monks*. The new dynamic note is sounded as early as the mid-eleventh century in a treatise by John of Fruttuaria. This pseudo-Bernardine work, which circulated widely under various titles, does not present a static ideal of the virtuous monk. After a preface maintaining that old age reaps the fruit of virtues acquired in youth, the author carefully sets forth the virtues suitable to every age: modesty, silence, and obedience for boys; chastity, humility, and patience for adolescents; the four cardinal virtues for the mature; faith, hope, and charity for the perfect. To fire the novice's zeal, the abbot of Fruttuaria writes:

> If anyone then has a virginal soul and is a lover of chastity, he should not be content with modest achievements which quickly become obsolete, but strive for perfect virtues. . . . Keep growing, young man! . . . Do not falter or grow lukewarm, but scale the ladder of perfection, which cannot be attained without great labors. Well done, good brother, well done! Now transcend your beginnings and aim for higher things.[112]

Spiritual dynamism is especially pronounced among the Cistercians. For example, the seventh chapter of the Benedictine Rule sets forth twelve "degrees of humility" by which the monk is enabled to attain perfect love; but while arranging these steps in numerical order, St. Benedict never explains precisely how one step leads to another. Bernard's commentary on this chapter, *On the Steps of Humility and Pride*, fills in the missing psychology while satirizing contemporary monks. Maintaining, humbly enough, that he has more experience of descending the ladder through pride than of ascending through humility, Bernard shows with painful clarity how, step by slippery step, the perfect monk can slither downward into the abyss. Presumably, he has only to reverse the stages of his descent in order to climb back to the heights of humility. Another of Bernard's works, the treatise *On Loving God*, presents a progression from carnality to charity in four stages, as "our love advances by fixed degrees, led on by grace, until it is consummated in the spirit."[113] William of St.-Thierry, in his *Golden Epistle*, sets forth the slightly different schema of animal (or "psychological") man, rational man, and spiritual man.[114] Guigo's *Ladder of Monks* takes a set of traditional monastic exercises—reading, meditation, prayer, and contemplation—and uses them to construct a psychology of spiritual growth.[115] All these writers share a keen awareness of inner process corresponding to their knowledge that the monks in any community will run the gamut from raw novices through seasoned contemplatives. This diversity of attainments complements the diversity of origins noted by Honorius, Peter of Celle, and others.

It took much longer for the new dynamism to penetrate the literature of formation for women. There is no sign of it in the writings addressed to them by Abelard, Osbert of Clare, Aelred of Rievaulx, or Thomas of Froidmont. Neither does it appear in *Holy Maidenhood*. Since virginity is not a state to be achieved but a condition to be preserved, the dedicated virgin did not have to climb a ladder so much as she had to beware of falling from the high rung she already occupied. In the *Garden of Delights*, an encyclopedia of salvation compiled by the abbess Herrad of Hohenbourg for her nuns, a ladder does appear; but it is the exception that proves the rule. Its fifteen rungs are named for various virtues, but there is no clear progression from the lowest to the highest as in Bernard. And in the illustration, the rungs of the ladder represent different vocations, arranged according to a static hierarchy of class rather than a dynamic of spiritual progress.[116] Significantly, the "ladder" most frequently encountered in treatises for nuns is that of the three states of life—matrimony, widowhood, and virginity. A woman's spiritual rank on this scale is determined by her outward circumstances rather than her inner development—a measure about which spiritual writers themselves felt uneasy.

Nevertheless, the newly professed nun, unlike the monk, had the dubious advantage of beginning in the same state where she would ideally end. If we listen not to the striving, restless spirits in the vanguard of female monasticism—a Heloise, a Tenxwind of Andernach—but to the formative literature they were meant to read, the religious woman emerges as an iconic figure not unlike the heroine of romance. Hers is a static perfection rather than a quest: the knight errant must seek the Grail through perilous adventures, whereas the damsel has only to remain in the castle where it abides. This privilege is paradoxically set forth in the *Speculum virginum*, in many ways the most subtle of the works of direction for women. Here the author does attempt to define five grades of virginity. The first is integrity of mind and body; the second, renunciation of the world; the third, prompt obedience in the love of Christ; and the fourth, contemplation of the divine word with a pure heart. The last stage, however, consists in humble and vigilant preservation of the first. Aging virgins should be "like pregnant women about to give birth, who, walking in harsh and hilly terrain, fear a miscarriage at any moment."[117] Like Mary, the consecrated nun has only to give birth to her spiritual child, Christ, whom she has carried throughout the long pregnancy of her religious life. In this most gendered of metaphors, to grow in spirit is not to ascend but to remain quietly where one is. The final shattering of the earthen vessel will then be the filling of the golden bowl.

2. Authority, Authenticity, and the Repression of Heloise

In the annals of medieval scholarship, questions about the authenticity of sources are not rare. Few texts, however, have languished in the limbo of aporia as long as the letters of Heloise to Abelard. For two centuries now these three epistles have been subjected not only to suspicion, but to the most persistent and stubborn assaults on their authenticity, as well as the most spirited defenses. Whole forests have been felled in the quarrel over Heloise's writing, especially the first two letters that occupy a mere eleven pages in Muckle's edition.[1] Yet still there is no consensus, for it is more than the solution of a textual crux, more even than entrenched academic pride, that is at stake. It is the very battle of the sexes, or what we are now pleased to call the "discourse of desire." As Linda Kauffman has written, Heloise's letters, like other epistolary texts that follow in their wake, "have aroused centuries of controversy concerning origins, authenticity, legitimacy, paternity," for such texts raise a most dangerous question: "What does it mean to 'write like a woman'?"[2]

In the unlikely event that my title has left any suspense, let me state my own *parti pris* at the outset. My intention in this chapter is twofold. First, I will try to dispatch once for all the old hypothesis that Abelard forged the letters of Heloise as part of a literary fiction. Then, after concluding this fervent but no doubt futile attempt, I will show how the same questions that have vexed the scholarly debate over Heloise—questions of authority, authenticity, and repression of the female voice—are precisely the questions that most vexed Heloise herself in her pious and amorous wars with Abelard. There is, in short, an uncanny resemblance between the debate about the text and the debate within the text.

What, Heloise asks herself as well as her beloved, is the authority for her monastic *conversatio*, for the austere and undesired life that she chose "freely at his command"?[3] What kind of authenticity, given her undisguised lack of vocation, could she possibly aspire to or attain in that life? And what yoke of repression could she bear to impose, more than a decade into the course, on all that still displeased Abelard and God—her desire and her anger, her memories, her words? To the chagrin of many readers, the answer to all of these questions seems to be "obedience to Abelard's will." Yet if Abelard's mastery appears complete when the correspondence ends— perhaps more complete than it ever was in reality—it has been yet more fully realized by certain latter-day interpreters. There are those for whom Heloise's letters are "authentic" only as part of Abelard's oeuvre; their authoritative word is Abelard's message of conversion; and the cost of this would-be redemption from the limbo of thirteenth-century forgery and eighteenth-century legend is not only the repression of Heloise's desire, but the complete obliteration of her voice.

/ I will try to show here that this "grotesque hypothesis"[4] is grounded in a priori notions of what a medieval abbess could write, frank disapproval of what Heloise did write, and at times outright misogyny. Further, I want to demonstrate that the thesis of Heloise as Abelard's literary creature not only fails to resolve the textual problems it is invoked to explain, but creates new and ludicrous problems that have so far been neglected only because the proponents of this thesis have ruled whole realms of investigation out of court. Whatever the difficulties raised by Heloise as author, they are less troubling than the ones Abelard would pose if he were accepted as the fictive author of Heloise. Indeed, the sensual abbess who has proved unconvincing to some readers and scandalous to others should be far less repugnant than the priest/husband who could fraudulently paint such a portrait of his wife and spiritual daughter. Both Heloise and Abelard, I will argue, are more historically as well as psychologically plausible figures if we accept the least problematic hypothesis about them, namely that the letters we have are essentially theirs.

I. *Refutatio hereticorum*

Habitués of this debate will be quick to point out that not only Heloise's letters but also those of Abelard have been challenged. In 1972, John Benton created a furor by positing that the whole correspondence was the collaborative effort of two thirteenth-century forgers, who eased their burden by incorporating the work of a third forger who had written the *Historia calamitatum* a century earlier, as well as some hypothetical lost writings of Abelard himself.[5] But since Benton withdrew his own Ecovian hypothesis in 1980,[6] it has found little favor, and the *Historia calamitatum* with Abelard's letters is now almost universally accepted as genuine.[7] The same cannot be said of Heloise's, for reasons that are perhaps unwittingly suggested by Peter von Moos. Fifteen years ago, von Moos expressed relief at the vindication of the *Historia*. He referred to Benton's original forgery hypothesis as "ominous" because the loss of Abelard's famed autobiography would have changed the whole intellectual profile of the twelfth century. In contrast, however, von Moos chose to remain agnostic about Heloise's letters, calling their authenticity "a comparatively minor, if not exactly trivial question with respect to the history of women in the middle ages or, more generally, the 'history of sensibility.'"[8]

Now women are used to being minor, if not exactly trivial, but must we continue to accept this relegation to a realm of "sensibility" where it is impossible to ascertain the truth that, in any case, hardly matters? Less misogynist, but no more satisfying, is Paul Zumthor's claim that authenticity is a moot point, since the whole discourse unfolds in an airy realm of pure textuality, utopic spaces, and resonant echoes.[9] Pure textuality is all very well, unless we happen to be concerned with the actions of real men and women who lived in the past, that is, with history. For the historian, to accept Zumthor's ethereal resignation would be no more than a gesture of weariness at a controversy that has lasted too long and borne too little fruit.

Among those scholars who believe the question does matter, attempts to reinforce male authority are surprisingly frequent and overt. J. T. Muckle, the even-handed priest who edited the correspondence in the 1950s, patiently examined and dismissed all scruples previously raised about the letters, but raised one of his own when, unlike most subsequent readers, he found Abelard insufficiently stern with Heloise's passion: "One would expect that Abelard would have chided her and tried to set her right in regard to such extravagant and sinful dispositions." Because Muckle does not perceive such "chiding," he tentatively concludes that Abelard could not have seen the offending passages, and he doubts that such an esteemed abbess could have written them. Rather, it was some unknown redactor—albeit "a literary genius"—who rewrote the first two letters of Heloise and put the dossier into circulation after her death.[10]

The male and specifically clerical attempt to "set [Heloise] right" is also the guiding thread that links all three of Benton's successive positions on the correspondence. In 1972, he argued that Heloise's letters were the work of "a thirteenth-century author who wanted to put women in their place" and thus made Heloise out to be a submissive, sensual creature, whereas the documents of the Paraclete show that the real abbess "must have been an outstanding person."[11] In 1975, Benton again set the "sensual" woman of the letters against the holy abbess of history:

> That Heloise loved Abelard was of course no secret, in the twelfth century or later. [What matters most] is the question of *how* she loved him. She may have loved Abelard as a dutiful wife and proper abbess who prayed for her husband after his death, . . . sharing Abelard's belief that the Christian calling of monk or nun was higher than the sensual life of lovers, whether married or not.[12]

By 1980, Benton had decided that the "author who wanted to put women in their place" was in fact Abelard. When the philosopher established Heloise at the Paraclete, "he was the man in control," but as he became further removed from the abbey's affairs, "he began to fear that Heloise and the nuns needed male control from outside the convent" and so forged the letters to illustrate "the carnal weakness of a woman without proper male direction."[13] In his last published writing on the correspondence (1988), Benton extended his argument to other alleged "literary fictions" that Abelard ascribed to Heloise, most notably the *Problemata Heloissae*—a set of forty-two exegetical questions posed by the abbess and answered by Abelard. Benton insists that even here "Abelard had the final say over what was written,"[14] although Heloise survived him by twenty-one years and presumably copied the manuscripts of these texts written for her edification. One may perhaps be pardoned for asking if this preoccupation with putting women in their place, establishing male control, and giving a man the final say is exclusively Abelard's.[15]

The need to assert Abelard's authority by repressing Heloise's authenticity is still clearer in the work of D. W. Robertson, whose *Abelard and Heloise* appeared in the same year as Benton's first salvo. Robertson's condescension toward Heloise is blatant. He refers to her twice as "poor Heloise" and once even as "little Heloise"; at least half a dozen times, he calls her discourse on marriage in the *Historia calamitatum* a "little sermon."[16] In a display of stunning inconsistency, he manages to deny that "little Heloise actually said anything like" what Abelard records, and at the same time to ridicule her for saying it. Embodying all the negative stereotypes of the feminine, Robertson's Heloise is both minx and shrew. In her "little sermon" she is guilty of "completely abandoning logic with a somewhat alarming feminine flair," yet shows "distinct promise of becoming a very able Xanthippe."[17] The "real" Heloise, Robertson concedes, had by the

1130s "grown from a vain and amusingly unreasonable young girl into a mature and respected abbess"[18] who may have actually written letters to Abelard—but not the literary ones that survive. His opinion of these letters as they are usually read is even lower than his view of the "little sermon." The letters have indeed earned Heloise "a reputation for remarkable 'enduring human passion,'" which is, in Robertson's view, "a rather polite, if somewhat amusing way modern ecclesiastics have of referring to the persistence of lust centered on a single object."[19]

Robertson himself would read these letters, like all medieval texts that purport to celebrate erotic love, as witty and ironic; they form part of an exemplary conversion narrative authored by Abelard. If Heloise had anything to do with them at all, she perhaps "made useful suggestions" to her husband.[20] In this way we can still credit the "mature and respected abbess" with the lustful thoughts while denying her the dignity of writing. Yet we are told that Heloise deserves "some credit for nourishing Abelard's literary ambitions";[21] and as badly as he abused her, it is just as well that she succumbed to his seduction, for without Abelard "she would very probably have become just another matron, somewhat more learned than her gossips, . . . soon forgotten and lost to both history and legend."[22] Robertson's Heloise, whatever her status—the seductive and silly little minx, the proper but silent abbess, or even the hypothetical bourgeois wife—is well and truly repressed.

The notion that Heloise was somehow involved in constructing the dossier without actually writing anything is also shared by Chrysogonus Waddell. Without discussing the erotic letters, Father Waddell would extend to them the same argument he has made about Heloise's letter on religious life. He "wonders whether, though the voice is Heloise's, the ideas may be, in the first instance, Abelard's—though these are ideas which Heloise is glad to make her own." Concerning Abelard's writings for the Paraclete, Waddell further asks "whether Heloise would have asked Abelard to write them if Abelard had not first wanted to do so."[23] The abbot may in fact have wanted to write a rule for nuns; but the idea that a woman would not ask a man for anything he did not already want to give her is wishful thinking of a high degree. And the odd claim that Heloise consulted with Abelard about personal letters that he then wrote in her name rests on nothing more substantial than a sense that women did not write— in spite of ample evidence to the contrary. As Peter Dronke has remarked, such theories further betray "the notion that in all that Abelard and Heloise shared intellectually, Abelard was exclusively the giver, the active partner. And this is purest prejudice."[24]

A final example of prejudice is supplied by Hubert Silvestre, the sole critic to uphold Benton's thesis of thirteenth-century forgery after Benton himself repudiated it. Before Silvestre decided that the thirteenth-century forger was Jean de Meun, he had described this personage as a "vindictive and not very commendable" character who forged the *Historia calamitatum* in order to mount attacks on his own enemies via the screen figures of Anselm of Laon, William of Champeaux, and others who had lived a century and a half before him. As for Heloise, Silvestre offers an equally outlandish theory that he himself terms a "venomous little hypothesis." According to Silvestre's fantasy, the forger had personally seduced and abandoned "a little Jeannie" who was demanding marriage, so in order to shake her off, he inserted Heloise's diatribe against matrimony in the *Historia*. But this little Jeannie is assumed—unlike Heloise!—to be capable of following a complex argument in Latin and objecting that *her* seducer was no eunuch, so had no excuse not to marry her. Therefore the forger made his fictional Abelard downplay the effects of his castration.[25] In a later contribution, Silvestre speculates about Abelard's "loose lifestyle" and possible homosexuality, and he accuses the literary Heloise of "an unpardonable sin"—preferring the creature to the Creator.[26] Such arguments do not deserve serious refutation; they are cited here only to demonstrate the gratuitous sexual fantasy that has accompanied some of the more forceful repressions of Heloise.

Embarrassing as it is to expose these unwarranted, often misogynist assumptions, it is essential to do so. In some quarters there still lingers a nineteenth-century bias against the very idea that medieval women wrote, but the scholarship of the last two decades leaves no excuse for this misconception.[27] It is ironic that Heloise in particular should be subjected to such a prejudice, for in her own day she had a reputation as a distinguished literary scholar even in her teens. Abelard states that he was first attracted to her because "in the extent of her learning she was supreme" and had already become famous throughout the realm.[28] Peter the Venerable confirms this account in a letter he wrote to Heloise after Abelard's death, remarking that even as a young man, he used to hear laudatory tales of her—"the woman who, although still caught up in the obligations of the world, devoted all her application to knowledge of letters . . . and to the pursuit of secular learning, [so] that not even the pleasures of the world . . . could distract her from this worthy determination to study the arts."[29] Even Abelard's bitter enemy Roscelin refers to Heloise as a *puella prudentissima* who had the philosopher as her tutor[30]—a fact that in itself testifies to the degree of her achievement, since not many teenaged girls in the 1110s were studying privately with renowned professors. From Heloise's mature years, we have the witness of Hugh Métel, a canon who had not actually met her but knew by hearsay that she had "surpassed the feminine sex" in writing, specifically of verse.[31]

Some scholars have objected not to the prospect of a woman writing per se, but to an abbess writing in praise of erotic love. Yet one of the most celebrated erotic writers of the twelfth century, Marie de France, may also have taken orders. We have no firm evidence about her identity, but a persistent hypothesis identifies her as a royal Anglo-Norman abbess— either Marie of Shaftesbury or of Romsey.[32] If one of these wealthy and prestigious houses was in fact headed by the poet, no scandal seems to have attached to her administration. Yet in Marie's lai of "Le Fresne," a convent-educated girl sleeps with her lover within the abbey walls, and later elopes with him, without incurring the slightest authorial reproach. And in "Yonec," a fairy knight transforms himself into the shape of his lady, a married woman, and receives communion in that form in order to convince the lady that he is worthy to become her lover.[33] In this story, too, the narrator is extremely sympathetic toward the couple. From a strict ecclesiastical point of view, these two lais are as shocking as anything in Heloise's letters—and unlike the private writings of Heloise, Marie's poems enjoyed a widespread and immediate vogue.[34] Could she have been chosen for high religious office in spite of them? It may be that at least some twelfth-century audiences were less fastidious in these matters than their modern interpreters.

Gender bias may have an insidious effect even on the choice of permissible methodologies. For many years, those who would write Heloise out of her letters have dismissed all arguments based on "psychology," claiming to find such considerations incurably subjective, unpersuasive, and unmedieval. Benton states that convincing arguments must be based on "the most technical and indeed unemotional issues," such as dating, *cursus* patterns, and computer-assisted word counts.[35] Psychological realism, he says, is a "risky basis" for any claims of authenticity.[36] According to Jean Jolivet, an agnostic on the letters, psychology is the weakest and least persuasive source of arguments.[37] Von Moos, the skillful critic of ideologies, also rejects the use of "psychological criteria for plausibility," although he allows that computerized studies can just as easily permit gross errors.[38] Robertson is especially vigorous in his assault on such villainous modern obsessions as personality, psychology, sentiment, sensuality, and "human understanding," which mar the appreciation of Abelard's exemplary dialogue on conversion.[39]

Now psychological arguments, like any others, can be used well or badly; they can be persuasive or unpersuasive. But two decades of argument over grammatical constructions, alleged anachronisms, and minute points of monastic observance have yielded no more consensus than the previous decades of argument over what Heloise or Abelard might have plausibly thought or felt. If our goal is to do justice to a text that offers, among other things, two of the most candid probings of conscience and consciousness that medieval sources preserve for us, we will hardly advance by renouncing any of the tools at our disposal.[40] More insidiously, these scholars' appeals to abjure psychology allow their own psychological assumptions to go unchallenged, especially on the subject of gender. Heloise's writing seems doubtful to those who find her sentiments dubious, but this ground for offense is no longer set forth plainly, as in Muckle's account. It still lurks in the background, however, masked by more "objective" and respectable concerns, so that repugnance for the literary Heloise need not be directly confronted.

Finally, if psychological arguments are ruled out of court, Abelard as the imagined author of Heloise is allowed to shield the reader from her blaze of recalcitrant passion, which is thereby reduced to the status of an edifying fiction, and we need not take the frightening spectacle of her struggles *au sérieux*. Yet by the same token, we need not imagine what kind of man, not otherwise known for his sensitive insight into other people's feelings, could have mothered such a hot-blooded yet cool-headed, tender yet passionately angry discourse on his own former mistress and wife, whom he was now taking pains to call his "sister in Christ." Significantly, the partisans of Abelard's sole authorship have focused on the *Historia calamitatum* and the monastic writings, paying little attention to Heloise's two erotic letters. No one has yet dared to read these epistles in detail as Abelard's literary creations, and even Robertson chooses to call their narrator " 'Heloise' for convenience."[41] Excellent close readings of these letters have in fact been offered,[42] but never on the supposition that Abelard wrote them.

The long-standing controversy over the letters, which has become a kind of institution in medieval studies, has brought many historians to a point of settled agnosticism. Yet we should bear in mind that, if the letters of Heloise are to be effectively challenged, the burden of proof rests squarely on the assailants, not the defenders.[43] For, surprisingly, none of the usual grounds for contesting authenticity is in fact present in this case. Nothing in the letters contradicts any documented historical fact, and alleged internal discrepancies have all been satisfactorily explained.[44] The manuscript tradition is late but solid, and can be traced back squarely to the Paraclete.[45] Given the scanty manuscript witness for Abelard's works in general and the number that are entirely lost—e.g., his commentary on Ezekiel, an exhortation to the monks of St.-Gildas, a *Grammatica* and *Rhetorica*, and a work on universals—the ten surviving manuscripts of the correspondence indicate that this text, once it was finally published, enjoyed a greater popularity than many of the master's philosophical and theological works. For our purposes, three facts about the manuscript tradition are especially significant.

First, all the MSS. ascribe the letters to Abelard and Heloise, never to anyone else or to Abelard alone, nor are they ever copied anonymously, like letters in a model collection.[46] Second, the tradition is strikingly uniform; the *Historia calamitatum* and the letters are always found together in the same order, without major variants (with the exception of Abelard's *Rule*, which only survives in one complete copy). This uniform text strengthens the case against Abelard as the final redactor, for finishing and polishing a book was not his strong point. By his own admission, he was the kind of scholar who was better at teaching than at publishing.[47] To illustrate, Abelard's *Theologia*, a work that he valued highly, survives in eighteen MSS. representing eleven redactions of three different versions, and his *Sic et non* is extant in ten MSS., every one of which preserves a different version.[48] It would have been very much against the grain for Abelard to retouch his own letters, much less those of Heloise, so as to cast them in definitive form for publication. Aside from the correspondence with Heloise, no other edited collection of Abelard's letters, such as we have for so many famous twelfth-century figures, has come down to us.[49] Moreover, even if Abelard had wished to "have the final say" about the literary form of these letters, in his last years he was more peripatetic than ever and had no permanent home in which to assemble a library. The manuscript tradition shows no connection with Cluny, where he spent his final year; and it has often been pointed out that Peter the Venerable, who knew both Abelard and Heloise, shows no acquaintance with the letters. They could have been preserved only at the Paraclete, where it was Heloise and not Abelard who had leisure to put them in publishable form.

The third salient point, however, is that Heloise did not in fact publish the letters. It has been conclusively shown that, although the story of Abelard and Heloise was well known to their contemporaries and inspired diverse responses among them,[50] the letters themselves remained unknown until the mid-thirteenth century. Jean de Meun translated them into French around 1280 and included a version of Heloise's diatribe against marriage in his *Romance of the Rose*.[51] Thereafter the volume of letters became a favorite text of the French and Italian humanists, admired by Petrarch and perhaps by Dante.[52] This long-delayed publication naturally gave rise to the suspicion of a thirteenth-century forgery; but that thesis had to be discarded when, despite diligent searching, Benton failed to expose anachronisms or historical errors of the sort that normally betray medieval forgeries.[53] It is, in any case, wildly improbable that any thirteenth-century writer would have possessed—or cared to possess—such a detailed and specific knowledge either of ecclesiastical and academic controversies in the 1120s or of the early history of the Paraclete.

On the supposition that the letters are authentic, does their non-publication in Heloise's lifetime constitute a problem? I think not. In her second letter, Heloise urgently pleads with Abelard not to praise her, attributing her untarnished reputation to "hypocrisy" and claiming that this "pretence" has deceived many, including Abelard himself.[54] In a celebrated passage of the *Historia*, Abelard indeed says that "bishops loved [Heloise] as a daughter, abbots as a sister, the laity as a mother; while all alike admired her piety and wisdom, and her unequalled gentleness and patience in every situation."[55] If Heloise had earned and maintained such a reputation, to which Peter the Venerable also bears witness,[56] over so many years and at the cost of such anguish as she describes, she would certainly not have been fool enough to destroy it by publishing her intimate confessions to the world. Scrupulous honesty before her own conscience and before Abelard, whom she now viewed as her spiritual father, was one thing; but the wanton destruction of her own reputation, which would have endangered the Paraclete and all its priories, would have been quite another.[57] Recent history shows that the dossier of letters can be read as an edifying narrative, but it has been more often read as witness to a scandal, and even the possibility of provoking such a response would have been enough to restrain a prudent abbess from publishing the confessions she was too candid and too desperate not to write.

Why, then, if they were not intended for publication, are Heloise's letters so "literary"? One might as well ask why Abelard was a teacher or Bernard of Clairvaux a monk. Literature was Heloise's first vocation, well before pregnancy, marriage, and their sequel had put such a sudden end to her studies. As prioress and later abbess she no doubt had many occasions for writing, but perhaps little chance to practice the vivid, stylized *ars dictaminis* she had learned as a girl. Is it any wonder that, when the opportunity to renew a correspondence with Abelard arose, she should have given her learning and artistry free play? If Heloise used every rhetorical device at her disposal, the hope of moving and winning consolation from Abelard alone fully justified her best efforts.[58]

It is worth noting that in this regard there is a marked difference between Abelard's letters and those of Heloise. Abelard's *Historia* is a quasi-public document, perhaps written to prepare the way for his departure from St.-Gildas and return to a teaching career in Paris,[59] although we have in fact no evidence that it ever circulated apart from the letters. The *Rule* along with Abelard's epistle on the history of nuns, and to a lesser extent even his two personal letters to Heloise, which include prayers for the Paraclete, are intended to edify the whole community as well as its abbess. But Heloise's letters are relentlessly private; they are addressed "to her only one," *unico suo*, "to him who is especially hers, from her who is uniquely his."[60] The famous salutations underline Heloise's theme of exclusive mutual belonging—of the marriage debt, in fact, which she transmogrifies into a demand that Abelard take full responsibility for her emotional and spiritual welfare in the life he has imposed upon her. While Heloise, like an Ovidian heroine, gestures toward the whole world as witness to her woes, she addresses her appeal to Abelard alone. There was no need for her to imagine a wider public—although it is just possible that, with her fine histrionic sense, she might have hoped for the appreciation of posterity once she had passed "where, beyond these voices, there is peace."

The simplest hypothesis concerning the letters, then, is that Heloise collected, preserved, and perhaps retouched them at the Paraclete, where the last three at least would have furnished useful reading for the nuns; but she did not publish them, nor was their existence suspected for more than a century to come. Some unsolved mysteries remain. We do not know, for example, how or if Heloise came upon Abelard's *Historia* "by chance," or how Jean de Meun stumbled on his great literary find. Such questions, however, are no more than the inevitable lacunae we confront in tracing the transmission of any medieval text. They are in no way comparable to the enormous, not to say insuperable, problems raised by the specter of Abelard as sole author of the letters.

Let us return now to this unlikely prospect and confront these problems head-on. Doubt about Heloise's authorship arose in the first place from reluctance to believe that she could have felt, or at any rate set in writing, the sentiments expressed in her first two letters. Let us then suppose, for the sake of argument, that she did not find such follies in her heart or inscribe them on her parchment. With Robertson, let us imagine that she "devoted herself energetically, with only occasional uncomfortable lapses, to the settled routine of her new career."[61] With Muckle, let us assume that Heloise was inwardly all that she appeared to be outwardly: "a person of sincerity, zeal and holiness and not a self-confessed hypocrite whose heart has all the while been possessed of a spirit of sensuality."[62] Let us recall the exemplary abbess whose virtue, as Peter the Venerable wrote, crushed the head of the serpent and made "a laughing-stock of the proud prince of the world."[63] This is the abbess who told Abelard "with the highest exultation" how Bernard of Clairvaux had paid her a long-desired visit and preached to her nuns "not as a man, but as an angel."[64] This is she whose administration was so effective that under her rule her abbey's "worldly goods were multiplied more in a single year than [Abelard's] would have been in a hundred."[65]

Heloise as abbess must indeed have been a remarkable figure. Her monastic foundation had begun beneath the shadow of a double scandal— first the long-remembered love affair, and then Suger's eviction of the nuns from Argenteuil on the pretext of their gross misconduct.[66] When Heloise and her daughters first moved to the Paraclete, they had little more than an abandoned oratory and a few huts that had been hastily erected on the site by Abelard's students. In her thirty-five-year reign, however, Heloise not only won the personal esteem that is so well attested, but attracted enough gifts and vocations to the Paraclete to attach five new priories and an abbey, La Pommeraye.[67] Her popularity is further suggested by the number of nuns and noblewomen who were named after her in the next generation.[68] These facts are uncontested, whatever one's position on the correspondence.

Assuming that Heloise was not the "hypocrite" she claimed to be and that she did not write her letters, what kind of man must Abelard have been to forge them? He had already wronged Heloise at least three times—when he seduced her, when he forced her into a marriage she opposed, and when he compelled her to precede him into monastic life because of sexual jealousy. If we believe Heloise's first letter (even on the theory that Abelard wrote it), he had wronged her yet a fourth time by ten years of studied neglect during her sojourn at Argenteuil. In 1129, however, Providence and Suger's greed gave him a chance to make amends, and he was able to provide for Heloise in her need with the gift of the Paraclete. Only at this point did Abelard renew his bond with her in the new guise of brother and sister in Christ, or father and spiritual daughter; but he took the new relationship seriously and began visiting the Paraclete often to preach and assist the nuns as best he could. His visits, in fact, were frequent enough to set scandal-loving tongues in motion yet again.[69] Abelard's subsequent devotion to the Paraclete is beyond question, not only as founder and patron but also as spiritual father. The extensive works he prepared for Heloise and her nuns include not only Epistles 7 and 8 (the *Rule* and tract on the history of nuns), but also a treatise on the study of Scripture (Epistle 9), the *Problemata*, a volume of hymns and sequences, a sermon cycle, and an unfinished commentary on Genesis.[70] Mary McLaughlin has shown plainly that in his last years, Abelard envisaged the Paraclete as a refuge and salvation not only for Heloise, but for himself.[71]

By 1132, the earliest likely date for the *Historia*, Heloise had been abbess of the Paraclete for at least three years. The new foundation had already turned the corner from abject poverty to the beginnings of prosperity and high esteem, and Abelard had already shown his willingness to cooperate with the nuns, although it seems that rumor had temporarily driven him to withdraw and return to his wretched life at St.-Gildas. As for Heloise, however, no breath of scandal had touched her at least since the move from Argenteuil. What demon, then, could have possessed Abelard to forge letters so compromising that they would jeopardize his own new foundation, which had begun to display such promise, by fueling the very rumors he deplored? In what demented frenzy would he defile the hitherto spotless reputation of Heloise as abbess, violating the honor of his "beloved sister in Christ" more grievously than he had done when he seduced her? What destructive and self-destructive madness could prompt him to heap ill fame on the cherished oratory that he had twice been forced to abandon, and now hoped to endow as his lasting monument to the God of all comfort? Finally, if Heloise was as far above reproach as he himself maintained in the *Historia*, what made him think that she could be driven to cooperate in such a peculiar fraud, much less that he could carry it off without her involvement or knowledge?

In short, Abelard could have had no sane or morally acceptable motive for forging letters in which Heloise is made to acknowledge sustained hypocrisy, luxuriate in self-pity, revel in erotic nostalgia, glory to be called a whore, belabor ancient grudges, accuse God of the harshest cruelty, avow an idolatrous devotion to her lover, declare her willingness to follow him even into hell, and express the gravest doubts about her own salvation] If she did not in fact harbor and give voice to such thoughts, anyone who made her confess them falsely would be committing an unforgivable calumny; and Abelard, in his newly chastened frame of mind and with his reviving hopes for the Paraclete, would have been the last person in the world to wish such a thing. It does not help the case to argue that the first two letters of Heloise are parts of a larger whole, which is meant to be didactic and edifying. If the entire dossier is supposed to bear witness to Abelard's pastoral skill in "converting" Heloise from her sinful thoughts, what should be the most important element of all is missing—namely a convincing proof of her conversion.[72] Moreover, although Abelard's replies to Heloise are effective enough in their way, no reader until Robertson ever pretended to find them nearly as memorable or moving as Heloise's "unconverted" letters.

We must ask finally, if we are to take the thesis of a conversion narrative seriously, whom Abelard could possibly have meant to instruct by it. Certainly not the monastic or clerical world at large, for he never published the letters; and in any case his own career as a monk had been so fraught with scandal that he was hardly the man to be taken seriously as a pastoral genius, even if his "exemplary" text had been less ambiguous and conflict-ridden than it is. Nor would the nuns of the Paraclete be edified by a public disclosure of the imagined mortal sins of their abbess, who had taken such pains to model an exemplary religious life for them in every way she could. Such a fabrication could only have been an act of the most irresponsible cruelty and folly on Abelard's part, wholly out of keeping with the concern and labor he was beginning to lavish on the nuns.

If anyone remains unconvinced, however, let us go yet a step further. Let us take the theory of Abelard's authorship more seriously than its own proponents have done, and try to read Heloise's first two letters as if Abelard had actually composed them. We must begin with the *Historia calamitatum*, assuming that when "Abelard" wrote his account of the quarrel he and Heloise had about marriage more than twelve years before, and when he described the events surrounding their monastic profession, he was already intending to correct this narrative with the subtle but significant alterations that "Heloise" would later make. This deliberately planned repetition-with-variation would suggest that it was Abelard, not Heloise, who assigned such deep significance to the question of whether she had wished to be called *amica* or *scortum*, and whether she preceded or followed him into vows. Surely these would be strange memories for him to revive and nuance so precisely when she had been a nun for more than a decade! But no matter. We must also suppose that when "Abelard" penned his flattering and idealized portrait of Heloise's piety, which comes near the end of the *Historia*, he was already planning to give it the lie by publishing her false confessions. The gracious tribute is thereby transformed into an artfully constructed façade that is worthy of Chaucer's Pardoner.

Turning to "Heloise"'s first letter, what sentiments do we find "Abelard" expressing therein? First a lengthy and, under the circumstances, pointless summary of his own previous epistle. He then covers himself with rebukes for not writing to Heloise—an odd maneuver for one who is writing to himself in her name—and proceeds to remind himself of serious obligations he had hitherto seemed to forget. Interspersed with these reproaches, however, are signs of a monumental vanity, for "Abelard" says of his own role at the Paraclete:

> You after God are the sole founder of this place, the sole builder of this oratory, the sole creator of this community. You have built nothing here upon another man's foundation. Everything here is your own creation . . . whatever was done, the credit was to be yours alone.[73]

Coming from Heloise, these remarks would be an eloquent testimony of devotion and gratitude; from Abelard, they can testify to nothing but an alarming monomania. Yet while taking such exorbitant credit for his venture at the Paraclete, "Abelard" then returns straightway to self-reproach on behalf of Heloise, berating himself for neglecting her "long ago," when she was newly converted.[74] In this ambivalent mood, he begins to profess Heloise's undying love for himself. Monk and eunuch that he is, he makes his mistress of fourteen years ago delight in calling herself his whore; in her person, he remembers and boasts of his own former attractions, praising the love songs he once wrote and making Heloise ask, "What matron, what virgin did not lust for you in your absence and flame with desire in your presence? What queen or powerful lady did not envy my joys and my bed?"[75] It is just possible that Abelard's sexual vanity was once so great—but fourteen years after his castration? Everything he wrote under his own name suggests that he had come to accept his mutilation as an act not merely of divine justice, but of mercy, and he claimed to have no regrets for his deliverance from the sins of the flesh.[76] Even assuming that he could still savor these past pleasures—which in his own letters he recalls only as base and shameful obscenities—would he have dared to attribute such feelings for his once-virile but now much-altered self to the venerable abbess? If Abelard had known that Heloise still cherished such passions, could he have written of her piety in such glowing terms, not only in the *Historia* but also in his subsequent letter? And if he did not suspect that she still felt this way, what response could he have expected this forgery to arouse in her except rage at his new betrayal?

Yet while making Heloise express this continued admiration and longing for him, and profess unbounded submissiveness to his will, "Abelard" also lets her accuse him of being shallow and manipulative: "It was desire, not affection which bound you to me, the flame of lust rather than love. So when the end came to what you desired, any show of feeling you used to make went with it."[77] Now it would be one thing for a man to exult in imagining a woman's boundless desire for him, although, as I have suggested, nothing indicates that this was Abelard's frame of mind at the time of the letters. But even if it were, would he be able in the same breath to imagine the same woman's vehement anger? In the *Historia* and the first letter written under his own name, Abelard expresses remorse for his past sexual indulgence, but never for the wrongs done to Heloise. The lament he utters over his castration contains no mention of her, or even of regret for their lost pleasures, nor does he betray any sense that he sinned in making her take the veil. What is more, in his reply to this letter he brushes off "Heloise"'s reproach so lightly, eulogizing her as the "good wife" whose prayers will be his salvation, that one would think he had not even yet suspected the depth of her anger, much less invented it himself and penned these bitter words.

To gain perspective on the unwonted sensitivity that Abelard is supposed to have shown in representing the thoughts of a wronged woman— one wronged by himself, moreover—let us contrast the *planctus* he wrote for Dinah, daughter of Jacob, whose rape is recounted in Genesis 34. Abelard cannot conceive of Dinah feeling any anger at all; rather, he has her blame herself for the rape, excuse her violator, and grieve that he has been so harshly punished.

Vae mihi miserae	Woe to my wretched self
Per memet perditae!	Destroyed by my own fault!
. . .	
Coactus me rapere,	Compelled to ravish me,
Mea raptus specie,	Ravished by my beauty,
Quovis expers veniae	You would not have gone unpardoned,
Non fuisses judice.	Whoever the judge might be.
. . .	
Levis aetas juvenilis	Your light-hearted
Minusque discreta,	And indiscreet youth
Ferre minus a discretis	Should have borne a lighter penalty
Debuit in pena.[78]	From those who were discreet.

Could the poet who portrayed a rape victim so forgiving have conceived Heloise, who loved him, to be so angry? More plausibly, it is the generous spirit of Heloise—but with all the rage carefully excised—that inspired Abelard's portrait of Dinah.

Let us turn to "Heloise"'s second letter. Aside from making her mouth the most profoundly ambivalent feelings toward himself, Abelard had already compromised the abbess's religion by letting her claim that she would blithely follow him to hell. But after inventing this scandalous protestation for her he compounded the mockery, in his reply, by commending himself devoutly to her prayers. Now, however, he gives her a powerful dramatic monologue filled with such anguish, such bitter lamentation, and such deeply divided yearnings that, if it is truly his, we must place him in the company of Ovid and Shakespeare among the great female impersonators of Western literature. It would be hard to find another twelfth- or thirteenth-century author who belongs in that company, for dramatic monologue was not a genre much cultivated at the time. The speeches given to their characters by such accomplished poets as Chrétien de Troyes and Jean de Meun are not at all like the monologues that Abelard ostensibly wrote for Heloise; they are much more allegorical and, oddly, more analytic and "dialectical" than these two letters ascribed to the prince of dialectic.[79] Moreover, it is hard to think what Abelard could have hoped to gain from such a virtuoso performance, even had he been capable of it. As the work of Heloise, this second letter could only be the fruit of an urgent and impassioned need for confession. As Abelard's fiction it could be nothing of the sort; it is hardly monastic or edifying; and, written under a pseudonym, it could not even earn him the literary fame that its brilliance deserves.

"Abelard"'s first remarks in the person of Heloise are flattering enough to his ego. He lets her insist that his name and rank should take precedence over hers, and he imagines her falling into despair at the prospect of his death, proclaiming that she could never live without him. But then he goes on to her famous Boethian *planctus*, inveighing against God and Fortune:

> O God—if I dare say it—cruel to me in everything! O merciless mercy! O Fortune who is only ill-fortune, who has already spent on me so many of the shafts she uses in her battle against mankind that she has none left with which to vent her anger on others. She has emptied a full quiver on me, so that henceforth no one else need fear her onslaughts . . . Of all wretched women I am the most wretched, and amongst the unhappy I am unhappiest. The higher I was exalted when you preferred me to all other women, the greater my suffering over my own fall and yours, when I was flung down; for the higher the ascent, the heavier the fall.[80]

These are strange sentiments for a priest-husband to place in the mouth of his abbess-wife. Heloise is made to reverse the expected Boethian progression, turning not from Fortune toward Providence, but from God back to Fortune; and her Lady Fortune has a quiver full of the arrows that belong more properly to Cupid. A topos often used to warn consecrated virgins of their precarious stature—the higher the ascent, the heavier the fall—is also turned on its head in this discourse.[81] "Heloise" represents herself as "exalted" when she was Abelard's mistress, but "flung down" and "fallen" into sacred chastity. She is made to continue in this vein at length, in passages that are yet more celebrated: venting her rage against God's injustice, avowing her lack of repentance, acknowledging the pleasure she still takes in erotic memories, and scorning her monastic life as a futile charade that cannot possibly earn merit in heaven. If critics have blanched at the idea of a Heloise who actually entertained such thoughts, even as abbess of the Paraclete, is it not twice as monstrous to imagine her spiritual father attributing them to her without warrant?

Scholars have occasionally proposed a compromise theory, namely that Abelard did not invent Heloise's confessions out of whole cloth but used remembered conversations and "actual fragments of authentic letters" to compose the epistles that we now have in her name.[82] These fragments are said to have been written much earlier, when Heloise was still at Argenteuil, so that we need not imagine her maintaining a stoic silence for twelve years and then bursting suddenly into speech. But this theory leaves the problem of Abelard's motivation untouched, and also fails to recognize the tightly unified structure of the sequence. Heloise's first letter is a detailed response to the *Historia calamitatum*—her own autobiography in return for Abelard's—complete with enhancements and corrections of the story he has already told; and her second letter responds just as directly to Abelard's first reply. The complaint that Heloise's letters are too long and full of quotations to be hers can only stem from a failure to acknowledge the depth of her learning or from an ignorance of twelfth-century style.[83]

I have chosen not to analyze Heloise's epistle on religious life in this context, since it has been drawn only incidentally into the authenticity debate and has been fully discussed and defended elsewhere.[84] But I hope I have shown that any attempt to read her first two letters as a fiction by Abelard, far from saving her reputation or enhancing his, would only make her the victim of an incomprehensible fraud and betrayal. To posit such an act, we would need not only to credit Abelard with a degree and type of dramatic skill that is otherwise unattested in his era, let alone his works, but also to entangle him in a web of psychological absurdities, including the sabotage of his own and Heloise's best interests at a time when the "history of their calamities" was just taking a turn for the better. By the same token, we would deprive Heloise herself of due credit for her learning, her unforgettable prose, and her devastating honesty in the service of truth. So, having laid the ghost of pseudo-Abelard at last, we can now reread these same letters as the work of a much more interesting author, namely Heloise, who was neither fiction nor legend but the writer whose ambiguous glory inspired more than her share of each.

II. *Accessus ad auctores*

Not a few students of English literature first encounter Heloise in those puzzling lines written by a real "female impersonator," Chaucer's Wife of Bath. The Wife is reminiscing about her husband Jankyn's Book of Wikked Wyves—the book she would later make him cast with his own hand into the fire, as Abelard had been forced to burn *his* book at Soissons—and she rehearses its contents for her hearers:

> He cleped it Valerie and Theofraste,
> At which book he lough alwey ful faste.
> And eek ther was somtyme a clerk at Rome,
> A cardinal, that highte Seint Jerome,
> That made a book agayn Jovinian;
> In which book eek ther was Tertulan,
> Crisippus, Trotula, and Helowys,
> That was abbesse nat fer fro Parys,
> And eek the Parables of Salomon,
> Ovides Art, and bookes many on,
> And alle thise were bounden in o volume.[85]

It seems that the misogynist appropriation and repression of Heloise began early. When we meet her in these lines she is already enmeshed in a textual net subtler than the one Vulcan used to ensnare Mars and Venus. An ironic male poet impersonating an angry feminist impersonating a jealous husband gives him an authoritative book on female evil starring Jerome, the famous misogynist whose best friends were women and whose "book agayn Jovinian" was a favorite text of both Abelard and Heloise. Behind Jerome stand a few of his own *auctores*—the Stoic woman-haters Chrysippus and "Theophrastus," the Jew Solomon, and the Christian Tertullian. There are also two women in the list of antifeminist authors—Trotula, whom Chaucer probably knew only through the title of the book ascribed to her, *De passionibus mulierum*, and Heloise, an avowed expert on the same subject. Strangely but fittingly, Heloise finds herself canonized midway between Jerome, the master of asceticism, and Ovid, master of the art of love—the two *auctores* who also left the deepest traces in her own writing. In this context, however, her authentic voice is overwhelmed by their dissonant but mutually reinforcing discourses that harmonize, for the misogynist reader, in the unity of "o volume." In much the same way, the Wife herself is contained between the bounds set by her creator Chaucer and her creature Jankyn. She is allowed to speak authentically "on the passions of women," but only in the safe space between two contrasting structures of male authority, one created by her husband's brutality and the other by the poet's irony.

Behind Chaucer's parade of manifest authors there lurks, as usual, a concealed *auctor*—in this case Jean de Meun, who was the first to discover and exploit Heloise for poetic ends. The abbess appears in Jankyn's Book of Wikked Wyves because she had first appeared in the *Romance of the Rose* as an exemplum cited by the Jealous Husband, a character invented by the lover's Ovidian friend. Yet in spite of this character's antifeminism, the Jealous Husband depicts Heloise not as a "wikked wyf," but as a good woman who undermines his own case for the perfidy of all wives. Thus, while the abbess is appropriated, on one level, by a misogynist discourse, on another level she is allowed to subvert the Jealous Husband,[86] just as the Wife of Bath is permitted to vanquish Jankyn on his own turf by mutilating his book. Jean's admiration for Heloise, whose writing he knew firsthand, shines through even the Jealous Husband's hostility. The speaker represents her as:

> Bien entendans et bien lettree,
> Et bien amans et bien amee . . .
> Car les livres avoit veüs
> Et estudiés et seüs,
> Et les meurs feminins savoit . . .
> Mes je ne croi mie, par m'ame,
> C'onques puis fust une tel fame;
> Si croi je que la lettreüre
> La mist a ce que la nature
> Que des meurs feminins avoit
> Vaincre et donter miex en savoit.[87]

> Wise and well-educated
> And most loving and beloved, . . .
> For she had looked at books
> And studied them and knew them well,
> And understood a woman's ways . . .
> But I don't believe, by my soul,
> That such another woman ever lived;
> Indeed, I suspect that learning
> Taught her how best to vanquish and subdue
> The woman's ways she knew by nature.

Jean's Heloise had both authority and experience on her side, as the Wife of Bath would have said. Her wisdom was supreme in Jean's eyes because she knew both *les livres* and *les meurs feminins*, and was able to conquer the latter through the former. In the headings sprinkled through his translation of the letters, Jean calls her *la belle Heloys*, *la bonne Heloys*, and (four times) *la saige Heloys*—epithets worth contrasting with those of Robertson.[88] In the *Romance*, however, Jean gives her wisdom a peculiar twist. Her stated reasons for opposing marriage are hardly the ones a Jealous Husband would be expected to endorse; they look ahead not to the *Wife's Prologue* but to the *Franklin's Tale*. Heloise wants a union based on freedom and equality, "sans seignorie et sans mestrise" (l. 8780). Jean ignores the historical Heloise's ecstasy of submission to Abelard's will and suppresses everything Abelard wrote in the *Historia* about her concern for his own reputation. On the other hand, Jean picks up one of her arguments that is obscured by modern translations. In the *Romance* Heloise is made to abjure marriage:

> Si qu'il peüst estudier
> Touz siens, touz frans, sanz soi lier,
> Et qu'el rentendist a l'estuide,
> Qui de science n'iert pas vuide.[89]

> So that he could give himself to study,
> Wholly hers yet wholly free, without binding himself,
> And she too could resume her studies,
> For she was not devoid of learning.

These lines draw on a plea that, according to the *Historia*, Heloise actually made:

> What harmony can there be between students and nursemaids, writing desks and cradles . . . ? *What man* bent on sacred or philosophical thoughts could endure the crying of children, the nursery rhymes of nannies trying to calm them, the bustling throng of male and female servants in the household? *And what woman* will be able to bear the constant filth and squalor of babies?[90]

Although this text is Abelard's, the discourse may indeed have been Heloise's. A year before this argument took place, she had been the private student of the most distinguished philosopher in France, as she believed; now she was the teenaged mother of an illegitimate son to whom she had just given birth on a remote provincial farm, where books were undoubtedly few. There is every reason to believe that Heloise, the precocious convent scholar, did prefer books to "feminine ways" and agreed with Abelard when he later wrote, "How unseemly for those holy hands which now turn the pages of sacred books to have to perform degrading services in women's concerns!"[91] No *auctor*—neither Ovid nor Jerome nor her beloved Stoics—would have taught Heloise to value the joys of motherhood. And as a good medieval scholar, she could scarcely conceive of an authentic life beyond the ken of *auctoritas*.

| Both Chaucer and Jean de Meun point, in their different ways, to a side of Heloise that more recent interpreters have neglected. Theirs was a Heloise fully immersed in the world of books and learning, herself an *auctor* whose authority could be cited in complex and ambiguous ways| More tellingly, they both introduce Heloise at one of the weakest yet most tenacious points of the learned tradition: its appeal to misogyny. It is interesting in this regard that the feminist Christine de Pizan did not mention Heloise in her comprehensive encyclopedia of good women, the *Book of the City of Ladies*, where she could have been included among the learned writers, the nuns, or even the heroines of love. We know that Christine was familiar with Heloise's story; in a letter she cited the abbess's celebrated claim that she would rather be Abelard's whore than a crowned queen. Christine may have known that text only through Jean de Meun, given that she had engaged in a pamphlet war over the *Romance of the Rose* with two of Jean's partisans, Gontier Col and Jean de Montreuil. Yet both of these French humanists were also noted admirers of Abelard and Heloise, and knew their correspondence firsthand.[92] Under the circumstances, Christine's silence is eloquent, for it suggests that she was already reading Heloise through misogynist lenses. Although she did not shrink from feminist rewritings of Dido and Medea, she could not view the abbess of the Paraclete as either a good woman or a useful *auctor* for feminists. In short, Heloise could not be admitted to the City of Ladies because she had already been canonized in the Book of Wikked Wyves. Her letters had become fit reading only for the likes of Jankyn and the Jealous Husband.[93] |

III. *Expositio in Heloissam*

The issue of authority vis-à-vis misogyny has been central to the reception of Heloise, whether medieval or modern, because it was in the first place central to Heloise herself. If she does not belong in the antifeminist canon where Chaucer placed her, she does belong in that uneasy realm where

Ovid makes common cause with Jerome. Most readers have been inclined to favor either Ovid's Heloise or Jerome's, valorizing the one and suppressing the other: either we accept the tragic and impenitent *grande amoureuse*, or else the practical abbess with her zeal for authentic religious life.[94] But if Heloise's letters are genuine, we cannot exclude either persona, nor can we divide her career neatly into an "Ovidian phase" and a "Jeromian phase." In her youthful diatribe against marriage she is already citing *Against Jovinian*, and in her letter on monastic life, no sooner has she "set the bridle of [Abelard's] command on [her] words of unbounded grief"[95] than she is quoting a choice passage from the *Ars amatoria*. Both *auctores* helped to lay the foundations of that misogynist prison that constrained her life and letters as well as the terms of her reception.

It is likely that Heloise had read both Ovid and Jerome, as well as Seneca, Lucan, Cicero, and a variety of ecclesiastical authors, before she ever laid eyes on Abelard. In addition to the convent library at Argenteuil, she would have had access through her doting uncle to even richer resources at Notre Dame of Paris. What imaginative possibilities could such voracious early reading have opened before the young Heloise? On the evidence of her later writings, the question is not hard to answer. The path of virgin martyrs evidently held no appeal for her, although in time she was to prove that a determined Stoic could make a better abbess than many a pious Christian. But the classical *otium philosophicum* exerted a strong attraction, and she saw the life of contemplative leisure—which absolutely excluded marriage, though not lovemaking—as a real possibility for herself as well as Abelard. From the letters of Jerome, she had learned that such a life allowed Christian men and women to form close spiritual bonds, transcending the pull of mundane life. Yet this was not the only option, for she knew also of the pious Roman matrons, the Lucretias and Cornelias, with their endless willingness to sacrifice for the husbands they adored. And she knew of the passionate women in love, seduced and abandoned yet eternally ardent—Dido, Sappho, Medea, Oenone. These utterly committed lovers of the *Heroides*, rather than the playful and manipulative coquettes of the *Ars amatoria*, powerfully appealed to her. Further, she knew and endorsed Cicero's ideal of pure, disinterested friendship that asked nothing of the beloved save himself, "te pure non tua concupiscens."[96]

But finally Heloise could not escape the tradition of "wikked wyves" that virtually any author, pagan or Christian, was all too ready to invoke, and in moments of despair she was not beyond adding her own name to the annals of infamy. There is indeed a strong antifeminist streak in her writing, and her medieval readers were not slow to identify it. This tendency may explain why modern feminist scholars have been none too eager to insist on the authenticity of her letters, for there are passages in them that one would be only too glad to father on Abelard or some other male. Even if we discount the *Historia*, Heloise's second letter contains a misogynist set piece in which she compares herself to Eve, Delilah, Solomon's consort, and the wife of Job, saying that women have always been the downfall of great men;[97] and in her third letter she refers often (though not consistently) to the weakness and corruptibility of the female.[98] The roles of weak woman and temptress, like those of world-renouncing philosopher, tragic lover, heroic wife, and spiritual friend, were sanctioned by the full authority of the ancient texts.

Heloise, I submit, came to Abelard with not only her mind but her imagination already well-stocked. Her studies with him were doubtless intense, but they were brief and, as we know, interrupted by potent distractions. What Abelard enabled Heloise to accomplish, through the course of their lifelong relationship, was to actualize one after another—at least in writing—every one of the models that her splendid and thorough education had laid before her receptive spirit. Remarkably, she enacted each of these roles vis-à-vis a single beloved other who became in turn her Ovidian seducer, her Pompey, her Aeneas, her Jerome; she could be his Corinna or Cornelia, his Dido or his Paula. More than any ancient Roman, perhaps, Heloise fulfilled to perfection the classical ideal of the *univira*, the woman who belonged solely and wholly to a single man. Whatever the role she played, Abelard was always her *solus*, her *unicus*; he alone could grieve her, comfort her, instruct her, command her, destroy her, or save her.[99]

The greater the variety of positions she could take over and against her beloved, the more total and perfect the relationship.[100] Hence the exultant multiplicity of that greeting with which her literary record begins: "To her master, or rather her father, husband, or rather brother; his handmaid, or rather his daughter, wife, or rather sister; to Abelard, Heloise."[101] Still more roles are added to her repertoire at the beginning of her second letter, where she objects to Abelard's prior salutation, in which he had set "woman before man, wife before husband, handmaid before master, nun before monk, deaconess before priest and abbess before abbot."[102] Aside from the contest in courtesy here and the show of monastic (and perhaps erotic) submission, Heloise once again revels in the manifold bonds that bind her to Abelard: no identity she can possibly claim lacks its counterpart in a title of his. Without him she is nothing, but with him she can be all things. Her self-abasement is thus also a self-enrichment, a multiple enhancement and proliferation of the roles that constitute her feminine self.

One is reminded here of the Marian piety that was so swiftly developing in the liturgy and the Song of Songs tradition during Heloise's lifetime, a piety that celebrated the Virgin as at once God's mother and his daughter, Christ's exuberant bride and desolate widow, self-effacing handmaid and all-powerful consort. For twelfth-century writers Mary was becoming, in Ann Matter's suggestive phrase, "the woman who is the All"[103] through her totally fulfilled relation to the allness of God. The female mystics of subsequent generations would delight in imitating every aspect of her endlessly rich, varied, and all-absorbing union with him. Heloise is, in this respect, a precursor of Mechthild of Magdeburg and even Margery Kempe, finding a rich and full selfhood in the adoption of multiple imaginative roles. But the opposite number in *her* totalizing relationship was an earthly man, and for her, classical models would do just as well as Christian. Authenticity, for Heloise, lay in the whole-hearted embodiment of the feminine exempla that authority supplied her—even at times the exempla of evil—so long as they could be played out vis-à-vis the one man whom she had constituted as her sole living authority, in the things of heaven as in those of earth.

But while this mode of authentic living might satisfy Heloise the lover and the woman of letters, it could not meet the needs of her religious life, nor could it satisfy Abelard, whom she desired above all things to please. A double movement of renunciation and repression is therefore required of her. In the first place, there is the voluntary repression of her own desires, undertaken as a sacrifice of obedience to Abelard's will. Romantic readers are not mistaken in seeing a kind of mystical surrender, an ecstasy of abnegation about this sacrifice, which we can read as an anticipation of the female piety that would become widespread a century later. Mechthild of Magdeburg, for example, was to pray that God would send her to hell if he might through her torment "be praised beyond measure by all creatures."[104] Hadewijch, to flaunt the utter disinteredness of God's lovers, declared hell to be the highest name of Love,[105] and Marguerite Porete asserted that heaven and hell are as one to the simple, annihilated soul.[106] Heloise prefigures such adepts of abnegation in her boast that she would follow Abelard without hesitation to the depths of hell, finding strength at his bidding to destroy her very self.[107] Her love, she claims, "rose to such heights of madness that it robbed itself of what it most desired beyond hope of recovery."[108] The fact that her sensual desires continue unabated supplies the proof that she is truly in hell and not in some celestial calm of mind, all passion spent.

I have been arguing for Heloise as a kind of mystic manquée. Yet, however great her spiritual virtuosity, as long as Abelard remains the object of her love, that love is, in Abelard's own terms, no more than idolatry. Perhaps the most telling of his reproaches is the one that reiterates her own boast, only to cast it back in her face inverted:

> You who strive to please me in all things, as you claim, . . . that you may please me supremely, you must put aside this [bitterness against God]; for with it, you can neither please me nor come with me to bliss. You who claim you would follow me even to hell—will you suffer me to go to heaven without you?[109]

With this challenge Abelard demands that Heloise renounce the motive of her own renunciation. In the name of love, he asks her finally to surrender him, along with her love for him, into the hands of Christ—to abandon her misplaced mysticism for an ordinary monastic life.

This second movement of renunciation, with its dizzying emotional gymnastics, recalls nothing so much as the climactic meditation of Marguerite Porete's *Mirror of Simple Souls*. Seeking the ultimate sacrifice of self-will, the mystic has professed her willingness to suffer eternal torments and see the whole creation destroyed, rather than offend against Christ's will; she offers to forego God's grace forever for the sake of God's love; but then she confronts three renunciations that she dare not make.

> Suppose he asked how I would feel if I knew he wanted me to love another more than him. Then my wits failed and I knew not what to answer, what to wish or refuse. But I said I would think about it.
> Then he asked how I would feel if he loved another more than me. And here my wits failed and I knew not what to answer, what to wish or refuse.
> Again he asked what I would do, and how I would feel, if he wanted another to love me more than he did. Again my wits failed and I knew not what to answer. . . . I told him these three things were much harder than the previous demands. . . . And there I failed, for I could not reply to any of these, nor could I deny or refuse them, yet he constantly pressed me for an answer. And I loved myself so much along with him that I could not be contented at all. . . . I was held in distress and could not easily escape. No one can understand this who has not been put to the test.[110]

This is precisely the test to which Abelard now puts Heloise's love. If she truly desires to please him, he commands, she must desire to please Another more than him; if she loves him, she must let him love Another more than her; and to prove that he truly loves her, he admits that Another loves her more.

> Think of him always, sister, as your true spouse. . . . What has he seen in you, I ask you, when he lacks nothing, to make him seek even the agonies of a fearful and inglorious death in order to purchase you? What, I repeat, does he seek in you except yourself? He is the true friend who desires yourself and nothing that is yours. . . . It was he who truly loved you, not I. . . . I took my fill of my wretched pleasures in you, and this was the sum total of my love. . . . To him, I beseech you, not to me, should be directed all your devotion, all your compassion, all your remorse.[111]

The cruel pathos of Abelard's ultimatum lies in his transference of Heloise's own terms of love to the surrogate Beloved. Does she boast that she would suffer torments gladly? Christ has actually done so. Does she profess the Ciceronian ideal of pure friendship? Christ alone has loved her truly and not what is hers. Was she willing to atone with her own life for Abelard's fall? Christ has already atoned for them both. Where Heloise exults in the multiple bonds that bind her to Abelard, he insists on replacing her binary pairs with triads that include the Other, the new beloved that he would have her embrace in his stead. He writes as the servant of Christ to Christ's bride, for Abelard is but the eunuch who guards the king's harem in which Heloise is queen.[112] Or again, she is to be Martha, beseeching Christ to raise her brother Lazarus from the dead, or the wife of Nabal the Carmelite, interceding with King David to save her husband's life.[113] Abelard will even remove himself from the scenario entirely: she who would be but the reflection of his glory, taking her whole identity from him, is now to take her very name from Another, *Heloissa* from *Heloim* (Elohim).[114]

We do not know, of course, whether or how far Heloise succeeded in this second repression. In the first she sacrificed her desire; in the second she was asked to sacrifice her love, the consuming fire that had motivated her first immolation. Like Marguerite Porete, she found the final demands of her beloved too difficult for words and expressed her will to obey them only by renouncing words. Hence the famous "silence of Heloise"—which is not really a silence so much as the turning of a page, the end of one discourse and the beginning of another. Henceforth her frame of reference shifts into alignment with accepted monastic *auctoritas*—Scripture and tradition, Benedict and Jerome, Augustine and Gregory. The classics slip quietly into the background, Ovid remaining only to supply an *exemplum in malo*. Authenticity becomes a question of proper monastic observance under an appropriate Rule, with fitting worship in which the Spirit is not killed by the letter.

For many readers, however, Heloise's last letter is precisely the one where her spirit dies, or at least goes underground forever. While she wages impassioned war with Abelard under the guise of submission, she never ceases to fascinate; but when she actually submits, she dwindles into virtue as a heroine of romance might dwindle into marriage. The second repression of Heloise does entail a silencing, not only of her desire and her rebellion, but of all that is most "literary" about her. It is, from one point of view, the ultimate victory of the masculine over the feminine voice: not only a personal triumph of Abelard over Heloise, but a victory for the poetics of castration over the discourse of desire. Heloise's erotic discourse has in fact been repressed ever since it was uttered: by Abelard within the text itself, by Jean de Meun and Chaucer in their ambiguous appropriations of it, and by those modern scholars who have made Abelard its author so as to negate it all the more powerfully.

Heloise's monastic discourse has provoked fewer and less fervent responses. But its first reader, Abelard, was at least generous enough to consolidate his moral victory with a treatise that renewed and amplified the themes of Christian feminism, after a silence of centuries.[115] His radical exaltation of women in general, and nuns in particular, was his own way of celebrating the "nouvelle Héloïse"—the loving Bride of God that he had tried so hard to forge from the ruins of his former love. Having humbled herself to the limit in the realm of desire, Heloise was now fit to be exalted in the new realm that she had consented at last to enter. Had she actually become the woman that Abelard henceforth addressed, the exemplary abbess whose historical record we have already traced? We shall never know. But we can only hope that her double repression, in response to Abelard's doubled authority, led her finally to that moment of complete authenticity that Marguerite reached at the end of her trials:

> "If I knew without a doubt that you willed this . . . I would will it, without ever willing anything again. And thus, sir, my will comes to its end with these words; and therefore my will is martyred, and my love martyred. . . . My heart

once thought it could live by love forever through the desire of good will. But now these two have died in me; they have brought me out of my childhood."

Then the Land of Freedom disclosed itself. . . . And Love came to me filled with kindness, she who had so often driven me out of my senses and in the end had put me to death. And she said to me: "Friend, what do you wish from me? I contain all that ever was, is, and shall be; I am totally fulfilled. Take of me whatever you please. And if you wish all of me, I will never refuse."[116]

3. "Crueel Corage": Child Sacrifice and the Maternal Martyr in Hagiography and Romance

Once upon a time in India, we read in the *Jātaka* stories, the future Buddha was born as a prince named Vessantara, who distinguished himself by his great generosity. After giving alms of all that he owned, the prince with his wife and children went off to the Himalayas to live the life of an ascetic. One day a brahman came along and asked Vessantara to give away his children as slaves for the brahman's wife. The sacrifice was a cruel one, but

> As the generous Vessantara gave him the children, the earth itself quaked from the power of his spirituality, and he wished that by this most difficult gift he might at last win the state of perfect mind. The children were bound and beaten by the cruel brahman, even before they were out of their father's sight. The heartbroken Vessantara went into his hut and wept bitterly as the cries of his children faded into the distance. Meanwhile the gods detained the children's mother in the forest until nightfall.[1]

The frantic mother searched all night without finding her offspring, but she had little time to grieve, for the next day another brahman arrived and Vessantara gave her too away. Yet the story has a happy ending: the brahman turns out to be a disguised god who is only testing Vessantara, and because of his flawless generosity he is restored to his kingdom and the family is reunited.

In this Buddhist folktale, medievalists will recognize a distant analogue of the story of Griselda. The legends of both East and West are filled with tales of sacrifice in which a parent slays or abandons children in order to prove devotion to a god or allegiance to a principle. In one important respect, however, the Griselda story differs from both the Buddhist legend and most classical and biblical exempla of child sacrifice. It is Vessantara, not his wife, who gives up the children; she remains unaware of his deed and is horrified to discover her loss. This paradigm covers the great majority of Western examples before the thirteenth century: the mother is absent, or else she is inscribed in the narrative as a figure of grief or protest.[2] In medieval Europe, however, we find a whole class of tales, of which Patient Griselda is the best known, in which a mother proves her virtue by acquiescing in the sacrifice of children.

In this chapter I will investigate the shift from father to mother as the parent whose child is required of her. The motif originates as a hagiographic topos in early Christian sources, but gains increasing prominence in the lives of thirteenth- and fourteenth-century women saints. What I shall call the "maternal martyr" paradigm emerges as a tenacious literary convention that duplicates tendencies in the cult of Mary, but also responds to potent social forces acting on medieval mothers, especially young widows. The maternal martyr is a woman whose holiness is enhanced by her willingness to abandon her children or, in extreme cases, consent to their deaths as the Virgin did to Christ's. As a consequence of this renunciation, she is delivered from family ties and enabled to live for God alone. By the fourteenth century, when this hagiographic type has become well established, we begin to see "secular saints" like Griselda as romance heroines—"good women" who still establish their virtue by sacrificing their children, no longer for God's sake, but for their husbands. The maternal martyr plot in romance both perpetuates and subverts the hagiographic hierarchy of values, in that it continues to represent care for children as an inferior good to be subordinated to any "higher" good that may conflict with it; but since the higher good is now linked to conjugal loyalty, the motif of child sacrifice no longer undermines the patriarchal family but supports it.

While these conflicting versions of the mother's involvement are distinctive to the medieval corpus, the meaning of child sacrifice itself remains fairly constant from antiquity onward. As a supreme test of religious devotion or honor, the primitive command to slay a child presupposes intense parental love—no sacrifice could be more painful, and therefore more precious.[3] As Alcuin says in his commentary on Abraham and Isaac, God demanded a three-day journey to Mount Moriah in order to heighten the patriarch's anguish through a period of sustained intimacy, "so that at every moment, the pain of his son's impending murder might increase with the father's love."[4] But the idea of parental responsibility is absent: only Abraham's pain, not Isaac's, is expected to evoke sympathy. In accord with the law of *patria potestas*, the child is viewed as the father's absolute property and has no intrinsic rights. In ancient examples the child's feelings are rarely consulted, and those victims who are given a voice proclaim themselves willing. Attention is thereby directed toward the parent's dilemma and away from the victim's pain. Medieval treatments of these tales, reflecting a greater sentimental interest in children, sometimes heighten their pathos by allowing the child to lament or question its fate. In this way the morality of the sacrifice may be at least obliquely problematized. In no case, however, is it even implicitly condemned.

I. The Family Sacrifice

Two biblical and two classical stories can illustrate the ancient paradigm of child sacrifice as a project of the fathers. The most famous of these is the Binding of Isaac (Genesis 22), understood by medieval Christians to prefigure Christ's sacrifice.[5] Although Sarah plays a large part in the story of Genesis, she is absent from the episode of Isaac's barely averted slaying, in which God tests the faith of Abraham alone. But the following chapter begins with the death of Sarah, and both Jewish and Christian interpreters seized on this fact to inscribe her in the scene of sacrifice. In rabbinic midrashim, Satan tempts Sarah and it is said that she died of grief (or alternatively, of joy when she learned that Isaac had been spared after all).[6] The medieval Corpus Christi plays, instead of killing Sarah, imagine her protesting the cruel demand. In the Chester Cycle, Isaac wishes plaintively that his mother were there, for surely she would kneel at Abraham's feet and beg mercy.[7] And in a French revision of the Abraham play (1539), the patriarch holds an imaginary dialogue with his absent wife and projects his pity and grief onto her, the better to repress them. Here Sarah's unspoken words represent the silenced voice of "human affection," while Abraham promotes the superior claim of "the Sovereign's love."

> Veulx tu par ung regret humain
> Perdre l'amour du souverain?
> Yras tu a dampnation
> Par une humaine affection?[8]

The sacrifice of Isaac, required by an apparently ruthless God but remitted in the nick of time, can be paralleled with Euripides's tragedy of Iphigenia. Here, too, the sacrifice of the child is a paternal project carried out against a mother's protests, this time not imagined but vehemently uttered. Agamemnon lures his daughter Iphigenia to Aulis on the pretext of marrying her to Achilles, but he actually means to sacrifice the maiden in order to placate Artemis and speed the Greek fleet on its way to Troy. Like Isaac in the Corpus Christi plays, Iphigenia plays the part of willing victim: she forbids Clytemnestra to mourn and begs her to forgive her husband.[9] But nothing can appease the bereaved mother's rage, which motivates her subsequent murder of Agamemnon. Only in a separate play is it revealed that the goddess accepted a deer in place of the maiden, just as God substituted a ram for Isaac. Interestingly, *Iphigenia in Tauris* begins with a soliloquy by the rescued virgin, now High Priestess of Artemis, lamenting that she herself must offer human sacrifice. At the end of the play, Athena proclaims the end of this barbaric rite.[10] Thus both the Hebrew and Greek dramas, like the Buddhist tale of Vessantara, suggest that the gods do not actually desire human sacrifice; what they demand is the supreme proof of loyalty evinced by a father's willingness to kill a child.

In tales where the sacrifice takes place on the father's own initiative, however, no surrogate is provided. The story of Jephthah's daughter, sacrificed in fulfillment of a vow (Judges 11), unfolds in the absence of any maternal figure. Likewise, in Livy's tale of the maiden Virginia, beheaded by her own father to preserve her chastity, the mother is a narrative blank. This tale was retold as an exemplum by Jean de Meun, Boccaccio, Chaucer, and Gower.[11] In the *Physician's Tale*, Chaucer gives the girl a "mooder deere" (l. 119) who, however, is nowhere to be found at the time of her murder—even though the poet has moved this crime from the courtroom to the maiden's home. Virginius, like Jephthah, makes a self-pitying speech in which he blames his daughter for causing him such pain, thereby projecting his unacknowledged guilt onto the victim (Jdg. 11:35, *PhyT* 213–26). In her lament, the girl explicitly compares herself to Jephthah's child (ll. 240–44).[12] Both daughters meet their fates grieving but unresisting—the Hebrew girl mourning that she will die a virgin, the Chaucerian maid taking comfort in the same thought. Medieval commentators were divided over the merits of Jephthah's deed, in part because the epistle to the Hebrews (11:32) lists him among the heroes of faith. Early authors gave typological readings, evading the literal sense,[13] while Augustine argued that although divine providence made prophetic use of this and other sinful acts, Jephthah was no less wicked for vowing a sacrifice so abhorrent to God.[14] Rabanus Maurus, on the other hand, called Jephthah a saint and cited his vow to justify the monastic practice of child oblation.[15] Rupert of Deutz and most later exegetes found the story unedifying and read it as a warning to beware rash vows. God refrained from halting the sacrifice as he had done for Abraham, Rupert says, in order to punish Jephthah's recklessness.[16] Chaucer likewise may be covertly disapproving of Virginius when he lets the Physician moralize to parents, warning them to guard their children well:

> Ye fadres and ye moodres eek also,
> Though ye han children, be it oon or mo,
> Youre is the charge of al hir surveiaunce,
> While that they been under youre governaunce.
> Beth war, [if by ensample of youre lyvynge,
> Or by youre necligence in chastisynge,]
> That they ne perisse . . .[17]

The verses I have bracketed, with their egregiously misplaced advice, are typical Chaucerian red herrings. If they are ignored, however, the apostrophe is apt and warns readers that Virginius, like Jephthah, should be neither imitated nor admired for his act of specious virtue. On the contrary, the more his daughter is assimilated to a virgin martyr, the more the father falls into the stereotypical role of torturer.[18] With morally monstrous irony, he who had no pity on his daughter intervenes to save her would-be assailant from hanging. But even Jephthah and Virginius, who have no divine mandate for their brutal deeds, are not condemned as unambiguously as we might hope.

By excluding the victim's mother, letting her voice objections to the sacrifice, or using her to displace the father's unacknowledged grief, these plots imply that no real mother would consent to the death of her child. In hagiography, on the other hand, we enter a brave new world of equal-opportunity heroism. Men, women, and children alike could aspire to the supreme value of martyrdom—whether the "red martyrdom" of blood or the "white martyrdom" of penance—which superseded the mere carnal and worldly value of motherhood. Intertestamental Judaism had already exalted the mother of the Maccabees, who, after watching six sons tortured to death before her eyes, exhorted her youngest to bear martyrdom with equal courage and finally suffered herself (2 Maccabees 7). One of the most poignant Christian martyr legends is an account of two young mothers, the wealthy Perpetua and the slave Felicitas, who achieved sisterhood in death. At the time of their execution in 203, Felicitas had just given birth to a premature daughter and Perpetua had barely weaned her son. Perpetua's harshest temptation was not fear of death but compassion for the babe she must abandon. At one point in the narrative her grief-stricken father appeals, "Have pity on your baby," and the governor pleads, "Have pity on your father's grey head; have pity on your infant son!"[19] But Perpetua overcomes the last temptation and meets her death with triumphant joy. In this case it is the two mothers, not the children, who are slaughtered, but the emotional dynamics are similar: maternal love must be crushed underfoot in the name of faith.

Even better known in the medieval period were the letters of Jerome, that tireless foe of family life, who praised his friends Paula and Melania for "scorning their wealth and deserting their children [as they] lifted up the Lord's cross."[20] Jerome sketched a memorable portrait of Paula in the harbor taking ship for the Holy Land, hardening her heart against her small son and nubile daughter as they stood weeping on the shore, hands outstretched toward her.[21] Such portrayals of the "unnatural mother" as saint gave flesh to Christ's counsel: "Whoever loves father or mother more than me is not worthy of me; and whoever loves son or daughter more than me is not worthy of me; and whoever does not take up the cross and follow me is not worthy of me" (Matt. 10:37–38). The mother who abandoned her child, whether by choosing death in the arena or a life of prayer and fasting in the desert, not only followed Christ's counsel but showed in the process that she had "become a man," leaving frail womanhood with its earthly cares behind her. In Jerome's words, "As long as a woman is for birth and children, she is different from man as body is from soul. But when she wishes to serve Christ more than the world, then she will cease to be a woman, and will be called man."[22] Echoing Jerome's antifamily sentiments, Bernard of Clairvaux would remark that "it is the height of piety to be cruel for Christ's sake."[23]

With the diffusion of lay piety in the later middle ages, such hagiographic models took on new force as increasing numbers of married women joined the ranks of the devout. Even among wives and widows, such piety remained essentially monastic in spirit, favoring virginity over marriage and renunciation over secular toil, as we see clearly in the writings of such a boisterous and worldly mystic as Margery Kempe. She and her sisters who had "fallen from virginity" knew all too well that theirs could only be a second-best sainthood.[24] Yet a heroic willingness to forsake their children might atone, in some measure, for the misfortune of having borne them in the first place. Just as the virgin martyr preferred death to dishonor, the new maternal martyr preferred the loss of a child to a life of religious mediocrity. But when she followed Paula's holy example in abandoning young children, she no longer did so to attain a virile or gender-neutral state of equality with men. By a peculiar paradox, it was precisely this renunciation of her children that set a holy seal on her motherhood, reconciling it as far as possible with the ideal of sexless, sacrificial maternity embodied in the Virgin.

Clarissa Atkinson, in her recent study of Christian motherhood, has argued that the "good mother" in the later middle ages was perceived as a "mother of tears," defined more by her suffering and pain than by active care for her child.[25] By this criterion, the mother who abandoned a child or acquiesced in its death could still be considered a good mother as long as she did so for noble motives and with genuine though well-repressed grief. One such mother was St. Anne, who, according to medieval legend, offered her daughter Mary to the Temple at the tender age of three. One of the English cycle plays represents Anne as the typical grieving but virtuous mother, smitten to the heart as she nonetheless gives up her child to fulfill her vow.[26] But Mary herself is the supreme example. Although she was in no sense responsible for Christ's death, medieval religious lyrics not only cast her in the role of Mater Dolorosa, but elicited her reluctant consent to her son's sacrifice. The *planctus Mariae* lyric frequently takes the form of an argument full of role reversals: it is the Crucified who has pity on his mother's pain, while at the same time persuading her that, for her own good, he has to die. Mary's grief and her consent are both required if she is to attain the pinnacle of compassion.[27]

In the English lyric "Stond wel, moder, vnder rode," Christ tells the Virgin that although she gave birth without pangs, now at last she knows what it is to be a mother:

"Moder, nou þou miht wel leren
    whet sorewe haueþ þat children beren,
    whet sorewe hit is wiþ childe gon."
"Sorewe ywis y con þe telle;
    bote hit be þe pyne of helle,
    more serewe wot y non."

"Moder, rew of moder kare,
    for nou þou wost of moder fare,
    Þou þou be clene mayden-mon."[28]

True motherhood, this lyric implies, does not consist in giving birth or even caring for a child, but in grieving over one. Some lyrics displace such dialogue from the Passion to the Nativity, setting it within a lullaby: the infant Christ prophesies his death on the Cross, Mary attempts to dissuade him, but he consoles her and she tacitly assents.[29] The implausible context displays the divine Child's omniscience and at the same time places Mary in the position of Griselda, grieving but acquiescing in the death of her Son while he is still a tender babe because his Father's will demands it.[30]

The *imitatio Mariae* which figured in late medieval devotion also tended to conflate the Nativity with the Passion, imparting melancholy overtones even to the joyful Christmas scene.[31] The pain of loss was written inexorably into the script of motherhood. For Adelheid of Frauenberg, a Dominican nun at Töss, maternity and martyrdom were one. This noble widow made a virtue of suffering in silence when her son was beaten by the novice master. At the same time she reveled in masochistic fantasies about the Christ Child:

> She always had an especially great love and devotion to our Lord's childhood, and . . . she wished with heartfelt, loving desire for her whole body to be martyred in the service of that sweet little babe. She wished her skin stripped off to make our Lord swaddling bands, and her veins spun into thread to make him a jacket, and her marrow ground into flour to make him porridge. She wished her blood poured out to make him a bath, and her bones burnt to make him a fire; and she wished all her flesh to be consumed for all sinners. And she cried from her heart for a drop of the milk that our Lady had when she suckled our Lord.[32]

If these aspects of Mariology bolstered the maternal martyr paradigm, the literature of consolation encouraged the belief that renouncing affection for one's child might be a form of holy poverty. Preaching patient acceptance of the death of children, this discourse may also have undermined the sense of obligation to protect them. In one of his sermons, Jean Gerson served warning on fond parents with an exemplum wherein God takes the life of a little boy because his parents have invested too much care and wealth in his nurture, neglecting their debts to the Church and the poor.[33] To cherish one's own child is to nurse mere selfish ambitions, but to feed the poor is to feed Christ himself. Birgitta of Sweden (c. 1303–73), herself a mother of eight, records the words of an exemplary mother held up for her admiration by the Virgin Mary: "If I had bread in my hand, and all my children cried for bread, and [God] hungered, I should give him bread before them all."[34] In his immensely popular *Life of Christ*, Ludolf of Saxony explains that when Jesus told the daughters of Jerusalem to weep for their children (Luke 23:28), he meant that "in the Day of Judgment parents will say that they are condemned . . . through the excessive love they have borne their children, and . . . children will say that they are damned through overmuch love and imitation of their parents."[35]

) Care of children, then, presented a mean between extremes: too much affection could be as bad as too little. Although the average couple were required to nurture and protect their offspring—who, after all, supplied the chief justification for their marriage—parental duty occupied a halfway position rather like the "ethical level" in Kierkegaard's scheme. It stood above the level of mere personal indulgence, but just as far below the level of religious calling.[36] On one end of the scale was criminal neglect or infanticide, perpetrated by sinful mothers; on the other was benign neglect or abandonment, practiced by saintly mothers. The crucial factor, here as elsewhere in medieval ethics, was not the effect of an action on its object, but the motive of the agent.

Unfortunately, it is the motive that most often eludes a historian's gaze. Since we learn of saintly mothers who abandoned their children primarily through their hagiographers, we cannot know with confidence how they actually felt about this decision. It is probably safest to assume a variety of motivations and mixed feelings on the part of women who are said to have renounced their children or accepted their deaths with composure. But it is no accident that this motif often follows hard on the heels of another topos—the young girl who would have preferred to remain a virgin, but obediently complied with her parents' wish that she marry.[37] If these topoi give access to reality at all, even as refracted through an idealizing lens, it is likely that at least some of the mothers who eventually played Paula or Griselda to their young ones had borne them with reluctance from the start. After a survey of the evidence, we may be able to disentangle some of the complex strands of resentment, resignation, and idealism that transformed these "monstrous mothers" into maternal martyrs.

II. The Maternal Martyr as Saint

Tales of mothers sacrificing their children cluster in the hagiography of the thirteenth through fifteenth centuries, but one of the earliest dates back to the eleventh. In the memoirs of Guibert of Nogent (c. 1064–c. 1125), we see a rare child's-eye view of maternal abandonment. Guibert's hagiographic account of his mother, modeled on Augustine's portrait of Monica, blends the adult son's admiration with the aggrieved child's still-smoldering anger. A noblewoman, Guibert's mother was married as a girl and had such a "fear of God's name" that she remained virgin for the first three years of her marriage, leading her husband's kin to speak of bewitchment and divorce. But the union was finally consummated as the unnamed lady "submitted to the duties of a wife," thereby opening herself "not so much to endless misery as to mourning" for the sins of her offspring.[38] Guibert was her youngest and last surviving child, born only months before her husband died. She labored, as he writes, "almost the whole of Good Friday in excessive pain of childbirth (in what anguish, too, did she linger, when I wandered from the way and followed slippery paths!)"[39] This agonizing childbirth, synchronized with Christ's Passion, set the stage for the new widow's life as a mother of tears. Refusing a second marriage, she waited until Guibert was twelve before entering a monastery. At that time, he recalls,

> though I did not lack for the necessities of food and clothing, I often suffered from the loss of that careful provision for the helplessness of tender years that only a woman can provide. As I said, although she knew that I would be condemned to such neglect, yet Thy love and fear, O God, hardened her heart. Still, when on the way to that monastery she passed below the stronghold where I remained, the sight of the castle gave intolerable anguish to her lacerated heart, stung with the bitter remembrance of what she had left behind. No wonder indeed if her limbs seemed to be torn from her body, since she knew for certain that she was a cruel and unnatural mother. Indeed, she heard this said aloud . . . tenderness would then have been her ruin, if she, neglecting her God, in her worldly care for me had put me before her own salvation. But 'her love was strong as death,' for the closer her love for Thee, the greater her composure in breaking from those she loved before.[40]

Feeling bereft and angry, Guibert took to a rowdy life, mocking church and studies, until his mother grew alarmed enough to place him in a monastery, where he became a devout novice but was still plagued by nightmares. Though vividly remembering these youthful torments, Guibert as an adult approved of his mother's choice, since he had adopted the same monastic values. He may have *felt* that she was a "cruel and unnatural mother," but he *believed* it was God who had hardened her heart, for her own good and ultimately for his. By emphasizing her grief at their separation, he was able to preserve his sense of being a loved child while highlighting the depth of his mother's sacrifice, and therefore her holiness. Guibert's memoirs also introduce a third topos linked with the maternal martyr—that of the prodigal son. The youth in Christ's parable abandoned his father; this youth is abandoned by his mother, but responds similarly by "squandering his property in loose living" (Luke 15:13) until, saved by the same mother's prayers, tears, and example, he repents and makes a good end.

A similar pattern appears in the vita of a saintly recluse, Juette of Huy (1158–1228), composed by the canon Hugh of Floreffe before 1239.[41] Juette, like Guibert's mother, was a young and unwilling bride who loathed sex and marriage. Before the event she had already observed that "the law of matrimony was a heavy yoke: the distasteful burdens of the womb, the dangers of childbirth, the raising of children." Once wedded she fell into despair, longing only for liberty or death: "that she might be freed from her husband, she seemed spontaneously to wish for his demise: and truly it was so." Happily widowed at eighteen, Juette stayed for only five years with her two surviving sons before joining a lepers' hospice at Huy. The vita does not say what arrangements she made for the boys, but in the interim she had antagonized her father by giving their inheritance to the poor and fending off a promising suitor. After more than a decade with the lepers, she had herself enclosed as a recluse. Her younger child, who was about five years old when she left him, had meanwhile reached adolescence and, like Guibert of Nogent, became a classic prodigal. In her reclusion, however, Juette showed considerably more concern for his salvation than she had for his upbringing. According to the vita, she proved herself a good mother after all by dint of the tears, prayers, and punishments she lavished on the young rebel, until he was duly converted and became a Cistercian like his brother. Juette herself compensated for the loss of her children in ways that would become increasingly familiar: she cultivated a devotion to the infant Christ and gathered a new "family" of spiritual sons and daughters.

Far better known than Juette was her royal contemporary, Elizabeth of Hungary (1207–31), one of the few recent saints to be included in the *Legenda aurea*. After her husband was killed on Crusade, Elizabeth abandoned her newborn babe and two small children to embark on a life of charity rigorous enough to kill her by the age of twenty-four—and secure her canonization only four years later. For her, too, maternal love was ostensibly a temptation to resist in the name of God. Her versified Middle English life, based on the *Legenda*, conveys the typical idea of children as a form of wealth to be renounced in the quest for holy poverty. At the turning point of her life, Elizabeth prays to God:

That he hyr grauntyn wold of al temporal possessyoun
Contempt, & from hyr hert al delectacyoun
Of hyr chyldryn takyn in euery degre, . . .
    And whan she had preyid hertyly þis wyse,
To hyr maydyns she seyd: 'god my preyere
So hath herd þat I as dung now despyse
Al temporal þingis, & my children here
To me þan oþir mennys be no more dere.'[42]

The saint proved her point by caring with special tenderness for poor and
sick children, but only after God had sufficiently hardened her heart toward
her own. Once again we see the young widow emulating the virgin martyr:
she can be forgiven her sexual experience because she endured it only in
obedience to husband and parents, and her motherhood because she sacrificed her own children to look after God's. Charity could begin anywhere
but home.[43]

Maternal martyrdom is especially common in the vitae of Italian tertiaries and other urban widows, partly because the loss of children could
be assimilated to the Franciscan ideal of poverty, partly because the dowry
system made it difficult for these widows to keep their children in any case.
Blessed Umiliana dei Cerchi of Florence (1219–46) loathed wedded life so
much that when her two daughters were ill, she told them they would be
better off dying as virgins than growing up and marrying. In such a desperate wish we can see the unhappy wife's resentment and rage mingled with
a desire to protect her innocent girls from the dread fate of womanhood.
Once freed by her husband's death, Umiliana refused a second marriage
and angered her wealthy father so much that he confiscated both her dowry
and her children. Prevented from entering a convent as she desired, she became a domestic recluse and experienced her lingering maternal affection
as a snare of the devil. Thus a visit from one of her daughters became an
occasion of sin, because she was tempted to break her vow of silence. On
another visit, however, when the child fainted and appeared to be dead,
Umiliana prayed with tears to the Virgin until Christ, in the form of a "remarkable and handsome boy, came forth from a painting" and revived her
daughter.[44] Umiliana found the Holy Family more sympathetic than her
relatives on earth.

Margaret of Cortona (c. 1247–97) was not royal or even noble. A Tus-
can peasant girl, she bore a son out of wedlock to the local lord. When
the lord was murdered, she repented of her nine years as his mistress and

eventually sought admission to the Franciscan Third Order.[45] As a "fallen woman" of low birth with an illegitimate child, Margaret was a most unlikely subject for hagiography. But the peasant, no less than the princess or the urban patrician, won praise for neglecting the child whose very existence she had cause to regret. She established herself as a new Magdalene by devoting herself wholly to prayer, refusing to cook for or even speak to her son, whose allotment of food she gave to the poor. Unlike her noble sisters, she evidently had no relatives willing to take him in. At length he was sent away to be educated, but when his tutor appeared one day to give a progress report and collect his pay, Margaret refused to say a word to the man even on her confessor's orders. Her hostility was so pronounced that later, when the boy failed to appear at Cortona for his Easter vacation, villagers spread a rumor that he had drowned himself in despair.[46] To the hagiographer, on the other hand, Margaret's rejection of the unfortunate boy invoked Christ's blessing: "This is she who perfectly fulfilled the word of the Gospel [Matt. 10:37] when, for the love of her dear bridegroom Jesus, she cast out her only son, preferring to him poor strangers and companions for Christ's sake."[47]

Two other Italian tertiaries came even closer to the literal enactment of child sacrifice. Angela of Foligno (c. 1248–1309) and Michelina of Pesaro (c. 1300–1356), both widows, were enabled to enter the Franciscan Third Order because their children died. In the narratives of both mothers, the first dictated by the saint and the second composed by a hagiographer, the children's demise is represented as God's direct answer to prayers. Michelina, widowed at twenty, opened her home to a tertiary named Syriana, who encouraged her young friend to renounce the world and validated the message by levitating at prayer. When Michelina said she could not give away her wealth as long as she was responsible for a son, Syriana suggested that they pray together at the church of St. Francis. There Michelina vowed, "Lord, if you deliver me from the love of my son, I will serve you forever." A voice from the Cross replied, "I want your son with me in Paradise, so I release you from his love. Go in peace." Sure enough, Michelina returned home to find the child dead and angels carrying his soul to heaven.[48] Shulamith Shahar finds this tale repugnant and hard to believe: "If this was indeed the course of events, then, even in the context of medieval culture, the incidents belong in the sphere of psychopathology. But the actual facts are immaterial; even if the tale is imaginary, it reflects a certain cultural attitude."[49] In the light of that attitude the boy's death is a blessing, since he—

or more precisely, his love—stands in the way of Michelina's wish "naked to follow the naked Christ."

Angela, a celebrated mystic, had already received a vision of St. Francis and was well on her way to holiness before God liberated her from the toils of family life. Knowing the ascetic path, she also knew what she had to pray for: "It happened, through the will of God, that at that time my mother, who was a great hindrance to me, died; after that my husband and all my children died within a short time. Because I had set out on the path [of sainthood] and had asked God that they should die, I therefore had great consolation for their deaths. And I thought that from that time forth, since God had made these things happen to me, my heart would always be in God's heart, and God's heart would always be in mine."[50] Angela's beloved is the God of Abraham and Isaac, a jealous God who brooks no rivals for his lovers' hearts. In a later passage of her book, however, she allows herself to express grief for her mother and her dead children, though not her husband.[51] Behind the topos of willing sacrifice, in this case, there lurks a real ambivalence. Angela dwelt on the intense compassion that Christ felt for his mother's pain, and at a moment of profound desolation, she inverted his own prayer from the Cross and cried out, "My son, my son, do not abandon me!"[52] Like many women who followed the path of maternal martyrdom, Angela was able to reclaim and redeem her motherhood in a sublimated form, cherishing not only the infant Christ but numerous spiritual sons.

Although the Franciscans placed a high value on renunciation of family, they had no monopoly on that theme. At the Dominican convent of Unterlinden in Colmar, four of the forty-four sisters commemorated in the famous nuns' book had abandoned small children to enter religious life, while three more brought small children with them. Eligenta of Sulzmatt, married to a knight, prayed like Angela for her husband's demise so she could attend to God more freely. Gratified by a sudden fever that carried him off, she took her three daughters with her to Unterlinden. Once professed, she edified the nuns with her abstinence, giving the best food on her plate to anyone except her children lest, by feeding her own flesh and blood, she lose her reward from God.[53] Like Margaret of Cortona and Birgitta of Sweden, Eligenta viewed her children as extensions of herself to the point that her own abstinence could have no merit if she saw her offspring well fed.

The tone at Unterlinden was set early by its foundress, Agnes of

Herenkeim, a noblewoman who was forced into marriage but "had an incredible horror of her husband's bed as long as he lived, detesting his company."[54] Widowed, she lost no time in sending her two young sons off to the Dominicans, while she and a companion founded the monastery at Unterlinden in 1233. More audaciously, three other noblewomen abandoned their families to join the community while their husbands were still alive. Adelheid of Rheinfelden, prioress ca. 1255–64, "left her husband, a young knight very distinguished in the world, with her two small children"—a feat that her hagiographer, Catherine of Gueberschwihr, found "even more excellent and magnificent" than her desire for poverty.[55] Adelheid's infant son soon died in the care of a nurse, while her daughter Sophia was sent to join her mother in the cloister. As for the husband, who became a Dominican priest, Adelheid had the satisfaction of seeing him tortured in the flames of purgatory after death, but dutifully won his release by prayer.

Sister Catherine may not have understood what prompted another woman, Rilindis of Bissegg, to leave her marriage after eight full-term pregnancies. But she represents that choice as a heroic sacrifice through her glamorized portrait of the family Rilindis left behind:

> She was so divinely inspired that, for the Savior's name, she deserted her husband—a noble knight, distinguished and powerful in the affairs of this world, charming and extremely handsome too—along with the eight children she had borne him, equally good-looking, at a young and tender age. And although she cherished her husband as well as her children with the most affectionate love—so much that she held them dearer than life, above health and every pleasure, more precious than light—yet in spite of such feelings, the mighty and immoderate love of God could not grow cool in her heart. Rather, steadfastly bidding them farewell, she entrusted them to almighty God, all drenched in tears.[56]

Rilindis's husband Guntrammus, perhaps more attractive to Sister Catherine than he was to his wife, took his two sons and joined the Teutonic Knights—among whom he was murdered in 1283. Of the six daughters, two were sent to Unterlinden and the remaining four farmed out to other Dominican convents. But Rilindis meanwhile could find no rest for her tortured soul. Too scrupulous even by Unterlinden's standards, she astonished her sisters and wore out her confessors, "sobbing and weeping over the lightest faults . . . and miserably accusing herself on many occasions when she had incurred no guilt at all." Her anguish was calmed only after she received both a personal visit from Christ and an assurance from the prioress Adelheid, whom she sought out as a role model, that

she and her entire family would be saved.[57] Even through the veil of Sister
Catherine's idealism, Rilinidis's plight seems all too apparent. Like Angela
of Foligno, she was impaled on the dilemma of medieval motherhood:
"damned if you do, damned if you don't." Whatever doubt about her salvation she had experienced as a sexually active wife and mother, her guilt was
only exacerbated at first by her decision to leave. But in the end, if we trust
Sister Catherine, the nuns' collective affirmation enabled her to overcome
her ambivalence. We are told that Rilindis died laughing, her daughters by
her side.

Gertrude of Saxony, a contemporary of Rilindis and Adelheid, likewise abandoned a husband, two sons, and a daughter—perhaps prompted
by a fire that destroyed her family's home and all their possessions. "Following the example of the holy patriarch Abraham in all respects," she
left her native Westphalia for distant Alsace at the urging of an uncle, the
Dominican prior provincial, who probably viewed Unterlinden as a model
convent.[58] The author of Gertrude's vita records her familial anguish not
directly, as in Rilindis's case, but through visions. After the disastrous
fire, while Gertrude was vacillating about her intended conversion, her
uncle saw her in a vision—"not a painted image but her true face, with
skin, flesh and bones"—nailed to a crucifix. This apparition is said to have
brought him great joy. Later Gertrude's husband would take the habit of
a lay brother, but in the interim he too "tasted the sweetness of a celestial vision." Though eucharistic visions of the Christ Child abound in the
Unterlinden vitae, the one vouchsafed to Gertrude's husband is unique:
he saw Jesus as a three-year-old boy *on the Cross* with pierced hands and
feet.[59] This startling image goes a step beyond the Passion lullabies and suggests painful, if subliminal, fears for the couple's own portionless and now
motherless sons.

The themes of childbearing and child sacrifice play a tantalizing but
largely repressed role in the *Book of Margery Kempe*. Margery (ca. 1373–ca.
1439), like most of the religious women discussed here, adored the infant
Jesus—but she scarcely mentions her own fourteen children, the all too
obvious reminders of her lost maidenhood. In an ingenious article, Laura
Howes suggests that the English matron bore (and perhaps lost) her last
child during her pilgrimage to Jerusalem of 1413, an event that inaugurated the most intense phase of her mystical life as well as her notorious
screaming fits. If so, this unwelcome childbirth is evasively chronicled as a
period of six weeks' confinement, followed by a sudden illness and, later,
by rumors that dog Margery back in England.[60] Interestingly, however, the

two episodes in which she does explicitly mention her children occupy a privileged place: one appears at the start of her book and the other opens a supplement composed several years later. The first event signals childbirth as the commencement of all Margery's sorrows: she recalls a psychotic episode that followed her first pregnancy and labor. With the second incident, she measures the distance she has come—from tortured madwoman to confident saint—by relating her own prodigal son story.

Although this episode took place shortly after her conversion, she does not tell the story until many years later, after the son in question had died. We do not know if he was the same child whose birth had caused her such distress, or if he felt embarrassed by his flamboyantly pious mother. In any case, he was a teenager at the time, "a tall young man" who traveled abroad on business and disgusted Margery by his irreverent ways. Since he refused to take her advice—namely that he renounce the world or, failing that, stay away from women until he could marry—she prayed that God would chastise him. The son was duly stricken with a skin disease that made him repulsive, causing him to lose his position; nor was this illness cured until he vowed to amend his life. In the meantime, his troubles drove him meekly back to his mother's house with a promise of good behavior to come. If we read between the lines, the son's malady sounds like no more than normal adolescent hijinks compounded by severe acne: "What with the evil enticing of other people, and what with his own folly, he fell into the sin of lechery. Soon after, his colour changed, and his face grew full of pimples and pustules, like a leper's."[61] But Margery's dramatic presentation suggests a moral crisis and even invokes the rhetoric of child sacrifice: so great is her devotion that she would sooner curse her own son with leprosy than risk the damnation of his soul.

According to Margery's narrative, her son laid both the curse and the subsequent blessing at her door: "He supposed by her prayers our Lord sent him that punishment, and therefore he trusted by her prayers to be delivered of it." Their ever-present neighbors, hostile as always, ascribed the same power to Margery, "saying she had acted very badly, for through her prayer God had taken vengeance on her own child." Circumstances vindicate her in the end, however: the overwhelming force of her prayers is confirmed by the youth's transformation into an ideally devout and devoted son, whose edifying death rounds out the tale.[62] A somewhat less edifying parallel occurs in the Unterlinden nuns' book. Tuoda of Colmar, a widow, is so upset by her son's misbehavior that she asks God to "snatch him from the present life" unless he intends to repent. Since he does not, he is speedily taken off by a fever because—as Sister Catherine blandly concludes—the nun's "holy prayer was no doubt of great efficacy and virtue."[63]

Judging from the evidence I have presented, the topos of maternal martyrdom was a versatile one that could surface in any religious order or social class, and it endured for centuries across lands stretching from Belgium to Italy, from England to Hungary. Ideally, the maternal martyr was a virgin manquée who married for the sake of obedience; took little or no pleasure in sex; bore children to fulfill her conjugal duty; raised them with detachment; cared more for their souls than for their bodies; accepted their deaths with equanimity or abandoned them willingly, if not without grief; took advantage of her widowhood to serve God single-mindedly; and only then displayed her truly "maternal" character in compassion for the infant Christ, loving service to the poor, and zealous care for her spiritual sons and daughters.[64] Like erotic longings, which could more safely be lavished on Christ than on an earthly spouse, maternal feelings won praise if they were displaced from one's own children onto the Child of Mary and "the least of these" his brethren. As a hagiographic ideal, the maternal martyr—like the virginal bride of God—typified the ambivalence of the medieval Church toward conventional womanhood. Both the bridal and the maternal roles served as privileged metaphors for union with the Divine, but only for those who were willing and able to renounce their concrete reality. A woman who had experienced sexual union and parenthood before her conversion had no advantage over her virgin sisters, who knew only their metaphoric equivalents; rather, she had a liability to overcome. Hence Angela and Margery, the two mothers who dictated their own spiritual autobiographies, said a great deal about the infant Jesus but almost nothing about their flesh-and-blood children.[65]

In actual fact, the maternal martyr paradigm might have covered many types of women, including some who wished good riddance on children they had never wanted in the first place, others who consoled themselves for their youngsters' deaths in the conviction that God willed it so, and perhaps still more who believed, as their culture so loudly proclaimed, that it was impossible to combine the careers of motherhood and sainthood. The first scenario seems clearest in the case of Margaret of Cortona, who rejected her illegitimate son so coldly that even her confessor was upset, while laypeople blamed her for his alleged suicide. For this "new Magdalene," the inconvenient child must have been a constant, galling reminder of her previous sinful life and perhaps of his murdered father, who may have exploited her lowly status to seduce her in the first place. On the other end of the social scale, Guibert's mother, Juette of Huy, Umiliana dei Cerchi, and Agnes of Herenkeim were all forced as teenagers into marriages they despised.[66] Though these women failed in their resistance to a first marriage, they struggled with grim and successful determination to avoid a second. All of them seem to have had ambivalent feelings toward their children. Neither Guibert's mother nor Juette allowed maternal cares to impede her vocation, yet both maintained intense and stormy relations with the "prodigal sons" who ultimately followed them into religion. The wretched Umiliana, whose short life never led to the monastic status she desired, said she would rather see her daughters dead than married. Yet such a wish was "for their own good," as she believed, since marriage was a fate literally worse than death.

Angela and Michelina, like so many medieval women, watched all their children die. From the bald and shocking account in Michelina's life, it is impossible to say what she really felt about her son's death, which is rationalized as an act of God. Angela's memoirs allow us a glimpse of mingled grief and relief; the latter takes priority because, as a budding saint, she knew that she "ought" to feel detachment and even gratitude for this liberation from worldly cares. A similar sentiment is expressed in the vitae of Umiliana, Elizabeth of Hungary, and Rilindis of Bissegg, for whom maternal love was associated with guilt. The ordinary mother could perhaps afford to luxuriate in such feelings, but the woman who aspired to holiness must resist them in the name of God, just as fiercely as Perpetua, Felicitas, and Paula had hardened their hearts against their families.

Aside from the peasant Margaret of Cortona, all of our maternal martyrs were either noblewomen or the daughters of wealthy burghers. Upper-class women like these did not ordinarily devote much time to child care: their infants were usually entrusted to wet nurses shortly after birth. If they survived until the age of weaning they would be returned to their mothers, but only until age seven or so, when they were once again sent away—this time permanently—for education or fostering. As Nikki Stiller observes, "the estrangement of mother and child may well have contributed to a loosening, if not a severance, of the mother-child bond, a provision, albeit unconscious, by the patriarchy against the formation of a very strong loyalty between child and mother."[67] Given such institutions as wet-nursing, oblation, and fosterage, the aspiring saint who "abandoned" her child to relatives or placed it in a monastery might not have acted very differently from the ordinary mother of her class and station. Yet the rhetoric of sacrifice marked the future saint as special, elevating what may have been either routine neglect or inescapable loss to the status of heroic virtue. We have almost no information about the feelings of ordinary mothers—those who were neither queens nor saints nor the mothers of saints—but it is worth asking whether empathy for the maternal martyr's sacrifice, like identification with Mary's compassion, could in some way have consoled such mothers for the forced separation from their own young.

With the exception of Margery Kempe and three of the Dominican nuns, most of the maternal martyrs celebrated in our texts were widows.[68] In the case of the fugitive wives at Unterlinden, their surviving husbands and children also entered religious life, whether by persuasion or necessity. But even widows, as "freed" women, could have a hard time establishing their independence in real life. Christiane Klapisch-Zuber has shown how young widows with children, especially if they were wealthy, came under intense competing pressures from their natal and conjugal families.[69] Their surviving parents or other relatives would try to reclaim them, with their often substantial dowries, for a second marriage alliance. A widow who capitulated to this pressure and returned to her father's house, like the repudiated Griselda, would necessarily leave her children behind, for they belonged to her late husband's lineage and not her own. On the other hand, the husband's relatives and the children themselves, if they were old enough, would pressure the widow to remain in her conjugal household, raising her children and (perhaps even more important) letting her dowry remain as part of their inheritance. Such a system virtually guaranteed moral conflict for the young, widowed mother: if she opted to be an obedient daughter, complying with the wishes of her own lineage, she became a "cruel mother," while if she chose to remain with her children, she became a rebel against her father's house.

A strong-willed, pious widow who not only abandoned her children, but gave their inheritance to the poor, could alienate both families at once and thus often met with fierce opposition. Such women were able to succeed in their saintly careers only if they secured the powerful help of their new "conjugal family," the Church—for, in effect, such a widow took Christ as her second husband. Like any married woman, she was then bound more firmly to her spouse than she was obliged to either parents or children. As the saintly widow's father, God might claim her dowry to bestow it on his own family, the poor; and as husband, he might demand the sacrifice of her children in the interests of a more impartial and spiritual "motherhood." Yet Christ's brothers and sisters—the friars, confessors, tertiaries, and other religious with whom the aspiring saint came into contact—could validate her choices and insulate her, to some degree, against the competing claims of her earthly families.[70] At this point she entered a new social network, as well as a new affective world, in which previous family relationships could be sublimated or replaced by spiritual ties, and the death or abandonment of children might be rewarded by a special intimacy with Christ and his sorrowing Mother.[71] As an apologia for her conversion, which was as much social as spiritual, the maternal martyr's vita furnished propaganda for kinship with the Holy Family, as well as the ecclesiastical "family," at the expense of the paternal and conjugal families that she willingly left behind.

III. Cruel Mothers, Loyal Wives

The "cruel mothers" of romance, so chilling to modern sensibilities, bear a strong resemblance to the maternal martyrs of hagiography. The same ethic of renunciation, the same Stoic detachment from what most people, then as now, perceived as natural human feelings, determines the behavior of these heroines. But while their characterization displays hagiographic influence, the child-sacrifice plots themselves derive from folklore, not social reality, and preserve a strongly atavistic character. In the vitae, the motif of child sacrifice is softened to detachment, neglect, abandonment, or equanimity in the face of loss; in the romances, it is the child's actual murder that is required or threatened. The primitive material retains its shock value even after it is rationalized and historicized by the medieval poets. Indeed, it is precisely in their attempt to justify the horrific deeds their narratives code as virtuous that these narrators expose the fault lines in contemporary value hierarchies.

On the most obvious level, the romance of child sacrifice sets the undeniable value of parental love against (and beneath) other values like friendship, feudal honor, and fidelity to vows. Since the supreme good of devotion to God is no longer an issue, such plots clarify the value hierarchies governing conflicts between familial and male homosocial interests. More subtly, the demand for sacrifice also problematizes the woman's role, setting wifehood against motherhood and privileging the former. Faced with a call for child sacrifice arising from her husband's demands or commitments, the wife invariably wins narrative approval by placing obedience to her mate above the obligation to protect her child. Several romances make a point of including the mother's consent to the death of her child, a sacrifice entailed by her husband's loyalty to another man, even when her involvement does not seem strictly necessary to the plot. The wife's fidelity to her marital vow is thus made to parallel her husband's fidelity to the chivalric vow that precipitated the demand for sacrifice in the first place.

Problematic as we may find this ideal of wifehood, it testifies to a higher rather than lower valuation of the sacrality of marriage. In a traditional formulation based on Augustine, procreation was considered chief among the "three goods of marriage" and furnished the only sinless motive for sexual relations. But a mother's willingness to sacrifice her child for the sake of her husband calls this venerable ideology into question. The popularity of child-sacrifice plots, especially in the second half of the fourteenth century, seems to be correlated with a shift toward the alternative consensual model of marriage, based on the union of Mary and Joseph. According to this doctrine, which began to win favor in the twelfth century, the indissoluble loyalty of the wedded pair (characterized theologically as *fides* and *sacramentum*) takes precedence over their fertility.[72] Not surprisingly, it is the loyalty of the inferior party, the wife, that is dramatically tested, just as her husband's loyalty is tried in his capacity as knight. Child sacrifice functions in both cases as the ultimate loyalty test. A wife who meets this challenge, like Griselda, becomes an exemplar of conjugal devotion so absolute that it is no longer an alternative, but an analogue, for religious devotion.

The Griselda story is unique in that it is framed exclusively as a test of female obedience. Unlike the protagonists in the other romances, Griselda's husband Walter is not constrained by external pressure, but decides of his own accord to tempt his wife by feigning infanticide. In other respects, however, the famous tale belongs to a small group of stories that all culminate in episodes of real or apparent child sacrifice, and all idealize the maternal martyr in her guise of faithful and obedient wife. Seen in this light, the *Clerk's Tale* is no longer an isolated monstrosity, but part of a developing line of discourse that runs closely parallel to that of hagiography, yet points in the opposite direction.

Amis and Amiloun, based on a widely distributed folktale, is a late thirteenth-century English romance celebrating male friendship.[73] Two knights take an oath of brotherhood and then, like Tristan and Isolt, proceed to prove their *treuthe* by their willingness to violate all other bonds for the sake of their love. When Amis is challenged to a judicial combat because of his affair with the princess Belisaunt, he dares not meet the challenge because he knows himself to be in the wrong, so he asks his look-alike friend Amiloun to fight in his place. Before the battle, Amiloun is warned by a voice from heaven that if he perjures himself by pretending to be Amis, he will be stricken with leprosy within three years. Amiloun disregards this warning and carries off the victory, but the angel's prophecy is fulfilled and, as a leper, he must endure many years of exile, poverty, and abjection. Finally he arrives at the court of Amis and Belisaunt, who tenderly care for him. After a year has elapsed, Amis and Amiloun are both advised in a dream that if Amis is willing to slay his two children and bathe Amiloun in their blood, the leprosy will be cured.[74] Weeping, Amis carries out the sacrifice on Christmas Eve, as if to recall that Jesus too was born to be slain. When his wife returns home, he breaks the news to her:

> Leue leman,
> Be bliþe & glad of mode;
> For bi him þat þis warld wan,
> Boþe mi childer ich haue slan,
> Þat were so *hende* & gode . . . (ll. 2378–82)   [gracious]

Belisaunt, seeing her husband's sorrow, swallows her own grief in order to comfort him:

> "O lef liif," sche seyd þo,
> "God may sende ous childer mo,
> Of hem haue þou no care.
> ʒif it ware at min hert rote,
> For to bring þi broþer *bote*,   [remedy]
> My lyf y wold not spare." (ll. 2392–97)

After this proof of conjugal loyalty, Amis's loyal friendship is vindicated by two miracles: he and his wife find Amiloun healed and then discover their children alive and well, as if nothing had happened. Their resurrection, recalling the deliverance of Isaac, not only seals the poet's approval of Amis's choice but reassures the audience, averting potential guilt in the knowledge that all is well: the hard choice was only a test, not an irrevocable act.[75] Through the angelic message and the miracles, God both tests and rewards the hero, but he judges in accord with the values of male courtly society and does not, as in hagiography, offer an alternative to them.

The scene of Belisaunt's consent is not required by the plot; in fact, it does not appear in an earlier Latin version of the tale by Radulfus Tortarius. In that eleventh-century narrative, the hero Amelius sends his wife away before killing the children "lest sight of these things cause her death," and she returns to find nothing amiss, perhaps never learning of the sacrifice.[76] Belisaunt's partnership does not change the outcome of the story, but it characterizes her pointedly as a noble lady and makes her a foil to Amiloun's evil wife, who casts him out when he becomes a leper. The princess commits herself fully to her husband's loyalties and projects, setting the interests of his male friend above her children. For the audience, a clear hierarchy of relationships is established: the supreme bond is male friendship, followed by the loyalty of a good wife to her husband, with the parent-child bond in third place.

While Belisaunt consents to a *fait accompli*, Griselda in the *Clerk's Tale* is given a harder task. Playing Abraham to Walter's God, she must consent in advance to the slaughter of her children on two occasions, and unlike Belisaunt she suffers in silence for years before learning that her son and daughter are still alive. Griselda's role as exemplar of patience forbids the least sign of mourning, nor does she so much as mention the children once they are gone. Boccaccio, Petrarch, and Chaucer all note something suspect and unnatural about this refusal to mourn.[77] In Chaucer's words:

> This markys wondred, evere lenger the moore,
> Upon hir pacience, and if that he
> Ne hadde soothly knowen therbifoore
> That parfitly hir children loved she,
> He wolde have wend that of som subtiltee,
> And of malice, or for crueel corage,
> That she had suffred this with sad visage. (ll. 687–93)

Griselda indeed gives cause for wonder. Though she kisses and blesses her children on parting, she remarks to Walter:

> Naught greveth me at al,
> Though that my doughter and my sone be slayn—
> At youre comandement, this is to sayn.
> I have noght had no part of children tweyne
> But first siknesse, and after, wo and peyne.
>
> Ye been oure lord; dooth with youre owene thyng
> Right as yow list; axeth no reed at me. (ll. 647–53)

Amis had announced his action to Belisaunt with the words, "Both *my* children I have slain." Griselda refers to "my doughter and my sone," but she immediately goes on to disclaim any parental interest in them; she has no part in her children except "siknesse, wo and peyne," and no right to protect them because both they and she are Walter's "owene thyng."[78] Later, at her dismissal, she asks only a smock to cover "thilke wombe in which youre children leye" (l. 877). Technically, she views even her consent to the children's murder as gratuitous, since they are scarcely "hers" to give up; she has never been more than the unworthy vessel through which they passed. Wifely submission, a minor theme in *Amis and Amiloun*, is here the central issue, underscored by Walter's capricious tyranny. If, as the tale seems to imply, even the worst of husbands is entitled to such obedience from the best of wives, then conjugal loyalty is indeed sacred—a perfect analogue for the soul's obedience to God, and far superior to the sentimental love a mother may feel for her child.

The readiness of these fictional parents to let their children die by no means proves that real parents would have behaved in the same way. Both the child murder in *Amis and Amiloun* and Griselda's farewell scenes are suffused with pathos, and the private anguish displayed by Amis and Griselda is meant to magnify their heroism. In neither case, however, is the parent's struggle seen as a moral contest between two goods, the child's welfare and the ideal of loyalty. Rather, the love of children is represented as a powerful but essentially selfish emotion, and their loss as a deep narcissistic wound. It is still the grieving parent, not the silent and objectified child, who is expected to elicit the reader's admiration and pity. Amis, Belisaunt, and Griselda are heroic because they have overcome their selfish love, resigning themselves to pain for the sake of duty. But there is never any doubt that Walter and Amis have the legal right to do as they please with their "owene thyng." Underneath the new pathos and sentimentality, the ancient *patria potestas* remains in force.

Mothers, of course, were expected and under normal conditions obliged to cherish the fruit of their wombs. Infanticide by women was repeatedly condemned, not only in penitentials and confessors' manuals but in actual trials, where the motive was often discovered to be concealment of an illicit love affair.[79] The escalation in penalties for this crime, along with other trends like the reaction against monastic child oblation, the development of a didactic literature on child care and wet-nursing, and the growing interest in Christ's childhood, support David Herlihy's claim that European society was increasing its psychological as well as economic investment in children from the twelfth century onward. But Herlihy also points out that "alternative and even competitive sets of child-related values can coexist in the same society, perhaps even in the same household."[80] In test cases, when the claims of children conflicted with loyalty to a husband, there was no doubt where a wife's obligation lay. Duty to a superior overrode any obligation to inferiors.[81] Thus, if a father was bound to serve a principle—friendship, generosity, victory, chastity, honor—at the cost of his children's lives, a mother was doubly bound to serve the father of her children and accept his choices.

Amis chooses his friend's health over his children's lives; Belisaunt chooses both Amis and Amiloun over the dead children. Griselda submits wholeheartedly to Walter's murderous test despite her inner torment. Not only has she internalized society's view of her as a chattel; she has abdicated her will so thoroughly that the moral choices of a lifetime are subsumed in her single vow of subservience to Walter. If the goodness of that initial vow is accepted, Griselda becomes not less but more virtuous with each proof of her loyalty, and she shows herself not less but more than a woman as she subordinates the instinctual passion of mother love to the rational virtue of obedience. At this point her story discloses its antique hagiographic tinge. In admiring Griselda's apparently "cruel corage," Walter peers beneath her submissive wifehood to discover the *femina virilis* idealized by Stoic and patristic moralists. This aspect of the maternal martyr emerges even more clearly in my two remaining examples. The romances of *Sir Amadas* and *Le Seigneur du Chastel* both present fathers faced with a demand for child sacrifice yielding to helpless fits of emotion, while their wives courageously nerve them on to the deed. Such heroines supply a secular gloss on the familiar hagiographic claim that God chooses "weak women" to shame strong men (1 Cor. 1:27).

Sir Amadas, an English romance dated to the fourteenth century, borrows the folklore motif of the Grateful Dead. The hero, an impoverished knight, spends his last remaining funds to pay the debts and funeral costs of a merchant who has lain unburied for several months. In return for this boon, the merchant's ghost seeks out Sir Amadas in the guise of a white knight, who promises to help him regain his fortune if Amadas will divide his winnings with him. The mysterious knight directs Sir Amadas to the site of a shipwreck, where he enriches himself with the drowned men's garments and goes on to win a tournament and the hand of a princess. Later, after the birth of a son, the White Knight returns to claim his share. Disdaining gold, silver, and rich lands, he demands instead "half þi child, and halfe þi wyue." [82] Sir Amadas protests that it would be "grete synne" to slay his lady, who has until now remained an anonymous, generic tourney prize. But at the moment of crisis, the lady herself takes matters in hand. Bidding her lord to keep his covenant, she declares:

> "Sithun Crist will þat hit be so,
> Take and parte me euun in toe,
> Þu wan me and I am thine.
> Goddus forbotte þat ȝe hade wyuut,
> Þat I schuld ȝo a lure makette,
> ȝore wurschip in londe to tyne!"
>
> Still ho stode, withoutun lette,
> Nawthir changet chere, ne grette,
> Þat lady myld and dere.
> Bede, "Foche me my ȝung sun me beforne,
> For he was of my bodi borne,
> And lay my herte full nere." [83]

Like Griselda, this nameless heroine takes it for granted that she and her child are her husband's property ("þu wan me and I am thine"), and she prefers to die along with her son rather than see her lord's honor stained. While Sir Amadas carries on "as ho were wode" and his courtiers swoon, the lady alone maintains her calm, dispassionate mien: "Nawthir changet chere, ne grette." In one manuscript she tries, by word and example, to awaken her husband's manhood: "Syr, kyþe þat ye ar a knyȝt." [84] After sending for the child, she gives her lord a farewell kiss and lies down to be sawed in two. When the White Knight asks Sir Amadas which victim he loves more, he rewards her fortitude by responding without hesitation, "My wife, so dere!"—only to be told that he must kill her first. It is only after he has lifted his sword to strike, like Abraham at Mount Moriah, that the White Knight relents and discloses his true identity. Since Amadas (like the prince Vessantara) has already been characterized as generous to a fault, his willingness to divide his wife and son with the White Knight surmounts the ultimate challenge and thereby, as in the Buddhist tale, puts a definitive end to his bout with poverty and affliction.

In contrast to *Amis and Amiloun*, *Sir Amadas* downplays the theme of child sacrifice to emphasize the loyalty and self-surrender of the wife. Even before the sacrifice scene, the poet holds her up as a model because "All þat hur lord lufd wurschipput ho, / Alle suche wemen wele myȝte be" (ll. 695–96). Afterward the White Knight bids Sir Amadas to "lufe þis lady as þi lyue" (l. 820) because of her meekness, and the poet comments:

> Þer is ladis now in lond full *foe*   [few]
> Þat wold haue seruut hor lord soe,
> Butte sum wold haue sayd nay. (ll. 832–34)

Rarity that she is, the perfect patriarchal wife is more precious to her husband than his firstborn son, since she is willing to let the child, who lay "full near her heart," join her in martyrdom as a joint sacrifice to their lord's word of honor.

The final stage in this recruitment of mothers for patriarchy appears in the story of the Seigneur du Chastel by Antoine de la Sale, written in 1460.[85] This tale is set during the Hundred Years' War in France. Its hero, the Seigneur, commands a strategic fortress under siege by the Black Prince. Like many a feudal lord in reality, he is compelled to give his only son, age thirteen, as a hostage along with his pledged word that, if reinforcements do not arrive by a specified date, he will surrender the castle. Help does arrive, but the Prince unchivalrously reneges on his word and swears to execute the boy anyhow unless the Seigneur surrenders. At this point we are given an anguished dialogue between the Seigneur and his wife as they lie in bed. Asked to offer advice, Madame du Chastel at first demurs, avowing her Griselda-like submission: "Such things must issue from the noble hearts of brave men and not from the female hearts of women who, by God's command, are subject to you men." Her husband therefore commands her to state an opinion. Like the wife of Sir Amadas, Madame now takes the initiative: it is precisely *because* she is so attached to her son, she says, that she has both the right and the duty to give him up. Her statement, which begins with an affirmation of maternal love, ends in a total identification with feudal honor and patriarchal values:

> You, my lord, and every man and woman alive, know that by natural right and the experience of our eyes it is more apparent that children are sons and daughters of their mothers who have carried them in their loins and given birth to them than they are of their husbands. . . . And for this then he is my true son, who cost me very dear to carry nine months in my loins while I suffered throughout many a day many a great anxiety, and to give birth to whom I almost died, whom I so dearly fed and loved and cherished down to the day and the hour when he was given over. But now and for ever more I

abandon him into the hands of God and it is my will that he shall never more be anything to me, as though I had never seen him, but of my own free will, without force, constraint, or violence whatever, I give, cede, and transfer to you all the natural love, affection, and right which a mother can and must have for her only and dearly loved son. . . . And truly, my lord, here is a great choice. We are still of an age to have sons, if it pleases God. But your honor, once lost, alas, you can never recover.

After this speech the Seigneur thanks God "that from the heart of a female and weak creature could come such high and virtuous words as those Madame spoke, having thus entirely abandoned the love of her only and most beloved son and all for the love of him." The tale is pitiless, however: there is no stay of execution, no miracle of resurrection. The boy is led to the scaffold, weeping and resisting to the last moment as he cries out to his absent father and mother. By this point in our trajectory, virtue must be its own reward: the pathos of the boy's death is meant to strengthen our empathy with his suffering parents, not to challenge the rightness of their decision.[86] It is telling that Erich Auerbach, who analyzed this tale during the Second World War, remained thoroughly committed to its values. As he wrote, "Madame du Chastel's submissiveness, her humility, her obedient bowing to her husband's will, show only the more impressively the sterling force and freedom of her nature as it awakes in a time of need. . . . It is hard to decide what is most praiseworthy in this speech, its self-effacement or its self-control, its goodness or its clarity."[87] Auerbach's sympathetic reading reinforces the nexus that now inseparably links child sacrifice with wifely submission, paternal honor with maternal martyrdom.

Significantly, la Sale's tale forms part of a larger work, *Le Réconfort de Madame de Fresne*, written to console a mother for the loss of her son. As we have seen, the literature of consolation urged bereaved parents to resign themselves to God's will, and excessive mourning was taken as a sign of rebellion against him.[88] Since this conventional wisdom represented grief as both selfish and effeminate, the mother who repressed it could attain the specially exalted status of a virile woman. But the tales of Griselda, Sir Amadas, and Madame du Chastel go even further, conflating resignation after the fact with acquiescence in a death that could still be prevented. Likewise Dame Prudence, in Chaucer's tale of *Melibee*, gives her husband typical advice on mourning when their daughter is not even dead, but only wounded by her father's enemies: "Us oghte, as wel in the deeth of oure children as in the los of *oure othere goodes temporels*, have pacience. Remembre yow upon the pacient Job" (ll. 997–98). Simply because it is so stereotyped, this "consolation" is revealing in several ways. First, there is a grim if unintended realism in the conflation of a child already dead with one who is still in jeopardy at the hands of adults. From the perspective of most medieval women, acts of war or of abusive husbands might just as well be acts of God, for their power to influence them was scarcely greater. Second, the listing of children among "our other temporal goods" says as much about the nobility ascribed to child sacrifice as volumes of social history. Griselda accepts the death of her children and the loss of her jewels and gowns with the same composure, and Belisaunt and Madame du Chastel both find comfort in the thought that they can always have more children if God wills. The Christianized Stoic ethic of detachment reinforces a tendency to view children as precious but replaceable goods.

Finally, Dame Prudence recalls the exemplum of Job, who lost seven sons and three daughters to a deal between God and Satan. Griselda too paraphrases Job's words of resignation—"Naked I came from my mother's womb, and naked shall I return" (Job 1:21)—when she is sent back naked to her father's house (ll. 871–72). But after Job had sufficiently proved his patience, he was rewarded with seven more sons and three daughters, and Griselda likewise regains her lost offspring. Modern readers usually balk at these happy endings, like Ivan Karamazov who refused even paradise as a consolation for innocent suffering. For medieval readers, however, I suspect the moral carried weight. It is often objected that if Griselda signifies the faithful Christian, then Walter must represent God—but is that not precisely the point? In this Petrarchan allegory, which too many critics read as a mystification, we may find a last and perhaps more benign explanation for the popularity of child sacrifice plots. At a time when tenderness for children could do nothing to ease their appalling mortality, and when the apocalyptic mind perceived in the endless wars, famines, and plagues of the age a whole series of deals between God and Satan, God must often have seemed to bereft mortals like a celestial Walter.[89] I believe people took genuine comfort in the hope that, if they accepted his cruel and capricious exactions with the patience of Griselda, God their enemy would prove to be a true lover after all and restore their losses—if not here, then hereafter.[90]

As a strategy for coming to terms with loss, tales of sacrificed children, like the sermons on mourning, adopted the ideal of detachment from earthly goods to negotiate the distance between a fond attentiveness to children and the pathos of their precocious deaths. In this function the hagiographic and romance plots often coincide. With respect to the mother's role, however, they diverge sharply. In hagiography, the saint who abandoned her baby or prayed for her young child's death was following in Abraham's footsteps and obeying the call of Christ, providing a potent symbol of attachment to God alone—God above all and, if need be, against all. Such gestures, cruel as they are, could lift the widowed mother beyond the oppressive and often competing claims of her human families, bringing her as close as possible to the ideal of virgin singleness of heart and removing the telltale proof of her sexuality. In the meantime, the grief concealed behind her facade of heroic renunciation might fill her cup to overflowing, giving her cause to identify with the dolorous Mother who acquiesced in the Father's primordial sacrifice of her Son.[91] In secular fiction, on the other hand, the figure of the maternal martyr reinforced the values of conjugal loyalty over parental love and abstract principle over physical life. The Griseldas of medieval fiction, read either literally or allegorically, could only encourage women to internalize patriarchal demands.

For modern readers, there are few themes that mark the indelible difference of medieval culture so pointedly as this one. In contemporary fictions of child sacrifice, like William Styron's novel *Sophie's Choice* (1979) and Toni Morrison's *Beloved* (1987), the murdered children do not go peacefully to heaven, but haunt their mothers to the point of madness. The agonizing choices that eventuate in their deaths are not imposed by gods or noble causes, but by the brutality of inhuman regimes (Nazism in one case, slavery in the other).[92] And Abraham, whom Kierkegaard could still read as a hero of faith "by virtue of the absurd," has in our century become a figure of horror. The poet Wilfred Owen, in his "Parable of the Old Man and the Young" (1917), made the sacrifice of Isaac a metaphor for the slaughter of a whole generation in the First World War. Feminist theologian Dorothee Soelle unmasks the old typological reading of Abraham and Isaac as an apologia for theological sadism, since if we read Christ's sacrifice as the "fulfillment" of Isaac's, the humane progress away from child murder in Genesis is reversed: "A theology of suffering that is developed from this starting point will necessitate worshiping the executioner."[93]

Finally, to call a stop to the glorification of Abraham's choice, Eleanor Wilner rewrites the tale and imagines God speaking to Sarah, who gives him a very different response:

"No," said Sarah to the Voice.
"I will not be chosen. Nor shall my son—
if I can help it. You have promised Abraham,

through this boy, a great nation. So either
this sacrifice is sham, or else it is a sin.
Shame," she said, for such is the presumption
of mothers, "for thinking me a fool,
for asking such a thing. You must have known
I would choose Isaac. What use have I
for History—an arrow already bent
when it is fired from the bow?"[94]

Isaac protests, for if he is not sacrificed, he will no longer be God's chosen, and the whole grand design is imperiled. But the matriarch, no longer Griselda, answers:

"It's time," she said. "Choose now."
"But what will happen if we go?" the boy
    Isaac asked. "I don't know," Sarah said
"But it is written   what will happen   if you stay."

4. On the Threshold of the Dead: Purgatory, Hell, and Religious Women

> Tanto giù cadde, che tutti argomenti
> alla salute sua eran già corti,
> fuor che mostrarli le perdute genti,
> Per questo visitai l'uscio de' morti,
> e a colui che l'ha qua su condotto
> li preghi miei, piangendo, furon porti.[1]
> —*Purgatorio* 30.136–41

In the middle of the way from the savage wood to the face of God, at the summit of purgatory, on the threshold of heaven, Beatrice reminds Dante of another threshold long since crossed. Like Persephone, like Isis, like Inanna, she once "visited the threshold of the dead." A blessed spirit, she has walked among the lost. Descending from the throne of joy, she has offered up prayers with tears. By this means alone is Dante saved, as indeed he already knows. Virgil had given him courage to embark on his journey with the news that "three such blessed ladies / care for you in the court of heaven."[2] Now, having completed his tour of purgatory by doing penance for his own sins, Dante is freed by Beatrice and another lady, Matelda, who baptizes him in the rivers of paradise.

In this uniquely moving scene we encounter more than Dante's personal history, reverberating with echoes of *fine amour* and ancient myth. His gracious, enigmatic Matelda has been identified by several scholars with Mechthild of Hackeborn, a mystical nun of Helfta (d. 1298) whose visions link her closely with purgatory and the earthly paradise.[3] But whether or not the poet intended that reading, his Matelda shares with Beatrice a role that appears time and again in medieval texts: the holy woman as medium and mediatrix, the psychopomp whose compassion takes her through the portals of hell and heaven that she may lead souls out of purgatory. If those redeemed spirits could speak to us now, how many would cry with Dante: "Oh pietosa colei che mi soccorse! O compassionate she that succored me!"[4]

Since the publication of Jacques Le Goff's landmark study, *La Naissance du Purgatoire*, in 1981, purgatory has emerged from the backwaters of *Dogmengeschichte* to become an almost fashionable subject.[5] But Le Goff's work and the many articles inspired by it leave half the story untold./For of all Catholic doctrines, none has been more deeply shaped by female piety than the notion of purgatory, which filled an overwhelming place in the visions, devotions, and works of charity undertaken by religious women! Le Goff gives only a few tantalizing hints about the importance of purgatory for beguines and cloistered women./In this chapter, following the lead of Caroline Bynum and Jo Ann McNamara, I would like to explore the theory and practice of women's purgatorial piety, which I will call an "apostolate to the dead." In the second part I will turn to a surprising and hitherto neglected offshoot of this piety: the witness of a small group of mystics who, with Beatrice, crossed the threshold into the beyond, but returned with a daring challenge to eternal hell.|

I. Religious Women as Apostles to the Dead

Like many of Le Goff's readers, I am skeptical about the high importance he ascribes to the emergence of *purgatorium* as a noun circa 1170, with the accompanying shift he perceives from a binary to a ternary model of the otherworld.[6] Thus, rather than defining purgatory in Le Goff's sense as a "third place" with a local habitation and a name, I will adopt a more traditional and theological view of it as the condition of suffering, both punitive and redemptive, undergone by elect souls between the moment of death and their eventual admission to heaven. This conception of purgatory had existed in inchoate form since the subapostolic age, and in a more or less rationalized form since Augustine. Is it coincidence that the two most woman-centered texts to come down to us from the whole early Christian period are also the first two witnesses to purgatory? These texts both assert that martyrs-designate, by virtue of their present and future torments, had a special right to deliver the helpless dead from torments by their prayers.

Such a belief is first attested in the popular *Acts of Thecla*, a second-century text from Asia Minor that circulated in Greek, Latin, Syriac, and Ethiopic versions.[7] This controversial work, used by some Christians in antiquity to legitimize women's teaching and baptizing, glorifies female characters and vilifies men to such a degree that some scholars have proposed female authorship for it.[8] The heroine, Thecla, is a virgin convert of Paul. In the course of her adventures she is adopted by a sympathetic queen whose daughter, Falconilla, has died. Falconilla reveals to her mother in a dream that Thecla can get her "translated to the place of the righteous," so the queen asks Thecla, on the eve of her battle with wild beasts, to "come and pray for my child, that she may live forever." As a pious adopted daughter, Thecla at once intercedes with Christ and Falconilla's deliverance is implied, though not explicit.[9]

A similar incident occurs in the better-known *Passion of Saints Perpetua and Felicitas*, dating from 203.[10] Perpetua, the wealthy young matron who submits to martyrdom with her slave Felicitas, overshadows their three male companions, for the narrative incorporates her first-person prison diary punctuated with a series of poignant dreams. Filial piety has been a source of anguish for Perpetua, who must reject her father as well as her infant son because they bind her to the world of the living. When she has done so, she is unexpectedly haunted by a memory of her brother, Dinocrates, who died at the age of seven. Realizing that because of her elect status as martyr-to-be she is both worthy and obligated to pray for him, Perpetua does so and receives a vision of Dinocrates in torment—thirsty, ill-clad, still afflicted by the ravages of his cancer. After days of fervent prayer and weeping, she is consoled by a second dream of Dinocrates now healed and happy, at play in the immortal fountain that has quenched his thirst.

Peter Dronke has rightly noted that the landscape of this vision is classical, not medieval, and the central elements of purgatory are lacking: there is no indication that the little boy was especially sinful, that he repented on his deathbed, or that he is being purged by fire.[11] Nevertheless, Augustine took Perpetua's vision in a "purgatorial" sense when he argued that Dinocrates must have been baptized in order to benefit from his sister's prayers.[12] Moreover, even if the child does not fit the medieval paradigm of a soul in purgatory, Perpetua's role prefigures that of the medieval holy woman. In renouncing this world and its orderly march of generations, symbolized by her father and her baby, she achieves a liminal status and gains entrée to the otherworld. There her agonized renunciation of the live child is transmuted to compassion for a dead child, whose deliverance both prophesies and rewards her success in the ordeal of martyrdom. Perpetua thus becomes the model of a new, Christian *pietas* that could utterly transform the devout woman's relation to her family. Repudiating the roles of wife and mother, hence guarantor of an earthly lineage, she takes on a new role as patroness of her kin hereafter. The care she withdraws from the living, she bestows upon the dead, and what she denies in the flesh she is prepared to grant in the spirit.

Visionary women, though always few in comparison to the host of clerics, seem at the very least to have served as midwives at the birth of purgatory, and their concern with it only grew stronger in the course of time. During the period Le Goff signals as crucial, the final third of the twelfth century, women may have anticipated men in their purgatorial witness. A decade before Le Goff's "birth date," Hildegard of Bingen devoted a whole book to purgatory—her neglected *Liber vitae meritorum* (1158–63)—returning to the subject in her *Causae et curae* and again in the remarkable cosmology of her *Liber divinorum operum*.[13] Her friend Elisabeth of Schönau prayed for sisters in purgatory and worried about her own potential sojourn there.[14] Even Marie de France devoted her sole religious writing to this domain, translating the knightly adventure of *St. Patrick's Purgatory* composed by an English monk.[15] It is true that neither the visionary texts of women nor the lives of female saints constituted more than a small proportion of medieval religious writing. Yet both of these genres suggest that purgatorial piety, while not the exclusive preserve of women, occupied a privileged place and took on a distinctive character in their religious lives. Both positive and negative factors may help to account for this phenomenon.

On the positive side, intercession for souls in purgatory seems to have been especially recommended to devout women by their directors and highlighted by their hagiographers. Such prayer constituted a safe, invisible, contemplative mission that could put women's devotion and compassion to work without violating any gender taboos. At the same time, it could be construed as a work of active charity, an apostolate requiring the same zeal for souls that men could express by preaching or hearing confessions. Thomas of Cantimpré, as Robert Sweetman has shown, composed his life of Christina Mirabilis to represent her bizarre, perhaps deranged behavior as a living sermon on purgatory.[16] After a near-death experience (or "return from death") during which she received a vision of souls in torment, Christina chose a life of dramatic and eccentric sufferings that would free souls from purgatory and at the same time make its tortures visible on earth, winning the conversion of sinners. Her lived purgatory was as powerful as the word of any preacher: "What else did Christina proclaim in all her life than that people should do penance and be prepared at all hours? This she taught with many words, with tears, with lamentation, with unending cries, with the example of her life—and she shouted louder than anyone."[17] Her apostolate to the dead became a witness that the living could not ignore.

Thirteenth-century beguine literature emphasized prayer for those in purgatory as a central obligation. A series of sermons preached to the beguines of Paris in 1272–73 frequently appeals to the women's pity, stressing the harshness of purgatorial pains and the helplessness of souls imprisoned there, especially dead relatives.[18] From about the same period comes the *Règle des Fins Amans*, a rule of life composed for a French beguine community, which lists among the "four parts of prayer" a duty to pray "for the dead who await mercy, that God may relieve their torment and hasten their glory."[19] Mechthild of Magdeburg sums up the responsibilities of the gifted soul as "to work for sinners and those in purgatory and to consider the need of everyone, living or dead."[20] Anna of Wineck, a thirteenth-century nun of Unterlinden, likens her apostolate to the dead to the ministries of preaching and nursing. Frustrated in her desire to be a hospital sister, she "constructed three hospitals spiritually in her mind"—one for sinners, one for the dying, and one for souls in purgatory—and ministered to these three groups continually in prayer.[21] This apostolate could also be understood as an *imitatio Mariae*, for the Virgin's well-known compassion made her the supreme hope of souls in purgatory and those that would otherwise be damned.[22]

Laymen and religious males were also concerned with the fate of their dead relatives, but even in this most private of ministries, they had options that women did not have. The most significant of these was of course the ability to say mass, acknowledged to be the most effective suffrage for the dead. Requiem masses furnished a major activity and a prime revenue source for male monasteries, aside from the more specialized institution of chantry priests.[23] Women, however, could at most commission priests to offer masses on behalf of their friends in purgatory. Barred from ordination, women were also less equipped to bestow the spiritual favors money could buy. Jo Ann McNamara observes that from the twelfth century onward, with the trend toward primogeniture and other changes in family structure, many women lost control of economic resources and thus of the ability to win merit and serve others through almsgiving. Determined "to remain in the giving class," McNamara argues, devout women began "to experiment with spiritual almsgiving to complement or replace corporal charity."[24] If they could not purchase indulgences for cash, they might buy them with their tears.

Finally, men had the option of helping their beloved dead by going to war. Although crusade indulgences remained highly controversial, popular preachers were in the habit of signing up recruits by promising them indulgences not only for themselves, but for any souls they might choose, living or dead. Caesarius of Heisterbach, in a sermon of 1225, harshly criticized this practice:

> They do not care what they preach as long as they take many recruits. There are some crusade preachers today who promise those willing to take the cross as many souls as they ask—from purgatory or from hell, which is even more insane—as if they held them shut up in their net. Since souls freed from their bodies are not under the jurisdiction of the living, with what effrontery do the living presume to sell them? [25]

Albert the Great also knew of crusade preachers who promised indulgences "for two or three or sometimes ten souls whether living or dead, at the choice of the crusader—but those souls are sometimes in hell, sometimes in purgatory, sometimes still among the living." In Albert's view, wild promises of this sort were invalid: authorized indulgences always stipulated that the beneficiary, whether living or dead, must be in a state of grace.[26] The audacious claim that crusaders could free the damned was never accepted as orthodox. It is nonetheless paralleled in the pleas of a few mystical women, who fought not with infidels but with God himself on behalf of the souls in hell. Despite their gender-specific liabilities, religious women offered what they had—their prayers and tears, their compassion and determination, their propensity for visions, and above all their sufferings—to ease the pain of the indigent dead.

II. Purgatorial Piety and Familial *Pietas*

From the beginning, the idea of purgatory had the potential to support a Christian cult of the dead, although such a cult was not fully established until the feast of All Souls' Day was introduced in 997 or 998.[27] In the New Testament, as in Protestant and Orthodox Christianity, there is little to mediate between the sharp alternatives of heaven and hell. Whether at the moment of death or on Judgment Day, the soul stands naked before the justice and mercy of God. Even the cult of saints and martyrs, with their established role as intercessors, could not meet the needs of ordinary Christians who, though not exceptionally holy, nonetheless wished to help their beloved dead. This desire could be satisfied only if two conditions were met: first, there had to be some intermediate state (not necessarily a "third place") in which the dead could benefit from help, and second, there had to be concrete actions the living could perform to help them. Purgatory and the associated idea of suffrages met these conditions.

Through the cumulative testimony of ghost stories and otherworld visions, the sufferings a deceased sinner could expect to meet on the way to heaven became an item of popular belief well before theologians had worked out all the juridical implications of purgatory.[28] The more concrete and graphic the images of such torment, as reported by seers and revenants, the more urgency would attach to prayers for the dead. In his *De cura pro mortuis gerenda* (circa 422), Augustine had already recommended sober prayers and masses as a substitute for the lavish funerals and commemorative feasts of the pagans. Suffrages of this kind offered not only hope for the less-than-saintly dead, but also the comfort of constructive action for the bereaved, with the promise that death could not break the bonds of mutual aid. Purgatorial piety thus supplied an outlet for familial *pietas*, prolonging the kind offices of kinship and friendship into the hereafter.[29] In the case of religious who, like Perpetua, had renounced the reproductive claims of family, an apostolate to the dead furnished an alternative way to remain a dutiful and valued member of the kin group. For laywomen, offering suffrages served to extend into the spiritual realm the traditionally female responsibilities for laying out the dead and mourning.

The most prominent of all themes in purgatorial piety is solicitude for members of one's family, whether natural (like Perpetua and Dinocrates) or spiritual (like Thecla and Falconilla). A consistent pattern emerges in saints' lives, exempla, and vision literature: the deceased appears to the survivor in torment, explains why he or she is suffering such pains, and asks for help. After a period of ardent prayer, accompanied by tears, fasting, and other penitential exercises, the seer is rewarded like Perpetua with a second apparition of the deceased, grateful and glorified. These experiences both frighten and comfort the bereaved, since the deceased is in pain yet assured of ultimate salvation, and they give survivors a positive role to play long after the corpse is buried. At the same time, the visions may reinforce the values of a religious community, assuring the seer that her own, spiritual way of life is superior to the carnal, worldly life for which the deceased is being punished.

A daughter in religion always provided a kind of life insurance for her parents. Saints as different as Odilia in the eighth century and Catherine

of Siena in the fourteenth are said to have prayed their fathers out of punishment, Catherine typically by taking his pain on herself.[30] Among the
nuns of Unterlinden, Mechthild of Winzenheim kept her two murdering,
pillaging brothers out of hell by praying for their deathbed contrition,
then went on to secure their early release from purgatory. Margaret of
Brisach released both her mother and a brother who would otherwise have
languished until Judgment Day.[31] Such apparitions often highlighted the
discrepancy between the reward of fellow religious and the punishment of
worldly kin. The prioress Adelheid of Rheinfelden saw the souls of her fellow nuns in glory, but her ex-husband (whom she had abandoned to enter
religious life) appeared to her "in the places of punishment, enveloped in
flames and harshly vexed." Even though he had become a Dominican friar,
he still required his wife's tearful prayers for deliverance.[32]

From earliest times, there was a special, complex relationship between
purgatory and marriage. On the one hand, clerics were always suspicious
of marriage because it involved sexual activity and other worldly pleasures
worthy of punishment. Augustine set the tone when he named excessive
conjugal love as the type of sin for which purgatorial fire was invented, and
others followed suit.[33] Caesarius of Heisterbach told of a matron, known to
be a good woman, who wound up in purgatory because she had used magical arts to retain her husband's love.[34] On the other hand, marriage itself
could be a purgatory on earth: if happy marriages deserved punishment,
unhappy ones deserved a reward, at least for the abused and long-suffering
spouse. Saintly wives like Dorothea of Montau, following the Griselda
paradigm, bore their husbands' abuse with patience enough to win the
martyr's crown in heaven.[35] But there is a telling asymmetry in accounts of
the purgatorial marriage. The abused wife is a figure of hagiography, while
the abused husband is a figure of misogynist satire. Nevertheless, he too
merits a heavenly reward.

Purgatorial marriage became a familiar comic topos in later medieval
literature. In the thirteenth-century poem *De conjuge non ducenda*, wedlock
is already characterized as "vel tartara, vel purgatorium."[36] The notorious
Lamentations of Mathéolus, translated by Jehan Le Fèvre, allowed the poet
to blaspheme against God for creating women and to accuse Christ of
not daring to take a wife, since a woman would have led even the Savior
into sin. But God replies that on the contrary, marriage is a proof of his
mercy, for it is the greatest purgatory on earth—and he shows the poet his
own designated throne in heaven, where husbands will have a higher place
than celibates because they have suffered more.[37] The same motif governs

Justinus's ironic advice to Januarie in the *Merchant's Tale*: the lecherous old man need not fear that the joys of marriage will preclude the bliss of heaven, for it may be just the opposite.

> Dispeire yow noght, but have in youre memorie,
> Paraunter she may be youre purgatorie!
> She may be Goddes meene and Goddes whippe;
> Thanne shal youre soule up to hevene skippe
> Swifter than dooth an arwe out of a bowe.

Reasoning in the same vein, Chaucer's archwife turns a confession of her own marital mischief into a eulogy for her fourth husband: "By God, in erthe I was his purgatorie, / For which I hope his soule be in glorie."[38] The motif attains an even richer development in Boccaccio, whose delicious parody assumes an audience thoroughly familiar with the themes of purgatorial marriage and otherworld visions. A hypocritical abbot, lusting after the peasant Ferondo's wife, uses a potion to cast the man into a death-like sleep, then imprisons him and, when he wakens, makes him believe he is in purgatory, where he is treated to daily beatings. Meanwhile the abbot impregnates Ferondo's wife. When the peasant finally "returns from the dead" to raise the abbot's son as his own, he is reckoned a saint, "and he himself made up some of the most beautiful fables about the workings of the world of Purgatory."[39]

Bad or good, then, a wife was supposed to secure her husband safe passage to heaven. The bad wife did it by nagging, cheating, and squandering to make him a martyr of marriage; the good wife by her devotions as a widow. As early as the third century, Tertullian had advised Christian widows to pray for their husbands' *refrigerium* instead of remarrying.[40] Medieval literature is filled with exemplary tales of such wifely intercession. Among the most gripping is Guibert of Nogent's ambivalent account of his mother, who had been miserable in marriage yet exerted herself "with almost daily masses, prayers, and tears, and much almsgiving" on behalf of her husband's soul. But none of these efforts freed him, and she was continually beset with visions of his soul in torment. At length she adopted a troublesome orphaned baby in order to atone for her husband's sin of begetting a bastard, who had died unbaptized. The tale has many startling features, not least of which is the widow's determination to go on paying, even after his death, for her husband's infidelity. Released from a purgatorial marriage, she freely returns to the purgatory of motherhood—for

Guibert construes the baby's crying as a direct intervention of the devil. Just as the damned infant's wailing torments its father in the underworld, the orphan's wailing torments his widow on earth in a redemptive exchange, uncannily reversing Perpetua's exchange of a live child for a dead one. In this case, "the more [the widow] happened to experience the eagerness of the Devil in the irritation of the child, the more she was assured that his evil sway over the soul of her husband was being countered."[41]

Caesarius tells another tale of extraordinary vicarious penance by a widow. A usurer of Liège died in such ill repute that the bishop refused to bury him in holy ground; but his wife, after pleading successfully for that favor in Rome, assumed his penance by having herself shut up as a recluse beside his grave. There, for fourteen years, she strove in prayer and fasting to deliver his soul from purgatory.[42] In a popular Middle English text, a ghost is asked why he sought help from his wife rather than a religious house, for as their prior affirms, "hit hadde be more resoun that thou hadde schewid thee to clerkys then to thy wyf that is a woman." But the ghost responds, "I loue more my wyf than ony man of relygioun and therfore y yeode first to hure. . . . that y myght schewe to my wyf here perel of that priue synne that we diden."[43] In a similar context of sexual shame, the newly widowed Birgitta of Sweden—who had been happier in her marriage than most female saints—had a gruesome vision of the torments she deserved for past pleasures. If God punished her in strict justice she would be torn limb from limb, rot with disease, and suffer such hunger that she would eat her own excrement. But the Lord in his mercy would accept mere earthly penance in lieu of these torments.[44] For her husband, a devout man consigned to purgatory for venial sins (such as excessive love of their son), Birgitta purchased redemption with a year's worth of masses and generous alms to the poor.[45] As for the wayward son, who with the Virgin's help had barely escaped damnation, even greater offerings were required: a gift of thirty chalices to the Church, thirty chosen priests each to say thirty masses, thirty poor men to be fed and clothed, dowries for maidens and widows, plus a special penance to be assigned by the pope himself.[46]

All these familial rescue missions have a personal, idiosyncratic character. In each case there is visionary contact and dialogue between the deceased and the bereaved, and the suffrages are not routinized but specially tailored to each soul. Yet not everyone could expect to receive such visitations. While the damned might appear to their comrades in sin to warn them of their fate, those in purgatory were more likely to approach friends in religion or devout relatives who could help them. If no apparition was forthcoming, survivors might consult a specialist to request one. Hildegard of Bingen wrote several letters in reply to queries about particular souls in purgatory, although she expressed some reservations about this role.[47] Birgitta often told inquirers what alms, prayers, and sacrifices were required to deliver their dead from torment.[48] Margery Kempe, a less-respected seer, angered one widow by claiming that her husband was in purgatory and annoyed a second by urging her to spend more than she wished on masses.[49] But in spite of Margery's talent for alienating people, a woman with a gift for seeing into the beyond was a precious resource for the bereaved. In effect, she was not only mediator but medium, supplying longed-for news of lost friends and relations.[50] Unlike the nineteenth-century medium, she needed no technology to commune with the dead, nor did she experience possession by their spirits. The soul's ability to return and manifest its state aroused little skepticism.[51]

In some religious contexts, the extraordinary became ordinary, and apparitions the normal way to say farewell. Many sources record a "mutual vision pact" in which two friends promised that the one who died first would appear to the survivor and reveal his or her state.[52] In certain monasteries the deceased were expected as a matter of course to return, appearing either to a close friend or to another religious who specialized in such visions. At the English Gilbertine house of Watton, the nuns continued to pray for each dead sister until she revealed her glory or her punishment in a vision,[53] and the prioress of Unterlinden spent so much time communing with the dead that it was considered an especially virtuous act when she left them to celebrate the divine office.[54] At Helfta, Gertrude the Great saw such a multitude of souls liberated at the annual mass for departed relatives that she could not believe the nuns had so many kinfolk. Christ explained that, since he himself was their next of kin, all his friends were also their relations and thus included in their prayers.[55] Women like Marie of Oignies,[56] Lutgard of Aywières, and Mechthild of Magdeburg prayed both for special friends in purgatory and for hundreds of nameless, needy souls. Mechthild's clients included a friar, a beguine, a priest, and a murdered profligate; Lutgard was visited by Abbot Simon of Foigny, Pope Innocent III, Duchess Mary of Brabant, Jacques de Vitry, and her own sister.[57] A century later, the Dominican Margaret Ebner read Mechthild's revelations with great profit. She took so much joy in her own mission to the dead, who were not only her clients but her comforters and faithful informants about the beyond, that she was filled with gratitude toward them all, confessing that "the Poor Souls were the beginning of all the good that God has worked in me." [58]

III. Co-Redemption

Whether the souls in need were queens and popes, friends and relations, or anonymous spectral crowds, the apostle to the dead fulfilled her mission by suffering. "Redemption" in modern theology has become a dead metaphor, but medieval Christians understood the term in its original sense: it meant "buyout." The ransom for original sin had been paid by Christ on the cross, but each new sin established new debt, for which justice set a price and mercy paid—sometimes with money, sometimes with masses to bathe the souls in Christ's blood. But the most common currency of women was their pain: tears wrung from the heart, prayers poured like blood from wounded spirits, fever and chills, hunger and sickness and savage blows to the flesh. The Christ of purgatorial piety did not care who paid each sinner's debt: it might be God's mother or his saints, his special friends or the friends of the deceased—or he himself might pay by applying his own sacrifice to their account. Nor did he care about the venue: souls might atone in the "purgatory of mercy" (sickness and tribulation in life), the "purgatory of grace" (expiation as ghosts), or the "purgatory of righteousness" (otherworldly fire)—unless or until someone bought them out. [59] But payment there must certainly be. As in Anselmian atonement theory, the aim of purgatorial piety was to reconcile justice with mercy, not override it.

These notions of injured justice, satisfaction, and vicarious suffering set the medieval cult of the dead apart from spiritualism as well as the ancestor cults found in numerous other religions. Caroline Bynum has called attention to "the characteristically Christian idea that the bodily suffering of one person can be substituted for the suffering of another" as "one of the most puzzling, characteristic, glorious, and horrifying features of Christianity." [60] In scholastic theology, that idea found expression in the image of a "treasury of merits" disbursed by the pope as comptroller of spiritual revenues. [61] In women's piety, the alternative metaphor of the mystical body supplied a more congenial vehicle for the same idea. Ultimately, the whole Church was but a single body, perpetually dying, perpetually raised. Its members might seem scattered—some glorified in heaven while others suffered in purgatory and on earth—but the body remained one, the indivisible, broken flesh of Christ. For this reason the devotions to Christ's sacred heart, his wounds, and his eucharistic body could furnish means for the redemptive transfer of pain from one suffering member to another. The body of Christ was, in an almost literal sense, the medium of exchange.

There is no clearer exposition of this theology, even in medieval sources, than the work of the twentieth-century Anglican writer Charles Williams. In Williams's view, the heart of Christianity is what he calls "one of the open secrets of the saints": the doctrine of substitution, exchange, and coinherence, or the mutual interpenetration of souls within the mystical body.[62] Williams's extraordinary novel, *All Hallows' Eve* (1945), is the kind of fiction medieval mystics would undoubtedly have composed if the novel had been invented. Its central characters are three young women, two recently dead and one living. One of the dead women, incapable of selfless love, works out her own damnation. But the other, like the ghosts in medieval apparitions, inhabits a realm that is at once purgatory and the "real world," in this case contemporary London. Her friend, a chronic invalid and a visionary, is able to commune with the revenant. Through their exchange of love and pardon, the two friends achieve an act of co-redemption that brings about the living woman's cure, the dead woman's entry into heaven, and the liberation of numerous souls from the clutches of a devil-figure. At one point, when the dead woman offers her own "body" to intercept a curse that threatens her friend, the cross of Christ mysteriously interposes itself to cushion the blow and reverse the intended evil.[63]

In spite of its modern setting and semi-realistic style, Williams's novel is a complex reworking of a paradigmatic medieval plot. In the narrative of co-redemption, both the dead and the living profit from their exchange, which is enabled by the original substitution of Christ for Adam. Thus a devout woman's self-offering for souls in purgatory and her imitation of—or better, participation in—Christ's passion were on the deepest level not two actions, but one. Le Goff fails to see this intrinsic unity when he denies "any explicit link" between Lutgard's devotion to the sacred heart and her intercession for souls.[64] But any suffering accepted in union with Christ for the relief of souls—even the involuntary suffering of illness or persecution—could make the sufferer a co-redeemer. Perpetua made a gift of her martyrdom, and Guibert's mother of her child care. Lutgard of Aywières offered the dead a seven-year fast, Alice of Schaerbeke the agonizing pains of leprosy, and Christine of Stommeln her weird torments at the hands of demons.[65] Such remedies for souls occasionally suggest a kind of homeopathic medicine. Since the pains of purgatory were known to involve alternating fire and cold, the vicissitudes of a feverish illness (or self-inflicted equivalents) might be an especially fitting way to share and thereby relieve the sufferers' ordeal. Thus Christina Mirabilis jumped into hearth fires, baking ovens, boiling cauldrons, and icy rivers,[66] while Lidwina of Schiedam offered a fever of twelve years' duration.[67]

A late and particularly bizarre example comes from the life of Madre Juana de la Cruz, a Spanish Franciscan superior (d. 1534). Madre Juana, devoted like many women to helping souls in purgatory, also suffered constant illness. One day, when she was heating stones in a brazier to warm her chilled limbs, a stone cried out to her from the fire, revealing that a soul from purgatory was imprisoned within it. It turned out that not one but many stones were thus animate, comprising a "hospital" for souls in pain, and Juana could help them by making her own ailing body into another such hospital. Thenceforth the practice she had begun as a way to relieve her symptoms became a new method of self-torture. Juana had her sickbed heaped with stones collected by her nuns, laying them on her body so she could absorb the purgatorial heat or cold that the imprisoned souls must feel. Some of these confessed that they had been in purgatory for hundreds of years, since all their relatives had died and there was no longer anyone to remember them. But Madre Juana earned the grace of presiding over their deliverance, and as soon as each soul was freed she replaced its stone with a new one. While she groaned in this vicarious pain for weeks on end, her sisters fortified her by reading Christ's passion at her bedside.[68]

In their exertions on behalf of souls, saintly women undoubtedly strove to outdo one another, engaging in behavior that could strike observers as masochistic, insane, or (in Madre Juana's case) decidedly heterodox. But when its theological underpinnings are laid bare, the psychological and social motivations of such piety become easier to see. Several motives have already been suggested: the need to give, to fill a valued niche within the family or community, to maintain contact with lost friends and kinfolk, to win fame as a tireless apostle and bountiful patron despite the limitations of gender and class—in a word, to earn respect from the living and gratitude from the dead. Such gratitude need not remain hidden in the depths of a quiet conscience, for visions and revelations made it plain. Aside from the individual apparitions I have cited, the prestige of an especially potent intercessor could be displayed in sheer numbers. When Lutgard of Aywières died—as her spirit told a friend soon after—she felt such compassion as she passed by the souls in purgatory that God let a whole troupe of them follow her into paradise. Mechthild of Magdeburg was assured that her intercession had freed seventy thousand souls, and Margery Kempe, not to be outdone, delivered "many hundred thousand."[69] A holy woman at prayer, knowing the extent of her own largesse, must have felt not unlike a feudal magnate surveying his hall filled with banqueters, or a queen distributing alms from her balcony to the clamorous crowd below.

Like many ascetic practices, penance undertaken for souls in purgatory could also be a way to exert control over the slings and arrows of outrageous fortune, to wrest meaning out of otherwise inexplicable pain. Alice of Schaerbeke's leprosy, Lidwina of Schiedam's wasting sickness, Madre Juana's fevers, the mental instability of Christina Mirabilis and Christine of Stommeln—all defied medical help and cried out, not for healing as they would in our therapeutic society, but for consecration. The intricate connection between illness and women's piety becomes especially clear in such cases: if sickness is offered as a gift, then pain can be transmuted into the complex pleasure of generosity, amplifying the erotic pleasure of union with Christ.[70] Understood from this perspective, the theology of coredemption is a kind of theodicy: it not only justifies the fact of physical pain, but transforms it into a blessing. As McNamara writes, "Christ gave [his brides] pain and they took it as a gift to bestow on beggars in the afterworld."[71] By so doing they might intensify their own suffering, but they also abridged it, for the devout woman who wept, prayed, and suffered for souls was often assured that she herself would bypass purgatory and go straight to her reward.[72] A victim united to the supreme Victim, she earned merit in heaven even as she harrowed hell.

Christ, however, was righteous judge as well as suffering victim, while his bride was victim only. For this reason mystical texts and vitae sometimes put women in the anomalous, even embarrassing position of appearing more merciful than God himself. In the context of prayer for the dead, the familiar stereotypes of masculine justice and feminine compassion, far from keeping women "in their place," could exalt them in defiant humility to God's place. I submit that the more daring and theologically sophisticated mystics were aware of this potential and struggled with it, reflecting on their purgatorial piety to reach new and sometimes frightening insights about the paradox of justice and mercy. These explorations led them to challenge the limits of their devotion and at times, almost unwittingly, to question its very basis—God's sacrosanct right to punish.

IV. "Hell is the highest name of Love"

It all begins with a little harmless hyperbole. In courtly literature, so closely allied to beguinal mysticism, Christian rhetoric had been co-opted from the beginning: "penance" and "martyrdom" were ubiquitous tropes for the pains of erotic love. Further along that spectrum, the romance hero Aucassin in a famous theological outburst chose hell with his beloved Nicolette over paradise without her.[73] Heloise, poised on her knife-edge between Christ and Ovid, had expressed her fanatical devotion to Abelard by declaring herself ready to follow him even "ad Vulcania loca."[74] Dante thanked Beatrice that "you suffered, for my salvation, to leave your footprints in hell."[75] So it should not be surprising if mystical writers use the same trope to declare their loyalty to God. It is, at first blush, a straightforward paradox: better to experience the pains of hell for God's love than the joys of heaven without him.

The idea has a distinctly feminine cast, a note of extravagance and abjection, and it is voiced most often to express the mystic's perfect submission to the will of God. Mechthild says her soul, in its ecstasy of self-surrender, "wished that [God] would send her to hell, so that he might be praised beyond measure by all creatures."[76] Beatrice of Nazareth, consumed with longing, "would most willingly have supported the very pains of hell in her body . . . so long as she could have arrived at the fulfilment of this insatiable desire."[77] In Marguerite Porete's *Mirror of Simple Souls*, Fine Amour declares that to the free soul all fates are equal: "Shame is as precious as honour, and honour as shame; . . . and to be in Hell as to be in Paradise." In her quest for annihilation of the will, Marguerite consents to suffer everlasting pain rather than offend God in any way.[78] One of Tauler's spiritual daughters abandons herself to "the deepest torments of hell" and is thereby "drawn utterly into God's abyss."[79] Catherine of Siena muses that she would lovingly be condemned to hell for the honor and glory of God if all sinners could thereby be saved. But God replies that this is impossible: "Love of me cannot exist in hell, for that love would wipe hell out of existence." So much the better, Catherine answers: "If your truth and justice would permit it, I would love that hell should be wiped out; or at least that no soul should ever go there again. And if it were possible that, without losing love of you, I could be set upon the mouth of hell to close it, and so prevent any further souls from entering it, that is what I would like most of all."[80]

Catherine's dialogue cuts to the heart of the issue, revealing the true dynamics of the paradox. For heaven is defined as God's presence and hell as his absence, all of its torments being ancillary to the *poena damni* which, as theologians agreed, is the worst of all.[81] To endure the pains of hell out of devotion, compassion, or love of God is therefore, strictly speaking, an impossibility. When the mystic makes this boast she is really engaging in a *demande d'amour*: by sacrificing not only self-interest but reason itself to prove the extremity of her love, she challenges God to display an equal or greater love, first by delivering her from this voluntary hell but then, as Catherine puts it, by "wiping hell out of existence" altogether. Put another way, hell is necessary only as a point of reference, a *ne plus ultra* of suffering that the mystic can use, as Christ did his passion, to plumb the depths of her love. But it is no longer necessary "that any soul should ever go there again," because the mystic's sacrifice of co-redemption has exhausted that possibility. It would be unthinkable for the creature's charity to exceed the Creator's, so God is virtually bound to accept the challenge and forego his option of damning anyone ever again. Steering clear of dogmatic assertion, the logic of the mystical *demande d'amour* nevertheless leads covertly but inexorably toward universalism. A number of mystical women flirted with this realization, all of them expressing more or less discomfort as they glimpsed its far-reaching implications and perhaps a faint cloud of heresy looming on the horizon.[82]

Hadewijch of Brabant, mystical theologian and poet, dealt with the problematics of hell and purgatory in prose and verse, in theory and practice. Drawing on the courtly paradoxes of *fine amour*, she characterized love as a madness where hell and heaven meet, but hell predominates:

> To be wholly devoured and engulfed
> In her unfathomable essence,
> To founder unceasingly in heat and cold,
> In the deep, insurmountable darkness of Love:
> This outdoes the torments of hell.
> [One] who knows Love and her comings and goings
> Has experienced and can understand
> Why it is truly appropriate
> That Hell should be the highest name of Love.[83]

In view of this paradox, Hadewijch defines the soul mature in love as one who "did not fear hell / And did not serve for the hope of heaven, / And . . .

for hell's sake and for heaven's sake / [would be] equally glad and equally daring."[84] Since "hell" is no longer to be taken literally, but refers to one pole in the dialectic of love, Hadewijch can describe it paradoxically as a path by which the loving soul approaches God. In her difficult twenty-second letter she sets out four ways that souls may come to him: "through himself, through heaven, through hell, and through purgatory." The way of hell is called a "madness without hope" because souls on this path conform themselves to Christ's passion in their despairing self-condemnation: "They can neither believe nor hope that they would ever be able to content Love in her substantial being." Yet this path of abject humility "leads them very deep into God, for their great despair leads them above all the ramparts and through all the passageways, and into all places where the truth is."

Souls on the way of purgatory also suffer, but their torment is the gap between God's infinity and their own finite capacity. They "live in the land of holy anger" because they cannot bear their own inability to receive all that God desires to give. On this exalted plane, the mystical theologian joins hands with less sophisticated women like the nuns of Unterlinden by imagining a new form of purgatorial grace, an exchange of suffering more psychological than physical. The mere fact that the mystic acknowledges God's overflowing fullness and her own littleness, Hadewijch suggests, can channel the surplus grace toward indigent souls. For God may embrace "all his friends" with his right arm, but for their sake he also embraces "the strangers . . . with naked and scanty faith" in his left: "For the sake of his good friends and his beloved ones, he gives the strangers his glory and makes them all friends of the house."[85] The bride's exquisite purgatorial pain still showers largesse on the less fortunate.

In two of her visions, Hadewijch discloses what she took to be the practical implications of this teaching. In the tenth vision her soul is introduced into the New Jerusalem as bride and learns of the glory she has earned by suffering: "She shall be great, and she shall see her repose, and the voice of power shall be wholly hers." This "power" of the bride is co-redemptive, for she is told that the life of all creation will be renewed in her heavenly marriage. Even the "dead sinners who have come without hope, . . . and desire grace or entrance into purgatory," will attain fulfillment "if only they believe in the oneness of you both."[86] The saint's mystical union, like her suffering, is a redemptive event akin to the Passion in that all who merely witness it are saved *sola fide*. It is difficult to say whether Hadewijch is using "purgatory" literally or metaphorically in this passage; her "dead sinners" are probably reprobates on earth rather than damned souls. In the fifth vision, however, she confesses that she did in fact try to liberate souls from hell, and succeeded:

> In one thing I did wrong in the past, to the living and the dead, whom I with desire would have freed from purgatory and from hell as my right. But for this be you blessed: Without anger against me, you gave me four among the living and the dead who then belonged to hell. Your goodness was tolerant of my ignorance, and of my thoughtless desires, and of the unrestrained charity that you gave me in yourself for men. For I did not then know your perfect justice. I fell into this fault and was Lucifer because I did not know this, although on that account I did no evil in your eyes. This was the one thing because of which I fell among men, so that I remained unknown to them, and they were cruel to me. Through love I wished to snatch the living and the dead from all the debasement of despair and of wrongdoing, and I caused their pain to be lessened, and those dead in hell to be sent into purgatory, and those living in hell to be brought to the heavenly mode of life.[87]

Hadewijch's ambivalence is patent and unresolved. On the one hand, she is certain that she did wrong. She committed not only a "fault" but a satanic one, becoming "Lucifer" because she tried to deny God's justice. For this sin she deserved a heavy punishment—fall from leadership, persecution, and exile. Since her repentance, God has shown her that she must "hate and love wholly with" him, for he can "hate and love in one same Being." Justice must be preserved; there is no cheap grace. On the other hand, Hadewijch sinned in ignorance. God was not angry with her and she did no evil in his sight, since he himself gave her "unrestrained charity" and did, after all, deliver the souls she desired.[88] Her phrase, "I fell among men," even echoes Christ's prophecy that the Son of man must fall into the hands of men (Luke 9:44), as if her persecution could be expected to bear still more fruit for souls. Hadewijch's reassertion of divine justice thus stands as a sign of contradiction. Purgatorial grace has its limits, and she has gone beyond them. Yet she has done so with God's collusion and, so to speak, at his instigation. If Lucifer is divided against himself, how can his kingdom stand?

This perplexity is understandable in light of a piety eager to affirm both the hope of infinite mercy and the righteousness of heaven's judgment (in contrast to the all-too-earthly kind). Hadewijch may have been familiar with the celebrated legend of St. Gregory the Great and Trajan, which bears witness to the same dilemma. The Pope, knowing the pagan emperor's reputation for justice, is said to have taken pity and prayed for his

soul, which of course had been damned. But the *Golden Legend*, unwilling
to assert either that a soul could be freed from hell or that so great a saint
could have prayed in vain, summarizes no less than six alternative theories
as to what happened. In one version, Trajan was miraculously restored to
life long enough to become a Christian, and so was saved;[89] in other accounts, his punishment was only mitigated or delayed. The last theory in
the *Legend*, however, concedes that God did pardon the emperor, yet punished Gregory because he had prayed for a damned soul. Given the choice
between two days in purgatory and a lifetime of sickness, the saint chose
the latter.[90] Although Hadewijch wrote before Jacobus de Voragine, the
legend was already well-known and might have encouraged her to think of
her own sufferings as punishment for her audacious prayer.

It is possible, too, that even here Hadewijch intended "hell" in a metaphorical sense. Vekeman and Willaert have argued that the "souls dead in
hell" were none other than Hadewijch's close friends—contemplative beguines who had despaired of attaining mystical union until she secured that
grace for them through prayer.[91] In that case, Hadewijch's "fault" would
lie not in questioning God's absolute justice but in placing affection for
her friends above total surrender to his will. If she did mean her strong
language to be read in such a rarefied way, as a spiritual *trobar clus*, one
consequence would be an even further diminution of the "actual" hell. Re-
ducing God's ultimate sanction to a trope for the dark night of the soul, a
temporary trial reserved for his chosen brides, would make the possibility
of eternal, literal damnation seem more remote than ever.

Mechthild of Magdeburg, a younger contemporary of Hadewijch,
had a clearer sense of orthodox boundaries and a deeper engagement with
those outside her mystic circle. Several times she remarks that there is no
hope for the souls in hell, so God's lover must "never wish them well" even
though, if a pure soul could dwell among them, "it would be an eternal
light and a great comfort."[92] But from the other side the boundaries may
seem blurred, since many souls in purgatory have such sin that they "cannot know whether they will ever be redeemed."[93] For such desperate cases
Mechthild prays: "Give me, O Lord, the guilty souls out of purgatory; on
me alone be their ransom, all too dear."[94] Calling these anguished dead her
"children," she feeds them with her heart's blood yet remains careful, like
Hadewijch, to pay lip service to heaven's justice: "I suffer like a mother, yet
I am glad they are suffering pain justly for the honor of God."[95] Nonetheless, mercy and exchange have the upper hand. Mechthild's book is replete
with visions of purgatory, each crowned by her successful intercession.

On one occasion, the sight of tortured souls makes her "so fiercely angry" that she "takes purgatory in her arms" and stands waiting, while God tells her not to get upset because the pain is too hard for her to bear. Mechthild, showing her greater compassion, refuses to leave until God releases a thousand souls at her request. But they are still too filthy to enter heaven, so the mystic completes their purgation by bathing them in love's tears.[96] Like Abraham arguing with God over Sodom and Gomorrah, she personifies mercy outraged at the sight of vengeance. In a similar episode, Mechthild takes advantage of the eucharist to bestow the body of Christ where she thinks it will do the greatest good. She herself seems to initiate a vision of the otherworld, sweeping Christ along behind her like an imperious bride with her meek husband in tow: "Now she won such great might that *she* led *him* with his power, and they came to as gruesome a place as human eyes had ever seen"—purgatory, of course, filled with darkness and demons. Again Mechthild commands her beloved to take pity, he concedes that she has a point, and she gleefully presents him as ransom to the "sin-eaters," who are forced to flee as thousands of souls enter the earthly paradise.[97]

Near the end of her life, the beguine set forth her theology of exchange for a "spiritual friend"—perhaps a nun of Helfta—in terms reminiscent of Hadewijch. The soul, she explains, is like a small vessel that easily overflows when God fills it with grace, so the excess must be given to sinners and souls in purgatory:

> A small, full vessel can be emptied so often into a large one that the large vessel is filled from the small. The large vessel is the satisfaction God takes in our works. Alas, we are so small that one little word from God or from Holy Scripture fills us to capacity. So we pour the gift back into the large vessel, which is God. How can we do this? We should pour it with holy desire upon sinners, that they may be purified. . . . But as the vessel is filled again, we pour it on the need of poor souls suffering in purgatory, that God in his goodness may take their manifold pains from them. . . . Love makes suffering sweeter than one can say.[98]

In this way the soul can "lead God with God's own power" because the love she pours out is ultimately his own. But unless she channeled it to the needy dead, refusing to take no for God's answer, they would have to suffer for decades more. Without embracing universalism in theory, Mechthild strives for it in practice, giving the impression that if all God's brides were as fervent as she, purgatory would very soon be emptied.[99]

Marguerite Porete, third in the trio of literary beguines, no longer prayed for particular intentions (like the release of souls from purgatory) once she had become a free spirit and "taken leave of the virtues." But in her more theoretical way, she too developed a theology that, carried to its logical conclusion, implies the abolition of hell. Perhaps the most famous passage in her *Mirror*—next to the *demande d'amour* that closes it—is the paradox in which she declares herself to be "the very salvation of all creatures and the glory of God" because she is the sum of all evils. Marguerite's argument posits that God would be false to his own nature if he did not give alms to the poorest of the poor. But there can be none poorer than she herself, who in her created essence is only nothingness and the privation of all good. Therefore nothing less than the infinity of God's goodness can fill the abyss of her lack, so her evil no less than Christ's death becomes the supreme occasion for the display of his grace. "The goodness of God is made known to the human race by means of my wickedness, so it is clear that I am the everlasting praise of God and the salvation of humankind." [100]

Marguerite takes up a familiar neo-Platonic idea—evil as the privation of good—and couples it with the Pauline paradox of grace abounding to the chief of sinners. But in her flamboyant way she transmutes these commonplaces to arrive at a deliberately shocking and heretical claim: she is co-redeemer with Christ not because she is overflowing with charity, like other mystics, but because she is *not*. Marguerite's inquisitors may have accepted her claim to be "the sum of all evils" and hence worthy to be killed. Most Christians, however, would have defined that quantity as neither more nor less than "hell." According to the logic of Marguerite's paradox, God would then have to bestow his alms—the totality of his goodness—on hell itself, harrowing it once and for all and, indeed, obliterating it. It is interesting that Catherine of Siena, who wished to seal hellmouth with her own soul, operated on a theological maxim very similar to Marguerite's: "You are she who is not, and I am He Who Is." [101] On this point, the difference between saint and heretic is more a question of style than of substance. Both covertly assert power against God on the basis of their very nothingness, challenging him once more to use "the things that are not"—namely themselves—to confound "those that are"—namely the pains of hell.

In a text radically different from Marguerite's *Mirror, The Book of Margery Kempe*, we find a frank discomfort with the idea of damnation. Margery's piety is revealing precisely because she was not an original thinker like Hadewijch or Marguerite Porete but a virtual composite of feminine mysticism (of a Continental rather than English variety, for reasons that have yet to be sufficiently explained). Like Mechthild, Margery liberated sinners by the thousands; like Hadewijch, she was told that "the souls in purgatory shall rejoice at your coming home."[102] Like Catherine, she longed to abolish hell by her personal sufferings: "You would be chopped up as small as meat for the pot for their love, so that I would, by your death, save them all from damnation if it pleased me. For you often say in your thoughts that there are enough in hell, and you wish that no more men should ever deserve to go there."[103]

The most revealing passage, however, is one where Margery falls short of the sublimity that was her aim. Few will forget the episode in which, for twelve days, she fantasized about priests exposing their privy members to her and felt compelled, at the devil's instigation, to "prostitute herself to them all." These lurid sexual fantasies have, not surprisingly, distracted readers from the event that triggered them. Immediately before her "foul thoughts," Margery reports a conversation with Christ in which she had, uncharacteristically, refused a revelation. God wanted her to "hear of the damned as well as of the saved," but Margery rejected this painful knowledge, preferring to believe that "it was some evil spirit out to deceive her." As a punishment for her unbelief, God abandoned her to the devil and his "abominable visions" until she had learned her lesson.[104] Sexual pathology here overlies an acute conflict between Margery's desire for universal salvation and her orthodox belief that hell is essential to Christian faith. Having weathered many accusations and at least one formal heresy trial, she could ill afford to deny the eternal fires, whatever she might wish. Lacking Hadewijch's subtlety, Catherine's charisma, and Marguerite's will to martyrdom, she could only yield the point. Her "punishment" for refusing to witness one manifestation of hell's power was to be subjected willy-nilly to another, in the realm where she knew herself to be most vulnerable. Damnation became a frightening possibility, not in the ecstasy of vicarious pain she imagined herself embracing, but in the humiliation of untrammeled lust.

We come at last to the most celebrated case of universalism in medieval theology—Julian of Norwich's *Showings*. Julian's eloquence, her atypical optimism, and above all her famous refrain ("all manner of thing shall be well") have led many to interpret her as the clearest proponent of universal salvation since Origen. A close reading of the Long Text, however, shows that while the anchoress does urgently maintain that "all shall be well," this affirmation is just as unresolved and fraught with contradiction as the other forays against hell we have examined. As I also hope to have shown, Julian's resistance does not stand in splendid isolation; rather, she makes central to her theology a problem that has emerged as at least a subtext in a variety of women's religious writings. Doubts about damnation become critical to her handling of the problem of evil, which constitutes the cornerstone of her theology.

Unlike most of the women we have considered, Julian did not have a particular apostolate to the dead. Although she did wish, as a young woman, for sickness and the "wound of compassion," she was uninterested in ascetic feats and certainly expressed no desire to be damned for the salvation of others. Her mature perception of the human plight was universal rather than individual, so she did not single herself out as either extraordinarily evil or destined for extraordinary grace. To her mind "sin," conceived as a general state of alienation from God, did not so much justify as constitute the wretchedness of humankind. Hence, "if it were laid in front of us, all the pain there is in hell and in purgatory and on earth, death and all the rest, we should choose all that pain rather than sin. For sin is so vile and so much to be hated that it can be compared with no pain which is not itself sin. And no more cruel hell than sin was revealed to me, for a loving soul hates no pain but sin." [105] If this is the case, then hell is not denied, but relativized; instead of being the ultimate punishment for sin it becomes an ancillary pain, almost a distraction from the real cause and essence of human suffering. The perspective adopted is of course that of the "loving soul," which is the only one Julian ever seriously considers.

In her more developed treatment of hell, she adopts a rhetorical strategy diametrically opposed to Margery's. As Nicholas Watson has shown, the entire Long Text is constructed as a dialogue not so much between God and Julian as between Julian-the-inspired-visionary (who received the showings) and Julian-the-questing-believer (who struggles to understand them).[106] In this dialogue it is the questing believer, always obedient to Holy Church, who reasserts the orthodox belief in hell, while the inspired visionary, basing her faith on the showings, reiterates that all manner of thing shall be well. The two eventually arrive at neither compromise nor resolution, but a kind of truce: both affirmations are correct, but they can be reconciled only through the enigmatic "great deed" that God is to perform on the Last Day. Speaking as the dutiful daughter of Holy Church (or what Marguerite Porete would have called "Holy Church the Little"), Julian knows "one point of our faith is that many creatures shall be damned"—the devil and his angels, heathens, unconverted Jews, and wicked Christians. "All these shall be damned to hell without end, as Holy Church teaches me to believe." In confirmation of this teaching, Julian even desires "some sight of hell and of purgatory"—not that she doubts them, as she hastens to add, but in order to "live the more to God's worship." [107]

Margery refused to contemplate hell, yet had hellish visions forced upon her; Julian requests a showing of it, but her request is denied. In response to her desire—which is not recorded in the Short Text—she sees only that the devil is "endlessly condemned" and anyone who shares his condition will be "no more mentioned before God and all his saints." Thus the possibility of damnation remains open while the actuality is left uncertain, for "the revelation was shown to reveal goodness, and little mention was made in it of evil." This silence Julian-the-believer takes as confirmation of her orthodox faith, which demands that God will "save his word in all things." But Julian-the-visionary, who has no sight of hell, clings to the alternative truth of her divine assurance:

> And as to thys I had no other answere in shewyng of oure lorde but thys: That that is vnpossible to the is nott vnpossible to me. I shalle saue my worde in alle thyng, and I shalle make althyng wele. And in thys I was taught by the grace of god that I shuld stedfastly holde me in the feyth as I had before vnderstond, and ther with that I shulde stonde and sadly beleue that alle maner thyng shall be welle, as oure lorde shewde in that same tyme. For thys is the grete dede that oure lorde god shalle do, in whych dede he shalle saue his worde in alle thyng. And he shalle make wele all that is nott welle. But what the dede shal be, and how it shall be done, there is no creature beneth Crist that wot it.[108]

Julian's aporia, or double truth, expresses on the scale of humankind what Hadewijch had maintained with respect to particular souls in hell. On the one hand, God will "save his word in all things": if he pronounces a soul to be damned, then damned it shall be. If Scripture and Holy Church threaten hellfire, then hell assuredly burns. On the other hand, God "will make all things well": whether here and now or on the Last Day, whether individually or collectively, the damned may yet be set free. Hadewijch felt harshly punished for her success in liberating them, yet she somehow knew God was not angry. Julian sees sin as utterly hateful, far worse than any hell; but she also knows that in heaven, God does not blame sin but turns it to bliss and honor.[109] Because the voice of Julian-the-visionary proclaims this consoling message, and because modern readers prefer inner authority to that of Holy Church, it is easy to interpret the protestations of Julian-the-believer as heresy insurance, proof against real or imagined prosecutors. Indeed, if we accept the revisionist dating of the Long Text proposed by Watson, persecution of Lollard anchoresses was actually taking place as

Julian composed her book.[110] Yet it would be dangerously anachronistic to assume that it was only her "even Christians," and not also herself, that she needed to assure of her orthodoxy.

We have seen that articulate women from a variety of religious milieux doubted, challenged, or wished to disbelieve in eternal punishment, although not one of them denied it outright. These women were not part of an organized movement and did not develop their doubts in the same manner or build on the same theological foundations, despite some underlying similarities. Nor were they inspired by any current in scholastic theology or popular preaching, to which the doctrine of hell was essential.[111] A straightforward denial of it would have contradicted the express word of Scripture and undermined the foundations of traditional Christianity (as may be demonstrated from the history of the modern Church). What, then, was the source of these doubts—doubts that clearly provoked anxiety and ambivalence in the women that harbored them? I would like to suggest three possible answers.

First, I have argued that discomfort with the idea of eternal torment may be an outgrowth of orthodox purgatorial piety, which religious women cultivated to a high degree. Their apostolate to the dead, whether undertaken for family members, friends in religion, or anonymous suffering souls, required them to feel empathy for those in pain regardless of their moral stature—indeed, all the more because these sinners deserved the torment they endured. Visions of afflicted ghosts, or of purgatory in all its horror, typically inspired not the self-righteous shudder of alienation ("there but for the grace of God go I") but renewed activity on behalf of the *arme Seelen*. If it was reckoned a special triumph to liberate the most despicable wretches, to free thousands of souls with a single prayer, or to cut decades off a poor sinner's sentence, should it not be an even greater triumph to liberate the "hopeless cases," the damned themselves? All were sinful, all suffering; could there be so great a divide between fire and fire? As visionaries often remarked, the only difference between purgatory and hell was that one was temporary, the other permanent, while several maintained that the worst sinners in purgatory had no assurance of their salvation.[112] To a dispassionate observer—still more, to a compassionate one—the boundaries might well appear blurred. Mary, the Mother of Mercy, did not care for such niceties: the more sinful the soul, the more confidently it might trust in her prayers. Imitating her, an audacious spirit might pursue the competitive edge in piety, the special *frisson* to be gained from daring to wrestle with God and to prevail. The prevalence of this mentality is attested by Gilles d'Orléans's sermon to the beguines of Paris in 1272: the friar admonished them specifically to pray "for those who are in purgatory, not those in hell."[113]

In the second place, doubts about hell seem to follow from the conception of God held by many religious women. God is Charity, as St. John and the univocal witness of the Church proclaim; but to mystics and devout souls of every kind, God was Lover and Beloved in a peculiarly intimate way. To be sure, the variations even among the small group of women here studied are considerable. Catherine of Siena's supportive Father and crucified Bridegroom do not speak with the same voice as Margery Kempe's partner and bedmate. Julian's homely Servant, courteous Lord, and gracious Mother are most unlike the aristocratic, all-consuming Frau Minne of Hadewijch and Mechthild. Nevertheless, all these women experienced God in their most private and passionate selves as unbounded Love. It is only because they knew his compassion from experience that they dared to challenge it in their prayers and visions: they did not expect to be refused, whatever the reservations of Holy Church. From the intensity of their own sacrificial passion and compassion, they found it inconceivable, on some level, that the God who had died for them might be less merciful than they. So, whatever the theoretical necessity of hell, its practical possibility repelled them.

At this point, some readers may be nervously wondering if I have embraced a sentimental and essentialist version of female piety. I must state emphatically, therefore, that most religious women whose lives are known to us did *not* question God's right to punish. The records of feminine piety that circulated widely in medieval England—the *Life of Marie of Oignies*, Birgitta's *Revelations*, the anonymous *Revelation of Purgatory*—promulgate an orthodox purgatorial piety without expressing any doubts whatsoever on the subject of eternal punishment.[114] We are dealing with a very limited and extraordinary group of writers. It is worth noting that all of these doubters were religious "irregulars" or solitaries: three beguines, a tertiary, a recluse, and a freelance pilgrim. Hadewijch and Mechthild were both harassed and driven from their beguine communities; Catherine exercised an unusual and much-criticized apostolate; Margery Kempe was tried for heresy and Marguerite Porete burned for it; and Julian took pains to avoid suspicion—pains that included the non-publication of her book.

It looks very much, therefore, as if the marginality of these mystics, both as women and as irregulars, fueled their doubts. Women in general, but freelance religious women in particular, had little to gain from the enforcement of universal law. Powerless themselves, they had no involvement in the administration of secular justice, and unlike nuns, no opportunity to hold office within a well-established hierarchy of obedience. Sin for them was not a juridical problem, but a way of talking about human pain, estrangement, and lack of love. Even the figure of God as King was not primarily lawgiver but romantic lover (as in Marguerite Porete's fable of King Alexander) or model of gracious condescension (as in Julian's parable of the lord and the servant). Hell as the ultimate sanction in a system of cosmic justice, the place that both eternalizes rebellion against God's law and forever excludes the rebels, may have seemed superfluous to these women who were, in so many ways, outside the social mainstream yet felt themselves to be profoundly included and even privileged in the realm of God. It is interesting that none of the doubts about damnation come from cloistered nuns, even in monasteries like Helfta and Unterlinden, where the apostolate to the dead was pursued with zeal. Women who actually ruled or founded monasteries—Hildegard of Bingen, Birgitta of Sweden, the Carthusian prioress Marguerite of Oingt[115]—might be deeply concerned with freeing souls from purgatory, but had no thought of questioning God's right to damn.

Most atypical, then, were these women who alternately embraced hell for themselves as a means to free others and struggled with God over its very existence. Or perhaps it would be more accurate to say that the survival of their witness is atypical. William of Auvergne, the heresy-hunting bishop of Paris (1228–49) contemporary with Hadewijch and Mechthild, was deeply troubled by the "ignorant and unbelieving"—the majority of his flock—who had questions of their own about hellfire:

> Here is one cause of this error that disturbs and bewilders many: the huge numbers that are to be damned and the few that will be saved. Why, they ask, did the mercy of God choose so few for salvation, but leave so many in perdition—especially since he is believed to be more ready to save than to condemn? . . . It can even seem presumptuous for a few Christians to think they alone will be saved, and the whole rest of humankind left to perdition—that is, bad Christians (who far outnumber the good), as well as Jews, Saracens, and pagans . . . Does it seem fitting for the King of kings and Lord of the ages to have more subjects bound in prison, hung on the gallows, and delivered to torture than he has in his loyal service? Can the mercy of God, which is infinite and beyond measure, endure so painful a slaughter? Why, they ask, did he create such a multitude of the damned? . . . It upsets the ignorant and unbelieving that sin is momentary and takes only a short time to commit. How, they ask, can it be just to inflict eternal punishment for it?[116]

William heaps scorn on the "intolerable stupidity" of the masses and goes on to defend hell at length, citing its utility as a deterrent to crime and its admirable justice in avenging God's honor. Anyone who truly loves God, he says, should also love his justice, for "hell is not an evil; rather it is very good and ought to be highly valued."[117]

None of our women mystics were ignorant or unbelieving, and their doubts about hell should not be confused with the strain of skeptical materialism that has been documented from a variety of sources.[118] On the contrary, it was in the context of a largely orthodox and unusually fervid piety that these women questioned eternal justice. Indeed, their professions of willingness to be damned themselves for God's love prove that they were not seeking easy grace. Yet their objections, far from being silenced by arguments like William's, may be only the most vocal and courageous testimonies to an unease that was more widely shared. It is no accident that such doubts, if they were to survive in writing outside of inquisitorial records, could find a niche only in the literature of visions and revelations—the genre of women's writing par excellence. Exceptional as they were, then, these mystics' limited numbers should not blind us to the importance of their witness. With respect to medieval piety, they may represent the tip of an invisible iceberg. With respect to the history of Christian thought, they form the narrow end of a wedge that did not make substantial inroads until the nineteenth century.

Significantly, not a single woman who had her doubts about damnation cited the classic theological defense of it—God's respect for human freedom, with its capacity to persist forever in a posture of rejection. These devoted lovers of God could not imagine a Miltonic Satan, a Faust; it was inconceivable to them that any soul could finally resist the blaze of God's love, or that God could withhold his favors forever. Not for them the chilling inscription on the gate of Dante's hell:

> Giustizia mosse il mio alto fattore:
>   Fecemi la divina potestate,
>   La somma sapienza e'l primo amore.[119]

Justice and power might indeed have fashioned an eternal hell; supreme wisdom, possibly; but primal love? Never.

5. *La mystique courtoise*: Thirteenth-Century Beguines and the Art of Love

Around 1250 a German poet, Lamprecht of Regensburg, wrote about women's mysticism under the telling name of *kunst*—knowledge or art. He expressed the usual consternation over female hegemony in this sphere:

diu kunst ist bî unserm tagen
in Brâbant und in Baierlanden
undern wîben ûf gestanden.
herre got, waz kunst ist daz,
daz sich ein alt wîp baz
verstêt dan witzige man? [1]

("Knowledge" has in our days sprung up among women in Brabant and Bavaria. Lord God, what knowledge is this that an old woman understands better than a learned man?)

Lamprecht gives a familiar and no doubt comforting explanation: women, because of their soft hearts and simple senses, could be "kindled more brightly" than men by desire for God.│They were wiser mystics because they were better lovers.│But when such women made their desire into an art, they belied the naïveté that Lamprecht wished to foist on them. To contemporaries, the sophistication of writers like Hadewijch, Mechthild of Magdeburg, and Marguerite Porete was as disconcerting as it was seductive, for here were "celibates with a real love life, . . . religious women who knew desire and [its] fulfillment" and had the hauteur of a courtly *domna*.[2] It was an artful knowing, not mere desire, that made them into those dangerously subtle creatures, *beguines clergesses*. And it is art that must guide us in reading their desire today.[3]

│*La mystique courtoise* was a distinctive creation of the thirteenth-century beguines, not just a pretty new bottle for the same old wine, and once it appeared on the scene, mysticism would never be quite the same.│

Here was a new movement both religious and literary, an *ars subtilior* of the spirit, a *dolce stil religioso*[4] in which the monastic discourse on love converged with the courtly. As adepts of *fine amour* who were also theologians, the beguine mystics needed to discern as finely as Chrétien de Troyes anatomizing Lancelot's heart or Aquinas disputing Pecham on the soul. Characteristic of beguine writings far more than of monastic or anchoritic texts, *la mystique courtoise* defies the mainstream view of medieval theorists (and medievalists) for whom the "two loves" were quite simply opposite.

The originality of the beguines' self-understanding is missed if it is treated solely as a version of *Brautmystik*, the eroticized contemplative practice based on allegorical reading of the Song of Songs and popularized by Bernard of Clairvaux.[5] This exegetical tradition had long been central to formative literature for nuns and virgins, including such well-known texts as the *Ancrene Wisse*. In its origins, bridal mysticism was a narrative devised by male authors for a female protagonist: the virgin bride of Christ, who could be understood collectively as the Church, individually as the Virgin Mary or any loving soul, or more concretely as the female recluse or nun. If monks wished to play the starring role in this love story, they had to adopt a feminine persona—as many did—to pursue a heterosexual love affair with their God. It might be assumed that when women began to compose their own mystical texts, they could more easily have followed the path already laid out by men. But rather than stepping neatly into the role designed for them, some women forged a more complicated, less stereotypical way that allowed them a wider emotional range. In adopting the language of *fine amour*, the prevailing ethos in courtly lyric and romance,[6] they drew on a discourse that assumes a male protagonist and a female object of desire. Since this literature offers only rare expressions of female subjectivity, it could encourage women writers to experiment with gender roles just as monks did within the Song of Songs tradition.

What is remarkable about the beguines is that they appropriated both forms of discourse, using them in counterpoint to express contrasting if not contradictory movements in their all-consuming love. Each tradition is in itself supple and nuanced. In juxtaposition, *Brautmystik* and *fine amour* can convey strikingly different views of the lover, the beloved, the emotional and ethical praxis of love, and not least, the community in which the love-drama unfolds, with its carefully defined sets of insiders and outsiders. In combination, the two discourses may reinforce each other or they may work at cross-purposes, almost incidentally conferring dual gender on both the lover and the divine Beloved. It is this dialectic that gives *la mystique courtoise* its characteristic dynamism, broadening its resources to express the loving, volatile self's whole panoply of response to its ineffable Other.

I use the term *mystique courtoise* in lieu of the more familiar *Minne-mystik* to stress the influence of courtly literature as well as the ambiguous social location of this movement, which, like the beguines themselves, straddled the border between religious and secular life. It would be misleading, however, to insist on too strict a correlation between this new form of mystical discourse and beguinal status, for the analytical framework I develop here could be applied to a variety of thirteenth- and fourteenth-century texts. Among them are some little-known beguine writings—the poems of "Hadewijch II,"[7] the anonymous dialogue *Schwester Katrei*—but also the Cistercian Beatrice of Nazareth's *Seven manieren van minne* and certain works of Suso and Ruusbroec. Nevertheless, it is beyond doubt that the three great literary beguines—Hadewijch, Mechthild, and Marguerite—developed the art to its highest and subtlest pitch.

I. The Order of *fins amans*

About the same time that Marguerite Porete was polishing her *Mirror*, a French priest associated with a beguinage, perhaps that of Paris, did what the clerical friends of religious women had always done. He wrote them a rule, not so much to legislate as to articulate the ideals of their community.[8] This document, the *Règle des Fins Amans*, is an invaluable key to the self-understanding of beguines—not just the extraordinary mystics and writers, but the ordinary women whose daily lives, struggles, and aspirations were the ground from which they sprang. Since the author of the *Règle* wrote a century after the beguine movement began to attract wide attention, and perhaps fifty years after Hadewijch had formulated her full-blown *mystique courtoise*, he was hardly an innovator. His rule can be read as a typical or representative statement of a beguinal ethos that by 1300 was widely shared.

A century earlier, court poets and spiritual teachers alike might have been taken aback by the *Règle*'s succinct formulation: "Li ordres des fins amans est beginaiges."[9] An order was a religious fellowship vowed to poverty, chastity, and obedience, in which monks or nuns prayed, fasted, kept silence, donned unassuming garb in neutral colors, and studiously avoided the opposite sex. But *fins amans*, the flirtatious young gentlemen at court? What had St. Benedict to do with Sir Lancelot, or St. Bernard with la belle Isolt? Guinevere, that paragon of paramours, might become nun and abbess at Almesbury; but she repented first.[10] A broad stream of opinion, shared by ascetic and worldly writers, held the love of God to be incompatible with *fine amour* in any form. Andreas Capellanus, after expatiating wittily and bawdily on love in the courtly mode, turned and fathered the whole art upon the devil.[11] Ovidian palinodes like his *De amoris remedio* were a well-worn topos by the time that Chaucer, hoping for a pious death, found it prudent to retract "many a song and many a leccherous lay."[12] Clerical denunciations, not only of sexual love but of the courtly affectations and pastimes that glamorized it, were even more numerous. It was on the basis of this stolid conservative tradition that D. W. Robertson proposed his notorious reading of medieval culture as a crusade of Augustinian *caritas* against erotic *cupiditas* (by which he meant "courtly love").[13]

Nevertheless, rapprochement between the two great systems of desire was attempted from both sides. Gérard of Liège, a thirteenth-century author, wove passages from Augustine and Bernard, vernacular love lyrics, and the Song of Songs into a single *ars amatoria*, representing God as *li dieu damours*, Christ as *li biaus descouneus* (the Fair Unknown, a romance hero), and Augustine himself (*pace* Robertson) as *li anguisseus damours*.[14] In the *Règle des Fins Amans*, a comparable synthesis of eros and agape takes shape (*pace* Anders Nygren) under the rubric of *fine amour*. Much of the *Règle* sets forth doctrine that could have been preached to cloistered nuns, and in fact it describes beguines as "religieuses de leur seigneur."[15] But the hallmark of the rule is its thoroughgoing, unabashed translation of monastic teaching into the idiom of secular love poetry. The writer begins with a definition of his key term, using conspicuously inclusive language to describe God's *fin amant* even though he leaves the phrase in its conventional masculine form.

> *Fin amant* is the name for men and women who love God *finement* . . . that is, purely, with all our heart, with all our strength, and with all our virtue. What marvel! This is the way he loved us. He showed us love of the heart when he wished to have his side opened right next to his heart, as if to say: 'I cannot speak, but I have opened my bosom to you. Fair sweet son, fair sweet daughter, put your hand in my bosom, take my heart! For it is yours.' . . . And he says through Solomon: 'Fair son, give me your heart!' He does not say 'lend it to me!' . . . Surely he would have too base (*vilain*) a heart who would refuse or deny so great a lord what he requires, since he asks so beautifully, so sweetly and honorably.[16]

Here Christ's "great commandment" (Matt. 22:37) is interpreted as *fine amour*, and the cult of the Sacred Heart is assimilated to the romance motif of lovers exchanging hearts.[17] The *fin amant* is exhorted to think of her lover often, to seek out his favorite haunts, and to receive the jewels he sends her gladly, although these consist of "poverty, diseases, maladies, and tribulations." She is given commandments by "Jhesucrist, l'abé des fins amans," in a scenario that conflates the Sermon on the Mount and the act of monastic profession with another romance topos, the lover's receipt of "commandments" from the *dieu d'amors* in a court of love or *locus amoenus*.[18] The queen of this amorous court is Mary, "sweet abbess of the convent of paradise," and the model *fin amant* is Mary Magdalene, "who loved Jesus Christ with such ardor."

Three features in particular connect the *Règle* with the practice of *la mystique courtoise*. First, the ancient monastic topos of earthly life as exile from God is given a new romantic coloring through the paradigm of *amor de lonh*, or love from afar.[19] Yearning at all times for her distant love, the beguinal *fin amant* can snatch only brief and furtive meetings. These are her moments of ecstasy, which is taken for granted as a stage of prayer that Christ's *amie* will achieve. It is the fruit of meditation on his glorified human nature, and the writer calls it "ravishing" (*ravisement*)—a term that originally meant "rape" but could refer at this period to both spiritual exaltation and sexual pleasure.[20] The author's exempla of *ravisement* culminate in King Solomon's *amie*, the queen of Sheba (1/3 Kings 10:1–13), whose romantic adventures could be dovetailed with that royal love story, the Song of Songs.[21]

> When a soul is fixed in such meditation, none of the bodily senses fulfills its function; and this is called "ravishing." . . . It is signified for us in the queen of Sheba, who heard tell of Solomon and his riches and came to him from the end of the world, and when she came, she said that whatever they had told her was nothing compared to what she had found. She could not endure the marvels she saw, and so she swooned. When a soul is in such a state, then she is in contemplation, the fourth type of prayer.[22]

The Queen of Sheba is a perfect exemplum because she typifies both the mystic in ecstasy and the ideal *fin amant*—falling in love with a noble king "from the end of the world," giving and receiving immeasurable gifts, and finally losing herself in total surrender to her beloved.[23] At the beginning of her book, Marguerite Porete compares her experience of *fine amour* to the adventure of a noble princess who falls in love with King Alexander, sight unseen, and consoles herself by painting his portrait—which is both her lover's gift and her own imaginary *Mirror* of this distant love.[24]

A second courtly aspect of the *Règle* is its stance on community. In the aristocratic game of love, the amorous couple never stood alone; they were surrounded by courtly friends and jealous foes. A fulfilled relationship could overcome the solipsism of immature lovers and blossom into what Chrétien de Troyes called the Joy of the Court. In his *Erec et Énide*, high festival is held when mature lovers achieve the integration of private desire with social responsibility.[25] So also with the beguine and her beloved: ecstasy finds its locus in community, and spiritual friends must be fiercely cherished. On the other hand, the elite circle had to guard its borders by excluding lesser breeds without the law of *fine amour*. In the *Règle*, the beguine community is defined both positively and negatively with respect to the wider world. Unlike thirteenth-century legislators for nuns, who were obsessed with claustration, the author of the *Règle* permits the beguines a harmless 'Joy of the Court': "I do not forbid you to play and celebrate with good people in safe and public places, and to honor and love good people and especially those through whom God has done [you] good. For all this one can do with God."[26] But the writer expects his charges to have more persecutors than benefactors: the world hates *fins amans* because it first hated their "abbot," Christ. After citing the Beatitudes on persecution, he tells his beguines not to fear those who slander them, because their Beloved is worth the pain: "Fair sweet Jesus Christ, how little I would fear the whole world if it had made war on me and wished to do me the worst harm it could, if I had you as a helper! . . . Fair sir God, take from me everything; if you give me yourself alone, it will suffice me."[27]

This complex of attitudes—loyalty to the Beloved at any cost, intimate friendship with the circle of *fins amans*, and contempt for the uncomprehending masses—is discernible in all the extant beguine texts. Their striking elitism is in part a simple transposition of the courtly ethos into religious terms. But more important, it sets a limit to the democratization of mystical piety that beguines themselves were promoting. Without the physical and symbolic protection of the cloister, these women were left painfully vulnerable to their enemies, and their attitude of lofty disdain can be seen as a cultural barrier raised to compensate for the lost privilege afforded by monastery walls. Since even large beguinages in the thirteenth century were not cloistered, the beguine was expected to mingle with a diverse public, dividing her associates into the few "good people" who appreciated *fine amour* and the hostile crowd to be despised or pitied, but never feared. Humble as she was, she assuredly knew her worth. Hers was a vernacular mysticism, but vulgar it was not.

Competition with the established orders surfaces again in the remarkable conclusion of the *Règle*. The text ends with a scenario that is impeccably traditional (for it is an allegory of Christ and the Virtues) yet stunningly secular (for it is an homage to the *Roman de la Rose*). The heroine Conscïence ("Desire") wakes up one morning, like the bride in the Song of Songs, to find her lover absent. Jealousy claims that the monks and nuns (*li cloistriés*) have imprisoned him in their garden, as Jealousy herself imprisoned Fair Welcome in Guillaume de Lorris's poem. With the help of Hope, Charity, Fine Amour, and other virtues, Conscïence breaks into the monastery garden, sees her lover, and swoons, like the Queen of Sheba in ecstasy. This mini-romance leads into a poem in which the beguine, identifying with the heroine, laments that she is so far from her Beloved *en estrange païs* and begs to join him in paradise. The diminutive sketch encapsulates its implied reader's self-consciousness as *fin amant*: she is expected to be fully conversant with the best-seller that was taking the Île de France by storm, and to respond to it by courting her divine Beloved as resolutely as the fictional Lover pursued his Rose.

Marguerite Porete may or may not have known the *Règle des Fins Amans*; the text has not been precisely dated. But she certainly knew the world of courtly romance and the *grand chant courtois*, as did Hadewijch and Mechthild before her. In reading these mystics, therefore, we must recognize that their new brand of eroticism was far from being a spontaneous manifestation of female desire. Rather, it grew out of a unique and specialized literary culture. A thirteenth-century hothouse plant, *la mystique courtoise* was a hybrid of court and cloister, of bridal mysticism and *fine amour*.

II. Bridal Self and Courtly Self

One of the salient characteristics of beguine mysticism is the variety of positions the loving self can occupy vis-à-vis Love or the divine Beloved. The mystic's polyvalent "I," like the troubadour's, is produced in part by the vicissitudes of erotic experience itself—in this case, the turbulent experience of loving God. It is also shaped by the performative context of her writing, for no matter how "autobiographical" her text, she is a representative lover whose experience is meant to provide a paradigm for others, illumining all the phases and degrees of love.[28] We can begin to discern some of these phases by distinguishing a "bridal self" and a "courtly self," and as variants of the latter, a masculine *fin amant* and a feminine *amie*.

The bridal self is the woman in love as she was imagined by generations of monks, and her exemplar is the Song of Songs as read by St. Bernard. While the bride lives out the rhythm of desire and fulfillment, meeting and parting, she has no doubts about her lover or her own status as beloved. She knows frustration, but not anger; she has moments of languor and abandonment (*quia amore langueo*), but not despair. On the whole she is joyous and confident in love, enjoying a measure of reciprocity with her bridegroom—a feature of the ancient Hebrew text that medieval exegetes preserved in spite of themselves. Of course she knows the distance between herself as creature and her divine Creator, yet so great is their love that in times of bliss, she forgets this difference and behaves as an equal. When the Beloved is absent she yearns for him and seeks him in prayer, but her basic posture is one of waiting; she knows that sooner or later he will return. It is important to recognize that this attitude is not "passive," however, for the bride eagerly demands fulfillment of her needs. She does not seek abjection but happiness, which stems from increasing intimacy and trust. As a "marriage," her union is viewed as fruitful: she becomes "mother" to virtues and spiritual children, who may include the poor and sick for whom she cares, the disciples who entrust themselves to her guidance, and the beneficiaries of her prayer. Though she constantly longs for union (ecstasy), she is content to occupy herself in the bridegroom's absence with her "maternal" duties (the works of charity).

The courtly self, on the other hand, can be expressed through either the conventionally male *fin amant* or his female partner, the *amie*. The *fin amant*, whose exemplar is the troubadour lyric or Minnesang, is typically unfulfilled and tormented by desire. Idealizing the object of his love, he sees her as vastly superior but inclined to be haughty, emotionally distant, and capricious. Hence the return of his love is often doubted. In the lover's complaint, moments of adoration and abject submission to the beloved alternate with moods of rebellion and rage, only to issue in renewed if melancholy professions of love. The *fin amant* does not simply wait for his beloved, but courts her by offering service—usually painful, humiliating, and prolonged. In divine love, this service may entail the same concrete activities as the bride's "motherhood" (with the addition of ascetic exercises); but instead of growing out of fulfilled love, service in the context of *fine amour* is a means of earning love. Its compensation lies not only in the ultimate hope of reward, but also in the knowledge that by persevering in *fine amour*, the lover has won a place among those noble, courtly few who alone are capable of its high demands.

Midway between the bride and the *fin amant* is the *amie*, whose exemplar is the courtly romance. In lyric the lady is merely a focal point for the poet's rhetorical energy; as a subject she is absent. Romance, however, supplies at least a few female lovers who are not mere prizes for the male hero, but must earn his devotion by undergoing parallel tests of fidelity and sacrifice. Among these are the loyal if antisocial Isolt, as well as more virtuous heroines like Chretien's Énide, the ladies in Marie de France's lais, and Perceval's sister in the *Queste del Saint Graal*. Like the bride in the Song of Songs tradition, the *amie* is already part of a couple and thus to some degree fulfilled in love. But her role is more heroic and uncertain, less maternal and nurturing, and it still savors of the glamorous, courtly world of *fine amour*. In the context of *la mystique courtoise*, the paradigm of the bridal self can only be the Virgin Mary. The paradigms of the courtly self, as in the *Règle des Fins Amans*, are Jesus and his lover, Mary Magdalene.[29]

In Mechthild's *Flowing Light of the Godhead*, a character called "Lady Knowledge" defines three roles of the *minnende Seele*: "You are a virile man in battle [*fin amant*], a well-dressed virgin in the palace before your Lord [*amie*], and a joyous bride in your bed with God."[30] These personae are not of equal importance to Mechthild, the most emphatically 'feminine' of the beguines, but they do lay out a spectrum of possibilities for *la mystique courtoise*. Not surprisingly, the three subject roles or models of the self prove to be correlated with object choices or models of God. In the traditional language of Christian spirituality, Mechthild would be labeled christocentric and Marguerite theocentric. Hadewijch, positioned midway between the two, is equally devoted to the human Christ and to the Godhead. This distinction has its correlative on the literary plane in the choice of erotic narratives. Mechthild, infatuated with the masculine Christ, identifies chiefly with the bridal self, while Marguerite, whose God is ambiguously gendered, identifies with the courtly self as both *fin amant* and *amie*. Hadewijch, the earliest of these writers, sees herself equally as bride and *fin amant*, and thus affords the clearest case of experimentation with gender and genre. In her oeuvre, the distinction between bridal self and courtly self proves to be correlated with a preference for *Brautmystik* in the prose visions and *mystique courtoise* in the letters and lyrics.

Hadewijch's bridal self, subject of the *Visions*, recounts experiences of ecstasy and union (*ghebruken*, or "fruitive oneness"). As the privileged bride, Hadewijch rejoices in her Beloved, contemplates her future glory in heaven, identifies with the Virgin, and expresses motherly care for her disciples as well as compassion for lost souls. Yet the visions, despite their aura of lofty spiritual attainment, belong to an early period in the mystic's life. In the first she refers slightingly to her youth, and the sixth takes place on her nineteenth birthday. Hadewijch may have recorded these experiences at a much later date, however, for they are carefully arranged to model the course of her progress from beginner to "full-grown bride." [31] As a novice, she states in her first vision, her whole desire was to be "one with God in fruition," but for this she was still "too childish" and had not yet suffered enough. Accordingly, the visions read in sequence teach that in order to become full-grown, the loving soul must first "live Christ's humanity" by imitating his patience with loyal devotion (*trouwe*). Only when she has accomplished this can she "become God with God" and enjoy the glorious union with Christ's divine nature in the Trinity.[32] Ultimately, God tells her, "you will be love as I am Love."[33]

"Becoming God" or Love denotes a process of psychological and spiritual growth rooted in a prior metaphysical truth. A good Christian Platonist, Hadewijch believed firmly in exemplarism, the doctrine of all creatures' real and eternal existence in the mind of God. Thus she took comfort in the thought that although her earthly, empirical self might still be immature and far from union, her eternal self was already glorified in the beatitude of perfect love. Her bridal experience, therefore, is staged as a series of encounters between her limited present self and her archetypal self, through whom she is united with the Beloved. These encounters entail a shock of recognition wherein Hadewijch realizes that "I" am "She"; a collapse of temporality, wherein the present self as experiencing subject meets the once and future self as ideal object; and the "bridal" union itself. In Vision 4, for example, Hadewijch sees two heavens of equal beauty: one belongs to her Beloved and one to her ideal self. Through a subtle shifting of voice, we are given to understand that she becomes what she beholds. Hadewijch's "I" at first denotes her empirical self, while "she" denotes the ideal self who already possesses a kingdom. The decisive moment of fusion comes when Christ begins to speak as "I." He addresses Hadewijch's ideal self as "you" while distancing her empirical self as "she":

> These heavens, which you behold, are wholly hers and mine; and these you saw as two kingdoms that were separated were our two humanities before they attained full growth. I was full-grown before; and nevertheless we remained

equal. And I came into my kingdom yesterday, and you became full-grown afterwards; nevertheless we remained equal. And she shall become full-grown today and come tomorrow with you into her kingdom; and nevertheless shall remain equal with me. You have wished, dear strong heroine and lady, . . . that she should attain full growth so as to be like me, so that I should be like her and you like myself.[34]

The apparent trinity here (cf. John 17:21–24) is in reality a couple. Hadewijch's two selves become one in the bridal union, which is a union of equals, of lovers both full-grown in their eternity. In the meantime her exemplary self, the "strong heroine and lady," asserts a benign maternal influence on her struggling earthly self.

Despite their allusions to suffering with Christ, the *Visions* on the whole tell a story of joy and triumph. In the most fulfilling moments of her life, Hadewijch identifies with the exalted bride. Yet for her this experience is not the end of spiritual life; it is only the successful completion of adolescence. Hadewijch's bridal mysticism is a narrative about "growing up" in every sense: discovering her "true self," exploring sexuality, learning to delay gratification, subjecting romantic dreams to the reality principle, acquiring confidence, preparing for leadership. So it is no wonder that as soon as she achieves the coveted title of full-grown bride, the mystic is also hailed as "strongest of all warriors."[35] Her letters and still more her lyrics are dominated by this chivalric persona acquired in the final vision. It is this model Hadewijch recommends to her young beguines: a love life characterized by struggle, not fulfillment, and poetically gendered male.

To a reader who has first encountered Hadewijch through the *Visions*, it is disconcerting to come upon passages like the following from Letter 13: "What satisfies Love best of all is that we be wholly destitute of all repose, whether in aliens, or in friends, or even in Love herself. And this is a frightening life Love wants, . . . miserable beyond all that the human heart can bear."[36] Hadewijch's courtly persona is unhappy and often bitter, but nonetheless determined to serve Love because no other life has any worth. It is better, she claims, to suffer for Love's honor than to feel love. Virtue, not sweetness, is the criterion of a true lover, and the most sublime life of all is to waste away and die in Love's pain.[37] The goal of the *fin amant* is "either to content God or to die in the attempt" because, "for the heart of the courtly lover, . . . that is the law of chivalry."[38] Union is sweet if Love grants it. But since this rarely happens, one must court God with humble service, "for the Beloved is courtly and understands courtliness in love."[39]

Hadewijch's voice in the lyrics is indistinguishable from the trouba-dour's. The twinned "I" and "she" of her visions are replaced by "I" and "he"—the generic *fin amant* or questing knight—but "he" and "I" share a common experience of desire, frustration, and stubborn hope. "She" in the lyrics is no longer the perfect Bride but Frau Minne, playing the role of courtly *domna*. Typical is the ninth poem, titled by Columba Hart "The Knight of Love," in which Hadewijch's persona runs through the gamut of troubadour moods: (a) scorn for the "ignoble persons" who are too timid for love; (b) promise that the true lover will "find his beloved and his country at the end"; (c) praise of the courtly knight's fine words, fine bearing, and fine garments; (d) complaint against the lady (Minne) be-cause she despoils those whom she "ought to clothe, honor, and nourish"; (e) reflection that this failure may, after all, be the lover's fault; and (f) hope that other *fins amans* will gain "a much better bargain in love / Than I have found so far."[40] So closely does Hadewijch follow the conventions of Minnesang that only initiates will recognize her Beloved as God.

Sometimes, again like the troubadours,[41] Hadewijch pretends for a while to abandon love:

> I bid farewell to Love now and forever.
> He who will may follow her court; as for me, I have had too much
> woe.
> Since I first chose her, I expected to be the lady of her court;
> I did everything with praise: I cannot hold out.
> > Now her rewards
> > Seem to me like the scorpion
> > That shows a beautiful appearance,
> > And afterwards strikes so cruelly.[42]

The mood of revulsion does not last, however. Although Hadewijch's "I" claims for a time to have "little part in Love," she is soon reaffirming her fellowship with more successful lovers: "he who was empowered," "who is high-minded," "who dares to fight" Love and so to receive her "full pardon." This warlike *fin amant*, though female, is no different from her male counterpart. What she experiences is not the bride's foretaste of glory but the knight-errant's arduous quest.[43] Others might call this life *imitatio Christi* or *vita apostolica*, and so it was. She called it *edele Minne*.

Mechthild's spirituality is very close to Hadewijch's, but her writing is more robust and exuberant, closer to folksong and romance than to the formal art of Minnesang. Her mystical drama centers on the heterosexual couple, and her favorite persona is the classic *sponsa Christi*:

> The bride has grown drunk from the sight of his noble countenance.
>> In the greatest strength she comes forth from herself,
>> in the loveliest light she is blind to herself,
>> and in the greatest blindness she sees most clearly.
> In the greatest clarity she is both dead and alive.
> The longer she is dead, the more joyfully she lives.
> The more joyfully she lives, the more she experiences.
> The more she is diminished, the more she overflows. . . .
> The deeper her wounds, the more stormily she rages. . . .
> The narrower the bed of love, the closer the embrace.
> The sweeter the kiss of the mouth, the more lovingly they gaze.
> The more painfully they part, the more he gives her.[44]

Such raptures, which abound in *The Flowing Light*, offer proof of the uninhibited sexual fantasy that the chaste could indulge with God's blessing. But Mechthild's transports, though intimate, are not private; they still have an "objective" dimension that anchors her personal experience in the collective. In one vision the Virgin Church calls Mechthild her "playmate" (*gespile*) because "we both have one Bridegroom"—a relationship that gives the beguine license to criticize the clergy as she sees fit.[45] A similar dynamic of identification unfolds in Hadewijch's twelfth vision, in which she sees a bride escorted to her Beloved. The lady is clothed in a robe of twelve virtues and might be taken for an allegory of Ecclesia, the Bride of the Lamb, led in royal procession. But after witnessing the spectacle as an observer, Hadewijch is told to "become the veritable bride of the great Bridegroom, and behold yourself in this state!"[46] At that moment she attains union and equality: no longer does she fall down and adore ("like an ordinary soul"), but stands in full confidence before the face of God. And like the bridal Church in Bernard's sermons, she becomes a nurturing mother to less exalted souls: "Behold, this is my bride, . . . whose love is so strong that, through it, all attain growth!"[47] Through her unitive experience, the beguine identifies with the Church not only as bride of Christ but as *mater et magistra*: she claims an authority that may be pastoral (for Hadewijch), prophetic (for Mechthild), or ineffably superior (for Marguerite).

The passionate bride takes the Virgin as archetype of her experience.

After the erotic passage cited above, the Mother of God explains to Mechthild that "when our Father's jubilation was grieved by Adam's fall, so that he had to be angry, . . . the Father chose me as a bride in order to have something to love, for his dear bride, the noble soul, was dead. And then the Son chose me as a mother and the Holy Ghost accepted me as a true love (*trútinne*). So I alone was bride of the Holy Trinity."[48] God's desire for "something to love," expressed in such touchingly human terms, is in Mechthild's view the motive for creation. Nor is this love pure altruism, as in scholastic thought; it is plain sexual longing. "I have desired you before the world began," God tells her. "Where two hot desires come together, there love is consummated (*vollekomen*)."[49] Again, Mechthild imagines the Father telling the Son, "I will make myself a bride who shall greet me with her mouth and wound me with her gaze; only then will there be loving." As soon as this bridal soul is created, he takes a marriage vow: "I am the God of all gods, you are the Goddess of all creatures, and I plight you my troth: I will never forsake you."[50] Mary, as paradigmatic bride, is also called "Goddess."[51]

Such daring language asserts the same equality that Hadewijch claimed between God and his bride, defying the gulf between Creator and creature. Since they are evenly matched if only in desire, their union is in that sense a marriage of equals. Even Mechthild's teaching on the pre-existence of the Virgin supports her erotic theology. It serves the same function as Hadewijch's exemplarism, conferring eternal fruition on a love affair that might, from an earthbound perspective, seem a hopeless failure. As everlasting bride, Mary's sinless soul fills the historical gap during which God's other "brides" are dead and forestalls what, for Mechthild, would be the unthinkable: a world without Minne, God without Goddess, a bachelor in heaven.

The most famous passages of *The Flowing Light* center on the Bridegroom as debonaire courtly *Jüngling* and Lord of the Dance.[52] Mechthild spices her bridal mysticism with a playfulness that belongs to her role as *amie*, along with an acceptance of frustration. Like a poor servant-girl, her soul comes to court and is welcomed by the noble, lovesick prince, who "greets her with courtly language" (*hovesprache*), dresses her in fine garments, and whisks her off to a secret place "to play a game with her that the body does not know, nor do peasants at the plow, nor knights at the tourney."[53] But this game must be abandoned at the height of its pleasure, because when two clandestine lovers meet, they must quickly part again.[54]

Often it is the *amie*, frustrated by her lover's distance, who plays the role of wooer. She sends messengers to heaven to say "Ich wolte minnen"; she hunts her Beloved with a giant's strength; she wishes to bind him with magic so he might find no rest but in her.[55]

Mechthild was a trinitarian mystic, but she made her desire her ontology: at the heart of the divine triad she always found a couple. In her quirky parables she names "Humanity" (rather than Son or Word) as the second Person of the Godhead, indicating the human Christ along with his mystical body or bride.[56] Thus she is able to set a divinized human pair on the throne of heaven—whether as God and Goddess, host and hostess, or even "brother Jesus and sister Mary."[57] As in classic christology, the ascription of pre-existence is used to assert the primacy of a theological sine qua non. To defend Christ's divinity, the fourth-century fathers maintained that their God could not be eternal Father without a co-eternal Son. Mechthild, defending her own soul's divinity, knew her God could not be eternal Lover without a co-eternal Beloved: the Virgin, the soul, *her* soul, herself. "Your childhood was a companion of my Holy Spirit," God tells her, "your youth was a bride of my humanity." And to comfort the querulous old beguine at Helfta he adds, "Now your old age is a housewife of my divinity."[58]

Marguerite Porete was more critical of *Brautmystik*, for her understanding of spiritual growth differed from Hadewijch's and Mechthild's. For the earlier beguines, the bridal union takes place near the outset of the mystical life, but only as a foretaste of consummation to come. Through the sweetness of this union, God or Minne seduces the soul, luring her into the wholehearted commitment that will prove bitter and painful later on. Minne (for Hadewijch) or the Bridegroom (for Mechthild) then withdraws, leaving the *minnende Seele* to prove her loyalty through a long period of suffering as she "lives Christ's humanity." First comes the sweet, then the bitter. But for Marguerite this painful service to the Virtues, resembling the love-service of Hadewijch's *fin amant*, corresponds only to the second and third of seven degrees through which the soul must pass.[59] If she attains the fourth stage she becomes a royal *amie*, what Mechthild would have called a full-grown bride:

> In the fourth state the Soul is drawn by the height of love into delightful thoughts through meditation, and abandons all outward labors and obedience to others in the height of contemplation. Then the Soul is so disdainful,[60]

noble, and delicate that she cannot bear to be touched by anything except the pure delight of Love, so she is singularly glad and full of charm. And this makes her proud of the abundance of love, of which she is mistress in that luster, that radiance of her soul.[61]

Yet such an intoxicated soul is deceived by Love's sweetness, for without knowing it, it is really herself that she loves.[62] Until she is divested of the last trace of self-concern, she can never be free.

Hadewijch and Mechthild would agree on the immaturity of a soul that wished to remain permanently in the delights of union, but they would advise her to grow up by following Christ in his life of humility, obedience, and pain. This is also the counsel of the *Règle des Fins Amans*. Marguerite, however, takes a different course. If the Soul is called to the truly free and noble life, she must not return from her ecstatic union to the beginner's exercises—prayer, fasting, masses, sermons, works of virtue. Instead, she "takes leave of the Virtues," undergoes a "death of the spirit," and "falls from love into nothingness," entering a state of permanent union with God. Her days as a struggling *fin amant* and exuberant *amie* are over, for she has herself become Fine Amour: henceforth she is one with the Trinity, "God by right of love."[63] The possibility of such a state was of course hotly contested.[64] In describing this as the highest life, Marguerite parts company with the earlier beguines and joins Meister Eckhart—who, like her, fell prey to inquisitorial wrath.[65]

Marguerite's ideal, the Free Soul or *ame adnientie*, gives all she is and has to her Beloved "sans nul pourquoy." She addresses Christ not as Bridegroom but as her "overflowing and abandoned love, courtly for my sake without measure"—not once or twice but thrice unbounded.[66] In the idiom of the *Règle des Fins Amans*, where the Ten Commandments meet the *Roman de la Rose*, Marguerite even names God the "treshault Jaloux," because he robs the soul of her very self, but gives in return "magistrale franchise."[67] This freedom, the central theme of the *Mirror*, is paradoxical in the extreme. Grounded in the soul's "annihilation" in utmost humility, it is exalted in language dyed through and through with aristocratic pride. One who would aspire to the status of a Free Soul must have a gentle heart and noble courage, keen and subtle understanding, a trenchant will and fervent desire—qualities, Marguerite says, that the sanguine and the choleric possess by nature.[68] Like Hildegard of Bingen, she admits a natural aristocracy in the realm of God, which conspicuously resembles a court.[69] Members of its spiritual—or natural or social?—elite can be known by their susceptibility to *fine amour*.

Beyond this charmed circle, the "beasts and asses" who follow Reason (ironically reversing the trope of "beasts who lack reason") cannot understand the secret language that free souls learn "in the privy court of that sweet land whose law is courtesy, whose measure is love, whose food is kindness."[70] There the Free Soul is queen and empress, eldest daughter of God, heiress of his kingdom, sister of wisdom, lady of the Virtues, elite bride of peace.[71] Though sunk in the abyss of humility, she is unspeakably noble:

> This Soul, says Love, is free, more than free, most free, transcendently free, in root and stock and all her branches and all their fruits. This Soul's inheritance is the purest freedom; each of her quarters has its blazon of nobility. She answers no one unless she wishes if he is not of her lineage, for a nobleman would not deign to answer a villein who called or summoned him from the battlefield. Therefore one who summons such a Soul does not find her; her enemies get no more response from her.[72]

One of the small ironies of the *Mirror* is that, while Reason and "Sainte Église la Petite" address Love and the Free Soul with exaggerated deference, these "courtly" figures respond with ridicule and abuse. In their case, *noblesse n'oblige point*. Silent before her inquisitors like Christ before Pilate, Marguerite proved she meant what she said.[73]

III. "Lady Love" as Mirror, Goddess, and Godhead

If contemplative and courtly literatures made a variety of subject positions available to the beguine, they offered an even greater range of options for representing her Beloved. Christ the Bridegroom is a familiar, unproblematic figure. God the Father, the Holy Spirit, and the undivided Trinity also appear, and Marguerite introduces someone she calls the "noble Far-Near" (*Loingprés*), who is God under the guise of the troubadours' *amor de lonh.* But the characteristic feature of *la mystique courtoise* is "Lady Love"—Frau Minne for Hadewijch and Mechthild, Dame Amour for Marguerite.[74] To the perennial frustration of critics, this potent figure resists the straitjacket of consistency, even in the writings of a single author. She appears in various contexts as a double for the mystic herself, her "transcendent I";[75] as a double for Christ, the Beloved; and as ultimate being, the Absolute, in which Lover and Beloved are one.

To appreciate the conceptual and affective range of "Lady Love," it is useful to review the figure's complex literary origins. Medieval Latin had three nouns for "love": *amor* (m.), *dilectio* (f.), and *caritas* (f.). *Amor* is personified in secular poetry as Cupid, the God of Love. From this refurbished classical figure springs the imperious Amors or *dieu d'amors* (m.), who plays a prominent role in the *Roman de la Rose* and its tributaries. But Old French *amour* (like Provençal *amors*) is usually feminine,[76] so that in troubadour and trouvère lyrics, personified Love and the beloved Lady could become poetically interchangeable. In German and Dutch, Frau Minne inherited the mantle of Venus, just as the *dieu d'amors* inherited Cupid's: she was by turns the lover's all-bountiful mistress and tyrannical dominatrix.[77] Like the troubadours, trouvères, and Minnesingers, Latin contemplative authors of the twelfth century chose to personify love as a female figure, Caritas. This choice was influenced by the universal representation of virtues and vices as female. But Caritas was not just one abstraction among many, thanks to the oft-quoted biblical text, "Deus caritas est" (1 John 4:8). Writers like Bernard and Hildegard elaborated this persona with great depth and lyricism, using her to represent God as mother and queen.[78] Sacred and secular met in *la mystique courtoise* when the aura of Caritas enveloped the originally profane figures of Amour and Minne, giving rise to the awesome Goddess of the beguines.

Of all the courtly mystics, Hadewijch had the most complex and multifaceted concept of Minne. By her own confession she spent two years of her girlhood asking obsessively—like how many other girls!—"What is Love? And who is Love?"[79] But the question she raised as a lovestruck teen, she answered as a theologian. Critics have been divided between "subjective" and "objective" readings of her poetry with good reason: her Minne denotes the human experience of loving, but also the Beloved as object and Love as a cosmic principle.[80] When Hadewijch ends a short, sober letter with the fierce cry, "De Minne es al!" ("Love is all"),[81] her outburst can be translated in at least three ways, as Tanis Guest observes. It is advice to the writer's young friends: "The only thing you can do, must do, is to give all the loving devoted service of which you are capable." It is a confession of Hadewijch's own experience: "To give love, and be loved in return, is the most wonderful thing in the world." And it is a metaphysical claim: "The One I love—whom we should all love—is literally everything, limitless and without bounds; . . . outside him there is nothing; worse, there is nothingness."[82]

At the simplest level, Minne or Fine Amour stands in a relation of specularity with the writer.[83] She is an alter ego, a projection of the ideal to which the *fin amant* or *minnende Seele* aspires, much as the *dieu d'amors* is a projection of the secular courtly ideal. Yet she remains sufficiently distinct to engage in dialogue with the empirical ego. Like Cupid and Venus, she can be perceived as hostile and destructive even though, in the end, the lover always submits to her. The specular Minne is what Hadewijch longs to become but desperately fears. Love is an irresistible force that swamps the frail ego, "terrible and implacable, devouring and burning"— the scourge of security, source of all joy and wellspring of pain. It is called *amor* "from death," *a morte*.[84] But even as a psychological force, Minne is never raw libido detached from its object. If Hadewijch is possessed by Minne, is in the act of becoming Minne, it is because she ontologically *is* Minne, a mirror of the unique, ubiquitous, omnivorous Love. As creative force, Minne separates subject and object only to effect a more conscious union. The endless to-and-fro of loving is signaled by an endless circle around the word:

Minne wilt dat minne al minne met minnen mane.
Love wills that love demand all love with love.[85]

O Love, were I but love,
And could I but love you, Love, with love!
O Love, for love's sake, grant that I,
Having become love, may know Love wholly as Love![86]

In Mechthild of Magdeburg, the specularity of Minne and the *minnende Seele* explains their frequent exchange of roles: Love is both mistress and handmaid of the Soul, and conversely, the Soul is queen and handmaid to Minne. They address each other with formal courtesy: "Lady Love," "Lady Bride," "Queen of My Heart."[87] These conversations sometimes recall the romance dialogues between lady and confidante—Laudine and Lunette, Isolt and Brangane—on the mysterious wiles of love. Like romance ladies, too, the women quarrel, as when the Soul reproaches Love for depriving her of childhood and youth, friends, riches, health, and honor; but Love counters that in exchange she has given the Soul freedom, virtue, and knowledge. Finally she offers herself and the Soul is reconciled, "repaid a hundredfold on earth," with God and heaven yet to come.[88] Minne can make such promises because the Bridegroom is like a passionate knight, supreme on the battlefield yet easily swayed by the will of a hot-blooded lady and the stratagems of her maid.

Since Mechthild's God is not self-sufficient but motivated by desire, his bride and her ally, Love, have power to compel or even kill him. Ulrike Wiethaus notes that Minne and the Bridegroom reverse conventional gender roles: "The opposite of the gentle adolescent Christ, [Lady Minne] seems a Western manifestation of the Hindu goddess Kali insofar as she is a divine force, fierce, unrelenting, and unmerciful. . . . Lady Minne, as image within an image, appears to reflect back to the mystical onlooker a notion of femininity that is strong-willed, single-minded, fiery."[89] Stepping into Minne's imperious role, Mechthild gains authority for her own strong-willed womanly self, for she too could be fierce and unyielding. Yet, embracing her "gentle adolescent Christ," she exults in the sexual freedom that only her lover's permanent bodily absence could bestow.

The world of Marguerite's *Mirror*, true to its title, is a realm of pure specularity. Its chief speakers, Fine Amour and the Free Soul, can be compared with the "I" and "he" in Hadewijch's lyrics or Minne and the *minnende Seele* in Mechthild. Their intermingled voices express the same experience of love in the first person and the third: the Soul describes the Love she has become, while Love describes the Soul she inhabits. The specularity of "Dame Ame" and "Dame Amour" is apparent even from their names, which point to one of Marguerite's key themes: the annihilated soul becomes literally divine. Lady Love is God because "Deus caritas est," as she explicitly states: "I am God . . . for Love is God and God is Love," with the corollary that "this Soul is God by condition of love."[90] Marguerite explains that she deliberately uses the humble name of "âme" (f.) even though "esperit" (m.) denotes a higher state of grace,[91] and she chooses Amour as her divine mouthpiece in lieu of Christ or the Holy Spirit. The feminine gender of Love is accentuated by her epithet, Mother and Mistress of Knowledge[92]—a role that Marguerite was consciously wresting away from male theologians. Her choice of female personae poetically underscores and perhaps subconsciously heightened her own conviction of oneness with the Divine.

For Hadewijch and Mechthild, who understood mystical union as a temporary rather than a permanent state, Minne denotes the divine Other as well as the ideal or divinized self. In this context Lady Love affords a verbal icon of God as female, like Eternal Wisdom in the life of Henry Suso.[93] In Hadewijch's lyrics she is both the troubadour's *domna* and the invincible Caritas—"noble maiden and queen," "lady," "mother of the virtues."[94] Occasionally she is Jesus, the Son concealed in the Father's bosom and born of Mary.[95] At times the two representations merge to create an androgynous figure, as in the thirteenth vision where Hadewijch sees one who is both Goddess and apocalyptic Christ (Rev. 1:12–16):

> Upon [the throne] sat Love, richly arrayed, in the form of a queen. The crown that rested on her head was adorned with the high works of the humble . . . From Love's eyes proceeded swords full of fiery flames. From her mouth proceeded lightning and thunder. Her countenance was transparent, so that through it one could see all the wonderful works Love has ever done and can do. . . . Her right side was full of perfect kisses without farewell. Her body was wholly full of ever-welling marvels; and in the amplitude under her feet she had the seven gifts.[96]

Minnedienst can be construed as *imitatio Christi* because Minne herself is Christ, or more precisely, womanChrist.

Yet Minne seems elsewhere to prevail over Christ like an irresistible power behind the throne.[97] In metaphysical terms Love may denote pure transcendence: the Godhead or divine Essence as distinct from the three persons of the Trinity. For Marguerite, Fine Amour is the Absolute, the unbounded oneness corresponding to what Meister Eckhart called "the Godhead beyond God." In Mechthild's more figurative language, the transpersonal Minne similarly denotes the inexhaustible plenitude of deity, as in this image inspired by the "wine cellar" of the Song of Songs (2:4):

> When I recall that the heavenly Father is the blessed host there, Jesus the cup, the Holy Spirit the pure wine, and I think how the whole Trinity is the filled cup and Minne the mighty cellaress, God knows I would gladly accept if she invited me to the inn![98]

Hadewijch uses Minne to denote the Unity of God, which absorbs both the soul and the persons of the Trinity in "abysmal fruition." Her Neoplatonic theology distinguishes two movements within the deity—emanation and return, activity and repose. These correspond to the mystic's experiences as *fin amant* and as bride, living the dual life of active virtue and ecstatic union. The Son and the Holy Spirit, proceeding from the Father, represent the outward movement, the principle of creation, generosity, service, and sacrifice. In this sense, Christ laboring for the world's salvation is Minne incarnate, and *Minnedienst* is the soul's life of virtue. On the other hand, the Unity that calls the Persons home and "engulfs" them in the Father also demands and effects the created soul's return, or contemplative rest. It is this Unity, the point of convergence of the three

Persons and all creation, that Hadewijch names Minne in a special and absolute sense. This Minne is the devouring eternal Mother, counterpart of the abysmal everlasting Father, whose embrace swallows up the Son and the Bride alike. She is the lightning flash of vision and the voice that sounds in thunder: "This is I! I am the all! I give the all!"[99]

IV. "Violent Charity" and the Abject

In all three beguine mystics, an intensely privileged self-awareness and class-consciousness are sustained in and through pain, humiliation, persecution, self-abnegation, and exile—a complex of sufferings summed up in the term "abjection." Historically, there have been two schools of thought about the mystic's abject stance. According to most theological interpreters, what she experiences is in fact the infinite ontological gap between Creator and creature, which is bridged only by divine love. Her perceptions of nothingness, estrangement, and union are described metaphorically in terms that may be more or less vivid, more or less exact, but are in some sense literally true. Following post-medieval norms for the assessment of mystical experience, most interpreters have felt more comfortable with the formulations of Hadewijch and Mechthild, which can be assimilated to such classic mystical concepts as infused grace and the "dark night of the soul," than with Marguerite's annihilation cum deification. But all three women can be understood as fulfilling the Beatitudes here on earth: the poor in spirit possess the kingdom of heaven, mourners are comforted, the pure in heart behold God.[100]

Psychoanalytic interpreters, less inclined to read the mystics on their own terms, have seen in their texts either the masochistic woman's self-abasement before a dominant male or a form of female narcissism. Luce Irigaray, in her famous rhapsody on "La Mystérique," celebrates what she perceives as the mystic's autoerotic union with "that most female of men, the Son."[101] For Margret Bäurle and Luzia Braun, the core of the mystic's passion is a kind of death wish, a desire for "unbecoming" that will dissolve the mundane self, its world, and its limits. In the empty spaces where ecstasy fails, it is writing that offers a place of repose between past and future bliss, the medium of words enabling a "delirious transference of what happens without words."[102] The most persuasive reading in this vein is that of Wiethaus, who remarks that in the divine game of Minne, "delicious scenarios of the imagination allowed for the return of the re-pressed or unattainable, that is, freely expressed sexuality and, especially for women, self-determination."[103] But the sexuality (as Wiethaus also notes) was turned inward, and the self-determination was used knowingly and deliberately to pursue the way of martyrdom.

These two schools of interpretation take opposite starting points and differ on essential questions. Their divergence is clearest in the points most embarrassing to each: theologians have felt bound to apologize for the mystics' unabashed sexuality and aristocratic hauteur, while their extreme self-abasement led older critics to diagnose psychopathology and now dis-tresses feminist readers. The interpreter who would confront the alluring and alien beauty of their texts must address some uncomfortable ques-tions, beginning with the most basic: Was the beguine mystic seeking self-fulfillment or self-destruction? I believe that, like most human beings, she sought fulfillment; but her desire would be falsified if we were to construe it primarily in terms of empowerment or *jouissance*. For what she desired was the goal held up by the most advanced contemporary theorists of love: a condition in which lover and beloved are no longer two selves, but one. This understanding of love as fusion required her to negate not so much the body as the separate, individual ego; and to that end pain and pleasure, exile and ecstasy, could alike be bent.

One of the most influential theorists of love, well known to both Hadewijch and Marguerite Porete, was the twelfth-century contemplative Richard of St.-Victor. A contemporary of Andreas Capellanus and Chré-tien de Troyes, Richard closed a distinguished career with his study of erotic obsession, *On the Four Degrees of Violent Charity* (circa 1170). In this provocative treatise the Victorine parts company with Bernard of Clair-vaux and the Cistercians, who set a wide gulf between carnal and spiri-tual love. Instead he maintains that while the mystic's "violent charity" is the moral opposite of untamed sexual passion, the two are psychologi-cally identical. Central to both is the lover's descent into abjection, which terminates in the complete negation of self.

Regardless of their object, according to Richard, all lovers experience the same maelstrom of painful feelings as they progress from "wounding love" through the degrees of obsession he labeled "binding," "languishing," and "fainting love."[104] Beginning in desire, love increasingly paralyzes thought and action until the lover is totally incapacitated and can no longer be appeased even by the presence of the beloved. Desire at this point has become infinite, spurning all finite gratifications and turning perforce into its opposite. Richard's account of the endpoint is an astute piece of psychology:

> There are often outbursts of temper between lovers in this state, they work up quarrels and when there are no causes for enmity they seek false and often quite unlikely ones. In this state, love often turns into hatred since nothing can satisfy the lovers' mutual desire. Hence arises what we have often seen in some people, namely that the more ardently they seem to love one another at first, the more they persecute each other afterwards with passionate hatred. Indeed, and this is even more astounding, at one and the same time they hate and yet do not cease to burn with desire for each other.[105]

Tristan and Isolt might well be bound by such a love—tinged with hatred, despairing of peace, propelled ineluctably toward death. But Richard goes beyond all his predecessors in suggesting that God's lover, too, must endure such torrents of desperation and rage at the higher reaches of the mystic life.[106]

Only the first degree of love, Richard states, is wholesome in earthly relations such as marriage. Subsequent stages are pathological, making the soul "not only bad but miserable also," giving her a foretaste of the hell for which she is bound. In spiritual love, on the other hand, the deeper a soul plunges into the vortex, the higher she rises. The four stages of divine love correspond to meditation, contemplative vision, ecstasy or ravishing, and the descent from glory into humble love. In the third stage the soul is liquefied, or as Marguerite would say, "annihilated": she passes entirely into God and has no more will or self to call her own. But for Richard—as for Hadewijch and Mechthild—this is not the summit. In the final stage, the soul now "conformed to the humility of Christ" leaves her glorious union for her neighbor's sake and sinks below herself in works of compassion. Alternatively, having died with Christ in the third stage, she rises with him in the fourth to a life that is no longer hers but God's. This in itself is standard monastic teaching: charity takes precedence over ecstasy. What is new in Richard is the comparison, more implied than stated, between this supreme, Christlike love and the erotic madness of a Tristan.

Denis de Rougemont, taking *Tristan* as the paradigm of Western erotic experience, emphasized the lovers' mystic yearnings for the infinite as well as the antisocial, death-seeking character of their love.[107] In Gottfried of Strassburg's famous lines:

Ein ander werlt die meine ich,
diu samet in eime herzen treit
ir süeze sûr, ir liebez leit,
ir herzeliep, ir senede nôt,
ir liebez leben, ir leiden tôt,
ir lieben tôt, ir leidez leben.
dem lebene sî mîn leben ergeben,
der werlt wil ich gewerldet wesen,
mit ir verderben oder genesen.[108]

(Another world I have in mind, which together in one heart bears its bitter-sweet, its joyous grief; its heart's joy, its longing's woe; its joyous life, its painful death; its joyous death, its painful life. To this life let my life be given: this world I will make my world, to be lost or blessed with it.)

An illuminating gloss on this creed is offered by the poet Robert Pinsky's tale of "Jesus and Isolt."[109] Bored in heaven, Pinsky's Jesus assumes the form of a mythical beast, flies down to Tintagel, and befriends Isolt. After the famous Liebestod, he reveals himself and tries to save her at the very gates of hell. But just when she begins to pay attention, Tristan appears, and of course Isolt takes his hand at once and descends into the pit. For the Ricardian mystic no less than the fated lovers, consummate love is precisely this choice of hell over heaven. "In this degree of love," Richard says, "the [human] soul might seem to be mad . . . Is it not complete madness to reject true life, to accuse the highest wisdom, to resist omnipotence? And if a man desires to be separated from Christ for his brethren's sake, is that not a rejection of true life?"[110] Yet Moses and Paul desired to be cast out for the sake of their people, and Abraham accused Wisdom and resisted Omnipotence when he interceded for Sodom and Gomorrah. Such "madness" of love, which burns with desire while making passionate war on God, is what Richard called "violent charity." In this state the self plumbs the utmost depth of abjection, and precisely there it achieves a proud, exultant defiance. Using rejection of their own beatitude as a weapon to procure that of others, women mystics in such madness begged to be damned if the world could be saved thereby.[111]

"Violent charity" often took the form of penance on behalf of sinners or the dead, but any form of pain could mold the lover's body into an image of her crucified Love. Indeed, all bodily experience might serve that end: encounters with the Divine under the forms of sexual union, mystical pregnancy, or eucharistic frenzy could dissolve the hated ego just as surely as hunger, sickness, or self-torture.[112] The goal in either case was to destroy the sense of individual selfhood, of any "I" but the divine. It was widely acknowledged, however, that the most effective means of union were the most painful, for those were the means Christ chose. Poverty and persecution were to be embraced with fervor. But beyond social ostracism and corporeal asceticism, the beguines devised an exquisite form of self-negation that cut to the heart of their identity as lovers. Since a lover can take no joy except in her Beloved, the supreme sacrifice must lie in the willed choice of absence over presence—the same choice that led Isolt and Tristan to their misery and death, and to eternal union beyond death.

"Love's nature," wrote Mechthild, "is such that she first flows with sweetness, then becomes rich in knowledge, and in the third stage she is greedy for abjection."[113] For Mechthild as for Hadewijch, this peculiar "greed" is a characteristic of the full-grown bride. God's very absence, once bitterly lamented, now becomes a sign of union with the abandoned Christ. In the end the *minnende Seele* ceases her wooing, because she has come to prefer God's alienation to his presence. She welcomes new handmaids, Blessed Estrangement and Lady Pain, and she puts on her "wedding garments" of sickness, temptation, and heartache.[114] Hadewijch portrayed the *fin amant* in this state as half troubadour and half Grail knight. For Mechthild, the abjectly loving soul no longer seeks her Beloved because she is identified with him, imitating Christ's passion so perfectly that she becomes herself a womanChrist.

> She is nailed so fast to the cross with the hammer of mighty love that all creatures cannot call her back. On the cross of love she feels a great thirst, for she would gladly have a drink of pure wine from all God's children. So they come one and all and give her vinegar. Her body is killed in living love, while her spirit is exalted above all human senses. After this death she descends into hell with her power and comforts the grieving souls with her prayer, by God's goodness, without her body's knowledge. She is pierced through her side by a blind man with a sweet spear of innocent love; then many holy teachings flow from her heart. She hangs high in the sweet air of the Holy Spirit, in the everlasting sun of the living Godhead, on the cross of high love, until all that is earthly has withered away in her.[115]

Marguerite's brand of abjection is, once again, a novel variant on a familiar theme. Instead of embracing the Beloved's absence as the means to a more perfect union, she chooses to be "absent" herself—to vacate the psychological space she had occupied once and for all, so that Fine Amour alone can hold court there. Her *Mirror* recounts two versions of this metaphysical suicide, one cast in philosophical and the other in courtly language. In the first version, the Soul is illumined by a vision of God's plenitude and her own nothingness. At once she perceives that she is "the sum of all evils," so that no amount of good will or virtue could ever repay the smallest fraction of her debt to God. Therefore she renounces her will to do good and her desire to enjoy it, and by virtue of No-Will, she is "annihilated" and at the same time possessed of Love's "only freehold"—oneness with God that is no longer a fleeting ecstasy but an everlasting peace.[116] Like Eckhart, Marguerite presents this call for annihilation in Neoplatonic terms. By the mere fact of existing as a distinct entity, even good will is a derogation from God and in some sense an illusion. Love has only bestowed free will that the Soul might surrender it and return to "where she was before she was made."[117] The act of renouncing will is therefore the negation of a negation. In Marguerite's repeated, almost liturgical formula, the *ame adnientie* is truly divine because Love alone works "in her, for her, without her."

In the second version, the most searing passage of the *Mirror*, Marguerite recalls how she became a Free Soul by imagining a series of savage *demandes d'amour*. Suppose God asked if she would consent never to have been created? Suppose he wanted her to bear eternal torments as great as his eternal power and goodness? Suppose she were equal to God: Would she give up that equality and vanish to nothing if it pleased him? Finally she invents three *demandes* painful enough to give her pause: What if God wanted her to love another more than him? What if he wished to love another more than her? Or what if he wished another to love her more than he did? The mystic aims here at a crucifixion of desire itself, in a move eerily similar to the real-life demands that Abelard once made upon Heloise, a lover no less uncompromising in her pursuit of the abject.[118] Having reached this point of no return, it is only by consenting to the unthinkable that Marguerite can find peace. "If I knew without a doubt that your will would will [these three things] without diminishing your divine goodness, I would will them, without ever willing anything again. And thus, Lord, my will comes to its end in saying this; and therefore my will is martyred, and my love martyred."[119] With this death of her desire, she adds, "I began to leave childhood and my spirit grew old"—no more amorous *joie* or courtly *jouvence*—but thereupon "the Land of Freedom disclosed itself."

Marguerite's abjection is, in an ontological sense, absolute. As an annihilated soul, "she" no longer exists. Yet by the same token, she is God, so there is no need for the bodily torments or public displays of humiliation so common in saints' lives. Abjection and exaltation are no longer alternating states, as they are for Hadewijch and Mechthild, because the Free Soul and Fine Amour are no longer separate selves. Rather, they coalesce in a Zenlike tranquility that orthodox mystics, from Richard of St.-Victor to Hadewijch to Ruusbroec, would judge to be a dangerous self-delusion.[120] From an ecclesiastical point of view Marguerite was indeed a heretic, fixated in stubborn pride far beneath the highest, humblest, and most Christlike love. But from her own standpoint as a Free Soul (or Free Spirit, as those of her persuasion came to be called), it is "Sainte Église la Petite" that falls short, clinging in pitiful bondage to the tyrant Reason. Only souls who dare the final lovers' leap into the void find there the fullness of peace and the end of desire.

V. *Ars subtilior*

In this chapter I have outlined an approach to the beguine mystics that takes them seriously both as theologians and as connoisseurs of courtly literature. Troubadour lyric, Minnesang, and romance had forged a language that glorified the lover's endlessly desiring, exquisitely self-conscious and recalcitrant subjectivity, but also celebrated the ecstatic fusion and dissolution of boundaries in consummated love. In this literature, too, some of the key elements of *la mystique courtoise* are already present: the glamor of love at a distance, the pursuit of amorous fusion through abjection, refinement in love as a badge of class solidarity, exaltation of Love as a goddess or cosmic principle, representation of the Beloved as a mirror of the self, and gender inversion or exchange between lovers as a proof of perfect union.

All these features could—with some daring and not without strain—be adapted to what Christians since Origen had seen as the ultimate love affair. Despite the androcentric bias of courtly literature, therefore, it supplied an irresistible new aesthetic for these female artists of desire.[121] But the currents run in both directions: the influence of Cistercian mysticism on *La Queste del saint Graal* and on Gottfried's *Tristan*, for example, has already been well studied. As an experiment in "reading backward," I would like to close with two secular analogues to the dynamics inherent in *la mystique courtoise*, teasing in their resemblance and in their difference.

The thirteenth-century *Roman de Silence* has captured the postmodern imagination because its transvestite hero/ine evinces a remarkable self-consciousness about gender.[122] To evade a royal law forbidding women to inherit, the girl-child Silence is raised as a boy (with the collaboration of the narrator, for whom she is always "he"). Silence grows up male despite the fury of Nature, who twice appears in person to debate with Nurture. Upon reaching puberty our hero aces two out of three tests of courtly virility: like Tristan he becomes first a skilled minstrel, then a knight of prowess. But a third test has ambiguous results. A villainous queen tries to seduce Silence, who pleads feudal honor as an excuse to flee her embraces. Silence thereby proves his virtue but casts doubt on his virility, prompting the enraged queen to send him on a quest that should be his undoing, as it can only be accomplished by a woman. By succeeding, Silence is both vindicated and exposed: her "true" gender is restored and, without further ado, she is married to the very king who initially disinherited (and so unwittingly masculinized) her.

Silence is full of sophisticated games that question the naturalness of gender. But perhaps the largest question raised by the romance is that of Silence's missing sexuality. Nature does not allow him to feel desire as a man, but Nurture has not taught her to experience it as a woman. At the end of the romance, therefore, the newly feminized Silence becomes a bride without the least hint of eros, even though the narrator is not normally fazed by female desire. The upshot of the experiment is that Silence acquires both genders but neither sex: s/he is accomplished and valiant as a man, beautiful and chaste as a woman, and utterly without desire.

From an odd but interesting point of view, Silence's career runs parallel to Hadewijch's. The mystic, "disinherited" not by gender but by the Fall, adopts verbal masculinity as a stratagem to regain her lost heritage and win favor at her chosen court. There she becomes minstrel and knight, preserving chastity until she can be reunited as bride to her king. Hadewijch's eschatological visions indicate that she perceived her true, eternal self to be female; her literary and spiritual cross-dressing is a temporary disguise. But where Silence achieves androgyny at the expense of desire, Hadewijch has a surplus of desire. Silence plays neither *fin amant* nor *amie*. Hadewijch, whose Beloved is male and female and beyond either, plays both parts: she has the minstrel's art, the knight's valor, the bride's embraces, and the lover's inexhaustible passion for the sole inexhaustible object.[123] For her, *la mystique courtoise* solves the riddle of gender and sexuality from which the

Roman de Silence finally retreats, bound despite its daring by the constraints of its own secularity.

Alternatively, we can read Silence's silence as the passivity of one who has renounced her will and identity along with her active virile persona. No longer man, has she in fact become woman, or some bewildering neutral creature whose soul, beneath her malleable body, has been freed from the whole masquerade of sex and gender? Could one who has been a female knight or, worse, a female theologian still be a woman at all? A hostile chronicler once referred to Marguerite Porete as *pseudomulier*.[124] We recall that she too was silent in the face of death, the mystic's alternative name for union—that consummation most devoutly to be wished. On Marguerite's terms, the fulfillment of all desire can only be granted to one who no longer has a will to desire it.

Another suggestive text, rare in its focus on female subjectivity, is Marie de France's "Yonec."[125] The heroine of this lai, imprisoned by her jealous husband in a tower, recalls romances she has heard and fantasizes about "adventure," praying for a secret love—who hears her appeal and materializes at once. Like Marguerite's princess who was smitten with Alexander, this lady has "dreamed the king himself" out of her own desire. Her fantasy lover has the fairy-tale gift of shape-shifting: he first appears as a hawk to fly through the tower window, transforms himself into a handsome knight, and finally, to deceive the lady's chaperone, takes on her own form. In that guise, to prove he is a Christian and no devil, he receives the eucharist. The love affair continues until the lady becomes pregnant. Eventually the husband discovers her secret and sets a trap to kill the hawk-knight, who is impaled on spikes placed in the window. At this point the grieving lady mysteriously attains powers of flight herself: she survives a twenty-foot leap from the tower and follows her beloved to his own land, an otherworld of fantastic silver spattered with real blood. Dying, he gives her a magic ring, a sword, and a promise of revenge.

Marie's mythical hawk-knight, the perfect lover of her heroine's fantasy, is strikingly like the Christ-knight of *la mystique courtoise*. The lover in "Yonec" appears as bird, man, and woman: he seeks the lady in her own land to answer her prayer, and only when he has incurred a bloody death for love is she freed to visit his land, a place of surpassing richness and beauty. Christ too is a shape-shifter—resplendent God, newborn child, mortal man, eucharistic host. Once, in a single vision, Hadewijch receives him in all these forms.[126] Of particular interest is the knight's transformation into his lady's shape, a gendered variant on the theme of incarnation.

Performed in the lady's own bed, this act enables a sacramental union to precede the sexual. For the mystical beguines there is a similar exchange: God becomes woman as Minne or Fine Amour, God's bride becomes man as *fin amant* or womanChrist, and communion supplies the metaphor and means for erotic union. But gender inversion is not the ultimate goal. It is only a symbol of the intoxicating fusion, the Liebestod wherein the lover assumes the full identity of the Beloved. Now her soul receives wings: she can leave the *estrange païs* of her imprisonment and fly to the land of freedom, even if she must return, like Mechthild, to endure a lifetime of exile in hope and patience.

La mystique courtoise was an art of consummate subtlety, a play of imagination no less fantastic than Marie's lais. It was an erotic game with a bewildering variety of moves: one could become the bride of a God or the lover of a Goddess, or merge utterly with the Beloved and become oneself divine—but only at the price of being no longer "oneself." For beyond all the strategies, the brilliant variations of desire, the object of the game was that "condition of complete simplicity, costing not less than everything." About a generation after the martyrdom of Marguerite Porete, as legend has it, a beguine known only as "Meister Eckhart's daughter" came to the Dominican cloister one day and announced herself to the doorman as "neither a girl, nor a woman, nor a husband, nor a wife, nor a widow, nor a virgin, nor a master, nor a maid, nor a servant." For all these positions, taken allegorically, entailed virtues that the speaker claimed to lack.

> If I were a girl, I should be still in my first innocence; if I were a woman, I should always be giving birth in my soul to the eternal word; if I were a husband, I should put up a stiff resistance to all evil; if I were a wife, I should keep faith with my dear one, whom I married; if I were a widow, I should be always longing for the one I loved; if I were a virgin, I should be reverently devout; if I were a servant-maid, in humility I should count myself lower than God or any creature; and if I were a manservant, I should be hard at work, always serving my Lord with my whole heart.

Thus bereft of the virtues and of gender, age, and class, what could she be but a simple, annihilated soul? So this daughter of Eckhart—and Marguerite—concludes, "since of all these, I am neither one, I am just a something among somethings, and so I go." As the free spirit departs, an illumined Meister tells his students, "I have just listened to the purest person I have ever known." [127]

Excursus 1. Hadewijch and Abelard

In the eighth of her visions Hadewijch is shown the "Countenance of eternal fruition" at the top of a mountain. There too she encounters a guide, a nameless saint, who offers to show her four ways to attain the summit. This man calls himself "the champion and vassal of this true Countenance" and boasts, "My beauty is that of one who conquers everything and has in his power the Thing heaven, hell, and earth serve." Nevertheless, he adds that there is a fifth way, the highest of all, which has been reserved for her because he himself did not master it. After she has been divinely taught, Hadewijch turns again to her guide.

> I asked him: "Lord Champion, how did you come to the beauty of your high witness, so that you led me upward and yet not to the end?" He told me who he was. After that he said to me: "I bear witness to you concerning the four ways, and I travel them to the end; in these I recognize myself, and I conquer the divisions of time. But the Beloved gave you the fifth way; you have received it where I am not. For when I lived as man, I had too little love with affection, and followed the strict counsel of the intellect. For this reason I could not be set on fire with the love that creates such a great oneness, for I did the noble Humanity great wrong in that I withheld from it this affection." [1]

This vision is unique in Hadewijch's corpus because her guide is human but unnamed. In most of the visions she is taught directly by God or angels, or else by allegorical figures. She meets John the Evangelist in the fifth vision, Augustine in the eleventh, and Mary in the thirteenth. After the fourteenth she appends a "List of the Perfect" that includes all her favorite saints, living and departed, and she places herself in their company. It was not spiritual modesty, then, that kept Hadewijch from identifying her Champion for the reader. Who was he, and why does she suppress his name?

In recent years two eminent scholars, working independently, have proposed a surprising candidate for the post: Peter Abelard. The name is startling for several reasons. A century after his condemnation at Sens, Abelard was hardly the well-known figure that he is today.[2] Manuscripts of his work were rare, and the chance that Hadewijch had read any of his authentic writings must be reckoned nil. Even if she had, it is unlikely that they would have appealed to her, and ludicrous to think she would have chosen the twelfth-century master of dialectic as her guide (albeit imperfect) in the mystical life.

But if the real Abelard was unknown to our beguine, one of his spurious works had made a deep impression on her. Abelard had considerable talent as a hymnographer, and several manuscripts ascribed to him the poem "Alpha et Omega, magne Deus," now attributed to his contemporary, Hildebert of Lavardin. This *rhythmus de Trinitate*, ending with a famous meditation on heaven, begins with the lines that inspired Hadewijch:

> Alpha et Omega, magne Deus, . . .
> Cujus virtus totum posse,
> Cujus sensus totum nosse,
> Cujus esse summum bonum,
> Cujus opus quidquid bonum. . . .
> Intra cuncta, nec inclusus;
> Extra cuncta, nec exclusus;
> Super cuncta, nec elatus;
> Subter cuncta, nec substratus.[3]

These four paradoxes, as Columba Hart has noted, form the heart of Hadewijch's Letter 22, which contains some of her most profound teaching on the Trinity, the divine nature, and the four paths to God (amended at one point to five).[4] The letter is in fact a mystical commentary on the hymn verses. If Hadewijch knew them as Abelard's, she would have thought of him as a theologian after her own heart, with a deep knowledge of divine mysteries. Vision 8, a closely related text, deals with the same four paths to God supplemented by a fifth, even if they are not described exactly as in Letter 22. Thus the author of the hymn expounded in the letter may well be the Champion encountered in the vision.

Why would Hadewijch withhold the name of her guide? The answer can only be that if she admired Abelard as a mystical poet, she also knew of his reputation for heresy and did not wish to avow him as her inspiration. Among the most important sources for her spirituality were Bernard of Clairvaux and his friend William of St.-Thierry. Both William and Bernard had campaigned vigorously against Abelard and succeeded, by fair means and foul, in procuring his condemnation. We know that Hadewijch had a manuscript of William's *De natura et dignitate amoris*, for she quoted it verbatim for two paragraphs of Letter 18.[5] The same manuscript (almost certainly under Bernard's name rather than William's) might have contained some of the Cistercians' polemical writings against Abelard. Among their numerous charges, both William and Bernard accused Abelard of teaching a Nestorian christology because he maintained that only the divine Word, not Christ qua God-man, could be considered a Person of the Trinity.[6] This may be the source of the Champion's confession that he had too little love for Christ's humanity. The charge of rationalism—allowing mere human reason to pry where angels fear to tread—is ubiquitous in the polemics against Abelard. Hadewijch's Champion regrets that he "followed the strict counsel of the intellect" and therefore lacked the fire of unitive love.

Despite this failing, he is described as one who has "conquered everything," even God. "To conquer" in Hadewijch's idiom means to wrestle like Jacob with the angel; in this life-and-death struggle with Love, victory and defeat are one. To be wounded, mastered, vanquished utterly by God is to conquer him.[7] Hadewijch hears herself too designated as "the unconquered one who has conquered all heavenly, earthly, and hellish champions."[8] From a different point of view, however, her portrayal of the Champion tallies remarkably well with Abelard's self-image in the *Historia calamitatum*. He is a knight-errant of dialectic, undaunted warrior of the schools, one who gives no quarter and takes no prisoners. Paul Mommaers observes that the Middle Dutch word for champion, *kimpe*, also means "bantam cock"—a brilliant image for Abelard's feisty if not downright cocky theological method.[9]

The resemblance is probably sheer coincidence, for Hadewijch could not possibly have seen the *Historia*. But she may, if she had read Bernard's or William's polemics, have known something of the persecution her poet-theologian had suffered. One of the four ways traveled by her Champion belongs to those who "suffer great opprobrium in unheard-of measure and are complained of by all; . . . men condemn them, and almost no one is merciful to them." If Hadewijch regretted the savagery of these polemics or suspected their unfairness, or if she knew anything of Abelard's humiliating end, she may have sympathized with him as a fellow victim of harassment and slander. Even if her "Abelard" was really Hildebert and her "Bernard" was really William, the beguine could have been aware that two spiritual writers she admired had fought a bitter conflict, without feeling any need to take sides. This woman, who herself suffered exile at the hands of "aliens" and who confessed to praying for the damned, was not one to be cowed by ecclesiastical protectionism.

The Champion's sole flaw is not heresy but a lack of human affection. Mommaers takes Abelard to be the prototypical scholastic theologian, the first to separate discourse about God from the experience of him as Beloved. When Hadewijch discusses the errors of reason in Letter 4, it is Abelard (and the Champion) that Mommaers envisions: "If reason fears God's greatness because of its littleness, and fails to stand up to his greatness, and begins to doubt that it can ever become God's dearest child, and thinks that such a great Being is out of its reach—the result is that many people fail to stand up to the great Being." [10] The rationalist, in short, can never attain the lover's and the mystic's invincible daring.

Let us carry the speculation of Hart and Mommaers one step further. Hadewijch, knowing little of the historical Abelard, probably knew nothing at all of Heloise. Yet these two impassioned intellectuals, so alike in their intelligence of love, so unlike in the course of their destiny—did they not reach the same opinion of that Abelard whom the one knew so intimately and the other not at all? In him they both saw a man of soaring intellect, a sublime reasoner in the things of God, one they worshiped as a saint—but he had, alas, "too little love with affection" and therefore "did the noble Humanity great wrong."

Heloissa vindicata? It is pleasant to think so.

Excursus 2. Gnostics, Free Spirits, and "Meister Eckhart's Daughter"

Among the many dubiously orthodox texts that circulated in Meister Eckhart's name is a tract called *Schwester Katrei*, which in some manuscripts bears the inscription: "This is Sister Catherine, Meister Eckhart's daughter of Strassburg."[1] The tract takes the form of a dialogue between a beguine ("Sister Catherine") and her confessor, a figure modeled on Eckhart. Since the master lived in Strassburg ca. 1314–23, the text can perhaps be dated to the second quarter of the fourteenth century. Its authorship is unknown, but Strassburg had a large population of beguines, and the writer was probably among them. Several features of the text suggest female authorship, especially its exaltation of the beguine's all-absorbing love at the expense of her confessor's churchly prudence. Although Sister Catherine begins by obediently following the confessor's advice, she soon leaves him to pursue "the fastest way" to God in exile and abjection. When she returns some time later, he no longer recognizes her, for in mystical contemplation she has "become God" and is soon "established in union." From this point onward the roles are reversed: the disciple becomes the mistress, delivering some remarkable sermons as the confessor listens until, following his daughter's advice, he attains ecstasy at last.

Schwester Katrei is suffused with Free Spirit ideas, but unlike Marguerite Porete's *Mirror of Simple Souls*, it escaped official repression. The dialogue survives in at least seventeen manuscripts with considerable variation. It was read and copied by monks and nuns as well as beguines, and a Benedictine, Oswald of Brentzahusen, found it worth translating into Latin in the fourteenth century. Oswald did not know who the author was, but assumed her to be a woman—"a certain young girl, noble and delicate."[2] That, of course, is the authorial image that *Schwester Katrei* and other beguine texts deliberately project. For the sake of convenience, therefore, I will refer to this anonymous writer as "Sister Catherine."

Despite its innocuous reception, *Schwester Katrei* now appears much further from orthodoxy than does Marguerite's book. Aside from its Free

Spirit motifs, the dialogue contains several ideas that savor more of ancient gnosticism than of Eckhart. Among these are an esoteric doctrine of the afterlife; skepticism about bodily resurrection, even Christ's; an apocryphal story in which Jesus tells his disciples to eat a corpse; the claim that St. Peter's profession of faith would have been more accurate had he said, "*I* am the Son of the Living God"; and the representation of Mary Magdalene as both virile woman and pure virgin. In particular, the mystical beguine's claim to deification, her role as *magistra*, her critique of Peter, and her choice of Mary Magdalene as a role model supply a link between the arcane worlds of Nag Hammadi and of heterodox beguinal piety. Much of this resemblance may be coincidental, though I will argue that at least some gnostic ideas reached "Sister Catherine" through the medium of apocryphal texts that are no longer extant. In any case, the dialogue represents a striking convergence of heresies old and new, crystallizing around the fiercely controverted (and dangerously related) tenets of female authority and mystical autotheism.

From a literary standpoint, the text can be divided into two parts: a frame story detailing the beguine's spiritual progress and her relationship with the confessor, and a series of mystical teachings delivered mainly by the daughter. In the frame story we can distinguish seven movements: (1) Sister Catherine initially seeks and follows her confessor's counsel until, (2) growing impatient, she demands a faster way to God. Father and daughter agree that the "fastest way" is that of the Cross: total poverty, exile, and renunciation of all comfort from creatures, including priests. But the confessor tries to dissuade Sister Catherine, insisting that this way "is not meant for women" and warning her not to make efforts beyond her strength. They quarrel. The daughter, citing the examples of Mary Magdalene and Mary of Egypt, proclaims that like them, she too can become a man and suffer as much as Christ did. She denounces her confessor and other clerics for wasting so much of her time and vows that henceforth she will obey the Holy Spirit alone. (3) In their next visit the two are reconciled. The father counsels Sister Catherine on the value of suffering; then she takes her leave and goes into exile.

(4) Some time later, the daughter returns so changed that the confessor no longer knows her and is not even sure if she is a human being or an angel. She reveals herself to him and discloses the sufferings and mystical experiences she has undergone in the interim. He is deeply impressed. (5) After this confession, Sister Catherine makes further progress. Having already "become God" in temporary union, she now experiences

a three-day mystical death, returning from her ecstasy to claim that she has "attained by grace what Christ is by nature" and enjoys her everlasting bliss: eternal union with God. (6) Fully accepting the daughter's claim, her confessor asks for instruction in turn. A lengthy mystical dialogue follows. (7) Repenting that he has thus far acquired only abstract, not experiential, knowledge of divine mysteries, the confessor is so overwhelmed by Sister Catherine's revelations that he too falls into ecstasy. When he returns, he yearns to be "established" in union as she is, but she explains that he is not yet ready and teaches him how to proceed until he becomes worthy of the ultimate goal.

The confessor in this tale may be the inferior party, but he is neither a fool nor a villain. Indeed, he is treated with far more respect than Marguerite Porete shows Reason and "Sainte Église la Petite." His doctrine in fact proves identical with the daughter's. The priest's only sin is his patronizing attitude: though he respects Sister Catherine, he underestimates her spiritual strength because she is young and female, and he wants to "protect" her from the suffering she must endure on the path to union. This is the sole cause of their quarrel, for which the father must atone by becoming his daughter's meek disciple. From this point of view, *Schwester Katrei* belongs to the same genre as a number of fifteenth-century exempla, such as "The Pious Beguine" and "The Young Woman of Two-and-Twenty," in which a simple woman's ardor surpasses the holiness of a learned theologian.[3] Eckhart, whose teaching kindled and shaped such ardor, was a logical candidate for the priest's role. In the legend of "Meister Eckhart's Daughter," an exemplum related to *Schwester Katrei*, the master is taught by a mysterious woman whose freedom from all identifying roles leads him to call her "the purest person I have ever known."[4] Such tales may reflect something of the real Eckhart's humility and admiration for *mulieres sanctae*. His intellectual debt to Marguerite has only recently been acknowledged,[5] and if he allowed himself to be swayed by the thought of a condemned heretic, why not by his own spiritual daughters? The frame story, then, gently rehabilitates friars like Eckhart (both Dominicans and Franciscans are mentioned) by showing that despite their tendencies to abstraction and paternalism, such men were not beyond hope if they had good women to teach them.

The doctrine ascribed to Sister Catherine is a miscellany cobbled from several earlier treatises.[6] Not all of it is heterodox: much is based on Eckhart's genuine writings, and there is an extensive polemic against false mystics, including antinomians and pious visionaries. Most interesting for our purpose, however, is the beguine's sermon on Mary Magdalene, which reinforces the frame story and provides a paradigm of the mystic's quest. Sister Catherine first names the Magdalene, along with Mary of Egypt and "Mary Salome," to justify her plan of exile, for these women obeyed God alone with no interference from priests. (It is of course the desert contemplative of medieval legend, not the Mary of the gospels, whom Sister Catherine has in mind.) Later, after her deification, the daughter offers a complete homily on the saint.

Magdalene, the perfect *fin amant*, "was a noble woman by birth and by nature, and therefore, she had a noble and loving heart. Because of it she had to love intensely whatever she loved."[7] Progressing from love of the world to love of Christ's noble humanity, she "did wonders through love (*minne*)" as long as he was with her—yet if she had gone no further than this, she "would have fallen to her eternal death." It was only after the *noli me tangere* that Mary, freed from attachment to Christ's carnal presence, "experienced her eternal salvation for the first time." Becoming truly virile, she now preached like the other apostles, accomplishing more than all the rest in a shorter time, for she "carried out everything a strong man should carry out." Yet the active missionary life was not her goal; it was only when she retreated into the wilderness that Mary "knew and loved God to the highest degree," for "one moment in the wilderness gave her more familiarity with God than the entire presence of Christ had offered her." Indeed, "the noble humanity of our Lord Jesus Christ" had been a downright obstacle to her knowledge of God. Alone in the wilderness, Mary needed neither priest nor sacrament, for here at last "she received God from God; she reached union and was established."[8] Thus far, "Sister Catherine" is in agreement with Marguerite and *la mystique courtoise*.[9] The Magdalene's journey typifies that of the elect soul, moving from the feminine role of *amie* to that of *fin amant* (*starck man* or virile woman) to perfect oneness without difference. Mary's preaching, her voluntary exile, and finally her deification provide the exemplar for Sister Catherine's life.

But the sermon continues in a more polemical vein. Unlike Mary Magdalene, who turned from her desire for Christ's physical presence to inward union with the Divine, Peter and the other disciples constantly fell short, for they failed to recognize the Father in the Son. Even Peter's celebrated confession of faith was in error. "Lord, you are the Christ," he said, "the Son of the living God" (Matt. 16:16). But from the point of view adopted by "Sister Catherine," "everything that was ever created may rightfully say, 'I am a child of God,'" for God is the universal Mother.[10] Had Peter truly

recognized "the great God" in the person of Christ, he would have proclaimed instead, "you are my Creator, . . . my eternal *Father*." This critique
of Peter and the apostles continues at length and includes the following
bizarre anecdote, ostensibly a parable against slander:

> [Jesus] told [his disciples] to go into a house and said, "Ask to be given food
> for us for the love of God!"
> The disciples found nothing in the house but a dead man. They returned to
> Christ and said, "There is no one inside but a dead man!"
> Christ said, "Then go and eat him!" The disciples said, "Alas, shall we eat a
> dead man?"
> Christ said, "It is better that you eat the dead than the living."[11]

After this gnostic interlude, the beguine unexpectedly turns to reach for
an orthodox conclusion. For "Sister Catherine" does not wish to condemn
the apostles outright: they need only be temporarily shamed, like her confessor, by the superior attainments of a woman. So the text goes on to say
that at Pentecost, the disciples too "became strong in the Holy Spirit" and
acquired the same grace that Mary Magdalene received.

   Even now, the dialogue is not quite finished with Mary. One revelation
remains, and although no doctrinal point is at stake, it is a dictum completely at variance with the saint's orthodox cult.[12] Hagiography had long
since resolved the confusion in the gospel narratives by making a composite
figure of Mary Magdalene, Mary of Bethany, and the "sinful woman" who
wiped Christ's feet with her hair.[13] The point of departure for the Magdalene's whole legend as penitent, preacher, and contemplative was her status
as a former prostitute.[14] But "Sister Catherine" will have none of this:

> Mary Magdalene had neither husband nor child. . . . I am sure you are aware of
> the fact that like loves like naturally. You know that Christ would never have
> loved Mary Magdalene so sincerely if she had not been a pure maiden, nor
> would he have been so intimate with her, nor would Mary Magdalene have
> been able to love Christ as much as she did if she had not been a pure human
> being. . . . She knew her lover and loved him and followed him virtuously and
> never turned away from him. These are true signs of a maiden![15]

Virginity as such plays no doctrinal role in *Schwester Katrei*, nor was it
essential to the cult of Mary Magdalene as *fin amant*. But "Sister Catherine"'s startling assertion resolves a tension that had been developing in the
saint's cult for over a century. Despite her well-known sexual past, Mary
Magdalene was named first among the *virgins* in a litany of saints widely

used by beguines. Moreover, since marriage was traditionally linked to the active life and virginity to the contemplative, the Magdalene's status as a mystical adept suggested that she had been at least metaphorically "revirginized" by penance and divine grace.[16] Claims about Mary's maidenhood represent an extreme, literal version of an idea in which devout matrons and widows took comfort: the hope that Christ the Bridegroom would confer a second virginity on his penitent lovers. By the fourteenth century, the Magdalene's contested status had become a focal point for the anxieties of the new devout: through penance and love, could sexually experienced women really achieve a status equivalent or even superior to the old ideal of *virginitas intacta*?[17] *Schwester Katrei* answers the question by dodging it: for this unorthodox writer, Mary Magdalene did not have to be revirginized because she had always been a pure maiden (*reine maget*). In a fifteenth-century English play, the Digby *Mary Magdalene*, the Queen of Marseilles even salutes the miracle-working Magdalene as if she were Mary the Virgin:

> *O virgo salutata*, for owr salvacion!
> *O pulcra et casta*, cum of nobill aliauns!
> O almyty maidyn, owr sowlys confortacion! . . .
> Heyll, thou chosyn and chast of wommen alon!
> It passith my wett to tell thy nobillnesse![18]

Schwester Katrei's claim that Mary was a maiden may also provide a clue to the genealogy or at least the spiritual affinities of the text. For the various roles "Sister Catherine" assigns to the Magdalene are precisely those that had been ascribed to her in gnostic tradition: "strong man," "pure maiden," intimate spiritual bride of Christ, preacher superior to the Twelve, perfected gnostic who can dispense with Church and sacraments. To gnostic Christians, a woman's attainment of perfect chastity (or figurative "maleness") was a corollary and a symbol of her initiation into gnosis: it conferred on her a charismatic authority fiercely repudiated by the orthodox. At least four gnostic texts—the *Pistis Sophia* and the "gospels" ascribed to Thomas, Philip, and Mary herself—cite versions of an argument between the Magdalene and Jesus's male disciples, who are jealous and resent her superior gnosis.[19] In the *Gospel of Philip*, Mary is the disciple whom Jesus "used to kiss often on her mouth," his companion in the divine bridal chamber reserved for "free men and virgins." When the men ask him why he loves Mary more than them, he replies that she alone sees the light of truth, while they remain in darkness.[20] The *Gospel of Mary* gives a fuller version of the quarrel: Peter asks Mary to share her esoteric knowledge, granted in a vision of the risen Lord, but after she has spoken he and Andrew reject the revelation. Andrew finds that "these teachings are strange ideas" and Peter asks, "Did he really speak with a woman without our knowledge . . . ? Are we to turn about and all listen to her?" But Levi defends Mary, asking, "if the Savior made her worthy, who are you indeed to reject her?" The brief text ends with a truce as the men resign themselves to Mary's privileged gnosis, and all go forth together to preach the gospel and "put on the perfect man."[21] In the *Dialogue of the Savior*, despite its antifeminist slant, Mary alone is praised as "the woman who had understood completely" (or "the woman who knew the All").[22] The late revelation dialogue *Pistis Sophia* carries this tradition of the Magdalene's superiority to its furthest point. Here Jesus repeatedly singles Mary out for praise, calling her "the pleroma of all pleromas and the completion of all completions," because she is always the quickest and deepest in understanding his mysteries. "The Saviour marvelled greatly at the answers to the words which she gave, because she had completely become pure Spirit."[23]

This tradition about Mary is consistent and enduring. Her role as perfect gnostic helps to clarify a notorious saying in the earlier *Gospel of Thomas*: "Simon Peter said to [the disciples], 'Let Mary leave us, for women are not worthy of life.' Jesus said, 'I myself shall lead her in order to make her male, so that she too may become a living spirit resembling you males. For every woman who will make herself male will enter the kingdom of heaven.'"[24] There is no contradiction between Mary's "virility" and her status as Christ's consort or chaste bride, for "becoming male" in gnostic tradition is tantamount to becoming spiritual, virginal, and supreme in the knowledge of God. Or as "Sister Catherine" puts it: "I know very well that women can never come into heaven; they have to become men first. It is to be understood like this: They must perform manly deeds and must have manly hearts with full strength so that they may resist themselves and all sinful things."[25] Such was Mary Magdalene and such is she. But with *Schwester Katrei* we have come full circle: the masculine unisex ideal of the gnostics converges with the beguines' courtly ideal of *fine amour*. At this juncture the virile woman *is* the womanChrist, the divine *amie* perfected to the point that she can "become God" for herself and others.

"Sister Catherine" 's use of these motifs poses a thorny problem of historical transmission. Apart from the unusual representation of Mary Magdalene, the text contains other motifs that suggest a direct if elusive literary debt to gnostic sources. The *Gospel of Philip*, which highlights Mary's intimate knowledge of Jesus, also includes a saying reminiscent of *Schwester Katrei*'s anecdote about eating a corpse:

> This world is a corpse-eater. All the things eaten in it themselves die also. Truth is a life-eater. Therefore no one nourished by truth will die. It was from that place that Jesus came and brought food. To those who so desired he gave life, that they might not die.[26]

In the *Gospel of Thomas*, too, Jesus tells his disciples that "The dead are not alive, and the living will not die. In the days when you consumed what is dead, you made it what is alive. When you come to dwell in the light, what will you do?"[27] Some gnostics, including the Manicheans, similarly taught that through their diet, the elect were able to release particles of light (or living spirit) from the "dead" matter of food.[28] Some such mythology may underlie the passage in *Schwester Katrei* where the confessor tells his daughter, now deified, that "if you want to enjoy all creatures you shall rightfully do so, because any creature you choose to enjoy is brought back to its origin."[29] The passage has sometimes been read as a temptation scene: the father tests the daughter by inviting her to antinomianism, which she rejects.[30] But although she vows "to be a poor person until [her] death," she acknowledges nonetheless that her confessor's words are true. The confusion here, as in the corpse-eating anecdote and its gloss, suggests that the author was trying to explain an esoteric tradition whose original meaning was lost to her.

Another gnosticizing motif appears in Sister Catherine's doctrine of eternal life. After expounding an esoteric view of hell, she adds that "even the best masters" have erred about the bodily resurrection. It is impossible that the Virgin Mary or the saints can be with God "body and soul for all eternity," because "nothing can be in God but God. There is neither mouth nor nose, nor hand, nor foot, nor any of the created parts that belong to the body," for the saints "do not take their materiality with them when they depart." The very idea is absurd and teaches us to understand even Christ's ascension in a spiritual sense. "You know well enough," Sister Catherine tells her confessor, "that food and everything coarse and material which Christ had taken into himself must be destroyed in the ascent. It remained in time. Thus, his being (*wesen*) came back into the Father."[31] The spiritualizing tendency at work here is characteristic of all dualistic and gnosticizing forms of Christianity. It is of a piece with "Sister Catherine"'s claim that Christ's physical presence hindered Mary Magdalene in her search for God, and more generally with the insistence on spiritual and interior as opposed to material, sensual, and institutional piety. In the same cluster of motifs we should place the daughter's voluntary exile, a literalizing of the familiar Pauline trope (shared by gnostics and Catholics) that life in the body is an exile from God (2 Cor. 5:6). But *Schwester Katrei* revitalizes the trope by dramatizing the beguine's "return" in a double sense: after exile she comes back simultaneously to her earthly home and to "the naked Godhead"— "where [she] was before [she] was created."[32] The same theme governs the gnostic *Hymn of the Pearl*, a fictional narrative included in the apocryphal *Acts of Thomas*.

To characterize *Schwester Katrei* itself as "gnostic" would be going too far. "Sister Catherine" is surprisingly orthodox on transubstantiation, a belief no true gnostic or dualist would accept. She also rejects antinomianism and universalism,[33] endorses ecclesiastical penance, and insists on the value of suffering, poverty, and *imitatio Christi* as vigorously as any fourteenth-century confessor could wish. Yet her central tenets are those of the Free Spirits: autotheism and liberation from the institutional Church. In other words, she claims that a total, permanent union with God is possible in this life, and that one who has attained it—even a laywoman—needs no further mediation or instruction from priests. Rather, she herself is able to teach with far greater authority. These are beliefs that medieval Free Spirits happened to share with ancient gnostics, and associated with the position are a number of subordinate themes, also shared: the elevation of the freelance Mary Magdalene above the hierarch Peter, the theology of exile culminating in a solitary spiritual ascent, and the absolute renunciation of creatures—a principle that here extends beyond orthodox asceticism to the rejection of corporeal visions and the denial of bodily resurrection. None of these beliefs requires the hypothesis of familiarity with gnostic texts, but they do reveal a doctrinal affinity that would have made such texts attractive to "Sister Catherine" if she had access to them. Moreover, rare motifs like the story of Jesus and the corpse, the virginity of Magdalene, and the claim that "women can never come into heaven," suggest that our author did have access. But to what texts, and by what means?

Some of the heterodox motifs in *Schwester Katrei* are shared with, perhaps even mediated by, the Cathars—dualists who likewise denied the resurrection of material bodies and affirmed that women entering heaven would be changed into men.[34] But the dialogue as a whole is far from Catharism. Nor is there evidence that any of the gnostic gospels, rediscovered only in the twentieth century, were known in the fourteenth. Yet the shadowy survival of gnostic ideas, sporadically and unpredictably encountered in medieval texts, is a real if baffling phenomenon. Some were transmitted by way of New Testament apocrypha, a vast and still poorly charted terrain. In her history of Mary Magdalene's legend, Marjorie Malvern notes that the cult itself could serve as a vehicle for the transmission of radical dualism.[35] The gnostic Magdalene of the apocrypha also found her way into medieval drama. In a fifteenth-century German Easter play, for example, the ancient motif of Mary's rivalry with Peter resurfaces in a context that is orthodox, but broadly comic and at least implicitly anticlerical. The apostle in the play not only rejects Mary's gnosis (in this case, her tidings of the resurrection), but threatens a beating and taunts her with misogynist insults: "Hurry home and mind your spinning! It is a disgrace that females run all over the countryside."[36] Peter's boorishness compounds his error, making him sound very much like an antifeminist cleric, while Magdalene's truth vindicates the authority of her sex. Although the esoteric context is lost, the social dynamics are identical with those in the *Gospel of Mary*.

Perhaps the best hypothesis we can reach about "Sister Catherine" at this point is that she was a literary and spiritual magpie. Her mysticism is characteristic of beguinal piety in the fourteenth century: it is permeated with the ethos of *la mystique courtoise* and still more with Meister Eckhart's ideas, carried to the radical extremes proclaimed by heretics of the Free Spirit. In addition to these currents, however, the writer knew apocryphal traditions of a markedly gnostic character. These sources are no longer possible to trace, yet their imprint is unmistakable. So too is the reason for their appeal. The gnostic Magdalene, that creature of paradox—pure virgin, noble lover, virile woman, peerless preacher, and solitary adept— "received God from God" and attained to that complete, perduring, and authoritative union that was "Sister Catherine"'s *raison d'être*.

6. WomanSpirit, Woman Pope

When Francesco Sforza married Bianca Maria Visconti, heiress to the Duke of Milan, in 1441, his family's fortune was made. Not long after their wedding, the couple celebrated by commissioning a deck of hand-painted playing cards, bearing the emblems of both families, from the bride's favorite artist. Such was the origin of the famed Visconti tarots, the earliest to correspond card for card with the modern tarot pack.

It is only fitting that these original tarots, treasured for centuries as a repository of esoteric lore, should commemorate an even more esoteric moment in the history of Christianity. Among the *trionfi* or Greater Trumps is a card known in modern lore as the High Priestess but in the Visconti deck as *la Papessa*, "the Popess." This lady is dressed in a nun's habit with a rope belt, white veil, and the triple tiara of the papacy; in her right hand she holds a scepter and in her left a book (Figure 1). Viewers might easily mistake her for Pope Joan of misogynist legend, but the tarot sleuth Gertrude Moakley has found a more likely model.[1] The Popess, who wears the garb of the Umiliati, can be identified as a sister of that order: Maifreda da Pirovano, cousin of the bride's ancestor Matteo Visconti. Sister Maifreda was actually granted the title of pope, vicar of the Holy Spirit upon earth, by a small heretical sect. After assuming a range of priestly duties over a period of twenty years, she celebrated solemn mass on Easter 1300, the year of the Jubilee. The mass was necessarily private, but Maifreda was to repeat the ceremony at Santa Maria Maggiore on Pentecost when the Holy Spirit—incarnate in a woman named Guglielma—would rise from the dead and confer blessings on her people. Instead of Guglielma, however, a troupe of inquisitors appeared, following up on prior investigations of 1284 and 1296. By September la Papessa and at least two of her congregation were dead at the stake.

The lengthy though incomplete records of the Guglielmites' trial were published as early as 1899,[2] and even earlier, H. C. Lea had devoted a chapter to them in his monumental history of the inquisition.[3] But until recently the sect has garnered little attention because it seemed so minor.

Figure 1. Maifreda da Pirovano as "La Papessa." From the Visconti-Sforza tarot cards painted by Bonifacio Bembo, circa 1450. Courtesy of The Pierpont Morgan Library, New York. M. 630, f. 4.

It never spread beyond a few tightly knit Milanese families and their affiliates; its hardcore believers never numbered more than a few dozen; and
after only two decades it was wiped out by inquisitorial zeal. Moreover,
the sectarians' beliefs were too anomalous to attract the interest of many
historians. They did not approximate the pattern of any "major" heresies—
Cathars, Waldensians, or even mainstream Spiritual Franciscans—and before Stephen Wessley's pioneering article of 1978, the ideas of a female Holy
Spirit and a feminine pope were deemed too ludicrous to be deserving of
study.[4] But in the light of newer research on medieval women's piety, it
is now possible to understand the Guglielmites and their teaching more
clearly. Given the unusual nature of their beliefs, it will be useful to situate
them in both synchronic and diachronic perspectives.

In one sense, the movement can be seen as a particular manifestation
of a perennial underground current within the Church. In this alternative
sectarian form of Christianity, which is as old as the second-century Mon-
tanists and as recent as the nineteenth-century Shakers, the esoteric motif
of a feminine Holy Spirit facilitates a critique of the establishment Church
and the elaboration of millennial hopes pinned on charismatic women.
Feminine deity, female leadership, and apocalypticism are ideas linked not
by theoretical logic but by their common fate: all three were repudiated
very early by the mainstream Church. Yet all can claim some biblical support and, perhaps more important, all seem to answer recurring needs of
the human psyche.[5] Hence these motifs have manifested themselves sporadically and unpredictably in the history of Christendom, almost always
in movements critical of the normative tradition. Sometimes such movements can be linked by direct historical descent, though more often we
have only tantalizing echoes. In the later middle ages a pervasive apocalyptic mood, combined with the disrepute of the papacy and the prestige some
men accorded to women mystics, created a particularly favorable breeding
ground for this type of religiosity. Apart from the Guglielmites, similar
ideas recur in the testimony of Lady Prous Boneta, an obscure heretic
burnt at Carcassonne in 1328, and two centuries later in the millennial fantasies of Guillaume Postel, woven around an Italian holy woman much
like Guglielma, whom he called "the Mother of the world." The periodic
outbreaks of such enthusiasm, notwithstanding the repression and ridicule
they aroused, suggest that in spite or indeed because of the Church's official androcentrism, the womanChrist paradigm remained firmly lodged in
the unconscious of Christendom. In the cases at issue here, it was activated
not only by the ferment of Joachite thought, with its typological vision of a

coming "Age of the Spirit," but also by a new ideal of gender complementarity rooted in the changing relationships of holy women and their male devotees. |

I. Two Heresies and Three Heresiarchs

"The Spirit blows where it will and you hear the sound of it, but you know not whence it comes or whither it goes." Fittingly, Guglielma's origins are veiled in mystery. A woman of means, already past fifty, she appeared in Milan sometime in the 1260s, bringing with her a son who leaves only the faintest trace in the record. Clothed in a plain brown robe and leading a "common life,"[6] she soon established herself as a freelance holy woman and attracted a band of disciples through her wise counsel, gradually gaining the reputation of a healer and miracle-worker. Her very foreignness gave her an extra cachet by raising her above the turmoil of local politics.[7] A saint was supposed to be a peacemaker, and among Guglielma's friends were members of both the rival Torriani and Visconti factions.[8] Her circle of admirers also included Maifreda and other Umiliati sisters from the convent of Biassono, along with ordinary men and women and members of the leading families of Milan. At some point Guglielma must have become an oblate of the Cistercian abbey of Chiaravalle, for by the time of her death in 1281, she lived in a house belonging to the monks, and it was to them that she willed her body and goods.[9] Like other beatae, she warned merchants against usury and fraud, encouraged the devout, comforted the distressed, prayed for the sick and received credit for their cures,[10] and, at times, waxed mysterious and oracular. She was said to bear the stigmata, though invisibly, and she confided to close friends that she had been born on Pentecost.[11]

It was even rumored that she was a daughter of the king of Bohemia—a belief that led two disciples to visit that realm after her death in the hope of reimbursement for funeral expenses and contributions toward their friend's canonization. Although they found the throne temporarily vacant, they claimed to have verified the royal birth of their saint.[12] Recent investigations have confirmed the fact: Guglielma was indeed Princess Blažena Vilemína, daughter of King Přemysl Ottokar I of Bohemia and his queen, Constance of Hungary.[13] Her brother Wenceslas I and his son, Přemysl Ottokar II, reigned during her lifetime. Her younger sister, St. Agnes of Bohemia, was the founding abbess of a convent of Poor Clares in Prague, which she entered on the significant feast of Pentecost, 1234;[14] she was canonized in 1989. Another half-sister, Margarete (Dagmar), married King Waldemar II of Denmark and was also widely esteemed a saint, though never canonized.[15] As for Guglielma, she presumably married a foreign prince, perhaps an Italian signore; but if she did, her husband and children have strangely eluded historians. Since she was born in 1210, we can assume that the son who escorted her to Milan was grown and did not remain in the city. If he had still been living there in 1300, he would surely have been remembered by witnesses and summoned by the inquisitors.

It seems most likely that Guglielma left her home as a widow, although she could have been a fugitive wife or even a penitent: her sojourn in a strange land might have been a flight from desperate circumstances at home. On the other hand, she may have been motivated by no more than the desire for obscurity and exile so highly valued by lovers of the apostolic life. In any case, high birth lent glamor to the life of renunciation. Although Guglielma was reticent about her past, her royalty must have contributed to the mystique of her holiness. Perhaps it reminded her devotees of the princess Elizabeth of Hungary, canonized within living memory. Elizabeth's example might even have had a direct influence on her cousin, for the dynasties of Bohemia and Hungary were closely related.[16] Only in death did Guglielma rejoin her royal parents, who like her were buried at a Cistercian monastery.[17]

We have no way of knowing whether the Bohemian princess was either mystic or heretic, for she left no written account of her life. Like other holy women, however, she chose one of her most intimate disciples to be the "only-begotten son" who would keep her teaching and memory alive.[18] In this case the elect son was not a priest or monk of Chiaravalle but a layman of modest wealth and stature, Andrea Saramita, who was familiar with the ideas of Joachim of Fiore. Instead of writing a conventional vita or transcribing Guglielma's visions as a cleric might have done, Saramita devised a literary record that was sui generis. For reasons we shall never fully know, he had come to believe that the mysterious king's daughter born on Pentecost was none other than the third person of the Trinity made flesh. Thus the appropriate memorial of her life would be a canon of new epistles and new gospels, some of which he composed himself, beginning with the words, "At that time the Holy Spirit said to her disciples . . ."[19] Maifreda, his steadfast partner in faith, composed litanies and hymns to the Holy Spirit in the person of Guglielma, while Francesco Garbagnate wrote *canzoni* to the same effect.[20]

These exalted claims were already in circulation during the saint's life-time, but witnesses differ sharply as to her own role in the matter. Most of her devotees saw in her only the humility befitting a servant of Christ. "Go away," she would tell miracle-seekers: "I am not God."[21] Confronted directly with Saramita's view of her, she denied it on at least three occasions, calling herself a wretched woman and a vile worm, mere flesh and bone, and citing her child as proof of her ordinary human nature.[22] If her devotees did not repent of this blasphemy, she added, they would surely go to hell. Saramita, on the other hand, told his fellow sectarians and eventually the inquisitors that Guglielma had indeed laid claim to deity. It was she herself who revealed how she had descended from heaven in a flash of lightning, and in days to come she would rise from the dead and ascend before the eyes of her disciples, send the Spirit upon them in tongues of fire, and bring salvation to the Jews and Saracens.[23] According to one witness, Sibilla Malcolzati, Guglielma told Saramita that she had come in the form of a woman because if she had been male, she would have been killed like Christ, and the whole world would have perished.[24] Francesco Garbagnate, the composer, had heard a strange oracle from Saramita and Maifreda. Guglielma allegedly told them that ever since 1262 the body of Christ had not been consecrated alone, but together with the body of the Holy Spirit, namely her own; and she did not care to be present at the sacrifice because she saw herself there.[25] In this gnomic saying lies a central clue to the Guglielmites' doctrine, and we shall return to it later. It is interesting, however, that Maifreda recalled no such conversations with Guglielma in the flesh. She claimed rather to have learned the saint's true identity through visions after her death.[26]

Given these discrepancies, two conclusions are possible. Either Guglielma entertained delusions of grandeur, but prudently concealed them from all but her chosen devotee; or else Saramita, fired by Joachite fever and entranced by the saint's charisma, devised the myth himself with Maifreda's help. I believe the latter is more likely, though the former cannot be excluded. There were rumors, for instance, that Guglielma had been investigated by inquisitors in her lifetime, although she was not found guilty of heresy.[27] Luisa Muraro speculates that she had been influenced by sisters of the Free Spirit, whom she could have encountered in Prague or in the course of her wanderings.[28] But the Guglielmites' developed doctrine bore little resemblance to anything Guglielma herself might have taught. On balance, the evidence points to Saramita and Maifreda as the joint creators and zealous missionaries of the sect. Carried away by enthusiasm, Saramita may eventually have convinced himself that he was the beneficiary of direct revelation from Guglielma. It is even clearer that the inquisitors, using all the means at their disposal, pressed hard for a confession of Guglielma's guilt. If the saint could be posthumously convicted, as she in fact was, the cremation of her bones would put an end to the orthodox cult that flourished at Chiaravalle, giving cover to more suspect devotions. In addition, her bequest to the monks could be confiscated.[29]

The sectarians' beliefs, unusual as they were, attest a reading of history far simpler than some of the scenarios proposed by other Joachite prophets.[30] Guglielmite doctrine, or at least Saramita's version of it, was created by transposing the familiar terms of biblical typology to the third age and the second sex. Just as the events and personages of the Old Testament were construed as types fulfilled in the New, these very "fulfillments" were demoted by the Guglielmites to another sequence of types, which would in their turn be fulfilled and transcended. Thus the conception of the Holy Spirit, "true God and true human in the female sex," was announced to her mother by the angel Raphael, just as Christ's birth had been foretold by Gabriel.[31] She would suffer, die, rise, and ascend just as Christ did, and as the Jew Christ had brought salvation to Gentiles and sinners, the Gentile Guglielma would bring redemption to Jews and outcasts. An altarpiece at Biassono represented the Trinity with Jesus and Guglielma side by side, "delivering the captives from prison"—i.e., harrowing hell.[32] After her ascension the Holy Spirit would found a new Church, superseding the corrupt institution in Rome. Maifreda would be the new Peter,[33] but there would also be a new Judas to betray the faithful, and the "apostles of the Holy Spirit" would be scattered and persecuted.[34] Saramita's literary production was central to this dispensation, since the gospels and epistles of the Holy Spirit would be to the New Testament what the New had been to the Old.

Summarized in these terms, the heresy sounds radical indeed. But given this bold preaching of a new age and a new incarnation, it is surprising to see that in some important ways, the sectarians were far from revolutionary. Unlike the Spiritual Franciscans, the lay Guglielmites neither preached nor practiced evangelical poverty. The leading members were mainly affluent citizens, to judge from the large outlays they spent on such goods as paintings, candles, gold-embroidered vestments and altar cloths, and liturgical fittings for the mass of Guglielma's resurrection.[35] In fact, it may have been the accumulation of such items in the spring of 1300 that first attracted an informer's or inquisitor's notice. The emphasis placed on liturgical splendor and the composition of new hymns and litanies indicates that the sectaries were neither anticlerical nor antisacramental. They were in fact high-Church ritualists, and they had no onus against the male sex. Although some writers have represented the proposed Guglielmite clergy as exclusively female, this view is mistaken. According to Saramita's plan, the first mass at Guglielma's grave was to be sung by a boy, Franceschino Malcolzati. The Gospel and Epistle at Maifreda's actual mass were read by men, Andrea Saramita and Albertone Novati, and participants of both sexes were vested.[36] But the sectarians' belief in charismatic rather than hierarchic ministry finally alienated two members. Saramita's friend Mirano da Garbagnate, a painter, had initially been a devoted follower, but after he was ordained a priest he kept his distance. He and another ex-member, Frà Girardo da Novazzano (a tertiary of the Umiliati), more or less willingly collaborated with the inquisitors and informed on the rest.[37]

Despite the apocalyptic features of their doctrine, the Guglielmites envisaged neither an imminent end of the world nor the coming of Antichrist. To be sure, at least some of them asserted that Boniface VIII and the bishops appointed by him were illegitimate, since that pope was elected while his predecessor was still alive.[38] But if contempt for the hated pontiff fueled the fires, it was hardly sufficient to kindle a heresy. Dante's *Inferno*, set in the same year as the Guglielmites' trial, calls Boniface "Prince of the new Pharisees," and in the *Paradiso* St. Peter denounces the pope from heaven as a usurper who has "made of my tomb a sewer of blood and filth," while in the eyes of God the papacy stands vacant.[39] Set beside these fulminations, the Guglielmite testimony against Boniface sounds mild and occupies only a minor place in the proceedings. Sectarians did not emphasize the subversive implications of their views; they did not proselytize beyond the small circle of Guglielma's devotees; and they expected Maifreda's enthronement to be accomplished through direct divine intervention without political or military action. Compared with the far more numerous and vociferous heretics who called for clerical divestment or with Fra Dolcino's armed rebels, the Guglielmites appear thoroughly aberrant, but harmless. The threat they posed was on the theoretical plane—for theirs was indeed, in Muraro's phrase, a "feminist heresy."

In the social realm, one of the most striking features of the Guglielmites is the closely knit unit they formed within respectable Milanese society. There is no sign that the members felt marginal or dispossessed or had any collective axe to grind. Women outnumbered men by about three to two, although ten of the most committed sectaries were male.[40] A mere seven families accounted for thirty of the members implicated, and the familial character of the movement was so clear that the inquisitors were frankly surprised by one devotee, the nobleman Danisio Cotta, who had no relatives in the sect.[41] But while heretical sympathies often followed kinship lines,[42] they divided more than one marriage. Andrea Saramita's mother, sister, and daughter, though not his wife, were all deeply involved. Bellacara Carentano, an enthusiastic believer, drew three daughters, a son, and two grandsons into the sect even though her husband remained aloof. Seven members of the Garbagnate family were active to varying degrees in the absence of their paterfamilias. Conversely, the physicians Giacomo da Ferno and his son Beltrame were fervent Guglielmites (Giacomo even gave sectarian names to two younger sons),[43] while his wife showed little interest. One couple had publicly quarreled over Guglielmite doctrine. At a dinner party, a woman named Adelina Crimella, professing her firm belief in Guglielma's deity, was sharply rebuked by her husband Stefano.[44] Although he too had participated in the sect's activities, the inquisitors decided because of this incident to treat him more as a complicit husband than as a heretic, punishing him for failing to exercise male headship.[45] Aside from the Crimellas, only a single married couple participated jointly in the movement.[46] At least seventeen women were able to take part without fear of marital strife: eight were widows, two were poor and unmarried, and seven more were sisters of Biassono.

This demography hints that the sect's active social life compensated some of its members for discord or loneliness at home. More important, it helps to explain their openness toward gender equality. Like the earliest disciples of Jesus, they had a strong sense of community heightened by a weakening or absence of marital ties, so that the female members enjoyed conspicuous freedom of action. The theological primacy ascribed to Guglielma and Maifreda facilitated a rare and genuine equality between the sexes. It is still more remarkable that this leveling occurred without the usual correlate of celibacy. No special privilege was ascribed to virginity, nor did renunciation of kin have any place in Guglielmite theology. Rather, there was a marked continuity between the members' ordinary social lives and their religious "conventicles," except that sectarians united by their common faith were willing to socialize across class barriers that would otherwise have been hard to breach. Membership ranged from the ruler's son Galeazzo Visconti to the poor seamstress Taria and the serving-maid Bianca.[47] On the ground that Guglielma had wanted her devotees to remain together as a family,[48] they held frequent commemorative meals in her honor at Chiaravalle, Biassono, and several sectarians' homes. These communal gatherings are reminiscent of the *famiglia* formed by Catherine of Siena's devotees a century later.

Many of the Guglielmites' activities suggest not so much reformist tendencies as common piety intensified to the point of deviance. Like the devotees of any saint, they paid visits to her shrine to light candles, ask favors, proffer gifts, and listen to the monks' preaching. The brothers of Chiaravalle were already keeping two feast days in her honor (Guglielma's death on August 24 and the translation of her relics in October), and initiates added a third, secret observance on Pentecost.[49] By 1300 at least four local churches had installed paintings of the saint.[50] In the one adorning her tomb at the abbey, St. Bernard was shown presenting the kneeling Guglielma to the Virgin—an impeccably orthodox motif except that Guglielma's face was painted a fiery red, the liturgical color of the Holy Spirit.[51] Crossing the blurred line between approved veneration and "superstition," some of the men surreptitiously placed hosts on the saint's grave, where they were "blessed" for later distribution by Maifreda.[52] The Popess also used one of the saint's relics in her ministry. Though the monks had Guglielma's body, the sisters of Biassono had the water in which it had been washed, and Maifreda employed this as a chrism to anoint the faithful.[53]

More cannily, she and other sectarians used the popular cults of St. Catherine and St. Margaret as a cover for their veneration of Guglielma. Mirano da Garbagnate confessed to painting an image of Guglielma under the title of Catherine, and the same virgin martyr was a favorite subject of Maifreda's sermons. The female devotees also had a custom of gathering at Biassono on Catherine's feast day.[54] As the inquisitors did not ask their reasons for this practice, we can only speculate. It is possible that Catherine's legend served in Maifreda's mind to validate her preaching, since the celebrated martyr was supposed to have converted fifty philosophers by her eloquence. Interestingly, Catherine and Margaret were also the saints whom Joan of Arc would identify under interrogation as the chief authors of her "voices." Joan, burnt as a heretic before she was canonized, was to invert the fate of Guglielma, buried as a saint before she was burnt. Catherine and Margaret, outspoken martyrs known to be the particular patrons of women, could have furnished mavericks like Maifreda and Joan with role models for their provocative free speech.[55]

If Saramita was the Guglielmites' theologian, Maifreda was their undisputed cultic leader. Her priestly actions, culminating in the fateful Easter mass, were acknowledged with honors befitting a pope: sectarians came to seek her blessing, kissed her hands and feet as they approached, and called her "Lord Vicar."[56] Reverence initially paid to Guglielma was gradually transferred to Maifreda, just as Christ's devotees consoled themselves for his absence by rushing to stand in St. Peter's shadow (Acts 5:15). Like the apostles of Jesus, too, the Guglielmites had been faced with the problem of a delayed Parousia, which they resolved through a subtle shift in their expectations. When Guglielma failed to return from the grave, the purple vestments and golden sandals prepared for her resurrection were supplemented with equally sumptuous vestments for Maifreda's mass.[57] As Patrizia Costa notes, the adoption of such clothing could be a sign of realized eschatology: ascetic garb was suitable for pilgrims and seekers, but luxurious vestments symbolized attainment of the goal—divinity present and manifest.[58] The Paschal mass thus marked a watershed for the sect, transposing future hopes to present reality and leading directly to prosecution. For it was Maifreda's mass that established the real significance of Guglielma's claims, or the claims made on her behalf. Without the Popess, Guglielma would have been just one more beata, canonized or not, with a few overzealous devotees.

Maifreda's attitude toward her role is of great interest. Interrogated four times between August 2 and August 20, she was understandably reticent at first and made a full confession only when death seemed inescapable. Thus, asked on August 2 whether she had known Guglielma in the flesh, she averred that Saramita had been the saint's closest friend and confidant; she herself had only a slight acquaintance with her.[59] On August 6, she named Saramita as the real heresiarch, claiming that she had initially ridiculed his beliefs and even later, "She sometimes doubted whether [the doctrines] were true, but never said a word of such doubt and revealed it to no one." After Saramita "taught" Maifreda where her own destiny lay, "sometimes she believed and sometimes she didn't."[60] On August 20, however, she confessed to perjuring herself in her previous depositions "out of simplicity and fear of offending St. Guglielma's other devotees," as well as fear for her life. The inquisitors, determined to scapegoat a single leader of the sect, now asked whom the believers heeded more—Saramita or herself? "She replied that the devotees paid a great deal of attention to Andrea, but even more to her, Sister Maifreda," and throwing futile caution to the winds, she acknowledged her own leadership and unswerving faith, grounded in posthumous visions of Guglielma.[61]

While Maifreda's testimony was colored by terror, a similar blend of boldness and diffidence can be seen much earlier in accounts of her preaching. Sometime around 1290, after a banquet in the house of Giacomo da Ferno, Maifreda reaffirmed her gospel amid a select company of Guglielma's devotees. Stefano Crimella, the skeptic, recalls her speaking "clearly and with great fervor, repeating her words many times." His wife Adelina, the believer, had more vivid recall:

> Sister Maifreda, sitting on a couch in the chamber, rolled the sleeves of her tunic up to the elbows, and after much further preparation and arrangement of her clothes, and with great spirit, she clearly told all who were present and able to hear: "I did not want to come here and I have come unwillingly, for there will be many Thomases here (that is, many unbelievers), and you will take great exception to what I say; yet I have acted like a person who wishes to obey. Our lady (she was speaking of St. Guglielma) has appeared to me and told me that I should come to you and tell you all that she, our lady Guglielma, is the Holy Spirit."[62]

Just how "unwilling" was this heresiarch? It would be possible to see her merely as Saramita's tool, a pliable instrument pressed into the role his fantasies required. Her account of hesitations and doubts, though given with ulterior motives, may not have been altogether fabricated: Saramita's convictions would have strained the credulity of virtually anyone. Moreover, in accepting the role of pope-elect, Maifreda ran undeniable risks. She already enjoyed an unusual degree of leadership at Biassono, where she preached on the Scriptures and saints' lives to a relatively large, mixed congregation.[63] But in consenting to serve as the Holy Spirit's vicar and propagate her doctrine, especially after the inquisitions of 1284 and 1296, Maifreda endangered her status as well as her life. Around 1297 she finally left the convent and moved to a private home for her own security and that of her followers.[64] Biassono, no matter how devoted to St. Guglielma, could not afford to jeopardize its reputation and its very existence by harboring a known preacher of heresy. Only conviction, purchased at considerable cost and strengthened by the loyalty of her devotees, could finally have sustained Maifreda as Popess.

As far as our evidence reveals, the Guglielmites' scenario for the millennium did not extend very far beyond Maifreda's papacy. She was to possess her see "in peace and quietness,"[65] preserving the ecclesial structures and sacraments intact, except that now they would be solemnized "in the name of the Father and the Son and the true Holy Spirit."[66] No fiery cataclysm, no revolution would follow, save the crucial one: a woman would be pope and under her reign the Jews, Saracens, and all "others outside Christendom" would come in.[67] It was for this sole reason that the Holy Spirit took flesh. We can say, with only slight anachronism, that the Guglielmites wished to make what they perceived as an exclusive Church inclusive, and they saw the first step in this process as the elevation of a female pope. They also saw—realists in this if in nothing else—that such a goal could not be accomplished without a new divine incarnation, who must herself be female. Reversing the perspective, we could say that gender equality in the Godhead was a necessary and sufficient condition for equality of religious leadership on earth; and once this equality was manifest, the full inclusion of outsiders would inevitably follow, resulting in a truly universal Church and salvation for the whole human race. The proximate means of redemption would be the same ones Christ and his Church already employed: nothing was to be subtracted from the old religion, but what was incomplete would be completed, the half subsumed in a greater whole. Woman, the most obvious of the excluded others, could by synecdoche represent and incorporate them all. Commitment to female leadership, in theory and in practice, was therefore the centerpiece of the Guglielmites' utopian dream.

Egalitarian in their own social and religious behavior, the small group of partisans who committed themselves to this program were in most ways quite ordinary. Whether religious or lay, they were not notably ascetic, and few of them inclined to visions and ecstasies. As solid citizens with families and property, many had a great deal to lose and showed no interest in martyrdom. On the contrary, the sectarians did their best to conceal their heterodox beliefs, and most of them confessed only after repeated interrogations, punctuated with torture of the principals.[68] The most damaging secret—the Easter mass—was not revealed at all until after the leaders had been sentenced. Because of the fragmentary nature of the record, the fate of many remains unknown. Only one condemnation survives, that of Sister Giacoma dei Bassani da Nova, relaxed to the secular arm on August 23, 1300.[69] Saramita's fate is revealed indirectly through the interrogation of his widow, and Maifreda undoubtedly met the same end. Having abjured in 1284, these three counted as relapsed heretics and could have found no mercy. The stake probably also awaited Bellacara Carentano and Sister Fiordebellina, the daughter of Saramita, who like Giacoma had abjured in the prior inquisition.[70] It is possible that the execution of Maifreda's sentence was delayed until the following year, when her cousin Matteo Visconti's power was temporarily eclipsed: some evidence suggests that the ruling family tried, albeit with limited success, to defy the inquisitors' power.[71] As for the rest, Sibilla and two other women escaped lightly, being merely excommunicated and absolved upon their plea. At least four men and four women were sentenced to wear yellow crosses, a penalty commuted after two or three months to a fine. In all likelihood, the same punishment was meted out to others. With these measures the sect was effectively extinguished, though not forgotten. As late as 1324, Pope John XXII cited the charge of aiding and abetting the Guglielmites in his campaign to discredit the Visconti family,[72] and the sad career of *la Papessa* lived on in the clandestine guise of the tarots.

Four years after John's bull against Matteo and Galeazzo Visconti, a second would-be avatar of the Spirit gave her life for the cause in Carcassonne. At the time of her arrest in 1325, Na Prous Boneta was an unmarried laywoman, about thirty years old, who lived with her sister Alisseta and a friend, Alaraxis, in Montpellier.[73] A longtime admirer of the Spiritual Franciscans, she had a special devotion to their leader Peter John Olivi, a revered Joachite prophet. Olivi had died peacefully in 1298, but his works were posthumously condemned and his followers relentlessly persecuted by John XXII. In 1323 that pope formally defined the Spirituals' teaching on the poverty of Christ to be heretical, earning for his pains the role of Antichrist in the friars' apocalyptic scenarios.[74] These antipapal sentiments were shared by Na Prous, who identified herself unreservedly with Olivi and his martyred disciples, including four Franciscans burnt at Marseilles in 1318. Arrested for favoring "the heresy of the burnt beguins,"[75] she embraced martyrdom fervently and used her deposition before the inquisitors as an opportunity for unabashed preaching and denunciation of the Roman Church.[76] As she steadfastly refused to abjure, she was judged an "impenitent and obstinate heretic and heresiarch" in August 1325, and later relinquished to the secular arm.[77]

Much of Na Prous's testimony is standard sectarian fare. God had sent St. Francis and Peter John Olivi into the world, she proclaims, to play the roles of Elijah and Enoch, the two witnesses of the final age (Rev. 11:3–12). When Antichrist—Pope John XXII—"slew" them by rejecting their testimony, he committed a sin as great as those of Lucifer, Adam, Cain, Herod, Caiaphas, and Simon Magus combined. Ever since the pope blasphemed by denying the poverty of Christ and condemning Olivi's writings, the sacraments have irrevocably lost their virtue, and all Christendom is spiritually dead. Since that apostasy, too, no soul has entered paradise; the saved must wait in the limbo of the fathers as they did before Christ's passion. Nevertheless, the Age of the Spirit has already dawned in spite of the present tribulation. Even now the Holy Spirit has descended anew to be crucified for the salvation of all—Christians, Jews, and Saracens—who will believe in the new dispensation. In fact, the Spirit has already ordained the long-awaited angelic pope, a friar named William Giraudi, who is to replace the apostate John. All these doctrines of Na Prous are supported by her allegorical exegesis of Revelation and of the story of Cain and Abel, whom she identifies with Aquinas and Olivi.

⏐ Na Prous, however, did not merely take her views as she found them. A visionary and prophet, she came to believe that she herself was the predestined bearer of the Spirit, hence the Spirit's passion was unfolding here and now in her own trial and in the destruction of Olivi's books./At this point her beliefs begin to resemble those of the Guglielmites. Like the Italian sect, Na Prous assumed that the earthly life of the Spirit in a female body must run parallel to that of Christ. As her convictions developed and matured, she identified sometimes with Jesus, sometimes with his mother, but most of all with the Holy Spirit who dwelt in them both. At the outset of her prophetic career she heard Christ assure her that "when you made a vow of virginity, all your sins were pardoned as completely as I pardoned my virgin mother [from the stain of original sin] in her mother's womb."[78] In a kind of overshadowing, Na Prous then received "the whole of the Godhead in spirit, as completely as God had given it to his virgin Mother and her Son." Just as the Blessed Virgin had been the *donatrix* of Christ, Na Prous was now appointed to be the *donatrix* of the Holy Spirit. And as Mary had been venerated by the apostles, she would be revered by the new apostles of the Spirit as the woman clothed with the sun.[79] Na Prous also claimed the Marian role of New Eve, for she was the one God had singled out as the "beginning and cause of salvation for all human nature."[80] First, however, she must be "crucified," or rather the Spirit must be crucified in her person. This is how she explained her arrest and interrogation: just as the Jewish lawyers had rejected Christ, so the Christian lawyers were rejecting and persecuting her. Na Prous stopped short of predicting her own resurrection, but she did claim that she held the keys of the abyss, so that all who failed to believe her words would die an eternal death.[81]

⏐Like the Guglielmites, too, Na Prous believed in a new pair of coredeemers, male and female, who would be to the third age what Adam and Eve had been to the first and Jesus and Mary to the second. The pairing of the sexes—not their union—was the essential point/ Saramita had seen himself as the "only-begotten son" of the Holy Spirit, Guglielma, and after her death he entered into a new partnership with her vicar on earth, Maifreda. Although he was prepared to subordinate himself to the two women, Saramita understood his own role as evangelist to be an essential part of the Spirit's dispensation. In practice, he and Maifreda were paired in the task of earthly leadership just as Christ and Guglielma were in the incarnation of deity. Na Prous, subscribing to a similar idea of gender complementarity, also had a male partner. For, aside from her complex and sometimes ambiguous identifications with Christ, Mary, and the Holy Spirit, she perceived herself as the female counterpart of Olivi. Even though the Franciscan leader had died when she was still a child, Na Prous believed that she and Olivi were in some sense a single person, one Spirit dwelling in two bodies.

> Christ told her, as she said and asserted, that there were nine months from the day she made a vow of virginity until the feast day of Friar Peter John [Olivi]. On the day [of her vow], the Lord God conceived Na Prous in the spirit; and on the day she was in Narbonne at the tomb of Friar Peter John, the Lord gave birth to her in the spirit.[82]

Olivi's end becomes Na Prous's beginning: just as the Virgin Mary conceived Christ through the Holy Spirit, it appears that Olivi has "begotten" the virgin Na Prous through the same Spirit. In fact she understood the ideal relationship between clergy and laity (Olivi and herself) to consist in the same spiritual friendship that Adam and Eve enjoyed when both were virgins in paradise.[83] Underlying her millennial hopes is the ancient idea of spiritual marriage: nothing can be accomplished without the equal partnership of male and female. This complementarity of gender persists despite the gradual attenuation of sexuality, proceeding from the carnal marriage of Adam and Eve, through the chaste but still corporeal union of Mary and Jesus, to the purely spiritual bond of Na Prous and Olivi. As befits the third age, the avatars of the Spirit are to be "crucified" in spirit through the mockery of their words—Olivi's writings and Na Prous's prophetic speech. Although she looked forward to being a glorious martyr in heaven, Na Prous seemed to regard her death at the stake as merely the seal set on the rejection of her message.

That rejection was crushingly thorough. Na Prous's disciples appear to have been limited to her sister, their friend Alaraxis, and a Friar Raymond John, both kin to Peter John Olivi.[84] All of these eventually recanted, and Friar Raymond denied that he had ever believed Prous's claims. The absence of a devoted male spokesman like Saramita no doubt sealed her failure as a heresiarch. In the end, hers was a solitary passion. But the heresies of Na Prous and the Guglielmites, though numerically insignificant, are more than footnotes to the history of enthusiasm. That two such similar heresies should have sprung up independently within a few decades sheds light not only on the discontent that fostered apocalyptic thought, but also on certain features of orthodox piety pursued by such sectarians to their logical conclusion. Among these are assumptions about the status of charismatic women, the place of gender in the economy of salvation, the holy woman's eucharistic assimilation to Christ, and the *imitatio Mariae* as a path to distinctive self-understanding for devout women. These assumptions, coupled with Joachite expectations for the third age, nourished both the Guglielmites and Na Prous. More significantly for the history of doctrine, they also breathed new life into the tenuous yet tenacious memory of a Godhead in which the Holy Spirit was no sacred bird, but the heavenly Mother. It is that memory, the dim recollection of a non-standard but not quite heretical Trinity, to which we now turn.

II. The Alternative Trinity

In the tiny Bavarian chapel of Urschalling, a place of no ecclesiastical importance, chance and whitewash have preserved a remarkable cycle of frescoes.[85] Among these paintings, executed between 1378 and 1395 but based on earlier works, there is a Trinity with the typological inscription "Abraham tres vidi[t] unum [ad]orav[it]" (Figure 2). The three persons are separate above the waist and joined below, and their unity is further indicated by the beams of a single cross inscribed in three adjoining haloes. To the viewer's right is the benign, gray-bearded Father; to the left, the golden-haired Son; and in the middle the smiling Spirit, who could be taken for Christ's twin sister. The Spirit is visibly "proceeding" from Father and Son, each of whom rests a hand on her shoulder as if to support her—or perhaps restrain her. Father and Son are wrapped in a single white mantle, while the Spirit wears a pleated rose-colored gown.

There are few clues to account for this unique iconography. The history of the little backwater church is so poorly documented that we know nothing about the patron or artist responsible for the frescoes. Certainly the region was not known as a center of heresy. According to Evamaria Ciolina, author of the fullest art-historical study to date, the paintings were created by an itinerant master from the south or east and are closely linked

Figure 2. The Trinity: a feminine Holy Spirit "proceeds from" the Father and the Son. St. James Church, Urschalling, near Prien-am-Chiemsee, Bavaria. Circa 1378–1395. Courtesy of Foto-Verlag Berger.

Figure 3. The Double Intercession: Christ offers his wound and Mary her breast for the salvation of sinful humanity. Florentine panel painting, circa 1402. Courtesy of The Cloisters, Metropolitan Museum of Art, New York.

Figure 4. Master I.M., Coronation of the Virgin by the Trinity. French panel painting, 1457. Courtesy of Öffentliche Kunstsammlung Basel, Kunstmuseum; photo Öffentliche Kunstsammlung Basel, Martin Bühler.

to the art of Bohemia[86]—the land of Guglielma's birth. In Ciolina's view, the middle figure in the Trinity is not a woman but a beardless youth, thus establishing a correlation between the three divine persons and the three ages of life.[87] This conception could be supported by literary evidence: Mechthild of Magdeburg linked the Holy Spirit with childhood play,[88] and one could even match the three ages with Joachim of Fiore's

Figure 5. Michael Pacher, Coronation of the Virgin by the Trinity.
Fifteenth-century panel painting. Courtesy of Alte Pinakothek, Munich.

Figure 6. Enguerrand Quarton, Coronation of the Virgin by the Trinity, 1453/1454. The Holy Spirit, proceeding from the mouths of Father and Son, doubles as the Virgin Mother's crown. Courtesy of Musée Municipal, Villeneuve-lès-Avignon.

three epochs, the age of the Spirit being last and therefore "youngest." But there seem to be no iconographic parallels, and the fact remains that, for most observers, the figure is plainly a woman, not a boy. Leopold Kretzenbacher more plausibly takes her to represent the Spirit as Wisdom (Sophia) and posits Byzantine influence, but this theory is countered by the Augustinian, "Filioquist" iconography, which would have been anathema to the Orthodox East.[89] Whatever its origins, the mysterious Urschalling Trinity may be placed alongside the teachings of the Guglielmites and Na Prous Boneta as a rare medieval witness to the feminine Spirit.

In spite of its marginal status, this alternative version of the Trinity turns out to be as old or older than the conventional version. The feminine

Figure 7. Celestial Court: Father, Mother, and Son share the throne of heaven. The dove of the Holy Spirit is perched inconspicuously to one side. From the Book of Hours of John the Fearless, Duke of Burgundy (1404–1419). Paris, Bibliothèque nationale, ms. lat. nouv. acq. 3055, fol. 195ᵛ. Courtesy of Bibliothèque nationale, Paris.

Spirit, an idea originating in Jewish-Christian theology, presupposes the grammatical femininity of "spirit" in Semitic languages (Hebrew *ruach*, Syriac *rûhâ*), as well as the common biblical identification of God's Spirit with Sophia.[90] In the wisdom literature, Sophia may appear as either God's consort or his daughter, so trinities of Father/Mother/Son and Father/Son/Daughter both occur in early sources.[91] The former is attested in the Syrian *Odes of Solomon* and the Alexandrian *Gospel of the Hebrews* (2nd c.), where Jesus refers to the Holy Spirit as his mother.[92] The latter occurs in the visions of Elkesai, a Jewish-Christian prophet (1st c.) who saw the Son and the Holy Spirit as a pair of male and female angels.[93] According to the *Macarian Homilies*, a Christian is someone who has God for a father, the Holy Spirit for a mother, and Jesus Christ for a brother.[94] Aphrahat, a fourth-century Syriac hymnodist, represents the Spirit as a maternal power who broods over the waters of baptism and descends upon the "newborn" soul.[95] In Syriac liturgical tradition, the Spirit's feminine gender even valorized a female ministry, for the triad of bishop, deacon, and deaconess were said to represent Father, Son, and Holy Spirit.[96] A number of writers drew analogies between the procession of the Spirit from the Father, the "birth" of Eve from the side of Adam, and the corresponding "birth" of Ecclesia from the pierced side of Christ.[97] In each case the symbolism of natural birth is inverted to display a female entity emerging from a male. Because of its androcentrism and typological neatness, this attenuated version of the motif survived longer than more explicit representations of the female Spirit, and it is ubiquitous in medieval iconography. Images of the "birth of Ecclesia" may even have shaped Na Prous's understanding of her relation to Olivi: she was "born" as an embodiment of the Spirit at the tomb of her male counterpart.

Another aspect of belief in a feminine Spirit has always been her association with female prophets and church leaders. In the best-known example, the ancient heresy of Montanism (or better, the New Prophecy movement) flourished in Asia Minor and counted among its leaders such women as Priscilla, Maximilla, and Quintilla. The fierce Tertullian was among their converts. Some features of this movement are strikingly similar to Guglielmite practice, though of course the Italian sectaries had no inkling of their precursors more than a thousand years before. Like the Guglielmites, the ancient heretics had a prominent male leader, Montanus, but gave precedence in their worship to two inspired women. (Epiphanius, a heresiologist who despised the sect, referred to it by the names of its female leaders; it was left for historians to foreground Montanus as heresiarch.[98]) The sectarians did not reject any doctrines or scriptures of the Catholic Church, but they added numerous books and prophecies of their own. Emphasizing women's leadership as a matter of principle, they "attributed a special grace to Eve because she first ate of the tree of knowledge,"[99] and cited Galatians 3:28 to justify their practice of including women in all ranks of clergy. Ecstatic prophecy formed a regular part of their services, which were led by "seven virgins dressed in white, carrying lamps." Interestingly, the sect made a custom of offering cheese along with bread in their eucharists—a substance that, like milk and honey, could symbolize the grace of a maternal Spirit.[100] This Spirit could be seen as Christ in female form, as Sophia, or as the closely related figure of Ecclesia as apocalyptic bride. The conflation of all three is apparent in Priscilla's famous vision: "Appearing in the form of a woman, radiantly robed, Christ came to me and implanted wisdom within me and revealed to me that this place is holy, and that here Jerusalem is to come down from heaven."[101] The millennial promise of this womanChrist resurfaces in the Guglielmites' faith in a new descent of the Spirit and a charismatic renewal of the Church by a female pope.

Epiphanius knew of another heresy, equally hateful, in which women presumed to serve as priests. His Collyridians, an all-female sect that spread from Thrace to Arabia, may have been affiliated with or descended from the New Prophecy movement.[102] They were said to worship the Virgin Mary as a goddess with gifts of bread and cakes—the ancient "cakes for the Queen of Heaven" once offered by the women of Jerusalem and deplored by Jeremiah (Jer. 7, 44).[103] These Collyridian women could have been recent converts perpetuating the rites of the Great Mother, Cybele, in a Christianized context. But the polemic Epiphanius launched against them shows that he feared some readers might take the idea of deifying Christ's mother seriously. Indeed, there are two late but interesting reports that among the heretics condemned at Nicea were certain "Marianites" who "affirmed that Christ and his Mother were two gods alongside the supreme God."[104] Collyridians seem to have survived in Arabia at least into the seventh century, for the Qur'an too denounces those who worshiped Jesus and Mary as gods.[105] When the Virgin was officially declared Theotokos ("Mother of God") at the Council of Ephesus in 431, mob violence threatened Christians who objected to the title, suggesting that a fervent popular goddess-worship undergirded the official dogmatic struggle over the Incarnation.[106] Though venerating Mary as goddess may seem a far cry from interpreting the Holy Spirit as female, the beliefs are linked in that both represent efforts to include a divine Mother in the Trinity, and in practice, both were used to justify priestly as well as prophetic roles for women.

At times the maternity ascribed to the Spirit led to her direct identification with Mary. For Marius Victorinus, a Neoplatonic theologian who influenced Augustine, the Holy Spirit is the mother of Jesus "both there above and here below" because she is the female principle of the Godhead in its descending, outgoing, life-giving phase. Conversely, Christ returning to the Father represents the ascending, contemplative, "masculine" phase.[107] This esoteric motif had little currency in the medieval period, but for mainstream theology as well, Mary as the bearer of Christ was necessarily the vessel of the Spirit (Luke 1:34). It has often been argued that, when the archaic doctrine of the Spirit as mother fell into disuse, Marian devotion implicitly preserved it to the extent that Mary came, in effect, to embody the third divine person. Both sapiential Mariology and the feminine Spirit have experienced a revival among Catholic and Orthodox theologians of the twentieth century.[108] In the medieval period, the dogmatic assertion of a hypostatic union between Mary and the Holy Spirit (to use Leonardo Boff's formulation) would surely have been deemed heretical. Yet this alternative Trinity is implicit in many expressions of medieval piety. Even though the Urschalling iconography is unique, "Marian Trinities" were not uncommon in late-medieval art. It would hardly have been surprising if laypeople, unschooled in the niceties of Trinitarian dogma, "read" such images as revealing the true objects of Christian worship: the Father, the Son, and the Virgin Mother.

Two types of Marian Trinity became especially popular in the fifteenth century. One of these was the Double Intercession, in which Christ and Mary appear as joint intercessors before God the Father. With parallel gestures, the Son bares his wound and the Mother her breast (Figure 3).[109] In such paintings the Holy Spirit is shown, if at all, as an inconspicuous dove; it is the three human figures who draw the viewer's attention. The logic of the representation thus runs counter to the official teaching that Father and Son partake of the uncreated Godhead, while Mary is merely a creature. A viewer might more easily take the Father alone to represent transcendent deity, with Mother and Son on a lower plane of equality. The Trinity altarpiece at Biassono was probably similar, showing the Father enthroned in heaven, while beneath him Jesus and Guglielma as the second and third persons were freeing sinners from hell.

An even more familiar theme, from the twelfth century onward, was the Coronation of the Virgin. Louis Réau notes the striking "iconographic crescendo" that marks the development of this motif: in the earliest examples Mary is crowned by an angel, in the twelfth century she usually sits beside Christ on his throne, and still later she receives her crown from God the Father. By the fifteenth century, we see the Virgin crowned by the entire Trinity.[110] Some paintings show the divine persons as three identical men, or as one old man and two younger ones, who graciously admit the Virgin to their fellowship (Figure 4). But in others the Spirit, in the form of a dove, hovers directly above Mary's crown (Figures 5, 6).[111] Such works could be taken to show Mary being crowned *with* the Spirit as the third person's unique, embodied revelation. The most radical instance of this iconography occurs in the Book of Hours of John the Fearless (1404–19), where an unusual Marian Trinity comes very close to the Urschalling fresco. In a miniature of the celestial court, depicting not the Virgin's coronation but its eternal outcome, Mary has completely displaced the Holy Spirit and sits enthroned in the center of the Trinity, on a level with Father and Son (Figure 7). The obligatory dove is reduced to barely decorative status. It perches on the golden circlet that surrounds the three figures, so tiny and inconspicuous that Ernst Kantorowicz, in his discussion of the image, missed it altogether.[112] It is no wonder that Sister Maifreda, in her sermon at the house of Giacomo da Ferno, proclaimed Guglielma's deity with Marian phraseology: "Our Lady is the Holy Spirit."[113]

Unfortunately for our argument, these iconographic types first appear a century later than the testimony of our heretics. But in this realm, as in so many others, mystical women seem to have anticipated a theme that would later become widespread. Mechthild of Magdeburg, a contemporary of Guglielma, called Mary "Goddess" and enthroned her as bride of the Trinity, just as artists two centuries later would depict her. Not coincidentally, Mechthild conferred the same title of Goddess on the elect soul—a bride who, like the Virgin, had been lovingly "greeted" by the Holy Spirit.[114] She herself was one such bride, and like many inspired women, she proclaimed that the words of her book were literally God's. Mechthild never laid exclusive claim to this privilege, yet there is a continuity between her thought and the more radical claims of Na Prous. In 1321, Na Prous confessed, she had a vision of the sacred heart, and God gave himself to her just as he did to the Virgin.

> Later on, she saw two other persons resembling God (*similes ipsi Deo*), who were joined in order one after the other. One of them began to run, and on the

way he positioned himself above her neck, and the second positioned himself above her right arm, saying: "You and I have become one, and now I have fulfilled that word that I spoke to you before when I gave you the Holy Spirit. You answered that such great things were not for you, and I replied that I would give you still greater things if only you were faithful to me. For now I have given you the other two persons, namely the Father and the Son; now that promise is fulfilled, . . . for now you have the whole Trinity." [115]

The iconography of this vision is so precise that Na Prous seems to have imagined her way into a painting, perhaps a particular image on which she was accustomed to meditate.[116] God the Father is stationed above her head, Christ is enthroned at her right, and she herself occupies Mary's place, embodying the Holy Spirit whom she has already received.

After prolonged meditation on this vision, Na Prous arrived at the conclusion that she was not only filled with the Spirit, but in a mystical sense *was* the Spirit. This conviction, even if it struck contemporaries as verging on madness, becomes intelligible in the light of Joachite thought. In their typological reading of history, the Spiritual Franciscans often equated Francis, Olivi, and other contemporary figures with Enoch and Elijah, Christ *redivivus*, the twelve apostles, and the angels of the Apocalypse. It might have seemed at least as plausible for the Holy Spirit, presiding genius of the third age, to have a personal and contemporary agent. That this figure should be a woman is explained, at least in part, by the close association of the Spirit with Mary and with female prophecy. If the second age began with the incarnation of the Word, should not the third begin with that of the Spirit? And if St. Francis was sent to recapitulate the life of Christ, should not a woman renew the career of Mary? How, after all, could the third Adam be fulfilled without a third Eve?

III. Chaste Partnerships and the Body Spiritual

While apocalyptic features may seem to dominate Na Prous's faith, and to a lesser extent that of the Guglielmites, both heresies are constructed around another idea that is independent of the Joachite theology of history, though not incompatible with it. That idea, as we have seen, is the belief that male and female must be paired as agents of redemption if all humanity is to be saved. Such a belief has nothing to do with the feminism of individual rights. It is, rather, an ontological belief about the nature of God and, consequently, of creation in God's image. In Western religion, it is most fully expressed in the systems of Christian gnostics and later of Jewish kabbalists, who conceived the Godhead as a complex unity of male and female dyads, or syzygies, all emanating from a single transcendent One. Since the material creation is a distorted image of the divine realm, it too is marked by the duality of gender: Adam and Eve are created "in the image of God" in a far more literal sense than orthodox commentators were willing to admit.

Certain modern scholars, notably Elaine Pagels, have posited a strong feminist slant in gnostic theology because of its emphasis on divine androgyny, female saviors, and the inclusion of women in religious leadership.[117] But while these elements are undeniably present, classic gnosticism has an equally undeniable misogynist bias. It associates the female with corruption, transience, and ignorance; defines salvation for both sexes as a process of "becoming male"; and even lauds its mother-goddess with the epithet of "thrice-male virgin." The mythic woman per se is neither good nor bad; it may be truer to see her as the destabilizing agent who alters the status quo for better or worse. Thus it is often a female entity who takes the initiative, whether in precipitating the cosmic fall (like the tragic Sophia) or in restoring gnosis and harmony (like the "Spiritual Eve" and Jesus's chaste bride, Mary Magdalene). Feminine evil signifies the fall into materiality: both men and women are "female" to the degree that they remain imprisoned by the body and the sensory world. Conversely, feminine good discloses the escape through gnosis. Women who have "become pure spirit," like the Magdalene, are ideally suited to proclaim the good news that liberation or "maleness" lies within reach of both sexes.[118] In the system of Valentinus, a second-century theologian who attempted a rapprochement between gnostic and Catholic Christianity, the task of cosmic redemption is assigned to the dyad of Christ and the Holy Spirit, a male-female pair who approximate the second and third persons of the orthodox Trinity.[119] Although maleness remains the sign of redemption, the collaboration of a female redeemer makes this goal accessible even to spirits trapped within women's bodies.

To a large degree, the ancient orthodox dichotomy of Eve and Mary replicated this gnostic gender system. Despite the ubiquitous cliché about active males and passive females, it was the woman who stood at the turning points of history: Eve's fall preceded Adam's as Mary's grace preceded Christ's. Likewise, "effeminacy" still epitomized evil, while the "virile woman" remained a powerful sign of redemption. In early Christianity, as scholars have often shown, this brand of antifeminism was correlated with a profound devaluation of the body, barely mitigated by the theology of incarnation. But by the later middle ages, the foundations of this theoretical bastion had begun to crack, even if the edifice showed no sign of crumbling. Insofar as a more fully incarnational Christianity managed to rehabilitate the body, the symbol of "woman" too could be rehabilitated, as Caroline Bynum has famously shown. If women continued to signify "the flesh" *in malum* for misogynists, they could also signify "the body" *in bonum*—especially the bleeding, suffering, eucharistic, redemptive body of Christ, for which many felt such irresistible desire. And in devout circles, "woman" might be construed as a sign of the Spirit, too—not the Spirit against the body, but the Holy Spirit as the source of those visionary, ecstatic, prophetic, and charismatic gifts of grace for which reform-minded Christians yearned. Only the Spirit offered hope of renewal, of that desperately needed complement to "organized religion"—the law, the letter, the Logos, and the whole apparatus of the *ecclesia terrena*, created by and for men. Thus the partnership of male and female in the work of redemption no longer had the same meaning as in the gnostic syzygies. By the thirteenth century, the redeemed and redemptive female no longer proved the availability of a unisex deliverance, but supplied a vital element that the male, by virtue of his gender and its privileges, *could not* supply.[120]

This abstract possibility is borne out by the evidence of actual religious life. From the twelfth century onward, close friendships between charismatic women and priests or friars are well documented. The Parisian *Règle des Fins Amans*, a text contemporary with the Guglielmites, includes an "ordinary" for entrance into the beguinage in the form of a dialogue between the prospective beguine and her spiritual director. In comparison with traditional religious rules, the *Règle* is remarkable for its emphasis on mutuality. Initiated by the chaste joining of hands, the contract of beguine and confessor is more reminiscent of marriage vows than of monastic obedience.

> Then the father should wrap his hands in something, take his daughter's hands and say: "Marie, I receive you as daughter in God and make you a companion in all my good deeds and all my prayers, that you may be partner in them as my spiritual daughter." The daughter says: "Sir, God reward you, and I receive you as father in God and make you a companion in my prayers and all my good deeds, and grant you to be partner in them as my spiritual father."[121]

Although the daughter alone promises to obey, it is assumed that each "companion" and "partner" will benefit from the other's holiness. In real life, such "couples in God" included Hildegard of Bingen and Volmar of St. Disibod, Ekbert and Elisabeth of Schönau, Christina of Markyate and Geoffrey of St. Albans, Jacques de Vitry and Marie of Oignies, Lutgard of Aywières and Thomas of Cantimpré, Henry of Halle and Mechthild of Magdeburg, Peter of Dacia and Christine of Stommeln, Henry Suso and Elsbeth Stagel, Dorothea of Montau and John Marienwerder, Angela of Foligno and "Brother A.," Catherine of Siena and Raymond of Capua.[122]

To this list we might add two exceptional pairs: Guglielma of Milan and Andrea Saramita, and Peter John Olivi and Na Prous Boneta. The cases are exceptional in many ways, not only in their heretical theologies and tragic dénouements. Saramita was atypical because of his lay status, Na Prous because she formed for herself a spiritual partnership with a man she had never met. Yet both these extraordinary relationships make explicit a dynamism that was often present, though implicit, in male-female alliances on the safe side of orthodoxy. In each case the woman was regarded, or regarded herself, as a physical and tangible sign of *both* the eucharistic Body and the Holy Spirit. Hence the unprecedented but oddly plausible notion that grew up around her: the thesis of a real incarnation of the Spirit in a feminine body. Official Christianity had never accepted that thesis either as historical claim or as millennial hope. It is a puzzling and instructive fact that, when the claim was actually made, its protagonists were female, even though the Spiritual Franciscans who speculated about an Age of the Spirit were no less male-dominated than the conservative hierarchy that repressed them. We have already explored the trinitarian aspect of the women's astonishing claim. It remains now to consider its eucharistic dimensions.

One of the few sayings the Guglielmites ascribed to their founder herself is the baffling remark—reported thirdhand by Francesco Garbagnate—that "from the year 1262 onward, the body of Christ had not been sacrificed or consecrated alone, but along with the body of the Holy Spirit, which was Guglielma herself. Hence Guglielma said that she did not care to see the body of Christ or the sacrifice, because she would see herself." This long-remembered quotation, like some of Jesus's more difficult sayings, can be accepted as reliable if only because the sect's theology fails to account for it. It seems rather to have been cherished as a mystery of faith, pregnant with unguessed meaning. Among the believers' guesses, scarcely less enigmatic was Adelina Crimella's profession of faith circa 1290: "I believe that Guglielma is that very flesh that was born of the blessed Virgin and crucified on the cross in the person of Christ."[123] Both these testimonies were withheld until late in the trial, after Saramita, Maifreda, and Guglielma's remains had already been burnt. They may therefore be counted among the sect's most dangerous and carefully guarded secrets.

In her subtle dissection of the believers' testimonies, Muraro has noted a veiled but significant difference between the versions of Guglielmite doctrine taught by Saramita and Maifreda.[124] Saramita, the Joachite, saw Guglielma as the center of salvation history; he crafted a future-oriented eschatology culminating in grandiose plans for the new Church of the Holy Spirit. Maifreda, on the other hand, taught a realized eschatology focused on Guglielma's living presence in her own ministry and sacraments. In Saramita's teaching, Guglielma's deity was manifest in her *life history*, replete with analogies that made her earthly life a mirror of Christ's. For Maifreda, however, Guglielma's divinity was revealed in her *body*, her "physical consubstantiality" with Christ. This was the doctrine so cryptically voiced by the Papessa's disciple, Adelina—who was also the only believer to claim she had actually seen and washed the stigmata in the saint's flesh.[125] While many mystics claimed or were thought to bear the five wounds, Guglielma's case was different. Far from revealing a devotion to the eucharist or the Passion, she expressed a desire to avoid mass because she felt that the sacrificed body on the altar was literally her own. This, at any rate, is what Adelina thought she meant; her confession would have been perfectly orthodox had she said, "I believe that *the sacrament of the altar* is that very flesh that was born of the blessed Virgin and crucified on the cross."[126] In other words, the claim that "Guglielma *is* the Holy Spirit" meant her body was, in a jarringly literal way, the body of Jesus. Just as the Son and the Holy Spirit were "one substance" in two divine persons, the man Jesus and the woman Guglielma were "one flesh" in two historical persons. This belief accounts for the sect's unusual practice of "blessing" hosts by placing them on Guglielma's tomb, as if to signify the identity of her body, Christ's body, and the eucharist.

The specific date of 1262 has given rise to much speculation. Marjorie Reeves noted its closeness to 1260, the year prophesied by Joachim of Fiore for the beginning of the *status tertius*—a coincidence that would have been particularly important to Saramita.[127] Wessley pointed out the political significance of the date: in 1262 Otto Visconti was elected archbishop of Milan, but the ruling della Torre family refused to let him enter the city, so the bishop retaliated with an interdict. Between 1262 and 1277 this sanction was repeated several times, while Milan remained without an effective bishop and often without the sacraments.[128] Perhaps Guglielma tried to console her devotees for this lack by offering the "sacrament" of her own Spirit-filled presence instead. But we do not know exactly when she settled in Milan: 1262 could have been the date of some traumatic personal event—a bereavement? a reversal of fortune? a conversion?—that spurred her decision to leave home and gave her a sense of chosenness. For her followers, the convergence of all three factors—a key date in prophetic revelation, a crisis in the local church, and Guglielma's mysterious advent—might have seemed such a marvel of synchronicity that it led them to receive the charismatic stranger as God herself.

It is interesting that despite their beliefs about the "body of the Holy Spirit," the Guglielmites saw no need to change the form of the mass. Maifreda followed the ordinary Catholic ritual, probably the Ambrosian rite of Milan. But the two witnesses who testified about her mass, pressed to implicate those who attended, revealed a striking fact about her congregation. Aside from the celebrant, six women and six men were named as participants, with two of each sex to serve as deacons.[129] Oddly, some of the most active sectarians were absent, while others with only marginal affiliation were present. Was it coincidence that precisely twelve disciples, carefully balanced according to gender, were invited to la Papessa's inaugural mass? Clearly her followers intended to imitate the Last Supper, but there is also a haunting literary parallel. In the Cistercian romance *La Queste del Saint Graal* (ca. 1225), twelve mysterious knights are summoned to attend the climactic Grail mass, while the companions of the Grail also hear a mystical "mass of the Holy Ghost" at which they witness the mysteries of the virgin birth and of transubstantiation. At the consummate point of their quest, Sir Galahad and his friends see with their bodily eyes how the host is, in Adelina's words, "that very flesh that was born of the blessed Virgin."[130]

The *Queste* author shared with the Guglielmites a kind of mystic literalism, a need to anchor the truth of the sacrament in material and tangible links with Christ. Thus the Grail is physically the same vessel used at the Last Supper; Joseph of Arimathea returns to celebrate the mass; and Galahad himself is a quasi-divine being, not Christ, yet more than a saint—in fact, something close to an incarnation of the Holy Spirit. Sinless and virginal, he arrives at Camelot on Pentecost—when else?—to take his place in the Siege Perilous. The Maimed King, whom he heals, salutes the knight as if he were the Virgin Mary: "You are the lily of purity, you are the true rose, the flower of strength and healing with the tint of fire: for the fire of the Holy Ghost burns in you so brightly that my flesh which was withered and dead is now made young and strong again."[131] Malory even makes Galahad a kinsman of the Savior, "the nyneth degré frome oure Lorde Jesu

Cryst." [132] In its awkward way, this claim of lineage is meant to convey the same kind of physical assurance as Adelina's insistence on the "one flesh" of Jesus and Guglielma. It is significant too that the *Queste*, despite its misogyny, gives a key role to its hero's *soror mystica*. Perceval's sister, a virgin and a king's daughter, is the one chosen to make Galahad a knight and to weave his sword belt from her hair. In the end she gives her life in a ritual of blood sacrifice: to heal a leprous maiden, she bleeds into a Grail-like dish until she dies. [133] This female mimesis of the Passion, a prelude to the Maimed King episode, also seems to be a necessary condition of the Grail Quest. It is not until the princess's incorrupt body has been recovered and solemnly buried that the companions can achieve their goal.

Thus the *Queste* romance, a touchstone of eucharistic orthodoxy, surprisingly illumines several aspects of the Papessa's far-from-orthodox sect. Here too we find a womanChrist, a royal lady linked by close spiritual ties to an elect male, who is a holy man though not a priest. By her passion and death she leads her companions to a new level of revelation and spiritual attainment. The Grail Quest itself binds a small sacred fellowship, all laymen, in a potent encounter with the Holy Spirit at a mystical mass. This rite differs from the ordinary mass not in form but only in the selection, careful preparation, and heightened consciousness of the invited guests. There they are initiated into a deep knowledge of the Christian mysteries, made accessible through the mediation of sacred persons and objects that supply a direct physical (not only metaphysical or metaphorical) link with Christ. Some such consciousness, I suspect, animated the twelve companions who kept the Paschal Jubilee at Maifreda's mass. Of course, the *Queste* romance displays neither the apocalyptic nor the feminist thrust of the Guglielmites. But it does shed light on some rarely explored dimensions of eucharistic piety that could, under very special conditions, inspire a real-life tragic romance.

In the heresy of Na Prous Boneta, a fervent but heterodox eucharistic piety is differently inflected. While we have virtually no information about Guglielma's personal beliefs, Na Prous's testimony is full enough to reveal her transformation from orthodox lay mystic to impassioned heretic. Na Prous took her vow of virginity in 1305, at the age of nine, and devoted herself from then on to an extra-regular religious life. She cherished such gifts as tears, sensations of spiritual fragrance, and inner warmth; experienced visions and ecstasies; prayed for the conversion of sinners, Jews, and Saracens; and cultivated a deep devotion to the eucharist. In fact, Na Prous believed at one time that "in the earthly paradise [the Church] a person could see the body of Christ, hear mass, or receive Christ's body with so much reverence that all sins would be forgiven, even unconfessed mortal sins." [134] On Holy Saturday of 1321 "God the Father appeared to her" at the elevation of the host, signaling the onset of a new and more intense phase in her mystical life. Not long afterward, Christ rebuked her for confiding in a cleric, revealing his desire to take personal charge of her soul. At this point she experienced union with the Trinity and began, like a Free Spirit, to think in terms of her own deification and mission to the world.

Even as a heterodox mystic, however, Na Prous might have stopped short of open rebellion if she had not been radicalized by a series of political crises. John XXII's condemnation of Olivi and the Spirituals, the burning of heretics at Marseilles, and the mass slaughter of beguins and lepers in 1321–22 all conspired to persuade her that the Antichrist was alive and furiously raging. Her piety then took a sharply heretical and apocalyptic turn, culminating in her decision to embrace martyrdom as the sole cure for the papal apostasy that had rendered Christendom spiritually dead. Nevertheless, Na Prous traveled a long way from her conviction that merely hearing mass with devotion had the power to remit unconfessed mortal sins, to her later belief that in the age of the Spirit the sacrament had been "totally annulled and ended." [135] I submit that in the course of her "heretication," Na Prous was able to give up her eucharistic piety only when she had found an adequate replacement for it. This replacement lay not only in the experience of mystical union, which enabled her to dispense with mediation, but also in the assurance that through her new role as *donatrix Spiritus sancti*, she had herself become a living sacrament. In other words, she now offered to the world in her own person the same characteristics she had once ascribed to the eucharist: identification with Christ's virgin-born, crucified flesh; the plenitude of the Holy Spirit; and the power to remit sins and thereby redeem the human race. If Guglielma's sacred body, in the eyes of her devotees, was identical with the eucharistic host, Na Prous believed that she and her *frater mysticus*, Olivi, had come to supersede the host. It was on the feast of the Purification of Mary—a cleansing she had experienced in her own self—that Christ told her she should no longer receive communion. [136]

When Christ took flesh in the Virgin, Na Prous testified, "he formed for himself a body of the purest and most precious blood that was in the Virgin; and there was no angel nor archangel nor saint in paradise who meddled in this, but Jesus Christ alone formed his own body." [137] Exactly the same gift was given to her, with one difference: "That divinity that

God gave her formed for itself a spiritual body (*unum corpus desperit*) of the purest and most precious intellect she possessed; and there was no angel nor archangel nor saint in paradise who meddled in this."[138] The Holy Spirit came upon her, but instead of becoming pregnant like Mary, she was, as it were, transubstantiated. Her interpretation of this experience combines three assertions, not easy to reconcile: (1) The grace given to her recapitulated Mary's virginal conception (2) while sublimating it, in a kind of Hegelian *Aufhebung*, from the physical to the spiritual plane and (3) forging a perfect, salvific union between her own "body of spirit" and Olivi's. The pivot of the ages thus turned on a double "incarnation," which was at the same time an anti-incarnation, not Spirit becoming flesh but flesh sublimed into spirit:

> The Lord God gave the Spirit completely to Friar Peter John, for otherwise men and women would not be saved. For (as she asserted God had told her) there was no mingling between the body of Jesus Christ and the body of his mother, the Virgin Mary: they were wholly the same (*totum esset idem*). Likewise, there is no mingling between the spiritual body (*corpore spiritus*) of Friar Peter John and the spiritual body of Na Prous (she said): Friar Peter John's spirit and her own spirit are the same, for the whole descended from God (she said). The Lord also told her that just as God ruled the Church through two bodies of flesh—the bodies of Christ and his mother, the Virgin Mary—in the same way he would rule the Church from now on through two bodies of spirit, given to Friar Peter John and herself, which spirits are both one (she said). She also asserted that the Lord had told her everyone who wished to be saved must believe the words of Friar Peter John's writing, which are written by the power of the Holy Spirit, and likewise believe the words of Na Prous, which are spoken by the power of the Holy Spirit (she said).[139]

The strange testimony is peppered with *sicut dixit*s, suggesting the puzzled notary's response to a doctrine he found barely intelligible. For us, the perplexity of Na Prous can be located in her ambivalence toward the body—incarnation, eucharist, the saving grace of flesh. On the one hand, she insists mightily on the importance of her female body—her virginity, her identification with Mary, her union with Olivi, supplying the partnership without which "men and women" could not be saved. On the other hand, "flesh and blood cannot inherit the kingdom of God" (1 Cor. 15:50). It is the Spirit that saves through the word—masculine writing, feminine speech—proceeding from transfigured "spiritual bodies." What the Apostle assigned to the resurrection, Na Prous assigns to the *novus status ecclesiae*, the age of the Spirit. In the course of her religious odyssey, this Provençal mystic had encountered Cathars and perhaps other dissidents as well as Spiritual Franciscans, and her troubled move away from sacramentalism reflects these diverse currents. For example, her claim that she "saw God in the spirit all day and night and at every hour, and he never departed from her,"[140] recalls the alleged Free Spirit doctrine that perfect souls enjoy permanent fruition of God and no longer need the mediations of grace. The Cathars too were known for their anti-sacramental views—and they were also heirs to the ancient gnostics. In the end, Na Prous sublimated her eucharistic faith into the form of a neo-gnostic syzygy without the sexism. She and Olivi would be paired redeemers, male and female informed by one spirit, revealing a word of illumination to free its hearers from the regimen of flesh and the oppressive powers-that-be. Her heresy, therefore, took an opposite turning from the Guglielmites. For the Papessa's followers, the incarnation of the Spirit enriched the eucharist with a new, esoteric meaning and transformed the priesthood, not the rite. For Na Prous, the coming of the Spirit mandated a firm if reluctant farewell to the adoration of the Body.

IV. The Mother of the World

Two hundred and fifty years after Guglielma's "only-begotten son" and her earthly vicar went up in flames, a strange phoenix rose from the ashes.

In 1553 there appeared in Paris a little book, dedicated to Princess Marguerite of France, entitled *Les très-merveilleuses victoires des femmes du Nouveau-Monde, & comment elles doibvent à tout le monde par raison commander*. Its author was one Guillaume Postel: brilliant linguist, kabbalist, ex-Jesuit, French patriot, impassioned Joachite prophet, and would-be angelic pope.[141] His tract on "the women of the new world" begins modestly enough, masking itself in the familiar guise of the *querelle des femmes* before taking a bizarre and unexpected turn.[142] Postel was no feminist, but he admired devout women for their ardent love of God, and he had a special esteem for Italian *beatae*—Angela of Foligno, Catherine of Siena, and Columba of Rieti, among others. Indeed, he goes on to say, he himself knew such a holy woman, a Mother Johanna, who lived a life of contemplation and charity first in Padua, then in Venice. Constant in prayer, tireless in her ministry to the poor and sick, astounding in miracles, she possessed an infused knowledge of mysteries that had been concealed for three thousand years, although she was quite unlearned. From her, Postel claimed to know many truths about the Kingdom to come, including the secrets of the *Zohar*, and she prophetically designated him her "firstborn son." The meaning of this honor did not become clear until two years after her death in 1549 or 1550. Shortly after Christmas of 1551, Postel experienced a miraculous rebirth—a total transformation of body and spirit, restoring his reason to its prelapsarian purity—as Mother Johanna's "substance and spiritual body" descended on him. Ever since then, he exulted, "it is she who lives in me and not I." Certain of his divine mother's superiority to "all creatures who ever were, are, or shall be," he triumphantly unveiled the new dispensation:

> It is most certainly decreed and determined in heaven that all the men who have ever been corrupted, destroyed, and set against God by the corruption of the old Eve, being no sooner born than damned, will be restored and re-mitted in their entirety, like me, by the substance of her spirit . . . for it is necessary that Jesus be the mental father and Johanna the spiritual mother of all: new Adam and new Eve, two in a single spiritual flesh.[143]

Postel's astonishing book was followed in short order by two more, *Le prime nove del altro mondo* and *Il libro de la divina ordinatione*, both in 1555. These works, together with his many unpublished manuscripts, supply fur-ther details about his "new Eve," whom he also called the "Venetian Virgin" and "Mother of the World." Madre Zuana (a dialect form of Johanna or Giovanna) was a historical person: foundress and director of the Venetian hospital of San Giovanni and San Paolo, where Postel served as chaplain between 1547 and 1549. At their first meeting, after watching him hear the patients' confessions and distribute communion, she begged the new priest on her knees to give her the same grace. "A little old woman of about fifty years," as he described her, she accepted Postel that day as both father confessor and spiritual son (*figliolo*), and he became her fervent disciple. Zuana's work was admired and supported by the Venetians, for like St. Catherine of Genoa, she seemed to embody the ideal of the mixed life: constant occupation in the works of charity together with absorption in the depths of God.[144] Surrendered to Christ and convinced of his indwell-ing presence, Madre Zuana permitted herself some remarkable statements, revealing more than a little familiarity with the prophetic and apocalyptic beliefs that flourished in her milieu. To Postel's offense and amazement (as he later wrote), she revealed to him that "I am the Lord because he dwells in me; and therefore I am—in him—the Holy Pope, the Reformer of the world."[145]

"Offended" or not, Postel soon found himself persuaded by Madre Zuana's miracles that she was indeed the feminine angelic pope, whose vicar he was personally called to be. Using the kabbalistic symbols he cherished, he called his Divine Mother the embodiment of the Shekinah and the chosen vessel of *tikkun*, the restitution of all things. Through her mystic papacy God would create a truly universal Church, offering baptism and forgiveness to all peoples and inaugurating the fourth and final age of the world. (This corresponds in fact to the Joachite *tertius status*, since Postel understood the first age as the state of nature, followed by the ages of law and grace.) As the archangels Michael, Gabriel, and Uriel had been linked with the first three ages, the healing angel Raphael heralded Mother Johanna in the fourth.[146] In her role as New Eve, the Mother of the World had ascended to heaven in her material body to be united with her spouse, the New Adam, in a "chemical wedding" whose fruit was Postel himself, the firstborn son of the restored creation—and its most zealous apostle.

Postel's thought is notoriously opaque, and we need not stray further into its labyrinths. For the rest of his troubled life, he continued to elaborate his key doctrines about Mother Johanna and the apostolic mission she bequeathed him. Toward the end of his *Victoires des femmes*, he had appended some "articles of eternal Reason" in which he avowed the necessity to sacrifice all—goods, life, and honor, if need be—for the sake of truth.[147] It should come as no surprise that this wayward prophet, who had already been evicted from the Society of Jesus, went on to an unhappy encounter with the Venetian inquisition. In 1555 he was condemned as an obstinate heretic and compelled to languish in prison for years. The inquisitors spared his life only because they judged him not malicious, but mad— a verdict that has been echoed by many historians.[148] Whatever its justice, however, the nature of Postel's "madness" should by now be familiar. Despite the intricate and baffling hedge of kabbala, his convictions about his Mother of the World cum angelic pope were, at heart, a more sophisticated version of the same doctrine for which Saramita and Maifreda died.

Is the resemblance merely coincidental—one of those inexplicable recurring ideas that bedevil the historian of esoteric thought? Did similar predispositions spontaneously lead the eccentric, erudite scholar to the same conclusions as the candid medieval enthusiasts? The answer is probably no. To be sure, Postel's thought was shaped by his own mystical experiences and psychological needs, and it was nourished by many streams, especially kabbalistic lore and Joachite prophecy.[149] Kabbalists were pre-

occupied with sexual polarity in the Godhead, and Joachites with the restitution of the Church by an angelic pope, but aside from Postel, neither
school of thought produced the idea of a female incarnation of the Spirit
(or Shekinah) who would inaugurate the new age—except, of course, for
the Guglielmites and Na Prous. In this case, it is possible to trace a direct
if circuitous link between the Milanese heretics and their humanist heir.

Between 1528 and 1534 three priests of Milan founded a society, called
the Confraternity of Eternal Wisdom, to promote evangelical reform.
Under the guidance of the controversial Fra Battista da Crema, the little
society (later known as the Congregation of San Paolo) came to include both men and women, the former called Barnabites and the latter
Angeliche. In their pursuit of apostolic perfection, members especially
stressed the collaboration of the sexes as a way of demonstrating their triumph over the flesh, and both men and women promised absolute loyalty
to their superior, Angelica Paola Antonia Negri, honoring her with such
titles as *maestra sanctissima* and *divina madre*. One young man, for example,
made his profession in 1544 with the following vow: "I give thanks to God
who has taken me from the slavery of the world . . . and illumined me to
seek his light . . . by revealing to me a true, faithful, and experienced guide,
Angelica—the truly angelic and divine Paula Antonia, most holy mistress
of the Angeliche of San Paolo in Milan . . . and I accept her as my only
Mother, into whose hands I absolutely, freely, and totally surrender all my
will and all my work . . . And because I consider myself reborn from this
hour, being but a little child I know not how to speak or what to ask . . . but
I entrust myself wholly to her, confident that she, like a good and faithful
mother, will know what is appropriate for the nurture of her little son." [150]

In 1539, the Barnabites and Angeliche were approached by the governing board of the Venetian hospital of San Giovanni and San Paolo,
founded by Madre Zuana almost two decades earlier. At the request of
these authorities, the Milanese order sent several of their women, including Madre Angelica Negri, to assist at the hospital in Venice and supervise
its female staff.[151] Not surprisingly, Madre Angelica and Madre Zuana did
not get along. Aside from a conflict over leadership, Marion Kuntz speculates that "the little hospital was . . . too small to house successfully two
feminine prophets." [152] Postel was keenly aware of the women's rivalry, de-
nouncing the Angeliche as "hypocrites and assassins of the poor." But more
to the point, it may well have been from her rival, the Milanese *divina
madre*, that Zuana learned of the divine feminine authority she too would

claim. According to Postel, it was in 1540—probably the year of Madre Angelica's arrival in Venice, and seven years before his own—that Madre Zuana experienced her "immutation," when the "spiritual or celestial body of Christ" came upon her and deified her.[153] After that event, she awaited only the coming of her own *figliolo*, who would offer her the same gratifying homage and obedience that Angelica received from her disciples. Postel, of course, found in his Venetian Virgin exactly the woman he needed both to give him a sense of personal mission and to flesh out the abstract ideas he had absorbed from the kabbalists and Joachites.

It remains only to add that Fra Battista da Crema, at whose initiative the Milanese order was founded, hailed from the same town as Carmeo da Crema, who appears fleetingly in the Guglielmite records. This Carmeo was dead by 1274, many years before Guglielma herself, so few of the sectarians could have known him. But he must have been a close friend of the saint, for he was instrumental in Chiaravalle's purchase of the house where Guglielma would spend her last years.[154] Danisio Cotta recalled that even then, he was proclaiming that she had come to save the Jews and Saracens. Carmeo was also a friend and perhaps a mentor of Andrea Saramita, who wrote a book in his name—the *Prophetia Carmei prophete ad tales civitates et gentes*.[155] Was Carmeo da Crema, then, among the earliest preachers of Guglielma's deity? It is likely. Was there an oral tradition in Crema, or in the families most deeply involved in the sect, that kept their beliefs and aspirations alive? It is possible.

The Visconti remembered: *La Papessa* was immortalized in the tarots 150 years after her trial (and a century before Postel's). There was also a legend about the Guglielmites, well-known in the sixteenth century, that transmogrified their history into a Boccaccian novella: it told of a clandestine affair between Guglielma and Saramita, an underground "synagogue" where women held nocturnal orgies, and the triumphant revenge of their injured husbands.[156] Muraro suspects a deliberate distortion on the part of anti-heretical preachers, who recast the story as a "popular" misogynistic fable from their pulpits to reinforce the lesson of the flames. But if this travesty remained current for centuries, why not the less-familiar truth? Oral memory may well have traced a path from Guglielma and her friends, through Battista da Crema and the "divine mother" Angelica, to Guillaume Postel and his Mother Johanna, the angelic pope and Mother of the World. In the priest Postel's version of the myth, as in the spurious legend, Maifreda's role has disappeared: his "womanSpirit" and woman pope have become a single person, whose mission can only be executed by her "son." Yet still, in the *Très-merveilleuses victoires des femmes*, there lingers a trace of that sister who, on the feast of the Resurrection, in the year of the Jubilee, in the name of the Spirit, "vested herself as a priest . . . and said mass" at the cost of her life.[157]

7. Renaissance Feminism and Esoteric Theology: The Case of Cornelius Agrippa

Of the myriad "defenses of women" produced in Renaissance Europe, the most flamboyant and fascinating is one of the first. Heinrich Cornelius Agrippa von Nettesheim (1486–1535), already a polymath and occultist of some fame, was but a young man of twenty-three, preparing to teach his first course at the University of Dôle in Burgundy, when in 1509 he delivered the brilliant inaugural lecture that became the kernel of his treatise *De nobilitate et praecellentia foeminei sexus* (On the Nobility and Superiority of the Female Sex).[1] The oration was dedicated to Margaret of Savoy, princess of Austria and Burgundy and *de jure* president of the university, whose patronage Agrippa wished to secure. Unfortunately for the young scholar's career, however, he roused the ire of the Franciscan Jean Catilinet with his ensuing course, a series of lectures on Reuchlin's kabbalistic text *De verbo mirifico*. Within a year the friar's diatribes would force Agrippa out of his post and out of town. After this summary denial of tenure, it was not until twenty years later that he published *De nobilitate*, with its original dedication, in the Antwerp edition of his works (1529).

Once in print the treatise enjoyed a virtual *succès de scandale*. A second edition appeared in 1532, others in 1567, 1603, and 1643. Shortly after its publication the work was translated into French and Italian; within fifteen years it was also available in German and English. A Polish version came out in 1575, a Dutch one in 1611. Between 1530 and 1801 at least eighteen separate translations appeared, not counting reprints and innumerable plagiarisms by other writers. But despite this enthusiastic reception, Agrippa's translators and publishers proved to be radically at odds over the interpretation of his remarkable tract. At the same time that seventeenth-century feminists were appropriating *De nobilitate* as a precursor text, misogynists were promulgating it as a satire on women.[2] Nor have modern interpreters reached agreement about its author's intentions. Its shifting tonal registers and teasingly contradictory arguments make this "defense of women" more than usually susceptible to interpretive bias.

Given its long and checkered reception history, the question of the work's original context is crucial. Understandably, most recent critics have read *De nobilitate* as a document in the *querelle des femmes*, that prolific and seemingly interminable pamphlet war between attackers and defenders of women. In her admirable study of Renaissance feminism, Constance Jordan takes *De nobilitate* as a serious work, "the most explicitly feminist text to be published in England in the first half of the [sixteenth] century."[3] Others have been less convinced. Ian Maclean maintains that while Agrippa's ringing finale "may appear to be a clarion call to radical change, . . . it would be safer to regard it as part of a rhetorical exercise in declamation."[4] In fact, the slippery genre of *declamatio* or paradox is responsible for much of Agrippa's ambiguity. According to Linda Woodbridge, paradox works by "over-correction, pointing up the untenable nature of one extreme position by demonstrating the feasibility of arguing its opposite." Agrippa's goal, in her view, was neither serious argument on behalf of female superiority nor ironic mock-praise of women, "but a graphic demonstration of the absurdities one must resort to if one claims superiority for either sex."[5]

The strategy of the *declamatio* is not to pursue a consistent line of argument, but to assemble all possible arguments, valid or invalid, that might support the case at hand. *De nobilitate* is a tour de force in this genre, handling its reasons and exempla deftly enough to keep the reader constantly guessing which are serious, which frivolous. Sliding between straightforward eulogy of women and bold inversion of misogynist topoi, the treatise escapes the usual confines of the *querelle des femmes*. Unlike most defenders, Agrippa expresses no outrage against antifeminist invective and makes no show of refuting some prior attack. His voice is not defensive or indignant, but supremely confident, now dazzling readers with his erudition, now entertaining them with hyperbolic claims, yet closing with what appears to be a sincere and carefully pitched appeal to reason.

Efforts to gauge Agrippa's seriousness through biographical criticism have been inconclusive. In 1900 Harriett McIlquham praised him as "a man of noble aspirations, unsullied life, of infinite genius and resources . . . Just and tender to all, he was especially so to women. He ever constituted himself their chivalrous champion."[6] As evidence that his feminism was sincere, she cited his two happy marriages (his third ended in divorce) and his successful defense of an accused witch in 1518. Agrippa also penned a treatise commending marriage, dedicated to Marguerite of Navarre—a work more traditional than *De nobilitate* but still radical enough to be un-kindly received in court circles.[7] On the other hand, in an apologia for yet another controversial text, the sly humanist observed that declamations like his *De nobilitate* contain many invalid arguments and jokes.[8] And in 1530, after quarreling with Louise of Savoy and falling from Princess Margaret's favor, he "[cried] out against the fickleness and gullibility of the sex."[9]

My purpose here is neither to decide whether Agrippa was sincere nor to determine whether, by present-day standards, *De nobilitate* is a gen-uinely feminist text. I would like instead to offer a new reading that may shed some light on its esoteric subtext as well as its deliberately ambigu-ous tone. For the slipperiness of *De nobilitate* is not a unique feature of this text or a trait due to its rhetorical genre alone, but a characteristic of Agrippa's oeuvre as a whole. We are dealing with an impish spirit who shocked contemporaries in what would seem to be two opposite ways at once: by compendious occultism and thoroughgoing skepticism. His two major works were a definitive handbook of the occult sciences (*De occulta philosophia*, 1510/1533) and a declamation on the vanity of all sciences, espe-cially the occult ones (*De incertitudine et vanitate scientiarum*, 1526). Seven years after he penned this exposé, Agrippa decided to publish the first edi-tion of his previously written handbook, undaunted by his own critique of the magical arts.[10] Adventurer that he was, he had a penchant for pursuing intellectual extremes without troubling unduly about the contradictions they might engender.

It is significant that both *De nobilitate* and *De occulta philosophia*, begun in the author's early twenties but later revised and expanded, were not committed to print until he had reached his mid-forties. In the interim he had become friendly with John Colet, Jacques Lefèvre d'Étaples, and other reform-minded Catholics whose biblical humanism came to balance his devotion to occult learning. The sweeping skepticism of *De vanitate* has been ascribed to the author's profound discouragement at a time of per-sonal, professional, and financial crisis;[11] but an alternative reading of this work is also possible. Frances Yates concluded from it that Agrippa was at heart not a true skeptic but an evangelical who, for all his learning, was finally prepared to know nothing but the Word of God.[12] Judging from his continued interest in magical and occult studies, however, it appears that none of these competing tendencies in Agrippa's thought ever succeeded in banishing the rest. Rather, he combined a lifelong thirst for esoteric wis-dom with a longing for the simple, biblical faith that would put all doubt to flight. Neither a Protestant nor a traditional Catholic, Agrippa gave vigorous expression to the intellectual and spiritual cross-currents of his tumultuous age. I will argue that in *De nobilitate*, his earliest known work, he was already balancing extremes, using the fashionable topic of women as pretext for a daring experiment in applied theology. Whatever he may have said at Dôle, in the published text of 1529 he adopted the eulogy of women to forge a link between his esoteric *prisca theologia* and a kind of evangelical humanism. In the process he distilled a rare and volatile elixir of feminist thought.

Most of Agrippa's critics, coming to *De nobilitate* from the standpoint of secular feminism, have failed to appreciate the scope and originality of his theological arguments. But his latest interpreter, Roland Antonioli, notes that Agrippa's feminism is part of a broader esoteric outlook: "It is illumined by a distant, kabbalistic, and Neoplatonic light, which sees in woman an immediate manifestation of the divine, a pure and original principle of life, capable of working miracles that manifest in her body the absolute power of spirit over matter." [13] In fact, the theology of gender set forth in *De nobilitate* is an amalgam of diverse materials: hermetic and kabbalistic lore, Neoplatonic reverence for ideal beauty, traditional and not-so-traditional praise of "good women," subversive counter-reading of the Eve myth, and evangelical feminist exegesis based on Pauline doctrine and early Christian praxis. Theoretically, these approaches can be reconciled only by the most generous accommodation, and to complicate matters, not all the arguments are set forth with equal seriousness. It is no wonder if the resulting blend, like the marriage of sulphur and mercury, is pungent as the one and unstable as the other.

The underlying conflict in *De nobilitate* stems from its two ultimately incompatible premises. On the one hand, Agrippa is arguing for a romantic, essentialist feminism that posits the innate superiority of women. This case is built partly on kabbalistic and hermetic grounds, partly on the Neoplatonic refinements of courtly love. On the other hand, he is arguing for an egalitarian, individualist feminism that posits the equality of the sexes. Christian Platonism in a different form comes to his aid here, assisted by some very un-Platonic arguments about evangelical freedom, the authority of the Spirit over the letter, and the successive ages of salvation history. Since these two conflicting strands of argument are intertwined throughout the text, even a sympathetic reader might be uncertain whether Agrippa was calling for a gender-blind, equal-opportunity Church or a form of woman-worship. Readers who noticed the contradiction might take the romantic case as a rhetorical overstatement meant to make the

egalitarian case more persuasive, or conversely, as a brilliant satire designed
to undermine it.

Both the conflicting premises are stated explicitly at the outset. In his
first paragraph Agrippa proclaims that there is absolutely no difference between the sexes except in their reproductive organs. As far as the "form of
the soul" and its faculties, reason and language, are concerned, men and
women are identical. What is more, both are gifted with the same "innate
freedom" and called to the same beatitude.[14] This platonizing stance assumes that the human person is essentially soul or mind; the ephemeral
body is of no ultimate importance. Buttressed by the biblical doctrine of
the *imago Dei*, this teaching was used by the Greek Church fathers to support the equality of the sexes in martyrdom, continence, asceticism, and
the pursuit of virtue. Although overlaid by androcentric bias, the idea of
the equality of souls had long been fundamental to Christian anthropology
and especially to the monastic ideal.[15]

But this doctrine does not advance Agrippa's purpose of proving
female *preeminence*, unless he should wish—as, incidentally, he does—to
assert the superiority of the female genitals. He adds, therefore, that "apart
from the divine essence of the soul," in all other respects "the noble feminine stock almost infinitely surpasses the harsh race of men." [16] Many of
Agrippa's "proofs" involve claims about the female body and its occult
properties, but others pertain to traits he has ostensibly excluded, namely
the intellectual, moral, spiritual, and even linguistic prowess of the two
sexes. The bulk of his treatise makes the novel case for female superiority at
the expense of human equality, although the latter would be the more serious and arguably the more radical claim. In his final peroration, however,
Agrippa hammers home the injustice of social and political constraints on
women, urging their liberation from all disabilities in both civil and ecclesiastical law. At this point the two strains of thought finally come together,
so that women's "natural superiority" becomes an argument for abolish-
ing sex barriers. If females are of such mettle that even untrained women
surpass trained men in such talents as eloquence, Agrippa asks, how much
more could women accomplish if they had free access to education and to
religious and political office? Thus the case for female superiority, although
philosophically at odds with the case for equality, is at last made to support
the same practical agenda.

The specifically esoteric features of *De nobilitate* include such doctrines
as divine androgyny; a kabbalistic interpretation of Eve; veneration of

Woman as the instantiation of God's partner, the divine Wisdom (Sophia) or Shekinah; adoration of feminine beauty as an act of worship; and reverence for occult virtues ascribed to the female body. These elements, although muted by Agrippa's characteristic skepticism and wit, nonetheless comprise a distinct subtext that most of his translators suppressed or missed altogether. A discerning occultist would note, in the very first sentence, a cunning conflation of Genesis 1:27 with the *Asclepius*, a hermetic dialogue in vogue among Renaissance mages:

> Deus Optimus Maximus, cunctorum genitor, Pater ac bonorum, *utriusque sexus foecunditate plenissimus*, hominem sibi similem creavit, masculum et foeminam creavit illos.[17]

> God the Best and Greatest, source of all things and Father of the good, *abundantly full of the fertility of both sexes*, created humankind in his likeness; male and female he created them.

The tag I have emphasized comes from a celebrated passage on the androgyny of God:

> —The sole God, therefore, like all things, *abundantly full of the fertility of both sexes*, always pregnant with her own will, constantly gives birth to whatever s/he wishes to procreate. . . .
> —So, Trismegistus, are you saying that God is of both sexes?
> —Not only God, Asclepius, but all animate and inanimate beings . . . For each sex is full of procreative power, and the joining of both or, to speak more truly, their incomprehensible unity, is what you could rightly call Cupid or Venus or both . . . in which the supreme charity, joy, gladness, desire, and divine love reside.[18]

Recalling this dialogue, our hermetic hermeneut might infer that Agrippa's text means more than it says. Woman no less than man is created in the divine image, not only because the *imago Dei* rests in the genderless soul, but more expressly because God is an androgyne. The *Asclepius* uses this idea to ground a theological affirmation of sexuality that also, however covertly, underlies Agrippa's celebration of erotic love, procreation, and motherhood. The notion of a dual-gendered God had already been used as an argument for gender equality in one of Agrippa's sources, Mario Equicola's little-known treatise *De mulieribus* (circa 1501),[19] and it was taken up again by Giuliano de Medici, the defender of women in Castiglione's *Corte-*

giano (published 1528).[20] Aside from these closely related texts, however, the teaching proved too esoteric and heterodox to become a staple of the genre.

Agrippa goes on to argue that Eve, the archetype of woman, surpasses Adam because her name means "life" while his means only "earth" (Gen. 2:7, 3:20). But he transforms this commonplace by adding that, "according to the mystical symbols of the kabbalists, the woman's name has a greater affinity than the man's with the ineffable name of the divine omnipotence, the Tetragrammaton, for the man's name does not accord with the divine name in characters, in figure, or in number."[21] This resemblance of the Hebrew names Hawwah (Eve) and YHWH (God) is invoked to suggest a kind of natural divinity in women. Its implications are spelled out in the important passage that follows. Woman is God's consummate creature, the nexus that unites and perfects the whole universe, and the final cause for which it was made.

> Then [God] created two humans in his likeness, first the male and then the female, in whom the heavens and the earth were finished, and all their embellishment [Gen. 2:1]. For the Creator, coming to the creation of woman, rested in her [Ecclus. 24:12], as he had nothing more noble at hand to create; and in her were enclosed and consummated all the wisdom and power of the Creator. Beyond her no other creature exists, nor can be imagined. Since woman, therefore, is the last of creatures and the goal, the most perfect completion of all the works of God, and the perfecting of the universe itself, who will deny that she is most worthy of preeminence over all creation . . . ? When the world was created, woman was the last in time among all created things, but in authority and dignity she was the first of all in the conception of the divine mind, as it is written of her by the Prophet: before the heavens were created, God chose her and foreordained her.[22] . . . As the final work of God, woman was brought into this world by God, led as its queen led to the palace already prepared for her, embellished and perfected with every gift.[23] Rightly, therefore, every creature loves, venerates and serves her, and all creation is rightly subject and obeys her, the queen and end of all creatures, their perfection and consummate glory in all respects. Wherefore the Sage says of her: he glorifies the noble birth of the woman who has cohabitation with God, for even the Lord of all has loved her [Wisd. 8:3].[24]

In this passage Agrippa makes two daring exegetical moves. First, he transfers theological tropes about man (*homo*) as the crown of creation to woman: she is the last to be formed because she is the goal of the entire process, the one for whose service and pleasure all things were made. Eve's belatedness thus becomes a proof of her superior rather than subordinate status.[25] Second, Agrippa takes biblical verses describing Sophia, the feminine persona of Divine Wisdom, and boldly applies them to woman per se. In patristic theology these texts had been referred to Christ, in whom "the Creator's power and wisdom" were totally enclosed (1 Cor. 1:24, Col. 1:15–20). From the seventh century onward they were gradually introduced into the Marian liturgy, fostering an assimilation of Sophia to the Virgin which eventuated, by the twelfth century, in the doctrine of Mary's eternal pre-existence in heaven.[26] By quoting the central texts of sapiential Mariology and applying them to Eve, that is to woman as such, Agrippa makes an audacious, original leap from the orthodox exaltation of one woman to a full-fledged esoteric feminism.[27]

As a kabbalist, Agrippa may have associated the biblical Sophia with the Shekinah, her descendant and counterpart in Jewish mysticism. The Shekinah or "glory of God" is the exiled feminine partner with whom the Holy One, blessed be He, continually seeks reunion. Frequently described as God's bride, she was also called the daughter or princess and associated with the Sabbath day. Thus the Creator's sabbath "rest" in the woman, to Christians a figure of Christ's incarnation through Mary, would to kabbalists also suggest the mystical union of the Holy One and his Shekinah. Pious Jews could advance this eschatological goal by fulfilling Torah and, more specifically, by obeying the sacred command of marital union on the Sabbath eve.[28] The kabbalistic rapprochement of YHWH with Hawwah had already suggested Woman's role as an embodiment of God's partner, the Shekinah/Sophia, and this identification is confirmed by the assertion that "the Lord of all has loved" not Wisdom or Mary, but simply "the woman." Their sacred marriage also reinforces the hermetic notion of divine androgyny.

From this esoteric praise of women, which an uninitiated reader might take for nothing but playful hyperbole, Agrippa moves on to another double-coded passage, a portrait of ideal feminine beauty. His enumeration of bodily features, each singled out for extravagant praise, has multiple roots in the rhetorical tradition of *ekphrasis*, the medieval courtly romance, and the Renaissance *blason*. From one point of view, it is the apotheosis of the male gaze, and many of Agrippa's translators took it in that sense, heightening the sensuality and eroticism implicit in his rather pedantic prose.[29] But the pedantry of the Latin text is not a stylistic lapse. As Antonioli observes, the description is constructed to emphasize scholastic canons of beauty—proportion and radiance—rather than sexual allure.[30] Agrippa tunes his praise to a standard Neoplatonic definition of beauty:

Beauty itself is nothing other than the splendor of the divine light and countenance inherent in things, shining through beautiful bodies; [this splendor]
plainly chose to dwell in women and fill them far more abundantly than
men. . . . No one who is not utterly blind can fail to see that God gathered
all the beauty of which the whole world is capable together in woman, so that
all creation might be dazzled by her, and love and venerate her under many
names.[31]

By enclosing the objectified female body within these theological brackets,
Agrippa implies that man's desire for woman is equivalent or at least parallel to his desire for God. His Neoplatonism makes explicit the quasi-
religious yearnings expressed in courtly adoration of woman, whether as
Lady or as Virgin. At the same time he traces a circular movement of divine/
human desire, complementing his earlier assertion that God's own desire
for woman is the source of her beauty. Even demons cannot resist loving
women, he adds mischievously, with a chain of mythological exempla.

Agrippa does not stop with external beauty, but goes on to celebrate
the internal mysteries of the female body, drawing on the discourse of biology and medicine. If women's souls are equal and identical to men's,
their bodies are remarkably different and superior, surpassing men in their
beauty, purity, fertility, and quasi-miraculous physical abilities. This idealized female nature is also credited with traits that would normally be ascribed to the spirit, e.g., women are said to be more eloquent than men and
more prophetic.[32] Many readers have taken the author's biological arguments to be frivolous, and some at least are undoubtedly so. Women, for
example, are said to be spared both the deformity of baldness and the sor-
did growth of facial hair; and their natural decency is proven by the "fact"
that drowned women float in a prone position, while men float supine.[33]

But even here, the broad humor masks a core of esoteric teaching.
Two examples must serve for many. Menstrual blood, Agrippa claims, is
not only a panacea for the sick but also "quenches fires, calms tempests,
wards off perilous floods, banishes all noxious things, destroys witchcraft,
and puts demons to flight."[34] Much more common, of course, was the
opposite view as taught by Pliny: the same blood "turns new wine sour,
crops touched by it become barren, . . . hives of bees die, even bronze
and iron are at once seized by rust, and a horrible smell fills the air."[35] In
his *De occulta philosophia*, Agrippa follows Pliny in listing curative as well
as harmful powers of the menses, but indicates that menstrual blood can
banish fevers, vermin, and serpents only because "the power of this poison is so great that it is a poison even to poisonous creatures."[36] Here as

elsewhere in *De nobilitate*, Agrippa gives his material a pro-woman slant by stating only the favorable aspect of a belief he expressed with greater ambivalence elsewhere. This strategy gives his claims a peculiar status, locating them midway between uproarious parody of received wisdom and genuine occult philosophy.

Following Galen and Avicenna against Aristotle, Agrippa also neatly inverts the scholastic biology of reproduction. He asserts that since the "female seed" provides the matter and nourishment of the fetus, the man's contribution is merely added to it "as an accident to the substance." Children, therefore, take after their mothers: a wise mother will raise smart children and a stupid mother, dull ones. "Nor is there any other reason why mothers love their children more than fathers do, save that mothers see and actually have much more of themselves in them. For the same reason, I think, we are also endowed with stronger feelings for our mothers than our fathers, so that while we may cherish (*diligere*) our fathers, we love (*amare*) our mothers alone." [37] Whether empirically true or not, this observation not only reverses conventional ideas of filial piety, but has potentially alarming consequences in the theological sphere. For even God's mother is no exception, but the crowning example that proves the rule. She is "Christ's true and natural mother" and he is called "son of man" (*filius hominis*) on his mother's account, not his father's. [38] This statement is not technically unorthodox, yet many translators felt compelled to alter it. One perceived danger may have been too naturalistic a view of the Incarnation, minimizing its unique and miraculous character. Another, more subtle threat lay in treating Mary (like Divine Wisdom earlier) as a normative woman, rather than the unique paragon who puts all others to shame.

Even when he is not infusing his defense of women with esoteric motifs, Agrippa refurbishes and exaggerates its standard topoi. In his obligatory remarks on Genesis, for example, he points out that Eve was fashioned in Paradise but Adam outside of it. [39] Moreover, Eve was made of a purer material than Adam (human flesh compared to mud). [40] The Virgin Mary, as the worthiest woman who ever lived, is nobler than the worthiest man (John the Baptist), while the worst man (Judas or Antichrist) is baser than the worst of women. [41] In another stock exemplum, Agrippa recalls that the risen Christ appeared first to Mary Magdalene and other women because they alone remained faithful to him in his passion. [42] Most of these observations date back at least as far as Abelard's proto-feminist epistle to Heloise (circa 1135) and possibly earlier. [43] They are concisely summed up in a late-medieval English manuscript:

> Woman is to be preferred to man, to wit: in material, because Adam was made from clay and Eve from the side of Adam; in place, because Adam was made outside paradise and Eve within; in conception, because a woman conceived God, which a man could not do; in apparition, because Christ appeared to a woman after the Resurrection, to wit, the Magdalen; in exaltation, because a woman is exalted above the choirs of angels, to wit, the Blessed Mary.[44]

But even these chestnuts receive a gourmet roasting at Agrippa's hands. From Eve's creation in Paradise he deduces that women do not suffer vertigo, since they are accustomed to heights, and from the story of Adam's rib, he concludes that man is a work of nature but woman the handiwork of God.

For Renaissance defenders of women, the task requiring the greatest ingenuity was exonerating Eve's conduct in Eden, since the normative exegesis of Genesis 3 formed the mainstay of their opponents' case. By Agrippa's time a number of options were available. One could protest that the Fall was fortunate because it "merited so great a Redeemer," as the Easter liturgy proclaims, and add that Eve's disobedience was outweighed by Mary's obedience. One could point out that Eve was but an individual woman who made a mistake, not an exemplar of all her sex; or one could excuse her by making Adam at least as guilty, if not more so. Agrippa took the final option, but typically carried it to a new and outrageous extreme. Citing Bernard of Clairvaux, he remarks that Satan tempted Eve out of envy, recognizing that her angelic beauty made her Adam's superior.[45] Moreover, Eve sinned only in the slightest degree because she was never subject to the prohibition in the first place:

> The fruit of the tree was forbidden to the man, not the woman, who had not yet been created; for God from the beginning wished her to be free. The man therefore, not the woman, sinned by eating; the man, not the woman, brought death. And we have all sinned in Adam, not in Eve, and we contract original sin from the male and not the female parent. For that reason the old law commanded every male to be circumcised, but let females remain uncircumcised, decreeing that the original sin should be punished only in that sex that had sinned.[46]

This exegesis cleverly plays up a pro-female aspect of the orthodox teaching on original sin, said to be transmitted through male concupiscence and semen and hence absent in the virgin-born Christ,[47] in order to draw the heretical conclusion that Eve was sinless. In his later treatise *De originali peccato* (1518/1529), Agrippa was to make the same assertion about Eve's liberty with a somewhat different but equally unorthodox twist, more clearly revealing the esoteric basis of his thought. Eve, he there remarks, is an allegory of reason (*ratio libera*), which is logically posterior to faith, symbolized by Adam. The tree of knowledge was forbidden to Adam lest we place our faith and hope in creatures, but permitted to Eve because human reason may speculate freely about all things. Adam's sin thus represents the seduction of pure Christian faith by speculative thought, in particular by the occult sciences.[48] This allegory expresses Agrippa's typically ambivalent attitude toward his favorite studies.[49] In a different vein, however, he goes on to name the original sin as carnal intercourse, for the serpent is none other than the phallus (*membrum reptile, membrum serpens*): "I think it was no demon but this one that tempted Eve."[50] This gnostic reading then leads to a celebration of virginity, conflicting with the praise of fertility and marriage to be found in *De nobilitate* and *De sacramento matrimonii*. The hobgoblin of little minds clearly did not trouble Agrippa's capacious spirit. But at least his interpretations are united in shifting blame for the Fall as far as possible from woman.

Agrippa's assertion about Eve, however radical, pales before the startling Christology he derives from it. Extending the Pauline concept of Christ as new Adam, he argues that the Redeemer was born male because the male sex stood in greater need of redemption, and also because of God's great humility: "Christ was born into this world most humbly, and in order to expiate the pride of the first parent's sin by his humility, he assumed the male sex as the humbler one, not the more sublime and noble feminine sex."[51] Given that Agrippa's God was androgynous and that the feminine Sophia was conventionally taken as a figure of Christ, a female incarnation would certainly have been conceivable. Hence it is, refreshingly, the Savior's maleness that needs explanation.[52] For similar reasons, the priesthood was committed to men: it is true that the male priest represents Christ, as orthodoxy claims, but only because Christ represents Adam, the first sinner. The supreme bastion of male privilege is thereby turned on its head. If Agrippa had taken his own reasoning seriously, he would have had to deduce that women need no sacrifice, no atonement, and no redemption.

Of course he does nothing of the sort. But if Eve's transgression and Christ's maleness can both be seen to prove the superiority of women, we should not be surprised to find lesser exempla turned on their heads as well. One of the most familiar and tiresome strategies in the *querelle des femmes* was the flaunting of endless catalogues, as if the moral stature of the female sex could be assessed by drawing up a balance sheet of good women against bad. Boccaccio's *De mulieribus claris* had supplied a large stock of biographies, mainly classical, that could furnish exempla on both sides of the quarrel, supplemented as need be with figures from biblical history or illustrious contemporary women. Christine de Pizan's *Livre de la Cité des Dames* relied largely on such exempla to refute misogynist libels. In her work, as in Agrippa's, the typical "good women"—virgin martyrs, faithful wives, biblical heroines—are of less interest than the rarer "bad women" who insinuate their way into the feminist casebook, challenging the criteria of judgment and expanding the scope of female achievement. Christine, for example, did not hesitate to rewrite Xanthippe and Dido as good. Agrippa includes several notorious "bad women" in his list of female paragons: thus the magicians Circe and Medea win praise for performing "deeds more miraculous than Zoroaster himself, the founder of this art."[53] The quality extolled here is not feminine or Christian virtue, but the Renaissance *virtù*, whose sole criterion is success.

Like that other ambiguous champion, the Wife of Bath, Agrippa inverts his exempla so brazenly that the nonfeminist reader will suspect satire, while the feminist may admire the ingenuity of his case. With the praise of famous viragos, as with his exoneration of Eve, Agrippa clearly risked straying across the invisible line into self-parody. But in the face of generic misogynist proof texts, ridicule may be the best if not the only refutation. The most egregious of the lot, the proverb that "a man's iniquity is better than a woman who does good" (Ecclus. 42:14), inspires Agrippa to open parody. He supplies a deliciously wicked list of cases where God punishes men for good deeds and rewards women for bad ones: Rebecca's cunning, Jael's treacherous murder of Sisera, and the incest of Lot's daughters are preferred to Cain's sacrifice, Esau's filial piety, and Uzzah's solicitude for the Ark. This display of divine favoritism issues in a rhetorical challenge to the whole threadbare tradition:

Ite nunc viri fortes et robusti, et vos praegnantia Pallade, ligata tot fasciis scolastica capita, et totidem exemplis contrariam illam probate sententiam, quod melior sit iniquitas viri quam mulier benefaciens.

Goe now yee stout and valiant men, go yee great Schollars, that have *Pallas* and the Muses most propitious to you, goe I say, & by as many examples (which all your Poetical helps are too few for) prove the contrary opinion, namely, *that the wickednesse of a man is better than a womans well doing*.[54]

Tweaking another stereotype by the nose, Agrippa takes up the Pauline motif that God chooses the weak to confound the strong (1 Cor. 1:27–29), a theme long favored by hagiographers to laud female saints.[55] In *De nobilitate*, however, the "weak women" are not pliant instruments through whom God providentially acts, but the very exempla cited by misogynists as destroyers of good men. No man has ever been more gifted than Adam, stronger than Samson, more chaste than Lot, more pious than David, wiser than Solomon: yet women overthrew them all. Satan himself could not shake the patience of Job, "yet a woman provoked him, superior to the devil and more confident."[56] Worse yet:

> If it is legitimate to call Christ himself into this comparison—and none is more powerful or wiser than he, the eternal wisdom and power of God—did he not allow himself to be vanquished by that little Canaanite woman? [Matt. 15:22–28] . . . for when Christ had seen that he could not get the better of her in argument, he blessed her, saying: Let it be for you as you wish. Who was more fervent in faith than Peter, the first of the apostles? A woman seduced him, not the lowliest pastor of the Church, into denying Christ.[57]

If this be praise, it rings with the echo of faint damns. But the purported eulogy of "weak women" actually demonstrates women's power, regardless in this context of their moral stature. Most writers predictably used exempla to prove either the excellence or the evil of women, but Agrippa marshals them to show that women have made their mark in history, for better and worse.

This revisionist strategy pulls his case in another direction as well. If historical exempla can subvert conventional definitions of "good" and "bad," they can also undermine supposedly timeless strictures on women's activity. For while Agrippa takes an essentialist view of female nature, he evinces a strikingly modern historicist outlook on gender in society. Thus, in the last section of *De nobilitate* he aims to prove that women's status has not always been subordinate, but has changed over time and can presumably change again. Entering into a legal debate that continued through the sixteenth and seventeenth centuries,[58] he maintains that women enjoyed equal or privileged status in Roman, barbarian, and feudal law before their disempowerment by the contemporary legal system and the Church. In defense of their right to religious authority, he mounts a two-pronged argument resting partly on exempla and partly on New Testament exegesis. This "evangelical" strand in Agrippa's feminism is as rare in the Renaissance *querelle des femmes* as it is common in the history of women's struggle for equality in the Church. Essentially similar arguments for female ministry recur from the egalitarian New Prophecy movement of the second and third centuries to the voluminous literature of contemporary Christian feminism.[59] At the time of writing, of course, Agrippa could hardly have expected such ideas to be taken seriously, and by inserting them in a witty *declamatio* he left himself a plausible line of defense in case of prosecution. But even if the times were not propitious, this line of argument suggests a serious theological purpose, and in subsequent eras, no element of *De nobilitate* was more vehemently attacked by champions of the status quo. Unlike the esoteric aspects, the evangelical arguments were impossible to dismiss as harmless window-dressing.

Agrippa does not pursue the dangerous logic of his Christology and proclaim that women have no need of Christ and the Church; he retreats to a safer but still controversial stand. Women, he declares, have always been Christ's most faithful followers and pillars of his Church, and are most unjustly deprived of the religious equality that is their due. Their greatest ecclesiastical disabilities were (and still are) exclusion from the priesthood and the prohibition ascribed to St. Paul: "Let a woman learn in silence with all submissiveness. I permit no woman to teach or to have authority over men" (1 Tim. 2:11–12). Agrippa challenges these proscriptions by claiming that saintly women in the past did serve as priests and teachers with authority. In the story of Priscilla (Acts 18:24–26, Rom. 16:3) he finds a perfect example: "What shall I say of that most holy woman, Priscilla, who instructed Apollos, an apostolic man and the very learned bishop of Corinth? It was no shame for an apostle to learn from a woman who was teaching in the Church."[60] As for female priests, Agrippa claims that Miriam, the sister of Moses and Aaron, entered the sanctuary with them and was therefore held to be a priest (Num. 12:4–5). He does not mention, of course, that God called her into the tabernacle only to smite her with leprosy for having dared to speak against Moses.

> But in our religion, although the function of priesthood is forbidden to women, we know nevertheless, as histories tell, that a woman who concealed her sex once rose to the pinnacle of the papacy. Nor are we ignorant of so many holy abbesses and nuns among us, whom antiquity did not scorn to call priests.[61]

I have been unable to locate any source that gives this title (*sacerdotes*) to nuns or abbesses, although holy women enjoyed a charismatic authority that could, in some cases, bypass the power of the clergy.[62] But Agrippa's female pope is well known. She is none other than the legendary Pope Joan, whose historicity was accepted widely enough to pose a problem for fifteenth-century writers on the papacy.[63] As usual with Agrippa, the exemplum is double-edged. He does not refer to the scandalous outcome of Joan's legend, as reported by Boccaccio and others: after taking a secret lover, she allegedly gave birth during a papal procession and was driven from office in disgrace.[64] The unsavory end of the tale, though suppressed in this allusion to it, might have persuaded readers that the exemplum was a jest. Yet on another level, it calls the maleness of the priesthood into question once again. If Agrippa's unconventional views on Eve and Christ imply that women do not *need* priests, the case of Pope Joan shows that all the same they can *be* priests, with no one apparently the worse for it. Thus Jean Wirth has argued that, under the guise of proving female superiority, Agrippa was really attacking the priesthood and orthodox Church discipline.[65]

Although he never left the Catholic fold, he closes his case for women's equality with an interpretation of St. Paul that would become typical of sectarian exegesis a century later. To counter the weight of standard antifeminist prooftexts, he invokes the authority of the Spirit over the letter and proposes his own version of dispensationalism. The charter text of Christian feminism, Galatians 3:28, is pressed into service too, in a way that challenges both historical precedent and patriarchal bias.

> Women are repulsed from preaching the word of God against the express statement of Scripture, wherein the Holy Spirit promised them through Joel: "And your daughters shall prophesy" [Joel 2:28, Acts 2:17]. It is known that even in the age of the Apostles women taught in public, like Anna the friend of Simeon [Luke 2:36–38], the daughters of Philip [Acts 21:9], and Priscilla the wife of Aquila [Acts 18:26].
>
> . . . Yet there are some who use religion to usurp authority for themselves against women, and they justify their tyranny by means of sacred Scripture. The curse of Eve is constantly in their mouths: "You shall be under your husband's power, and he shall rule over you" [Gen. 3:16]. If one answers them that Christ took away the curse, they will object again from the sayings of Peter, with whom Paul too agrees: "Let women be subject to their husbands" [1 Pet. 3:1]. "Let women keep silent in church" [1 Cor. 14:34].
>
> But anyone who knows the various tropes and dispositions of Scripture will easily discern that these texts are only superficially opposed. For there is an order in the Church by which men are set before women in ministry as Jews were set before Greeks in the promise. Yet God is no respecter of persons [Rom. 2:11]: for in Christ there is neither male nor female [Gal. 3:28],

but a new creation [Gal. 6:15]. Moreover, many things were permitted to men because of their hard-heartedness against women, as divorce was formerly conceded to the Jews [Matt. 19:8]; but these things in no way prejudice the dignity of women.

Indeed, when men fall short and go astray, women have the power of judgment, to men's disgrace. Even the queen of Sheba is to judge the men of Jerusalem [Luk. 11:31]. Therefore all men who, being justified by faith, have become sons of Abraham [Rom. 4], which is to say sons of the promise [Gal. 3:29], are subjected to woman and bound by the command that God gave to Abraham, saying: "Whatever Sarah tells you, listen to her voice" [Gen. 21:12].[66]

This dense biblical argument draws chiefly on Romans and Galatians, the epistles in which St. Paul had wrestled with problems of religious status and hereditary privilege in the nascent Church. Agrippa uses Paul's discussion of Jews and Greeks to propose an analogous case for men and women, as the apostle himself suggests in Galatians 3:28. By this logic, the age of male dominance parallels the age of Jewish exclusiveness in salvation history; but when Christ established a new, more inclusive dispensation accepting Jews and Gentiles on equal terms, he meant at the same time to abolish gender privilege. The male priesthood, like Jewish Christians in the Pauline Church, is declared to have only a historical and by no means a spiritual priority. If male supremacy still prevails in spite of Christ's intention, it is only because of the "hard-heartedness" of men, which women are entitled to judge and find wanting.

After citing precedents for the ministry of women in the time of Christ and the Apostles, Agrippa returns to the matriarch Sarah because, in Paul's allegorical reading of Genesis, she is the "free woman" who represents "the Jerusalem above," mother of the elect (Gal. 4:21–31). If Christians are metaphorically children of Abraham, "not according to the flesh but according to the promise," they must also be sons and daughters of Sarah: "We are not children of the slave but of the free woman" (Gal. 4:31).[67] Agrippa's originality lies in wresting a concrete political meaning—liberation for all women—from an allegory whose original sense had become obsolete. In this way Sarah's authority over Abraham, like the sapiential praise of Mary, ceases to be an exceptional or merely allegorical privilege and becomes a norm by which contemporary gender relations can be judged.

Despite the recurrence of this characteristic strategy, Agrippa's argument here differs markedly from the hermetic, kabbalistic, and sapiential theology that he had used earlier to establish woman's exalted status in creation. No longer is he drawing on esoteric lore or indulging in scandalous inversions of orthodox dogma, as he did in his account of original sin and redemption. Instead, he constructs an evangelical feminist argument that revolves around Luther's favorite epistles, relies on a humanistic style of exegesis, and incorporates historical criticism. On these grounds I would speculate that Agrippa did not include this passage in his oral declamation of 1509, but added it for the published edition after his prolonged immersion in biblical studies. The linkage he creates between women's authority and justification by faith, a key Reformation tenet, could have struck a particularly sensitive nerve in 1529.

Interwoven with the apologia for female priests is another novel line of argument that would remain central to feminist discourse from the sixteenth century through Mary Wollstonecraft and beyond. Following Equicola's *De mulieribus*, Agrippa launches a frontal attack on male tyranny that goes far beyond the conventional defense of women, for he explicitly disallows natural law and the will of God as sources of patriarchal privilege.

> Thanks to the excessive tyranny of men, prevailing against divine right and the laws of nature, the freedom given to women is now banned by unjust laws, abolished by custom and usage, and extinguished by upbringing. For as soon as a woman is born, she is kept home in idleness from her earliest years, and as if incapable of higher employment, she is allowed to conceive nothing beyond her needle and thread. Then once she has reached the age of puberty, she is handed over to the jealous rule of a husband or cloistered in a perpetual prison of virgins. Public offices, too, are denied her by law. No matter how intelligent, she is not allowed to plead in court. Women moreover are barred from jurisdiction, arbitration, adoption, mediation, administration, wardship, trusts, and testamentary and criminal cases.
>
> . . . So great is the wickedness of recent legislators that they have made void the command of God for the sake of their traditions [Matt. 15:6], as they pronounce women, who in other eras were most noble by virtue of their natural excellence and dignity, to be of baser condition than all men. By these laws, therefore, women are forced to yield to men like a conquered people to their conquerors in war, not compelled by any natural or divine necessity or reason, but rather by custom, education, fortune, and tyrannical caprice.[68]

A theological case for the "nobility and preeminence of the female sex" has laid the groundwork for this blunt defiance of patriarchy, challenging its ideological basis as well as its perpetuation by means of legal and domestic oppression. While many of Agrippa's arguments might be taken as arcane or flippant, there could be no mistaking the radicalism of this appeal. It could be resisted in theory and ignored in practice, but unlike the reversible topoi employed elsewhere in *De nobilitate*, it could not be bounced back and forth like a tennis ball between misogynist and feminist courts.

This reasoning may have been seriously meant and was at times seriously received, yet Agrippa himself was more interested in theology than in social change. I have argued that what is most distinctive and interesting about his tract is not its feminism per se, but its use of the "defense of women" genre to explore some novel implications of both esoteric and evangelical theology. Indeed, it is precisely because of this theological boldness that Agrippa, even allowing for his desire to shock and entertain, was nonetheless able to construct a feminist case more radical than anything that earlier or later defenders of the sex had to offer. But he was not the only theorist of his age to believe that, when a test case is needed for a hermeneutic experiment, "women are good to think." Late in the century, at least one other writer seems to have tried a similar project—from the opposite side of the court.

In 1595 there appeared in Germany a *Disputatio perjocunda qua anonymus probare nititur mulieres homines non esse* (Comic Disputation in which an anonymous author tries to prove that women are not human). This satire was reprinted as often as *De nobilitate*, frequently with a rebuttal, for a number of authors took it seriously enough to field a whole squadron of proof-texts against the anonymous writer's exegesis. It appears, however, that the satirist himself was not even fundamentally concerned with women. His real object was to skewer the anabaptists: using their absurdly literal hermeneutics, he would "prove" from the Scriptures that if Christ was not divine, neither were women human.[69] But the intended analogy failed to convey its point, for the satirist's "absurd" case struck many readers as no more or less absurd than Agrippa's case for female superiority. Anabaptists aside, his tract was received as an outrageous rant against women, while *De nobilitate* was received as an outrageous defense, its theological subtleties largely ignored or suppressed. In 1650 a Lutheran pastor, Johannes Bellin, played both sides against the middle, responding to a new edition of the *Disputatio* with a polemical translation of *De nobilitate*. In this defense of seventeenth-century "family values," he tried to strike a conventional balance between the satirist's misogyny and the esoteric humanist's feminism.[70]

Yet Agrippa's peculiar brand of feminist theology was not without successors. In one line of development, *De nobilitate* points toward the still stranger "feminism" of Guillaume Postel, like Agrippa a kabbalist and a scholar of prodigious and eccentric learning. Postel designed an apocalyptic scheme of world history wherein "the Mother of the World," a female savior heralded by Joan of Arc, was expected to complete Christ's work of redemption and inaugurate a new world order under feminine rule.[71] Agrippa's interest in divine androgyny would emerge anew in the theologies of such sects as the Behmenists, Philadelphians, Quakers, and Shakers. The first two groups, inspired by the esoteric mysticism of Jakob Boehme, cultivated visions of "the noble Virgin Sophia" and accepted the leadership of inspired women, in continuity with the late-medieval tradition of female prophecy.[72] For the Quakers and their offshoot, the Shakers, gender equality and female leadership were justified by Pauline exegesis in the same vein as Agrippa's: the new creation in Christ and the new dispensation of the Spirit overthrew the old barriers of sex and class.[73] Ironically, however, it was not these sectarians who appropriated *De nobilitate*, but a succession of mainline Protestants, liberal Catholics, and antireligious freethinkers with agendas that occluded precisely what is most original about that work. Contemporary feminist scholars can avoid the same error by turning from the clichés of the *querelle des femmes* to read Agrippa's tract in the highly charged religious context of its age.

Epilogue

> If a man who excels in beauty and stature, who surpasses others in the glory of his wealth and the nobility of his lineage, should chase the shadow of such vanity, it is no wonder, even if he has vowed the path of humility. But an arrogant woman is like a monster, for there is nothing more fragile than her sex.—*Speculum uirginum* (ca. 1140)[1]

> Christ was born into this world most humbly, and in order to expiate the pride of the first parent's sin by his humility, he assumed the male sex as the humbler one, not the more sublime and noble feminine sex.—Cornelius Agrippa, *De nobilitate et praecellentia foeminei sexus* (1529)[2]

Male pride, an understandable flaw; female pride, an unnatural vice. The *Speculum uirginum* was written around 1140, but with a few deft adaptations, these words could have been penned in 1540 or 1940. Indeed, there are large portions of the globe where they could be written still. "Plus ça change . . ." Agrippa's words, however, belong uniquely to his own historical moment and his peculiar theological daring. They presuppose the centrality of Adam and Eve, the still-normative theology of original sin and atonement; but they also bespeak a revolution in progress, both in religion and in the ideology of gender. Even in jest, such fighting words could not have been uttered a century before. Had they been written much later, the backlash of orthodox misogynism might have raised the specter of serious heresy, or the inroads of Enlightenment skepticism enfeebled their power to shock.[3]

Neither Agrippa's theology nor his feminism, both conceived "bitwixen game and ernest," was ever remotely mainstream. Yet the mere fact that such thoughts had become thinkable, albeit by a most extraordinary mind, testifies to a profound cultural change across the centuries that divide the *Speculum uirginum* from *De nobilitate*. That change is now recognized widely enough to have earned a name, "the feminization of Christianity," which I am hardly the first to declare. It was a movement more of hearts and souls than of religious institutions, although these too were involved. It emerges more profoundly from the witness of painters, poets, and mystics than from the tracts of academic theologians, though they also were affected. Lest we deceive ourselves, this "feminization" in no way abrogated the androcentric values of religion-as-usual. But it did complicate them; and despite the papal bulls, the persecutions and the pyres, late-medieval Christians gave ear to an unprecedented range of female voices.

These voices should not be flattened into unison, whether we would prefer to hear in them the serene monody of a Gregorian choir or the defiant chants of a picket line. No univocal discourse, no programmatic *écriture féminine* can encompass the commanding speech of Birgitta and Catherine of Siena, the subtle tones of Hadewijch and Julian, the impassioned cries of Angela and Mechthild, the fiery tongue of Na Prous Boneta. But each voice, whether strident or meek, struggled mightily to rise above the background noise of "the fathers" clamoring for silence.

Our knowledge of this struggle, still poignant on the umpteenth telling, can lure us into a facile but false assumption. We like to think it was because they were female, marginal, Other that such voices possessed a gratifyingly subversive éclat. It is mainly feminist scholarship that has brought them before the wider public they now enjoy, in some cases well beyond the confines of the academy, and the foregoing essays remain within this ambit. Yet I believe the time has come to break with at least one of its dominant paradigms. Medieval ecclesiastical authorities were preoccupied with binary classifications that often meant life or death to those on the receiving end: orthodox or heretic? obedient daughter or obstinate rebel? Generations of scholars, especially theologians and church historians, have followed in their wake, supplementing these oppositions with others more benign but frequently patronizing and misleading: *Wesensmystik* or *Minnemystik*? intellectual or affective? Regrettably, much feminist criticism remains within the old binary grid, though secularizing its labels and reversing its value judgments. Faced with the lives and texts of medieval religious women, we now ask: Is this oppression or subversion? self-destruction or empowerment? ventriloquized patriarchal ideology or proto-feminist revolt? The question is, within its own frame of reference, a valid one that has given rise to much useful analysis. Without the two decades of research motivated in part by such concerns, the essays in this book would not have been possible. Yet the "subversion question" is not finally adequate to the material at hand. For, if all historical questions are on some level mirrors of the historian's culture, this one is guaranteed to reflect, sooner and more fully than most, our own faces.

In lieu of this approach I suggest another, which may seem outrageous to some, self-evident to others. If modern readers perceive a baffling, beguiling "otherness" about the texts investigated here, it is not because their protagonists were women who set out to dismantle a hegemonic discourse, for that is a project deeply familiar to us. Their alterity lies rather in the fact that they were Christians. Of course their enemies were also Christians, and so too were the myriads who kept silence, the women history forgot. Christianity *was* the hegemonic discourse. Yet because this religion is *terra incognita* to most scholars in the postmodern academy, we forget too easily that neither "orthodoxy" nor "heresy"—much less "Christianity" or "the Church"—was ever a monolith. In pretending otherwise, we merely perpetuate the inquisitors' program of defining Insiders and Outsiders, even if we praise what they damned and damn what they praised. But once we acknowledge the capacious as well as contentious breadth of Christian discourse, we can move beyond the dichotomizing impulse to a fuller, freer understanding of medieval religious women. For it was not because of their commitment to feminism, self-empowerment, subversion, sexuality, or "the body" that they struggled and won their voices; it was because of their commitment to God. Thus only by taking their Christianity seriously can we hope to make sense of them. What matters is not how they were labeled, but how they articulated their beliefs, experiences, and practices in the texts that come down to us. In the most fortunate cases, we have their own words in their own language. In others we must make do with the complex layering of transcribed and translated texts, the praise of admiring confessors, or the queries of hostile judges. Even these texts, however, give access to a world of thought both more rewarding and more refractory than any dualities we might care to impose on it.

In the long run I believe a meticulous and attentive reading of the texts, with respect for their primary religious concerns, can tell us more even about questions of gender and power than an interrogation exclusively along those lines. Such a reading must also respect historical context—but not the artificial boundaries of academic disciplines. In the essays presented here I have deliberately examined the "orthodox" and the "heretics" together, and I have moved no less freely across the boundary between "religious" and "secular" literature. The disquieting phenomenon of child sacrifice, for example, is thematized in the genres of Marian lyric, drama, romance, and *consolatio*, but only in saints' lives do we see it functioning in the histories of actual women, however distanced and idealized by convention. These genres reciprocally illumine one another and show how women's Christianity both shaped and was shaped by their tragically alienated experience of motherhood. If the Christian ethos of redemptive sacrifice (along with nonreligious factors like arranged marriage, patrilineal kinship, the dowry system, and the high rate of infant mortality) helped to foster that alienation, it was also the sole consolation that medieval culture could provide for it. Indeed, it was to their Christianity that the exceptional women I have studied (and we must not forget how exceptional they were) brought not only their experience as mothers, but all their experiences. What made them *religious* women was not just their ambition, their eroticism, their illness and suffering, their artistic gifts, their yearning to be taken seriously, their rage at the abuse of power, their solidarity with the oppressed—but all of these transmuted by Christian faith, and in turn transmuting that faith into a decisively new form.

Gaining momentum over the course of centuries, this "new thing," this feminized Christianity, was crushed at last by the Reformation and constricted by the Counter-Reformation. But in the meantime it had changed the face of Christendom radically enough to make Agrippa's womanChrist fleetingly thinkable. Behind the heady contradictions of the Renaissance mage, we can now discern the lived paradox of innumerable religious women who, from the time of Heloise onward, wrestled in spirit with the conflicting gender ideals their masters set before them. On the one hand, the virile woman—fearless, outspoken, always ready for death—unmoved alike by family ties and tyrannical force. On the other, the bride of Christ—intimate, impassioned, always ready for love—and moved by every suffering creature's pain. But in the religion of the Cross, how long could death and love remain separate? The rhetoric is easy, but the living and dying were assuredly hard. Perhaps the last word should go to one, herself a master, who in obeying the traditional androcentric dictum—"conquer the woman"—found that in the process she had conquered God and man.

> Do not let lascivious mirth reduce you to your sex. Conquer the woman; conquer the flesh; conquer desire.—Osbert of Clare to the nun Ida of Barking (mid-twelfth century) [4]

> A voice of great thunder spoke to me . . . and said: "O strongest of all warriors! You have conquered all: you have opened the closed totality

that no creature ever opened, save by knowing with belabored and anxious Love how I am God and Man. O heroine, because you are so heroic and never yield, you are called the greatest of heroines: so it is right that you should know me to the full."—Hadewijch to a spiritual daughter (mid-thirteenth century) [5]

Abbreviations

AA.SS.	J. Bollandus and G. Henschenius et al., *Acta Sanctorum* . . . *editio novissima* (Paris: Palmé, 1863–)
CCCM	*Corpus christianorum: continuatio mediaevalis* (Turnhout: Brepols, 1966–)
CCSL	*Corpus christianorum: series latina* (Turnhout: Brepols, 1953–)
EETS	Early English Text Society
e.s.	extra series
MGH.SS	*Monumenta Germaniae historica. Scriptores rerum germanicarum* (Hannover: Hahnsche Buchhandlung, 1826–)
o.s.	original series
PL	J.-P. Migne, *Patrologiae cursus completus: series latina*, 221 vols. (Paris: Migne, 1861–64)
SC	*Sources chrétiennes* (Paris: Éditions du Cerf, 1941–)

Notes

Introduction

1. Gregory Lombardelli, *Life of the Blessed Aldobrandesca of Siena (1245–1310)*, ch. 3, trans. Elizabeth Petroff in *Consolation of the Blessed* (New York, 1979): 173.

2. I do not agree with R. Howard Bloch, *Medieval Misogyny and the Invention of Western Romantic Love* (Chicago, 1991), whose construction of misogyny as a monolithic discourse seems to me overstated and lacking in nuance. For critical responses to Bloch see the *Medieval Feminist Newsletter* 6 (1988), 7 (1989).

3. My interpretive standpoint has been diffusely influenced by contemporary feminist theology. I am indebted to such writers as Elisabeth Schüssler Fiorenza, Elizabeth Johnson, Sallie McFague, Rosemary Radford Ruether, and Dorothee Soelle. A useful anthology is Judith Plaskow and Carol Christ, eds., *Weaving the Visions: New Patterns in Feminist Spirituality* (San Francisco, 1989).

4. I borrow the term from Christin Lore Weber, *WomanChrist: A New Vision of Feminist Spirituality* (San Francisco, 1987). Its meaning is intentionally open-ended.

5. On this anthropology see especially Peter Brown, *The Body and Society: Men, Women and Sexual Renunciation in Early Christianity* (New York, 1988).

6. Jerome, *Commentarius in Epistolam ad Ephesios* III.5, in PL 26: 567a.

7. Kerstin Aspegren, *The Male Woman: A Feminine Ideal in the Early Church* (Uppsala, 1990).

8. See especially Averil Cameron, "Virginity as Metaphor: Women and the Rhetoric of Early Christianity," in *History as Text: The Writing of Ancient History* (London, 1989): 181–205.

9. Barbara Newman, *Sister of Wisdom: St. Hildegard's Theology of the Feminine* (Berkeley, 1987).

10. A good recent study is Brent Shaw, "The Passion of Perpetua," *Past & Present* 139 (1993): 3–45. See also Aspegren, *Male Woman*, 133–42.

11. By "constructivism," which I am rejecting only in its most extreme and uncompromising forms, I refer to the numerous brands of cultural and gender theory associated with Michel Foucault. For an eloquent defense of the position I am adopting here, see Nancy Partner, "No Sex, No Gender," *Speculum* 68 (1993): 419–43.

Chapter 1

1. "Cuius quidem rei defectu et indigentia nunc agitur ut ad eiusdem regulae professionem tam mares quam feminae in monasteriis suscipiantur, et idem institutionis monasticae iugum imponitur infirmo sexui aeque ut forti. Unam quippe nunc Regulam beati Benedicti apud Latinos feminae profitentur aeque ut viri. Quam sicut viris solummodo constat scriptam esse ita et ab ipsis tantum impleri posse tam subiectis pariter quam praelatis." J. T. Muckle, ed., "The Letter of Heloise on Religious Life and Abelard's First Reply," *Mediaeval Studies* 17 (1955): 242. The translation is from Betty Radice, *The Letters of Abelard and Heloise* (Harmondsworth, 1974): 159–60.

2. "Quippe sicut nomine et continentiae professione nobis estis conjunctae, ita etiam fere omnia nostra vobis competunt instituta." T. P. McLaughlin, ed., "Abelard's Rule for Religious Women," *Mediaeval Studies* 18 (1956): 243; trans. Radice, 184.

3. "Quippe quo infirmior est feminarum sexus, gratior est Deo atque perfectior earum virtus." Muckle, *Mediaeval Studies* 17 (1955): 268.

4. Mary McLaughlin, "Peter Abelard and the Dignity of Women: Twelfth Century 'Feminism' in Theory and Practice," in René Louis and Jean Jolivet, eds., *Pierre Abélard—Pierre le Vénérable: Les Courants philosophiques, littéraires, et artistiques en Occident au milieu du XIIe siècle*, Colloques Internationaux du Centre Nationale de la Recherche Scientifique, Abbaye de Cluny, 1972 (Paris, 1975): 287–333.

5. Jacqueline Smith, "Robert of Arbrissel: *Procurator mulierum*," in Derek Baker, ed., *Medieval Women* (Oxford, 1978): 175–84; Sally Thompson, "The Problem of the Cistercian Nuns in the Twelfth and Early Thirteenth Centuries," in ibid., 227–52; Kaspar Elm, "Die Stellung der Frau in Ordenwesen, Semireligiösentum und Häresie zur Zeit der heiligen Elisabeth," in *Sankt Elisabeth: Fürstin, Dienerin, Heilige* (Sigmaringen, 1981): 7–28; Jane Schulenburg, "Sexism and the Celestial Gynaeceum—from 500 to 1200," *Journal of Medieval History* 4 (1978): 117–33. For broader studies of women's monasteries in this period see Sharon Elkins, *Holy Women of Twelfth-Century England* (Chapel Hill, 1988) and Penelope Johnson, *Equal in Monastic Profession: Religious Women in Medieval France* (Chicago, 1991).

6. Peter Dinzelbacher and Dieter Bauer, eds., *Frauenmystik im Mittelalter* (Ostfildern, 1985); John Nichols and Lillian T. Shank, eds., *Peaceweavers*, vol. 2 of *Medieval Religious Women* (Kalamazoo, 1987); Gertrud J. Lewis, *Bibliographie zur deutschen Frauenmystik des Mittelalters* (Berlin, 1989); Elizabeth Petroff, *Consolation of the Blessed* (New York, 1979); eadem, *Medieval Women's Visionary Literature* (Oxford, 1986); Caroline Walker Bynum, *Holy Feast and Holy Fast: The Religious Significance of Food to Medieval Women* (Berkeley, 1987); Ulrike Wiethaus, ed., *Maps of Flesh and Light: The Religious Experience of Medieval Women Mystics* (Syracuse, 1993).

7. Many of these texts are discussed by Caroline Walker Bynum in *Docere verbo et exemplo: An Aspect of Twelfth-Century Spirituality* (Missoula, 1979). This volume is concerned with the differences between monks and regular canons, and consequently does not consider works written for nuns or solitaries.

8. See Appendix A for a listing. One text, John of Fruttuaria's *Tractatus de ordine vitae*, was written a few decades earlier, and Stephen of Sawley's *Speculum*

novitii may be slightly later than the period covered in this study. But both these works circulated under St. Bernard's name and were thus received by medieval readers as part of the mainstream of twelfth-century formative spirituality.

9. See, for instance, Volker Honemann, *Die Epistola ad fratres de Monte Dei des Wilhelm von Saint-Thierry: Lateinische Überlieferung und mittelalterliche Übersetzungen* (Munich, 1978); Giles Constable, "The Popularity of Twelfth-Century Spiritual Authors in the Late Middle Ages," in Anthony Molho and John Tedeschi, eds., *Renaissance Studies in Honor of Hans Baron* (DeKalb, 1971): 5–28.

10. Charles Dumont, introduction to Aelred de Rievaulx, *La Vie de recluse*, SC 76 (Paris, 1961): 34–36. The *Ancrene Wisse*, long anonymous, has now been attributed to Brian of Lingen, an Augustinian canon of Wigmore in Herefordshire: E. J. Dobson, *The Origins of Ancrene Wisse* (Oxford, 1976).

11. Matthäus Bernards, *Speculum virginum: Geistigkeit und Seelenleben der Frau im Hochmittelalter* (Cologne, 1955; rpt. 1982): 6–13; idem, "Die mittelrheinischen Handschriften des Jungfrauenspiegels," *Archiv für mittelrheinische Kirchengeschichte* 3 (1951): 357–64.

12. Cf. Tage R. Ahldén, *Nonnenspiegel und Mönchsvorschriften* (Goteborg, 1952), on the diffusion of a thirteenth-century text by David of Augsburg.

13. For Heloise's antifeminism, see the polemic against marriage ascribed to her in Abelard's *Historia calamitatum*, ed. Muckle, *Mediaeval Studies* 12 (1950): 185–89; the list of men destroyed by evil women in her second epistle, *Mediaeval Studies* 15 (1953): 79–80; and formulaic remarks about female weakness and corruption in her third letter, *Mediaeval Studies* 17 (1955): 242–43, 246, 262. Hildegard argued that woman, as a "weak and infirm habitation," was unfit for the priesthood: *Scivias* 2.6.76, ed. Adelgundis Führkötter, CCCM 43 (Turnhout, 1978): 290. On several occasions she referred to her own era contemptuously as an "effeminate age," PL 197: 167b, 185c, 1005ab. Cf. Barbara Newman, *Sister of Wisdom: St. Hildegard's Theology of the Feminine* (Berkeley, 1987): 238–47.

14. "Viros se nominant, sed inter effeminatos se moribus collocant." Peter of Celle, *De disciplina claustrali* 10, ed. Gérard de Martel, *L'École du cloître*, SC 240 (Paris, 1977): 186.

15. "Quae ubi perfectae rationis incipit esse, non tantum capax, sed et particeps, continuo abdicat a se notam generis feminei, et efficitur animus particeps rationis, regendo corpori accommodatus, vel seipsum habens spiritus. Quamdiu enim anima est, cito in id quod carnale est effeminatur; animus vero, vel spiritus, non nisi quod virile est et spirituale meditatur." William of St.-Thierry, *Epistola ad fratres de Monte Dei* 198, ed. Jean Déchanet, *Lettre aux frères du Mont-Dieu*, SC 223 (Paris, 1975): 306–8; translation adapted from Theodore Berkeley, trans., *The Golden Epistle: A Letter to the Brethren at Mont Dieu* (Kalamazoo, 1976): 79; cf. 35n.

16. "[L]asciuia mutat et dissoluit, titubatio effeminat et confundit, . . . delicie uirilem animum feminam reddunt. . . . Si uir forme prestantis et stature diuitiarum gloria, linea nobilitatis ceteris eminentior et clarus uanitatis huius umbram captauerit, mirum non est, etiamsi humilitatis callem professus est, quod uero mulier, quo sexu nihil fragilius est, in alta leuatur, monstro simile est. . . . Spiritus sanctus in hoc loco, mollicie uili solutam, et in opere dei desidem pro muliere posuit animam; que licet rectis intendat operibus, nihil tamen mercedis fere consequitur, studiis suis pigricia quadam fluitantibus. . . . Porro uirum animum uult intelligi uirilem

et sensum rationabilem, qui dum feruido spiritalis exercicii semper cursu mouetur, interdum in ipso recti studii zelo et si modicum offendere cogitur, que offensio quasi quedam in celestibus exerciciis macula iniquitatis nomen accepit." *Speculum uirginum* IV, VI, IX, ed. Jutta Seyfarth, CCCM 5 (Turnhout, 1990): 95, 173, 260. On the text from Ecclesiasticus see M. L. Arduini, "Il tema 'vir' e 'mulier' nell' esegesi patristica e medioeuale di Eccli. XLII.14," *Aevum* 55 (1981): 246–61.

17. "Non te lasciva iocunditas reducat ad sexum. Vince mulierem, vince carnem, vince libidinem." *The Letters of Osbert of Clare* 40, ed. E. W. Williamson (London, 1929): 139.

18. "[P]ura hominis meditatio sub viri nomine mystice describitur; infirma vero cogitatio mulieris titulo praenotatur. bona vero opera ad masculum referimus; actus autem noxios sexus inferioris charactere figuramus." Ibid. 42; Williamson, 170. Not long after receiving this letter from Osbert, Alice of Barking was accused by her archbishop of sexual misconduct: see Elkins, *Holy Women*, 148–49.

19. "[N]on enim expedit illi sexui proprii regiminis uti libertate, tum propter ejus naturalem mutabilitatem, tum propter tentationes extrinsecus advenientes, quibus mulieris infirmitas non sufficit resistere." Idung of Prüfening, *Argumentum super quatuor quaestionibus* 7, ed. Bernhard Pez, *Thesaurus anecdotorum novissimus* II.2 (Augsburg, 1721): 528; trans. Joseph Leahey in *Cistercians and Cluniacs* (Kalamazoo, 1977): 176.

20. Ambrose Wathen, *Silence: The Meaning of Silence in the Rule of St. Benedict* (Washington, 1973).

21. Philip of Harvengt, *De institutione clericorum*, PL 203: 665–1206. Most of the treatise *De silentio clericorum* deals with preaching. See Bynum, *Docere verbo et exemplo*, 50–55.

22. "Recte virum perfectum appellat, qui quasi vir viriliter stando in sermone suo offendendo non titubat; fragilis enim et quasi femineus esse convincitur, qui non solum otiosa vel levia proferendo, et quasi in minimis offendendo, huc illucque vacillando dilabitur, verum et impellente ira, praecipitante furore, nullo moderamine retinens fraenum linguae, . . . totus penitus conquassatur." Odo of St.-Victor, *Epistolae de observantia canonicae professionis recte praestanda* 4, PL 196: 1407ab.

23. "Nam si hoc ad quemlibet virum honestum pertinet, quanto magis ad feminam, quanto magis ad virginem, quanto magis ad inclusam?" Aelred of Rievaulx, *De institutione inclusarum* 5, ed. C. H. Talbot, CCCM 1 (Turnhout, 1971): 641.

24. "Quae quanto in vobis subtilior et ex mollitie corporis vestri flexibilior, tanto mobilior et etiam in verba pronior existit . . ." *Regula sanctimonialium* (McLaughlin, 245; trans. Radice, 188).

25. Abelard, *Epistola de studio litterarum*, PL 178: 332–33.

26. R. Howard Bloch, "Medieval Misogyny," *Representations* 20 (1987): 3.

27. Brenda Bolton, "Mulieres sanctae," in Susan M. Stuard, ed., *Women in Medieval Society* (Philadelphia, 1976): 141–58; eadem, "Vitae Matrum: A Further Aspect of the *Frauenfrage*," in Derek Baker, ed., *Medieval Women*, 253–73.

28. "Mulieribus tamen semper in penitentia iniungendum est quod sint predicatrices virorum suorum. Nullus enim sacerdos ita potest cor viri emollire sicut potest uxor. . . . Debet enim in cubiculo et inter medios amplexus virum suum

blande alloqui, et si durus est et immisericors et oppressor pauperum, debet eum invitare ad misericordiam; si raptor est, debet detestari rapinam; si avarus est, suscitet in eo largitatem." Thomas of Chobham, *Summa confessorum* 7.2.15, ed. F. Broomfield, *Analecta mediaevalia Namurcensia* 25 (Louvain, 1968): 375. See Sharon Farmer, "Persuasive Voices: Clerical Images of Medieval Wives," *Speculum* 61 (1986): 517–43.

29. "O Dina, quid necesse est ut videas mulieres alienigenas? . . . Tu curiose spectas, sed curiosius spectaris. Quis crederet tunc illam tuam curiosam otiositatem, vel otiosam curiositatem, fore post sic non otiosam, sed tibi, tuis, hostibusque tam perniciosam?" Bernard of Clairvaux, *De gradibus humilitatis et superbiae* 10.29, ed. Jean Leclercq and Henri Rochais, *Sancti Bernardi Opera* (Rome, 1957–1977): III, 39; trans. M. Ambrose Conway, *Treatises II* (Kalamazoo, 1980): 58.

30. Osbert, *Letters* 41 (Williamson, 143); Idung of Prüfening, *Argumentum* 7 (Pez, 525); Peter of Celle, *De disciplina claustrali* 4 (de Martel, 146); Hugh of Fouilloy, *De claustro animae* 3.1, PL 176: 1087–88; Stephen of Sawley, "A Mirror for Novices" 24, trans. Jeremiah O'Sullivan in *Treatises* (Kalamazoo, 1984): 117; *Speculum virginum* II (Seyfarth, 44).

31. "[H]eo is gulti of þe bestes deaðe biuoren vre louerd. 7 schal uor his soule onswerien adomesdei 7 ʒelden þe bestes lure. hwon heo naueð oþer ʒeld; buten hire suluen." *The English Text of the Ancrene Riwle* (London, BL Cotton Nero A.XIV), ed. Mabel Day, EETS 225 (London, 1952): 25; *Ancrene Riwle*, trans. Mary Salu (Notre Dame, 1955): 23–25.

32. On the consequences of this rule, see Jane Schulenburg, "Strict Active Enclosure and Its Effects on the Female Monastic Experience (500–1100)," in John Nichols and Lillian T. Shank, eds., *Distant Echoes*, vol. 1 of *Medieval Religious Women* (Kalamazoo, 1984): 51–86.

33. On women's use of inverted misogyny, see Peter Dronke, *Women Writers of the Middle Ages: A Critical Study of Texts from Perpetua (†203) to Marguerite Porete (†1310)* (Cambridge, 1984): 64–79; Barbara Newman, "Divine Power Made Perfect in Weakness: St Hildegard on the Frail Sex," in *Peaceweavers*, 103–22.

34. "[S]i in viris virtus rara est avis in terris, quanto magis in femina fragili et nobili? Denique mulierem fortem quis inveniet? Multo magis quis fortem et nobilem?" Bernard, *Epistolae* 113, PL 182: 256d. The *rara avis in terris*, a tag from Juvenal's Sixth Satire, exposes the antifeminist tradition on which Bernard drew even in his oblique praise of a woman.

35. Ibid., *Epistolae* 114, PL 182: 259c.

36. "[T]alem te fieri cupio, splendida et clara virgo, immo de viro Christo virilis et incorrupta virago." "Nulla ante illam femina huius praerogativae dignitatem obtinuit, neque post illam obtinebit ulterius." Osbert, *Letters* 40, 42; Williamson, 136, 155.

37. On the origins of the topos, see Rosemary Ruether, "Misogynism and Virginal Feminism in the Fathers of the Church," in *Religion and Sexism: Images of Woman in the Jewish and Christian Traditions* (New York, 1974): 150–83; Jo Ann McNamara, *A New Song: Celibate Women in the First Three Christian Centuries* (New York, 1983): 108–15.

38. Abelard, *De auctoritate vel dignitate ordinis sanctimonialium*, ed. Muckle, *Mediaeval Studies* 17 (1955): 253–81.

39. Both the text of this rule and its practical status are shrouded in confusion; its complete text is extant in only one MS containing the correspondence, and it differs in several particulars from a later rule apparently written by Heloise, PL 178: 313–26. Cf. Rudolf Mohr, "Der Gedankenaustausch zwischen Heloisa und Abaelard über eine Modifizierung der *Regula Benedicti* für Frauen," *Regulae Benedicti Studia* 5 (1976): 307–33; Linda Georgianna, "Any Corner of Heaven: Heloise's Critique of Monasticism," *Mediaeval Studies* 49 (1987): 221–53.

40. "Praepositum autem monachorum quem abbatem nominant sic etiam monialibus praeesse volumus ut eas quae Domini sponsae sunt cujus ipse servus est proprias recognoscat dominas nec eis praeesse sed prodesse gaudeat. . . . Omnes quoque fratres in professionibus suis hoc se sororibus sacramento astringent quod nullatenus eas gravari consentient et earum carnali munditiae pro posse suo providebunt." Abelard, *Regula* (McLaughlin, 259–60; trans. Radice, 212–13).

41. Abelard also followed Robert of Arbrissel's rule for Fontevrault in specifying that the abbess should be a matron with experience of the world, not a virgin raised in the cloister. On Fontevrault see Jacqueline Smith, "Robert of Arbrissel"; Penny Schine Gold, "Male/Female Cooperation: The Example of Fontevrault," in *Distant Echoes*, 151–68.

42. Among the exceptions are two letters from Anselm to a certain Robert and a group of women under Robert's direction, in *Sancti Anselmi Opera omnia*, ed. Franciscus Schmitt (Edinburgh, 1946–61): IV, 134–35 and V, 359–62, and Geoffrey of Vendôme's epistle 48 to the recluses Hervé and Eve, PL 157: 184–86. These letters contain nothing gender-specific, but all were addressed to a mixed audience. Caroline Bynum has argued that in the later middle ages, gender was a concern far more central to male writers than to female writers. "'. . . And Woman His Humanity': Female Imagery in the Religious Writing of the Later Middle Ages," in *Fragmentation and Redemption: Essays on Gender and the Human Body in Medieval Religion* (New York, 1991): 151–79.

43. Cf. Shulamith Shahar's classification of women as a "fourth estate" following the three traditional *ordines*. *The Fourth Estate: A History of Women in the Middle Ages*, trans. Chaya Galai (London, 1983).

44. "Huc accedit; quod virginitatem corporis per vim illatam potest perdere, quod in masculo ipsa natura repellit. . . . vasa quanto sunt fragiliora, tanto diligentiori egent custodia, illa scilicet, quae fit, ne vas frangatur, non illa, quae sit, ne furto vel rapina auferatur, quam aurea vasa magis requirunt, quam vitrea. Foemina vero Sanctimonialis exigit utramque, quia parabolice potest dici vas vitreum propter fragilem sexum, & vas aureum propter virginalis Sanctimoniae propositum." Idung of Prüfening, *Argumentum* 6 (Pez, 521–22; trans. Leahey, 168–69).

45. "Virginitas aurum est, cella fornax, conflator diabolus, ignis tentatio. Caro virginis, vas luteum est, in quo aurum reconditur, ut probetur." Aelred, *De institutione inclusarum* 14 (Talbot, 650).

46. "Þis bruchele uetles is bruchelure þene beo eni gles. uor beo hit enes to broken. ibet ne bið hit neuer. ne ihol ase hit er was." *Ancrene Riwle* (Day, 73; trans. Salu, 72).

47. This caveat is ubiquitous in the virginity literature. Cf. Augustine, *Enarrationes in Psalmos* 99.13, PL 37: 1280; Caesarius of Arles, *Homilia* 12, PL 67: 1074;

Speculum virginum II (Seyfarth, 56); Thomas of Froidmont, *Liber de modo bene vivendi ad sororem* 22.64, PL 184: 1239d.

48. "Cujus quanto superior est gradus, tanto gravior est casus. Cui perseveranti quanto felicior et suprema speranda est glorificatio, tanto cadenti miserior et extrema est timenda damnatio." Ivo of Chartres, *Epistolae* 10, ed. Jean Leclercq, *Correspondance* (Paris, 1949): I, 40–42.

49. "Et, cum omni peccato per poenitentiam medeamur, solus lapsus virginum restitutionis remedium non meretur." Peter of Blois, *Epistolae* 35, PL 207: 114c.

50. "Ah se þu herre stondest, beo sarre offearet to fallen; for se herre degre, se þe fal is wurse. Þe ontfule deouel bihalt te se hehe istihe towart heouene þurh meiðhades mihte, . . . ant scheote[ð] niht ant dei his earewen, idrencte of an attri healewi, towart tin heorte to wundi þe wið wac wil, ant makien to fallen, as Crist te forbeode!" *Hali Meidhad,* ed. Bella Millett, EETS 284 (Oxford, 1982): 7.

51. Ibid. 11–12.

52. "Divisit enim [Deus] inter te et me quasi inter lucem et tenebras, te sibi conservans, me mihi relinquens. . . . Quam miser ego tunc qui meam pudicitiam perdidi, tam beata tu, cuius virginitatem gratia divina protexit. . . . Verumtamen et me nolo aemuleris, valdeque putes erubescendum, si post tot flagitia, in illa vita tibi fuero inventus aequalis, cum saepe virginitatis gloriam intervenientia quaedam vitia minuant, et veteris conversationis opprobrium morum mutatio et succedentes vitiis virtutes obliterent." Aelred, *De institutione inclusarum* 32 (Talbot, 674, 676).

53. Marsha Dutton-Stuckey has shown that Aelred casts himself in the role of the prodigal son and thus places his sister in the invidious position of "elder brother." "A Prodigal Writes Home: Aelred of Rievaulx' *De institutione inclusarum,*" in E. Rozanne Elder, ed., *Heaven on Earth* (Kalamazoo, 1983): 35–42.

54. Clarissa Atkinson, " 'Precious Balsam in a Fragile Glass': The Ideology of Virginity in the Later Middle Ages," *Journal of Family History* 8 (1983): 131–43.

55. *Book of Margery Kempe,* 22, trans. Barry Windeatt (Harmondsworth, 1985): 88.

56. A rare exception is the romance hero Galahad, whose success in the Grail quest depends on his perfect virginity. But I have yet to discover an instance in the literature of formation where a male virgin is celebrated in the same way as a female virgin. An interesting proof-text is Rev. 14:4. The 144,000 virgins honored in this verse are male (they "have not defiled themselves with women"), yet in medieval usage the text was applied almost exclusively to females.

57. Bernard, *Epistolae* 113, PL 182: 258–59.

58. "[I]n illa enim superni imperatoris aula erunt paranymphi tui angeli, cives dei, ut te ad regis introducant cubiculum, et investiant purpura et bysso coloribus intinctis, sanctorum praerogativa meritorum: virginitas vero tua, quae in sacris nuptiis nescit dispendium castitatis, diademate coronata radiabit aureo, et pretiosi lapides tuo subtilius inserentur vestimento." Osbert, *Letters* 22 (Williamson, 91–92).

59. "Si vis nubere terrestri marito propter divitias, considera quod terrenae divitiae fallaces sunt et transitoriae, quia aut in praesenti vita transeunt, aut saltem in morte recedunt. Nube ergo illi, apud quem thesauri sunt incomparabiles, et divitiae immutabiles; quas nec fur furatur, nec tinea demolitur. Si autem vis nubere

terrestri viro, quia pulchritudine insignitur, considera quia pulchritudinem aut infirmitas extenuat, aut senectus exstirpat, aut saltem articulus mortis exterminat. Nube ergo illi, cujus pulchritudinem sol et luna mirantur." Alan of Lille, *Summa de arte praedicatoria* 47, PL 210: 195bc. The ultimate source of these comparisons is Wisd. Sol. 8, where it is argued that Wisdom is the most desirable bride. Alan simply reverses the genders.

60. Katharina Wilson, *Wykked Wyves and the Woes of Marriage: Misogamous Literature from Juvenal to Chaucer* (Albany, 1990).

61. *Speculum virginum* VII (Seyfarth, 195–97), gives several anti-marital exempla (David and Bathsheba, Samson and Delilah, Susanna and the elders, Solomon and his harem) in which men are undone by women.

62. "Nesciunt virgines quid ex maritali licentia mulieris sustineat infirmitas. Nesciunt, inquam, quibus uxor subjiciatur injuriis, quanta fecundam sauciet anxietas, quo sterilis moerore crucietur. Si formosa est, difficile caret infamia; deformem maritus aspernatur. Nunquam lectus est sine rixa, cujus vel pudet vel taedet conjugalem." Hildebert of Lavardin, *Epistolae* 1.21, PL 171: 194bc.

63. "Filiae hujus saeculi filiae Babylonis, quae de carnis immunditia sibi destinant successores, in peccato concipiunt, in dolore pariunt, in timore nutriunt, de viventibus semper sollicitae sunt, de morientibus inconsolabiliter affliguntur. Si vis parere, vis perire." Peter of Blois, *Epistolae* 55, PL 207: 167bc.

64. "Magna differentia est inter caelestes nuptias et terrenas. . . . [P]allida facies eius efficitur et oculorum claritas densa caligine concavatur: . . . pellicula rugas in facie contrahit et rotunditas digitorum in manibus tabescit: uterus intumescens impregnantis distenditur, et viscera intrinsecus gravidata dissipantur. . . . nec alio modo onusta gemmis et auro concipit aut parit in palatio quam inops et pannosa mulier in tugurio." Osbert, *Letters* 40 (Williamson, 136).

65. "[B]ikimeð þeow under mon, ant his þrel, to don al ant drehen þet him likeð, ne sitte hit hire se uuele." *Hali Meidhad* 2–3.

66. "Ant hwet ʒef ich easki ʒet, þah hit þunche egede, hu þet wif stonde, þe ihereð hwen ha kimeð in hire bearn schreamen, sið þe cat et te fliche ant ed te hude þe hund, hire cake bearnen o þe stan ant hire kelf suken, þe crohe eornen i þe fur— ant te cheorl chideð?" Ibid. 19.

67. The *trobairitz* lyric "Na Carenza al bel cors avinen" offers similar advice to women: one sister finds the thought of marriage depressing and another expresses the view that "having children is a penance," so the third counsels both to bear glorious seed by marrying "Coronat de Scienza," or Christ. Dronke, *Women Writers*, 101–3.

68. "For Gode, þah hit nere neauer for Godes luue, ne for hope of heouene, ne for dred of helle, þu ahtest, wummon, þis werc for þi flesches halschipe, for þi licomes luue, ant ti bodies heale, ouer alle þing to schunien." *Hali Meidhad* 17.

69. On its theory and practice see Georges Duby, *The Knight, the Lady and the Priest: The Making of Modern Marriage in Medieval France*, trans. Barbara Bray (New York, 1983); David Herlihy, *Medieval Households* (Cambridge, MA, 1985); Christopher Brooke, *The Medieval Idea of Marriage* (Oxford, 1991).

70. Peter Brown, *The Body and Society: Men, Women and Sexual Renunciation in Early Christianity* (New York, 1988).

71. M.-D. Chenu, "Monks, Canons, and Laymen in Search of the Apostolic Life," in *Nature, Man, and Society in the Twelfth Century: Essays on New Theological Perspectives in the Latin West*, trans. Jerome Taylor and Lester K. Little (Chicago, 1968): 202–38; Bynum, *Docere verbo et exemplo*.

72. Foundations of canonesses were analogous in name only, since these aristocratic houses—found chiefly in Germany—were often allied with noble families and lacked the apostolic impulse, as well as the clerical status, of the new canons.

73. Thompson, "The Problem of the Cistercian Nuns"; John Freed, "Urban Development and the 'Cura Monialium' in Thirteenth-Century Germany," *Viator* 3 (1972): 311–27.

74. Alan of Lille, *Summa* 43, 47, PL 210: 189–91, 194–95.

75. Peter of Blois, *Sermones* 62–64, PL 207: 741–50.

76. Abelard, *Regula* (McLaughlin, 252–54, 257). Abelard was obviously thinking of Heloise herself.

77. "Et sit [abbas] tamquam dispensator in domo regia qui non imperio dominam premit, sed providentiam erga eam gerit . . . Quae quibus officiis ipsa praeceperit et quantum voluerit praesint, ut sint videlicet istae quasi duces vel consules in exercitu dominico. Reliquae autem omnes tamquam milites vel pedites, istarum cura eis praevidente, adversus malignum ejusque satellites libere pugnent." Ibid., McLaughlin 259, 252; trans. Radice 212, 198–99.

78. "Si de fatuis [virginibus es], congregatio tibi necessaria est: si de prudentibus, tu congregationi. . . . Sive peccatrix, sive sancta sis, noli te separare a grege." Bernard, *Epistolae* 115, PL 182: 262ab.

79. "Cum sit inter alias sorores uirgo Christi maxima uel magisterio uel artis scientia siue nobilitatis linea seu uirtutum gratia, sit tamen omnium minima, mente sit omnium ancilla . . . Sed de his quid rogo dicendum est, qui leuato supercilio de linea generis inter alias sorores socialis gratie limitem excedunt conditionem diuidentes ac per hoc nature communi de priuato gloriando detrahentes? . . . Quod si carnem respicias, mira nobilitas est, mira generis claritudo, ubi uermis de uerme nascitur et putredo de puluere laudatur." *Speculum uirginum* IV, IX (Seyfarth 109–10, 265–66).

80. Hildegard of Bingen, *Epistolarium* 50r, 150r, 151, 159r, 186r, 237r (on perseverance in the abbatial role); *Epp.* 94r, 177r (against excessive abstinence). Ed. Lieven van Acker, CCCM 91–91A (Turnhout, 1991, 1993).

81. "Et quis homo congregat omnem gregem suum in unum stabulum, scilicet boves, asinos, oves, hedos, ita quod non discrepant se? Ideo et discretio sit in hoc, ne diversus populus in unum gregem congregatus in superbia elationis et in ignominia diversitatis dissipetur, et precipue ne honestas morum ibi dirumpatur, cum se invicem odio dilaniant, quando altior ordo super inferiorem cadit et quando inferior super altiorem ascendit." Hildegard, *Epistolarium* 52r, in Van Acker, CCCM 91, 129. Cf. Alfred Haverkamp, "Tenxwind von Andernach und Hildegard von Bingen: Zwei 'Weltanschauungen' in der Mitte des 12. Jahrhunderts," in Lutz Fenske, Werner Rösener, and Thomas Zotz, eds., *Institutionen, Kultur und Gesellschaft im Mittelalter* (Sigmaringen, 1984): 515–48.

82. Aloys Schulte, *Der Adel und die deutsche Kirche im Mittelalter*, 3rd ed. (Darmstadt, 1958).

83. "Boðe hit is riht þet heo dreden 7 luuien. auh þet ðer beo more euer of luue: þen of drede." *Ancrene Riwle* (Day, 195; trans. Salu, 191).

84. Honorius, *De vita claustrali*, PL 172: 1247–48.

85. Hugh of Fouilloy, *De claustro animae* 1.9–17, PL 176: 1033–49.

86. Peter of Celle, *De disciplina claustrali* 11–17; de Martel, 188–224.

87. Peter of Porto, *Regula clericorum* 2.28, PL 163: 730c.

88. "[O]stendendum est Deo auxiliante, quae in talibus Dei servis differentia, quae intentionis sit in diversis professionibus forma. Ad demonstrandum ergo quod istae diversitates professionum Deo placeant accingor." *Libellus de diversis ordinibus et professionibus qui sunt in aecclesia*, ed. and trans. Giles Constable and B. Smith (Oxford, 1972): 2–3. The treatise discusses different types of hermits, monks, and canons; a projected second book on the varieties of religious women was apparently never written.

89. Jean Leclercq, "Deux opuscules sur la formation des jeunes moines," *Revue d'ascétique et de mystique* 33 (1957): 390–91.

90. "Solent animi leves minimeque fundati, cum audierint quosdam in diversis virtutibus ac studiis bonis magnifice praedicari, ita eorum laude succendi, ut eorum imitari statum protinus desiderent. At frustra; nam ex hujusmodi mutatione ac varietate propositi, dispendium capiunt, non profectum; quia qui multa sequitur, nihil integre consequetur. Ideo hoc unicuique expediens est, ut secundum propositum quod elegit, et gratiam quam accepit, summo studio ac diligentia ad operis arrepti perfectionem pervenire festinet: aliorum laudes amet, et admiretur virtutes, ac nequaquam a sua, quam semel elegit, professione discedat. Multis namque viis ad Deum tenditur." Stephen of Sawley, *Speculum novitii* 24, ed. Edmond Mikkers, *Collectanea ordinis Cisterciensium Reformatorum* 8 (1946): 67; trans. O'Sullivan, 118. The passage cited is from Cassian's *Collationes* 14.5–6, PL 49: 959–60.

91. For Adam's career, see Jean Bouvet, introduction to Adam de Perseigne, *Lettres*, SC 66 (Paris, 1960): 7–29.

92. "Per lorum quippe promissae stabilitatis tanquam pia iumenta ad caeleste praesepium religamur." Letter 5 to Osmund of Mortemer, *De institutione novitiorum* 61, in ibid. 126.

93. See Brian McGuire, *Friendship and Community: The Monastic Experience, 350–1250* (Kalamazoo, 1988).

94. R. W. Southern, "Peter of Blois: A Twelfth Century Humanist?" in *Medieval Humanism* (New York, 1970): 123.

95. "[I]n rebus humanis nihil sanctius appetatur, nihil quaeratur utilius, nihil difficilius inveniatur, nihil experiatur dulcius, nihil fructuosius teneatur." "Dicamne de amicitia quod amicus Iesu Ioannes de caritate commemorat: Deus amicitia est?" Aelred, *De spiritali amicitia* 2.9, 1.69, ed. Anselm Hoste, *Opera omnia*, CCCM 1 (Turnhout, 1971): 303–04, 301; trans. Mary Eugenia Laker, *Spiritual Friendship* (Kalamazoo, 1977): 71, 65.

96. "[V]iginti simul vel triginta singulis diebus conferrent ad invicem de spirituali iocunditate scripturarum et ordinis disciplinis. . . . super grabatum illius ambulantes et decumbentes loquebantur cum eo ut parvulus confabulabatur cum matre sua. . . . Non sic infrunite agebat cum suis ut est quorundam consuetudo

abbatum insipiencium qui, si monachus socii manum tenuerit sua vel aliqua dixerit quod illis displiceat, cappam postulant, fratrem spoliant et expellunt. Non sic Alredus, non sic." *Walter Daniel's Life of Ailred*, ed. and trans. F. M. Powicke (London, 1950): 40.

97. John Boswell, *Christianity, Social Tolerance, and Homosexuality: Gay People in Western Europe from the Beginning of the Christian Era to the Fourteenth Century* (Chicago, 1980): 221–26.

98. Guibert of Nogent, *De virginitate* (PL 156: 579–80, 608bc). On Guibert's personality, see John Benton's introduction to *Self and Society in Medieval France: The Memoirs of Abbot Guibert of Nogent* (New York, 1970).

99. Ibid. 9, PL 156: 594–96.

100. "Nihil enim pulchrius, quam eos et magistros vitae habere et testes. Pulchra itaque copula seniorum atque adolescentium." John of Fruttuaria, *Tractatus de ordine vitae et morum institutione*, PL 184: 567a. For the attribution of this work to John, see André Wilmart, "Jean l'Homme de Dieu: auteur d'un traité attribué à saint Bernard," *Auteurs spirituels et textes dévots du moyen âge latin* (Paris, 1932): 64–100.

101. "Nascitur etiam ex amica frequenti et honesta collocutione commendabilis quaedam familiaritas, per quam magister efficitur ad corripiendum audacior, correptus ad disciplinam patientior, uterque ad intelligentiam Scripturarum eruditior." Adam of Perseigne, *Lettres* 5.57; Bouvet, 118.

102. "Neminem habeat familiarem. . . . Si autem familiaritas interdicitur hominum, quanto magis mulierum?" Arnulf of Bohéries, *Speculum monachorum*, PL 184: 1176–77. The antithesis of *homines* and *mulieres* is disturbingly frequent in the literature.

103. "Nullam certe personam te frequentius visitare vellem, nec cum aliqua te crebrius visitante familiare te vellem habere secretum. Periclitatur enim fama virginis crebra certae alicuius personae salutatione, periclitatur et conscientia." Aelred of Rievaulx, *De institutione inclusarum* 7; Talbot, 642.

104. "[S]ed vitiorum materias, gulam, somnum, requiem corporis, feminarum et effeminatorum familiaritatem atque convictum infra metas necessitatis cohibeamus." "Illa intuetur singulas, et inter puellares motus, nunc irascitur, nunc ridet, nunc minatur, nunc blanditur, nunc percutit, nunc osculatur, nunc flentem pro verbere vocat propius, palpat faciem, stringit collum, et in amplexum ruens, nunc filiam vocat, nunc amicam. Qualis inter haec memoria Dei . . . ?" Ibid. 23, 4; Talbot, 656, 640–41.

105. Ivo of Chartres, *Epistolae* 10; Leclercq, 42–48.

106. Thomas of Froidmont, *Liber de modo bene vivendi* 13, PL 184: 1222–24. This uninspired text was for a long time inexplicably ascribed to St. Bernard.

107. "Charissima soror, fuge societatem saecularium mulierum. . . . Sicut sirena per dulces cantus decipit marinarios, ita saecularis femina per suos deceptorios sermones decipit Christi servos. . . . Soror charissima, si tanto studio fugies feminas, quanto magis debes fugere viros? . . . moneo te, ut vir quamvis sit sanctus, nullam tamen tecum habeat societatem." Ibid. 57–58, PL 184: 1285–86.

108. "Vbi enim promiscuum sexum uirorum scilicet ac mulierum sanctitati licet assignatum paries unus distincte concludit, quamuis sanctitas utrorumque

miraculorum fulmine montes feriat, fide et precum maiestate montes moueat, tamen nisi timor et amor dei intercesserit, aduersariorum calumnie commanentia patebit." *Speculum uirginum* V; Seyfarth, 156.

109. "Sanctas igitur amicicias quere, unde possis adiuuari, si te constiterit aliqua aduersitate pulsari. Compedem pedibus suis innectit, qui se in amiciciam alterius, cuius mores ignorat, sine consideratione transfundit. Itaque morosa deliberatione morem eius et uitam, que eligenda est, precurre et sic probatam amicicie admitte. Que enim intemperata est ad amicicias, promptior erit ad inimicicias." Ibid. IX; Seyfarth, 277. Cf. Aelred, *De spiritali amicitia* 3.6; Hoste, 318.

110. "[H]oc te instruere sacra scriptura, femina virtutis, exemplo non desinit, ut cum sanctis viris familiarem et religiosam parias amicitiam, sicut cum beato papa Urbano virginem peperisse legimus gloriosam." Osbert, *Letters* 42; Williamson, 156.

111. In the letters of Hildegard, spiritual friendship is not discussed but presupposed. See Ulrike Wiethaus, "In Search of Medieval Women's Friendships: Hildegard of Bingen's Letters to Her Female Contemporaries," in *Maps of Flesh and Light*, 93–111.

112. "Si quis igitur habet animam virginalem, et amator est pudicitiae, non debet mediocribus esse contentus, . . . sed perfectas virtutes sequatur. . . . Adolescens, profice! . . . Desere ima quantum vales, et summa pete. Non deficias neque tepescas, ut gradum perfectionis possis ascendere, ad quam nonnisi multis laboribus pervenitur. Euge nunc, euge, frater bone, initia transcende, et ad superiora tende." John of Fruttuaria, *Tractatus de ordine vitae* 6, PL 184: 574ab.

113. "[N]ecesse est cupiditas vel amor noster a carne incipiat, quae si recto ordine dirigitur, quibusdam suis gradibus duce gratia proficiens, spiritu tandem consummabitur." Bernard, *De diligendo Deo* 15.39; Leclercq III, 152; trans. Robert Walton, *Treatises II* (Kalamazoo, 1980): 130.

114. William of St.-Thierry, *Epistola ad fratres de Monte Dei*, ed. Déchanet.

115. Guigo II, the Carthusian, *Scala claustralium*, ed. Edmund Colledge and James Walsh, SC 163 (Paris, 1970); trans. Colledge and Walsh, *The Ladder of Monks* (Garden City, NY, 1978): 81–99.

116. Herrad of Hohenbourg, *Hortus deliciarum*, reconstructed by Rosalie Green, Michael Evans, et al. (London, 1979): I, 352–53.

117. "Suspecta sit mortalis uite condicio his animabus precipue, que quasi pregnantes femine et iam pariture per cliuosa quedam et aspera gradientes aborsum momentis singulis metuunt." *Speculum uirginum* IX; Seyfarth, 291.

Chapter 2

1. For a history of earlier stages in the debate, see Peter von Moos, *Mittelalterforschung und Ideologiekritik: Der Gelehrtenstreit um Heloise* (Munich, 1974).

2. Linda Kauffman, *Discourses of Desire: Gender, Genre, and Epistolary Fictions* (Ithaca, 1986): 18.

3. "Ad imperium nostrum sponte velata," Abelard, *Historia calamitatum*, ed. Jacques Monfrin (Paris, 1959): 81.

4. Evelyne Sullerot, *Women on Love: Eight Centuries of Feminine Writing*, trans. Helen Lane (Garden City, 1979): 42. The "grotesque hypothesis" is part of a widespread pattern, as Sullerot notes: "Evaluations of women's writings on love are subject to two very common biases: an indulgence that borders on infatuation, on the one hand, and on the other a thoroughgoing skepticism, causing all texts attributed to women to be viewed as apocryphal, and in fact the handiwork of men" (41).

5. John F. Benton, "Fraud, Fiction and Borrowing in the Correspondence of Abelard and Heloise," in René Louis and Jean Jolivet, eds., *Pierre Abélard—Pierre le Vénérable: Les Courants philosophiques, littéraires et artistiques en Occident au milieu du XII⁰ siècle*, Colloques Internationaux du Centre Nationale de la Recherche Scientifique, Abbaye de Cluny, 1972 (Paris, 1975): 469–506.

6. John F. Benton, "A Reconsideration of the Authenticity of the Correspondence of Abelard and Heloise," in Rudolf Thomas, ed., *Petrus Abaelardus* (Trier, 1980): 41–52.

7. Two holdouts are Hubert Silvestre, who has argued that the whole dossier was forged by its eventual translator, Jean de Meun; and, more recently, Deborah Fraioli, who ascribes the letters to a contemporary enemy of Abelard and Heloise who forged the correspondence to ridicule them. Hubert Silvestre, "Die Liebesgeschichte zwischen Abaelard und Heloise: der Anteil des Romans," in *Fälschungen im Mittelalter*, Internationaler Kongress der Monumenta Germaniae Historica (Munich, 1986), Teil V: *Fingierte Briefe, Frömmigkeit und Fälschung, Realienfälschungen*, MGH.SS Bd. 33, V (Hannover, 1988): 121–65; Deborah Fraioli, "The Importance of Satire in Jerome's *Adversus Jovinianum* as an Argument Against the Authenticity of the *Historia calamitatum*," *Fälschungen*, 167–200. See also Peter Dronke's critique of these articles: "Heloise, Abelard, and Some Recent Discussions," in *Intellectuals and Poets in Medieval Europe* (Rome, 1992): 323–42.

8. Peter von Moos, "*Post festum*—Was kommt nach der Authentizitätsdebatte über die Briefe Abaelards und Heloises?" in Thomas, ed., *Petrus Abaelardus*, 81.

9. Paul Zumthor, "Préface," in *Abélard et Héloïse, Correspondance*, trans. Zumthor (Paris, 1979): 12. Cf. Jean-Charles Huchet, "La Voix d'Héloïse," *Romance Notes* 25 (1985): 271–87.

10. J. T. Muckle, ed., "The Personal Letters Between Abelard and Heloise," *Mediaeval Studies* 15 (1953): 59, 67.

11. Benton, "Fraud, Fiction and Borrowing," 501.

12. John F. Benton, "Philology's Search for Abelard in the *Metamorphosis Goliae*," *Speculum* 50 (1975): 202.

13. Benton, "Reconsideration," 51.

14. John F. Benton, "The Correspondence of Abelard and Heloise," in *Fälschungen*, 109n.

15. I hope I do not unduly disparage the late John Benton—a stimulating, careful, and versatile scholar—by pointing out what could be construed as an antifeminist slant in his work. For example, Benton devoted an earlier article to minimizing the influence of female patrons such as Eleanor of Aquitaine and Marie of Champagne, and a later one to demonstrating (effectively, in my view) that the

physician Trotula could not have written the medical works ascribed to her. See "The Court of Champagne as a Literary Center," *Speculum* 36 (1961): 551–91; "Trotula, Women's Problems, and the Professionalization of Medicine in the Middle Ages," *Bulletin of the History of Medicine* 59 (1985): 30–53.

16. D. W. Robertson, *Abelard and Heloise* (New York, 1972). For "poor Heloise" see 43, 60; "little Heloise," 51; the "little sermon," 50, 60, 90, 110, 135, 150.

17. Ibid. 50–51, 53–54.

18. Ibid. 97.

19. Ibid. 121. The reference to "modern ecclesiastics" is a gibe at Étienne Gilson, *Héloïse et Abélard* (Paris, 1938).

20. Robertson, 121.

21. Ibid. xiii. The author likewise thanks his own wife for "shield[ing him] from those domestic difficulties so vividly described by Heloise" and "patiently endur[ing his] . . . general intransigence" (xvi).

22. Ibid. 224.

23. Chrysogonus Waddell, ed., *The Paraclete Statutes Institutiones Nostrae: Introduction, Edition, Commentary* (Trappist, KY, 1987): 53.

24. Peter Dronke, *Women Writers of the Middle Ages: A Critical Study of Texts from Perpetua (†203) to Marguerite Porete (†1310)* (Cambridge, 1984): 142.

25. Hubert Silvestre, "Reflexions sur la thèse de J. F. Benton relative au dossier 'Abélard-Héloïse,'" *Recherches de théologie ancienne et médiévale* 44 (1977): 215–16.

26. Idem, "Die Liebesgeschichte," 140, 131.

27. In addition to Dronke, *Women Writers*, see Elizabeth Petroff, ed., *Medieval Women's Visionary Literature* (Oxford, 1986); Marcelle Thiébaux, ed. and trans., *The Writings of Medieval Women* (New York, 1987); Katharina Wilson, ed., *Medieval Women Writers* (Athens, GA, 1984); Karen Cherewatuk and Ulrike Wiethaus, eds., *Dear Sister: Medieval Women and the Epistolary Genre* (Philadelphia, 1993).

28. "Per habundantiam litterarum erat suprema. Nam quo bonum hoc litteratorie scilicet scientie in mulieribus est rarius, eo amplius puellam commendabat et in toto regno nominatissimam fecerat." *Historia calamitatum*, Monfrin, 71.

29. Peter the Venerable, Epistle 115, trans. Betty Radice, *The Letters of Abelard and Heloise* (Harmondsworth, 1974): 277.

30. Epistle of Roscelin to Abelard (Ep. 15), PL 178: 369c.

31. Hugh Métel, Ep. 16, ed. C. L. Hugo, *Sacrae antiquitatis monumenta* II (Saint-Die, 1731): 348; cited in Enid McLeod, *Héloïse: A Biography* (London, 1938): 125. Hugh Métel wrote Heloise two fulsome letters of praise, presumably to enhance his own reputation by reflected glory.

32. J. C. Fox, "Mary Abbess of Shaftesbury," *English Historical Review* 26 (1911): 317–26; Robert Hanning and Joan Ferrante, trans., *The Lais of Marie de France* (New York, 1978): 7, 26n; Sharon Elkins, *Holy Women of Twelfth-Century England* (Chapel Hill, 1988): 212–13, n. 21.

33. *Les Lais de Marie de France*, ed. Jean Rychner (Paris, 1973): 52–53 ("Fresne"), 107–08 ("Yonec").

34. Marie was also keenly aware that her authorship might be denied by "clerics" and took steps to prevent them from taking credit for her work: "Me

numerai pur remembrance; / Marie ai nun, si sui de France. / Put cel estre que clerc plusur / prendreient sur eus mun labur, / ne voil que sur li le die." Cited from the *Fables*, in Hanning and Ferrante, *Lais*, 6.

35. Benton, "Correspondence," 97. For a sample of computer-assisted analysis see John F. Benton and F. P. Ercoli, "The Style of the *Historia Calamitatum*," *Viator* 6 (1975): 59–86 (a study whose results Benton later rejected as invalid).

36. Benton, "Reconsideration," 52.

37. Jean Jolivet, "Abélard entre chien et loup," *Cahiers de civilisation médiévale* 20 (1977): 311.

38. Von Moos, *"Post festum,"* 81, 83.

39. "Sentimental humanitarianism, of which there are no traces in medieval Christianity, smothers the laughter of God in the lugubrious pieties of something called 'human understanding.'" Robertson, *Abelard and Heloise*, 111.

40. Cf. Nancy Partner's recent defense of psychohistory: "The objection that we are making an unwarranted assumption in thinking that the human mind was essentially the same over centuries of changing culture is a counsel of utter despair. If the deep structure of human experience could change so rapidly and profoundly, altered by the comings and goings of institutions and beliefs, then there could be no discipline of history at all, and our human endowment of memory would be a cruel deception. . . . The idea that imputing passionate and complex inner lives to persons we know through historical sources is an insult to them seems astonishing to me." "Reading *The Book of Margery Kempe*," *Exemplaria* 3 (1991): 61–62.

41. Robertson, *Abelard and Heloise*, 122.

42. See, for example, Gilson, *Héloïse et Abélard*; Dronke, "Heloise," in *Women Writers*, 107–39; Pascale Bourgain, "Héloïse," in *Abélard en son temps*, Actes du Colloque International, 1979 (Paris, 1981): 211–37; Peggy Kamuf, *Fictions of Feminine Desire: Disclosures of Heloise* (Lincoln, 1982): 1–43; Glenda McLeod, "'Wholly Guilty, Wholly Innocent': Self-Definition in Héloïse's Letters to Abélard," in Cherewatuk and Wiethaus, eds., *Dear Sister*, 64–86.

43. The use of methods like *cursus* analysis and word counts assumes the opposite, since these techniques would not be employed if the letters had not previously been held suspect on other grounds. In my own view these methods have not been sufficiently refined and tested on works of known authorship to be held reliable for use on doubtful texts. According to Benton, his own preliminary statistical analysis proved it more likely that Bernard of Clairvaux had written the *Theologia christiana* than that Abelard had composed the *Historia calamitatum*: "Reconsideration," 44. For a defense of Heloise's authorship on the ground of *cursus* patterns, see Peter Dronke, "Heloise's *Problemata* and *Letters*: Some Questions of Form and Content," in *Petrus Abaelardus*, 53–73.

44. On these discrepancies see Bernhard Schmeidler, "Der Briefwechsel zwischen Abaelard und Heloise dennoch eine literarische Fiktion Abaelards," *Revue bénédictine* 52 (1940): 85–95, with rebuttals by R. W. Southern, "The Letters of Abelard and Heloise," in *Medieval Humanism* (Oxford, 1970): 86–104, and D. E. Luscombe, "The *Letters* of Heloise and Abelard since 'Cluny 1972,'" in *Petrus Abaelardus*, 19–39. On the frequently noted contradictions between Abelard's *Rule* and the actual customs of the Paraclete, see Mary McLaughlin, "Peter Abelard and

the Dignity of Women: Twelfth Century 'Feminism' in Theory and Practice," in *Pierre Abélard*, 287–333; D. E. Luscombe, "From Paris to the Paraclete: The Correspondence of Abelard and Heloise," *Proceedings of the British Academy* 74 (1988): 247–83.

45. For an excellent and detailed study of the manuscripts, see Monfrin, ed., *Historia calamitatum*, 9–61, and idem, "Le problème de l'authenticité de la correspondance d'Abélard et d'Héloïse," in *Pierre Abélard*, 409–24.

46. Contrast the *Epistolae duorum amantium* edited by Ewald Könsgen (Leiden, 1974). Könsgen speculated that these anonymous Latin love letters may have been those exchanged by Abelard and Heloise before the discovery of their affair, but this hypothesis has found little favor.

47. Cf. the prefatory epistle to the book of sermons he wrote for the Paraclete: "Libello quodam hymnorum . . . nonnulla insuper opuscula sermonum, juxta petitionem tuam, . . . scribere *praeter consuetudinem nostram* utcunque maturavi. *Plus quippe lectioni quam sermoni deditus*, expositionis insisto planitiem, non eloquentiae compositionem," PL 178: 379–80.

48. Nikolaus Häring, "Abelard Yesterday and Today," in *Pierre Abélard*, 341–403; see especially 355–60.

49. E. R. Smits, ed., *Peter Abelard: Letters IX–XIV* (Groningen, 1983): 24–30.

50. Peter Dronke, *Abelard and Heloise in Medieval Testimonies* (Glasgow, 1976).

51. Jean de Meun, *Le Roman de la Rose*, ed. Daniel Poirion (Paris, 1974): 253–54, lines 8759–8832. For Jean's French version see Fabrizio Beggiato, ed., *Le lettere de Abelardo ed Eloisa nella traduzione di Jean de Meun*, 2 vols. (Modena, 1977).

52. Carla Bozzolo, "L'humaniste Gontier Col et la traduction française des Lettres d'Abélard et Héloïse," *Romania* 95 (1974): 199–215; Peter Dronke, "Francesca and Héloïse," *Comparative Literature* 27 (1975): 113–35.

53. See Benton, "Reconsideration."

54. "Diu te, sicut et multos, simulatio mea fefellit ut religioni deputares hypocrisim; et ideo nostris te maxime commendans orationibus, quod a te exspecto a me postulas." Muckle, 81.

55. Monfrin, 101; trans. Radice, 97.

56. See his letters to Heloise in Radice, *Letters*, 277–84 and 286–87.

57. Cf. Abelard's quotation from Augustine's Sermon 355, *De vita clericorum*: "Propter nos, consciencia nostra sufficit nobis; propter vos, fama nostra non pollui, sed pollere debet in vobis . . . Due res sunt consciencia et fama. Conscientia tibi, fama proximo tuo." *Historia calamitatum*, ed. Monfrin, 102–3.

58. Cf. Dronke, *Women Writers*, 108, 110.

59. Mary McLaughlin, "Abelard as Autobiographer: The Motives and Meaning of his *Story of Calamities*," *Speculum* 42 (1967): 463–88.

60. "Suo [*or* Domino] specialiter, sua singulariter." Letter V, Muckle, 94.

61. Robertson, *Abelard and Heloise*, 60.

62. Muckle, "Personal Letters," 63.

63. Peter the Venerable to Heloise, trans. Radice, 278.

64. Letter X: Abelard to Bernard of Clairvaux, in Smits, 239.

65. *Historia calamitatum*, ed. Monfrin, 100.

66. On this episode see Charlotte Charrier, *Héloïse dans l'histoire et dans la légende* (Paris, 1933): 154–74.

67. See Charles Lalore, ed., *Cartulaire de l'abbaye du Paraclet* (Paris, 1878).

68. Penelope Johnson, *Equal in Monastic Profession: Religious Women in Medieval France* (Chicago, 1991): 234.

69. *Historia calamitatum*, 101.

70. Damien van den Eynde, "Chronologie des écrits d'Abélard à Héloïse," *Antonianum* 37 (1962): 337–49.

71. McLaughlin, "Abelard as Autobiographer," 483; eadem, "Peter Abelard and the Dignity of Women," 317.

72. Dronke, *Abelard and Heloise*, 11.

73. Muckle, 69; trans. Radice, 111.

74. "Unde non mediocri admiratione nostrae tenera conversationis [*or* conversionis] initia tua iam dudum oblivio movit quod, nec reverentia Dei nec amore nostri nec sanctorum patrum exemplis admonitus, fluctuantem me et iam diutino moerore confectam vel sermone praesentem vel epistola absentem consolari tentaveris." Muckle, 70. This passage was among those that first cast doubt on the authenticity of the letter, since Heloise's charge of neglect seems to contradict our knowledge of Abelard's fairly recent comings and goings at the Paraclete. But she must rather have been recalling her early years at Argenteuil: "Your forgetfulness long ago caused [me] no little amazement at the tender beginning of my religious life." Even if she had been referring to her first years at the Paraclete, however, it would hardly have made sense for Abelard to describe his own activities there and then turn around and make Heloise accuse him of neglect when both knew the reproach was unfounded.

75. Muckle, 71.

76. On the contrast between the sexual sublimations of Abelard and Heloise, see Jean Leclercq, "Modern Psychology and the Interpretation of Medieval Texts," *Speculum* 48 (1973): 476–90.

77. Muckle, 72; trans. Radice, 116.

78. "Planctus Dinae filiae Jacob," PL 178: 1817. On the Dinah exemplum, see Chapter 1 above, p. 25.

79. On this point cf. Christopher Brooke's defense of authenticity in *The Medieval Idea of Marriage* (Oxford, 1991): 93–102.

80. Muckle, 78; trans. Radice, 129.

81. Cf., for instance, Ivo of Chartres, Epistle 10 on virginity: "Cujus quanto superior est gradus, tanto gravior est casus. Cui perseveranti quanto felicior et suprema speranda est glorificatio, tanto cadenti miserior et extrema est timenda damnatio." *Correspondance*, ed. Jean Leclercq (Paris, 1949): I, 40–42. See Chapter 1 above, p. 29.

82. This is the position of Charrier, *Héloïse*; quoted passage, p. 189.

83. See Giles Constable, *Letters and Letter-Collections*, Typologie des sources du moyen âge occidental, fasc. 17 (Turnhout, 1976).

84. See Dronke, *Women Writers*, 140–43; Rudolf Mohr, "Der Gedankenaustausch zwischen Heloisa und Abaelard über eine Modifizierung der *Regula Benedicti* für Frauen," *Regulae Benedicti Studia* 5 (1976): 307–33; Linda Georgianna, "Any

Corner of Heaven: Heloise's Critique of Monasticism," *Mediaeval Studies* 49 (1987): 221–53; and Chapter 1 above.

85. Wife of Bath's Prologue, lines 671–81, in *The Riverside Chaucer*, ed. Larry Benson (Boston, 1987): 114.

86. For a persuasive reading of this episode see Emmanuèle Baumgartner, "De Lucrèce à Héloïse: Remarques sur deux *exemples* du *Roman de la Rose* de Jean de Meun," *Romania* 95 (1974): 433–42.

87. *Roman de la Rose*, ed. Poirion, lines 8765–66, 8773–75, 8825–30.

88. Beggiato, *Le lettere*, 29, 31, 77, 84, 101, 115.

89. *Roman*, lines 8781–84.

90. "Que enim conventio scolarium ad pedissequas, scriptoriorum ad cuna-bula . . . ? *Quis denique* sacris vel philosophicis meditationibus intentus, pueriles vagitus, nutricum que hos mittigant nenias, tumultuosam familie tam in viris quam in feminis turbam sustinere poterit? *Que etiam* inhonestas illas parvulorum sordes assiduas tolerare valebit?" *Historia calamitatum*, ed. Monfrin, 76 [emphasis added]; contrast Radice, 71.

91. "O quam indecenter manus illae sacrae, quae nunc etiam divina revolvunt volumina, curae muliebris obscenitatibus deservirent!" Muckle, 90; trans. Radice, 150.

92. Bozzolo, "L'humaniste Gontier Col"; Charity C. Willard, *Christine de Pizan: Her Life and Works* (New York, 1984): 73–89.

93. Cf. Earl Jeffrey Richards, " '*Seulette a part*'—The 'Little Woman on the Sidelines' Takes Up Her Pen: The Letters of Christine de Pizan," in Cherewatuk and Wiethaus, eds., *Dear Sister*, 140–43, and Leslie Brook, "Christine de Pisan, Heloise, and Abelard's Holy Women," *Zeitschrift für romanische Philologie* 109 (1993): 556–63.

94. Cf. Peter von Moos, "Le Silence d'Héloïse et les idéologies modernes," in *Pierre Abélard*, 425–68.

95. Muckle, 94.

96. Ibid. 70.

97. Ibid. 79–80; Radice, 130–31.

98. J. P. Muckle, ed., *Mediaeval Studies* 17 (1955): 242–43, 246, 252; Radice, 161–63, 167, 176. For a fuller exploration of this topos see Chapter 1 above, pp. 22–23.

99. "Qui solus es in causa dolendi solus sis in gratia consolandi. Solus quippe es qui me contristare, qui me laetificare seu consolari valeas. Et solus es qui pluri-mum id mihi debeas et nunc maxime cum universa quae iusseris in tantum imple-verim ut cum te in aliquo offendere non possem me ipsam pro iussu tuo perdere sustinerem." Muckle, 70.

100. For the *sensus litteralis* see *Historia calamitatum*, Monfrin, 73: "Nullus a cupidis intermissus est gradus amoris, et si quid insolitum amor excogitare potuit, est additum."

101. Muckle, 68; trans. Radice, 109.

102. Muckle, 77; trans. Radice, 127. It has been left for modern scholarship to add even the relation of creator and creature to the complementary pairs.

103. E. Ann Matter, *The Voice of My Beloved: The Song of Songs in Western Medieval Christianity* (Philadelphia, 1990): 151.

104. Mechthild of Magdeburg, *Das fliessende Licht der Gottheit* I.5, ed. Hans Neumann (Munich, 1990): 11.

105. Hadewijch, *Poems in Couplets* 16, line 168, in *Complete Works*, trans. Columba Hart (New York, 1980): 357.

106. Marguerite Porete, *Le Mirouer des simples ames*, ch. 9, ed. Romana Guarnieri, CCCM 69 (Turnhout, 1986): 32.

107. "Aeque autem Deus scit ad Vulcania loca te properantem praecedere vel sequi pro iussu tuo minime dubitarem." Muckle, 72–73. On this topos in mystical writing see Chapter 4 below, pp. 123–29.

108. Muckle, 70; trans. Radice, 113.

109. "Quae cum mihi per omnia placere, sicut profiteris, studeas, . . . ut mihi summopere placeas, hanc depone, cum qua mihi non potes placere neque mecum ad beatitudinem pervenire. Sustinebis illuc me sine te pergere, quem etiam ad Vulcania profiteris te sequi velle?" Muckle, 87.

110. Marguerite Porete, *Mirouer*, ch. 131, pp. 384–86. Translation is my own.

111. Muckle, 91–92; trans. Radice, 151–53.

112. See Abelard's discussion of the Ethiopian bride (*nigra sed formosa*) in the fifth letter, Muckle, 83–85; Kamuf, *Fictions of Feminine Desire*, 28–31; Huchet, "La Voix d'Héloïse," 280–81.

113. Muckle, 74–75.

114. "Nam et tuae Dominus non immemor salutis, . . . te videlicet Heloissam id est divinam ex proprio nomine suo quod est Heloim insignivit." Muckle, 90.

115. "The Letter of Heloise on Religious Life and Abelard's First Reply," ed. J. T. Muckle, *Mediaeval Studies* 17 (1955): 240–81; McLaughlin, "Peter Abelard and the Dignity of Women." Radice does not include this letter in her translation.

116. Marguerite Porete, *Mirouer*, ch. 131–32, pp. 388–90.

Chapter 3

1. *Jātaka* no. 547, "The King Who Gave Away His Kingdom," in Roy C. Amore and Larry D. Shinn, eds., *Lustful Maidens and Ascetic Kings: Buddhist and Hindu Stories of Life* (New York, 1981): 116–18.

2. Cf. Plutarch on child sacrifice in ancient Carthage: Should the mother "utter a moan or let fall a tear, she had to forfeit the price of the sale, and her child was sacrificed nevertheless." *Moralia* XIV.13 (171C), in *Traités de morale*, t. II, ed. Jean Dumortier and Jean Defradas (Paris, 1985): 266.

3. Cf. John Boswell, *The Kindness of Strangers: The Abandonment of Children in Western Europe from Late Antiquity to the Renaissance* (New York, 1988): 140.

4. Alcuin, *Interrogationes et Responsiones in Genesin*, PL 100: 544–45.

5. For other biblical instances of child sacrifice see Boswell, *Kindness of Strangers*, 139–42.

6. Louis Ginzberg, *The Legends of the Jews*, I, trans. Henrietta Szold (Philadelphia, 1913): 286–87.

7. "Abraham and Isaac," *Chester Plays*, part I, ed. Hermann Deimling, EETS e.s. 62 (London, 1893): 76.

8. "Would you, through a human regret, lose the love of the Sovereign? Will you go to damnation through a human affection?" *Le Sacrifice de Abraham*, ll. 801–4, cited in John Elliot, Jr., "The Sacrifice of Isaac as Comedy and Tragedy," in Jerome Taylor and Alan Nelson, eds., *Medieval English Drama* (Chicago, 1972): 173.

9. Euripides, *Iphigenia in Aulis*, in David Grene and Richmond Lattimore, eds., *The Complete Greek Tragedies* (Chicago, 1969): IV, 297–380.

10. Euripides, *Iphigenia in Tauris*, in Grene and Lattimore, III: 345–46, 407–8. For a chilling revival of this motif see Ginette Paris, *The Sacrament of Abortion* (Dallas, 1992); Paris represents abortion in contemporary neo-pagan terms as a sacrifice to Artemis.

11. Livy, *Ab urbe condita* VI.1; Jean de Meun, *Roman de la Rose*, ll. 5589–5658; Boccaccio, *De mulieribus claris*, ch. 56; Chaucer, *Physician's Tale*; Gower, *Confessio amantis* 7, 5131–5306. Christine de Pizan, *Livre de la Cité des Dames* II.46.3, makes it Virginia herself who chooses to be killed rather than raped.

12. For a different reading of the allusion see Richard Hoffman, "Jephthah's Daughter and Chaucer's Virginia," *Chaucer Review* 2 (1967): 20–31.

13. The same brief interpretation, comparing Jephthah to God the Father and Christ, is ascribed to Isidore of Seville, *Quaestiones in Librum Iudicum* 7, PL 83: 388–89, and to Bede, PL 93: 428. According to John Chrysostom, "each one of us ought to be a Jephthah," sacrificing our "daughter" or soul to God after vanquishing our "enemies" (carnal desires). Cited by Rupert of Deutz, *De Sancta Trinitate et operibus eius, in Librum Iudicum* 12, ed. Hraban Haacke, CCCM 22 (Turnhout, 1972): 1168–70.

14. Augustine, *In Heptateuchum Locutionum Libri Septem*, VII.49, PL 34: 810–22.

15. Rabanus Maurus, *On the Oblation of Children*, PL 107:419–40, excerpts trans. in Boswell, *Kindness of Strangers*, 438–44.

16. Rupert, cited in n. 13 above; cf. Hugh of St.-Victor, *Adnotatiunculae Elucidatoriae in Librum Judicum*, PL 175: 92d.

17. *Physician's Tale* ll. 93–99, in *The Riverside Chaucer*, ed. Larry Benson (Boston, 1987): 191. All Chaucer citations are taken from this edition.

18. Cf. the well-known legend of St. Barbara, a maiden similarly beheaded by her father in the absence of any mother. An Old French version has been translated by Brigitte Cazelles in *The Lady as Saint: A Collection of French Hagiographic Romances of the Thirteenth Century* (Philadelphia, 1991): 102–12.

19. "The Martyrdom of Saints Perpetua and Felicitas" 6, ed. Herbert Musurillo, *The Acts of the Christian Martyrs* (Oxford, 1972): 112–15.

20. Jerome, Ep. 45 (to Asella), in *Lettres*, ed. Jérôme Labourt, 7 vols. (Paris, 1949–1961): II, 98.

21. "Et tamen siccos oculos tendebat ad caelum, pietatem in filios pietate in Deum superans. Nesciebat matrem, ut Christi probaret ancillam." Jerome, Ep. 108.6 (Epitaph of St. Paula), in ibid., V, 164.

22. Jerome, *Commentarius in Epistolam ad Ephesios* III.5, PL 26: 567a.

23. Bernard of Clairvaux, *Letters*, no. 378, trans. Bruno James (London, 1953): 449. Cf. Jerome, *Lettres* I, 35 (Ep. 14 to Heliodorus).

24. At one point Margery laments, "Ah, Lord, maidens are now dancing

merrily in heaven. Shall I not do so? Because I am no virgin, lack of virginity is now great sorrow to me." Christ reassures her that she is "a maiden in [her] soul," but she continues to doubt. *The Book of Margery Kempe*, ch. 22, trans. Barry Windeatt (Harmondsworth, 1985): 86–88.

25. Clarissa Atkinson, *The Oldest Vocation: Christian Motherhood in the Middle Ages* (Ithaca, 1991): ch. 5. I am indebted to Atkinson's fine work for many insights and examples.

26. "The Presentation of Mary" in *The N-Town Play*, ed. Stephen Spector (Oxford, 1991): 84. For alternative "pro-family" elements in the cult of St. Anne, see Kathleen Ashley and Pamela Sheingorn, eds., *Interpreting Cultural Symbols: Saint Anne in Late Medieval Society* (Athens, GA, 1990).

27. See Sandro Sticca, *The Planctus Mariae in the Dramatic Tradition of the Middle Ages*, trans. Joseph Berrigan (Athens, GA, 1988).

28. "Mother, now you can well learn what sorrow they have who bear children, what sorrow it is to go with child."—"Sorrow, indeed, I can tell you; unless it be the pain of hell, greater sorrow know I none."—"Mother, have pity on mothers' cares, for now you know of mothers' fate, although you are a pure virgin." G. L. Brook, ed., *The Harley Lyrics* (Manchester, 1956), no. 20, p. 57.

29. Carleton Brown, *Religious Lyrics of the XIVth Century*, 2nd ed. (Oxford, 1952): 56, pp. 70–75; James Ryman, "Mary and her Son Alone," in Celia and Kenneth Sisam, eds., *The Oxford Book of Medieval English Verse* (Oxford, 1970): 238, pp. 507–9.

30. As recently as 1953, a Sicilian bishop acclaimed a miraculous weeping image of the Virgin with the words: "Mary has wept! . . . Weeping is fecund. There has never been a sterile tear. As the rain that falls from on high irrigates the country-side and prepares it to receive, in all fertility, the crops and seed and fruit that will in time come to ripeness, so it happens in the realm of the spirit. A woman who weeps always becomes, in the very act, a mother." Salvatore Giardina, *Il Pianto di Maria a Siracusa* (Syracuse, 1971): 62; trans. Marina Warner in *Alone of All Her Sex: The Myth and the Cult of the Virgin Mary* (New York, 1976): 223.

31. Rosemary Hale, "*Imitatio Mariae*: Motherhood Motifs in Late Medieval German Spirituality" (diss. Harvard, 1992). See also Leah Sinanoglou, "The Christ Child as Sacrifice: A Medieval Tradition and the Corpus Christi Plays," *Speculum* 48 (1973): 491–509.

32. Elsbet Stagel, *Das Leben der Schwestern zu Töss*, ed. Ferdinand Vetter (Berlin, 1906): 52.

33. Jean Gerson, "Consolation sur la mort des amis," in *Oeuvres complètes*, ed. P. Glorieux (Paris, 1966): VII, 323. For more examples of such preaching see Shulamith Shahar, *Childhood in the Middle Ages* (London, 1990): 151–52; on Gerson see Françoise Bonney, "Jean Gerson: Un nouveau regard sur l'enfance," *Annales de démographie historique* (1973): 137–42.

34. Birgitta of Sweden, *Liber celestis* VI.50, Middle English text, ed. Roger Ellis, EETS 291 (Oxford, 1987): I, 438. For Birgitta's experiences and teachings related to motherhood see Atkinson, *Oldest Vocation*, 170–84.

35. *The Hours of the Passion, Taken from the Life of Christ by Ludolf the Saxon*, trans. H. J. Coleridge (London, 1887): 239. The infamous *Malleus maleficarum*,

II.2.8, warns that devils sometimes steal babies and replace them with changelings "when the parents dote upon their children too much, and this is a punishment for their own good." Jacobus Sprenger and Henricus Institoris, *Malleus maleficarum*, trans. Montague Summers (London, 1948): 192.

36. Kierkegaard, not coincidentally, developed this scheme in the course of his reflection on Abraham and Isaac; see his *Fear and Trembling*, trans. Walter Lowrie (Princeton, 1941).

37. This motif also appears in the lives of saintly widows without children, such as Bl. Gherardesca of Pisa (c. 1207-c. 1267) and Aldobrandesca of Siena (1245–1309). See Elizabeth Petroff, *Consolation of the Blessed* (New York, 1979): 85, 167.

38. Guibert of Nogent, *Autobiographie* I.12, ed. E.-R. Labande (Paris, 1981); trans. C. Swinton Bland and ed. John F. Benton, *Self and Society in Medieval France* (New York, 1970): 64, 67. For discussion see Mary M. McLaughlin, "Survivors and Surrogates: Children and Parents from the Ninth to the Thirteenth Centuries," in Lloyd deMause, ed., *The History of Childhood* (New York, 1974): 105–12; Georges Duby, *The Knight, the Lady and the Priest: The Making of Modern Marriage in Medieval France*, trans. Barbara Bray (New York, 1983): 140–47.

39. Guibert I.3; Labande 16, Benton 41. The hyperbolic Latin reads, "Totam ferme quadragesimam sub nimii doloris insolentia parturiens mater exegerat."

40. Ibid. I.14; Labande 102, Benton 74–75.

41. Hugh of Floreffe, *Vita Ivettae Reclusae*, AA.SS. January, tom. 2 (Paris, 1867): 145–69; Isabelle Cochelin, "Sainteté laïque: l'exemple de Juette de Huy," *Le Moyen Âge* 95 (1989): 397–417; Jennifer Carpenter, "Juette of Huy, Recluse and Mother (1158–1228): Children and Mothering in the Saintly Life," in Jennifer Carpenter and Sally-Beth MacLean, eds., *Power of the Weak: Studies on Medieval Women* (Urbana, 1995). This saint is also known as Yvette or Ivetta.

42. Osbern Bokenham, *Legendys of Hooly Wummen* (ca. 1447), ll. 10,292–301, ed. Mary Serjeantson, EETS o.s. 206 (London, 1938): 280. There is a translation by Sheila Delany, *A Legend of Holy Women* (Notre Dame, 1992). Cf. Jacobus de Voragine, *The Golden Legend*, trans. William Granger Ryan (Princeton, 1993): II, 309.

43. On this theme see the important article by Jo Ann McNamara, "The Need to Give: Suffering and Female Sanctity in the Middle Ages," in Renate Blumenfeld-Kosinski and Timea Szell, eds., *Images of Sainthood in Medieval Europe* (Ithaca, 1991): 199–221.

44. Vito of Cortona, *Vita Umilianae* I.6, IV.43, AA.SS. May, tom. 4 (Paris, 1866): 387, 396; Petroff, *Consolation*, 61–62, 202; Donald Weinstein and Rudolph Bell, *Saints and Society: The Two Worlds of Western Christendom, 1000–1700* (Chicago, 1982): 52–53; McNamara, "The Need to Give," 209.

45. On Margaret see Petroff, *Consolation*, 39; Weinstein and Bell, *Saints and Society*, 106–07; Daniel Bornstein, "The Uses of the Body: The Church and the Cult of Santa Margherita da Cortona," *Church History* 62 (1993): 163–77.

46. Giunta Bevignati, *Vita Margaritae de Cortona* II.26, AA.SS. February, tom. 3 (Paris, 1864): 308.

47. "Haec est illa, quae Evangelicum verbum perfecte implevit, quando prae amore dilectissimi sponsi Iesu, unicum filium expulit, et illi pauperes peregrinos

et notos pro Christo praeponens, rebus sibi deputatis ad usum se diligenter saepe privavit." Ibid. II.16, p. 307.

48. Mariano Florentino, *Vita Michelinae Pisauri* I.4, AA.SS. June, tom. 4 (Paris, 1867): 777.

49. Shahar, *Childhood*, 11.

50. *Il libro della Beata Angela da Foligno, Memoriale* I, ed. Ludger Thier and Abele Calufetti (Rome, 1985): 138. Cf. Angela of Foligno, *Complete Works*, trans. Paul Lachance (New York, 1993): 126.

51. Ibid., *Memoriale* III, 186; Lachance, 143. An illuminating paper by Catherine Mooney, "The Editorial Recreations of Margaret of Cortona and Angela of Foligno," traces modern editors' attempts to soften the reader's perception of such "unwomanly" (or "unsaintly") behavior.

52. *Instructions* III.1; *Memoriale* VIII; Lachance, 231 and 198.

53. Jeanne Ancelet-Hustache, ed., "Les '*Vitae Sororum*' d'Unterlinden," *Archives d'histoire doctrinale et littéraire du moyen âge* 5 (1930): 452–56. Written by Catherine of Gueberschwihr in the early fourteenth century, this collective hagiography memorializes nuns of the first two generations at Unterlinden.

54. Ibid. 385.

55. Ibid. 394.

56. Ibid. 460.

57. Ibid. 461–62, 404–05.

58. The uncle, Hermann of Havelberg, held this office in 1251–54 and again in 1260–65. It was during one of these periods that Gertrude came to Unterlinden. Her life is contained in an anonymous supplement to Sister Catherine's collection.

59. "Unterlinden," 480–83.

60. Laura Howes, "On the Birth of Margery Kempe's Last Child," *Modern Philology* 90 (1992): 220–25.

61. *Book of Margery Kempe* II.1, p. 266.

62. Birgitta of Sweden, whom Margery admired, prayed her own prodigal son Karl out of the clutches of hell even though he died unrepentant. Atkinson, *Oldest Vocation*, 177–79.

63. "Unterlinden," 430. Tuoda witnessed the death of her other son (from illness) in a eucharistic vision.

64. For a different perspective on this hagiographic type, see Dyan Elliott, *Spiritual Marriage: Sexual Abstinence in Medieval Wedlock* (Princeton, 1993), chapter 5. This durable paradigm continued to influence women (and hagiographers) well beyond the middle ages. We find it, for instance, in the life of the French Canadian saint Marie of the Incarnation (1599–1673), another unwilling bride who was widowed at twenty and entered a convent at thirty-two, despite the impassioned pleas of her young son.

65. I am intentionally omitting Birgitta of Sweden, a rare exception to this rule. Also interesting is Dorothea of Montau, a "maternal martyr" who burned her breasts with a candle to make nursing her nine children painful; she eventually lost eight of them to the Black Death. Among her mystical experiences (shared with many virginal adepts) was that of mystical pregnancy. On Dorothea, see Atkinson, *Oldest Vocation*, 184–90; Elliott, *Spiritual Marriage*, 213–16 and 227–

31; Richard Kieckhefer, *Unquiet Souls: Fourteenth-Century Saints and Their Religious Milieu* (Chicago, 1984): 22–33.

66. The Unterlinden book includes vitae of four other nuns who successfully avoided marriage: one prayed herself into madness (Stephanie of Ferrette), one withstood prolonged abuse by her relatives (Hedwig of Gundolsheim), and two defended their vows of virginity in court (Adelheid of Muntzenheim, Mechthild of Colmar). A similar account is given of the English recluse Christina of Markyate: C. H. Talbot, ed. and trans., *The Life of Christina of Markyate* (Oxford, 1959).

67. Nikki Stiller, *Eve's Orphans: Mothers and Daughters in Medieval English Literature* (Westport, CT, 1980): 6.

68. For a variety of perspectives see Louise Mirrer, ed., *Upon My Husband's Death: Widows in the Literature and Histories of Medieval Europe* (Ann Arbor, 1992).

69. Christiane Klapisch-Zuber, "La 'Mère cruelle': Maternité, veuvage et dot dans la Florence des XIVe–XVe siècles," *Annales* 38 (1983): 1097–1109. See also James Ross, "The Middle-Class Child in Urban Italy, Fourteenth to Early Sixteenth Century," in Lloyd deMause, ed., *History of Childhood*, 200–202.

70. See John Coakley, "Gender and the Authority of Friars: The Significance of Holy Women for Thirteenth-Century Franciscans and Dominicans," *Church History* 60 (1991): 445–60.

71. Cf. Atkinson: "When their children died, or the women sent them away or left them behind, the loss represented an opportunity to experience an intense form of the poverty and pain required of holy persons . . . Instead of blocking access to the sacred, motherhood made it available through sorrow and suffering, permitting women to share the tears of Mary and the pains of Christ." *Oldest Vocation*, 192.

72. Hugh of St.-Victor, *De sacramentis christianae fidei*, II.xi.3–8; Penny Schine Gold, "The Marriage of Mary and Joseph in the Twelfth-Century Ideology of Marriage," in Vern Bullough and James Brundage, eds., *Sexual Practices and the Medieval Church* (Buffalo and New York, 1982): 102–17, 249–51. Cf. Duby, *The Knight*, 181–83, and James Brundage, *Law, Sex, and Christian Society in Medieval Europe* (Chicago, 1987): 274–75.

73. *Amis and Amiloun*, ed. MacEdward Leach, EETS o.s. 203 (London, 1937). For more recent discussion see Ralph Hexter, *Equivocal Oaths and Ordeals in Medieval Literature* (Cambridge, MA, 1975): 27–37; Diana Childress, "Between Romance and Legend: 'Secular Hagiography' in Middle English Literature," *Philological Quarterly* 57 (1978): 311–22; W. R. J. Barron, *English Medieval Romance* (London, 1987): 199–204.

74. Two earlier romances, Hartmann von Aue's *Der arme Heinrich* and the anonymous *Queste del Saint Graal*, display a variant of this motif in which a nameless girl offers her own blood to heal a leper. Hartmann makes her a child of about eight whose parents oppose her plan of self-sacrifice. In the *Queste* she is a nubile virgin and the sister of Perceval, who fights to defend her.

75. Certain Jewish exegetes, influenced by Christian typology, taught that Isaac was actually killed by Abraham but then miraculously raised. See Jeremy Cohen, "Philosophical Exegesis in Historical Perspective: The Case of the Binding

of Isaac," in Tamar Rudavsky, ed., *Divine Omniscience and Omnipotence in Medieval Philosophy* (Boston, 1985): 137–38.

76. Translation in Leach, Appendix A, pp. 104–05. On the other hand, the wife's consent does figure in the folktale of "The Faithful Servitor," which Leach sees as the prototype for *Amis and Amiloun*, liv–lv, lxv, lxxxviii.

77. Cf. Boccaccio, *Decameron* X.10 (1353); Petrarch, *Epistolae de rebus senilibus* 17.3 (1373).

78. I cannot agree with F. X. Baron, who maintains that Griselda in the sacrifice scenes is "preeminently the anguished mother and quite secondarily the submissive wife." "Children and Violence in Chaucer's *Canterbury Tales*," *Journal of Psychohistory* 7/1 (1979): 87.

79. Yves Brissaud, "L'infanticide à la fin du moyen âge, ses motivations psychologiques et sa repression," *Revue historique de droit français et étranger* 50 (1972): 229–56; Barbara Kellum, "Infanticide in England in the Later Middle Ages," *History of Childhood Quarterly* 1 (1974): 367–88; Shahar, *Childhood*, 126–29. An instructive literary example is Marie de France's lai of "Le Fresne," in which a mother wishes to kill one of her twin daughters to avoid even the appearance of shame, but is persuaded to expose the infant instead.

80. David Herlihy, "Medieval Children," in Bede Lackner and Kenneth Philp, eds., *Essays on Medieval Civilization* (Austin, 1978): 112.

81. The same principle governs Thomas Aquinas's reasoning on the marriage debt: A menstruating wife may not initiate sexual relations lest she conceive a deformed child; but if her husband solicits her she may not refuse, lest he be tempted to fornicate. The husband's moral and sexual needs take priority over the good of the child, while the wife's own desires are not consulted. *Summa theologica*, Supplement, quaest. 64, articles 3–4.

82. *Sir Amadace*, line 731, in *Sir Amadace and The Avowing of Arthur*, ed. Christopher Brookhouse (Copenhagen, 1968): 55. Brookhouse edits both the extant manuscript versions of this romance; the hero's name is spelled "Amadace" in one and "Amadas" in the other.

83. " 'Since Christ wills that it be so, take and part me even in two; thou won me and I am thine. God forbid that you had married so that I should make you a liar, to lose your honor in the land.' Still she stood, without hindrance, neither changed her countenance nor wept, that lady mild and dear. She bade, 'Fetch me my young son before me, for he was of my body born, and lay full near my heart.' " *Sir Amadace*, lines 763–74.

84. *Sir Amadas*, line 692, p. 131.

85. Antoine de la Sale, *Le Réconfort de Madame de Fresne*, ed. Ian Hill (Exeter, 1979); excerpts and translation in Erich Auerbach, *Mimesis: The Representation of Reality in Western Literature*, trans. Willard Trask (Princeton, 1953): 232–47 (quotation, 236–37).

86. In an earlier romance, *Jourdain de Blaye* (late 12th or early 13th century), a vassal sacrifices his only son at his wife's urging in order to ransom his lord's son from captivity: *Jourdain de Blaye*, ed. Peter Dembowski, rev. ed. (Paris, 1991): 19–24. *Jourdain* is closely related to the French *Ami et Amile* and follows it in the unique manuscript.

87. Auerbach, *Mimesis*, 245.

88. For a rare fifteenth-century protest against this topos see James Banker, "Mourning a Son: Childhood and Paternal Love in the *Consolateria* of Giannozzo Manetti," *History of Childhood Quarterly* 3 (1976): 351–62.

89. Shahar estimates the average rate of child mortality at 20 to 30 percent within the first year and 50 percent within the first five years, with the death rate soaring even higher in times of war, famine, and plague. *Childhood*, 149–50.

90. On the spirituality of patience see Kieckhefer, *Unquiet Souls*, ch. 3.

91. For a trenchant theological critique of this tradition, see Joanne Carlson Brown and Carole Bohn, eds., *Christianity, Patriarchy, and Abuse: A Feminist Critique* (New York, 1989).

92. On *Beloved* see especially Judith Wilt, *Abortion, Choice, and Contemporary Fiction: The Armageddon of the Maternal Instinct* (Chicago, 1990): 157–66.

93. Dorothee Soelle, *Suffering*, trans. Everett Kalin (Philadelphia, 1975): 28–32.

94. Eleanor Wilner, *Sarah's Choice* (Chicago, 1989): 21–24.

Chapter 4

1. "So low he fell that all means for his salvation now came short, save to show him the lost people. For this I visited the threshold of the dead, and to him who has led him here, my prayers were borne with tears." I have used the edition of John Sinclair, *Purgatorio* (New York, 1961): 398.

2. "Dunque che è? perchè, perchè restai? / perchè tanta viltà nel cuore allette? / perchè ardire e franchezza non hai? / poscia che tai tre donne benedette / curan di te ne la corte del cielo?" *Inferno* 2.121–25.

3. John Sinclair, ed. and trans., *Purgatorio*, 374; Mary Jeremy Finnegan, *The Women of Helfta: Scholars and Mystics* (Athens, 1991): 56–61. The other leading contender for the role is Countess Matelda of Tuscany, although that imperious warrior lady seems most unlike Dante's gentle, flower-gathering singer.

4. *Inferno* 2.133.

5. Jacques Le Goff, *La naissance du Purgatoire* (Paris, 1981); trans. Arthur Goldhammer as *The Birth of Purgatory* (Chicago, 1984).

6. Cf. Adriaan Bredero, "Le Moyen Âge et le Purgatoire," *Revue d'histoire ecclésiastique* 78 (1983): 429–52; Aron Gurevich, "Popular and Scholarly Medieval Cultural Traditions: Notes in the Margin of Jacques Le Goff's Book," *Journal of Medieval History* 9 (1983): 71–90; review by Alan Bernstein in *Speculum*, 59 (1984): 179–83; Graham Edwards, "Purgatory: Birth or Evolution?" *Journal of Ecclesiastical History* 36 (1985): 634–46; review by Peter Dinzelbacher in *Ons Geestelijk Erf* 61 (1987): 278–82; Brian McGuire, "Purgatory, the Communion of Saints, and Medieval Change," *Viator* 20 (1989): 61–84.

7. *Vie et miracles de saint Thècle*, ed. and trans. Gilbert Dagron and Marie Dupré La Tour (Brussels, 1978). The text is sometimes cited as the *Acts of Paul and Thecla*.

8. Stevan Davies, *The Revolt of the Widows: The Social World of the Apocryphal*

Acts (Carbondale, 1980): 105–9. Dennis MacDonald, in "The Role of Women in the Production of the Apocryphal Acts of the Apostles," *Iliff Review* 41 (1984): 21–38, argues that the account is a product of women's storytelling if not authorship. Even the female beasts in the arena protect Thecla, while the male beasts attack her.

9. *Acts of Thecla* 28–30, trans. in Ross Kraemer, ed., *Maenads, Martyrs, Matrons, Monastics* (Philadelphia, 1988): 285. See also eadem, *Her Share of the Blessings: Women's Religions Among Pagans, Jews, and Christians in the Greco-Roman World* (New York, 1992): 150–54.

10. "The Martyrdom of Saints Perpetua and Felicitas," ed. and trans. Herbert Musurillo, *The Acts of the Christian Martyrs* (Oxford, 1972); Le Goff, *Purgatory*, 49–51.

11. Peter Dronke, *Women Writers of the Middle Ages: A Critical Study of Texts from Perpetua (†203) to Marguerite Porete (†1310)* (Cambridge, 1984): 11–12.

12. Augustine, *De anima et eius origine* I.10, PL 44: 481; Dronke, *Women Writers*, 284. For Augustine's reading of Perpetua as a *femina virilis* see Brent Shaw, "The Passion of Perpetua," *Past & Present* 139 (1993): 36–41.

13. Hildegard of Bingen, *Liber vitae meritorum*, ed. J.-B. Pitra in *Analecta sacra* 8 (Monte Cassino, 1882), passim; *Causae et curae* V, ed. Paul Kaiser (Leipzig, 1903): 233; *Liber divinorum operum* II.5.1–13, PL 197: 901–13. See also Dronke, *Women Writers*, 179, 247; Sabina Flanagan, *Hildegard of Bingen, 1098–1179: A Visionary Life* (London, 1989): 71–79; Barbara Newman, "Hildegard of Bingen and the 'Birth of Purgatory,'" *Mystics Quarterly* 19 (1993): 90–97.

14. Anne Clark, *Elisabeth of Schönau: A Twelfth-Century Visionary* (Philadelphia, 1992): 111–17.

15. Marie de France, *Saint Patrick's Purgatory*, ed. and trans. Michael Curley (Binghamton, 1993).

16. Robert Sweetman, "Christine of Saint-Trond's Preaching Apostolate: Thomas of Cantimpré's Hagiographical Method Revisited," *Vox benedictina* 9 (1992): 67–97; Thomas of Cantimpré, *Vita Christinae mirabilis*, AA.SS. July, tom. 5 (Paris, 1868): 650–60; translation by Margot King, *The Life of Christina of Saint Trond* (Saskatoon, 1986).

17. *Vita Christinae mirabilis* V.56, 659.

18. Nicole Bériou, "La prédication au béguinage de Paris pendant l'année liturgique 1272–1273," *Recherches augustiniennes* 13 (1978): 124, 129, 140. See also Michel Lauwers, "'Noli me tangere': Marie Madeleine, Marie d'Oignies et les pénitentes du XIIIᵉ siècle," *Mélanges de l'École Française de Rome: Moyen Âge* 104:1 (1992): 228–31.

19. Karl Christ, ed., "*La Règle des Fins Amans*: Eine Beginenregel aus dem Ende des XIII. Jahrhunderts," in B. Schädel and W. Mulertt, eds., *Philologische Studien aus dem romanisch-germanischen Kulturkreise: Festgabe Karl Voretzsch* (Halle, 1927): 201.

20. Mechthild of Magdeburg, *Das fliessende Licht der Gottheit* VI.13, ed. Hans Neumann (Munich, 1990): 221.

21. Jeanne Ancelet-Hustache, ed., "Les '*Vitae Sororum*' d'Unterlinden," ch. 31, *Archives d'histoire doctrinale et littéraire du moyen âge* 5 (1930): 425.

22. Peter Damian, *De variis apparitionibus et miraculis* 3, PL 145: 586–87; R. H. Bowers, ed., *The Gast of Gy: A Middle-English Religious Prose Tract, Beiträge zur englischen Philologie* 32 (Leipzig, 1938): 25–26; William Cumming, ed., *The Revelations of Saint Birgitta* I.50, EETS o.s. 178 (London, 1929): 54–55; Annette Garnier, "Autour de la mort: Temps de la dilation et Purgatoire dans les *Miracles de Notre Dame de Gautier de Coinci*," *Le Moyen Âge* 94 (1988): 183–202.

23. See Eamon Duffy, *The Stripping of the Altars: Traditional Religion in England c. 1400-c. 1580* (New Haven, 1992): 368–76.

24. Jo Ann McNamara, "The Need to Give: Suffering and Female Sanctity in the Middle Ages," in Renate Blumenfeld-Kosinski and Timea Szell, eds., *Images of Sainthood in Medieval Europe* (Ithaca, 1991): 212, 221.

25. Caesarius of Heisterbach, *Fasciculus moralitatis* III.46 (Cologne, 1615), cited in Robert Shaffern, "Learned Discussions of Indulgences for the Dead in the Middle Ages," *Church History* 61 (1992): 369 n.7.

26. Albert the Great, *Commentarii in IV sententiarum* IV.20.18, *Opera omnia* 29 (Paris, 1894): 852–56.

27. McGuire, "Purgatory," 74; Le Goff, *Purgatory*, 125, gives a date ca. 1024–1033. The solemnity was inaugurated by Abbot Odilo of Cluny and spread rapidly.

28. Gurevich, "Medieval Cultural Traditions."

29. McGuire argues that a deepening emphasis on purgatory and the communion of saints is associated with a "greater optimism about the possibility men and women have to shape their own lives"—with a little help from their friends: "Purgatory," 68. On death rituals and kinship see John Bossy, *Christianity in the West, 1400–1700* (Oxford, 1985): 26–34; Duffy, *Stripping of the Altars*, 348–54.

30. *Vita Odiliae Abbatissae Hohenburgensis* 12, ed. Bruno Krusch and W. Levison in MGH, *Scriptorum rerum merovingicarum* 6 (Hannover, 1913): 44; Raymond of Capua, *Life of Catherine of Siena* II.7, trans. Conleth Kearns (Wilmington, DE, 1980): 209–11. There is a striking parallel in the medieval legend of Miao-shan, an avatar of the Chinese goddess of mercy, Kuan-yin. This bodhisattva refused marriage to live the life of a Buddhist nun. Later she not only sacrificed her arms and eyes to heal her persecuting father, but also visited hell in a vision and delivered its suffering souls from torment. See Glen Dudbridge, *The Legend of Miao-shan* (London, 1978): 85–98.

31. "Unterlinden" ch. 15, 52; pp. 368, 503–4.

32. Ibid. ch. 23, pp. 398–99; Chapter 3 above, p. 90.

33. Augustine, *De civitate Dei* 21.26, CCSL 48 (Turnhout, 1955): 797. The seventh-century *Liber de ordine creaturarum*, ch. 14, mentions "the idle use of legitimate marriage" first in a list of sins deserving purgatorial fire: ed. Manuel Diaz y Diaz (Santiago, 1972): 192. Cf. Le Goff, *Purgatory*, 100.

34. Caesarius of Heisterbach, *Dialogus miraculorum* XII.27, ed. Joseph Strange (Cologne, 1851): II; trans. C. C. Swinton Bland (London, 1929): II, 316–17.

35. Richard Kieckhefer, *Unquiet Souls: Fourteenth-Century Saints and Their Religious Milieu* (Chicago, 1984): 22–24.

36. "Quid dicam breviter esse conjugium? / certe vel tartara, vel purgatorium. / Non est in tartara quies aut otium, / nec dolor conjugis habet remedium." "Golias de conjuge non ducenda" (ca. 1222–50), ed. Thomas Wright in *Latin Poems*

Commonly Attributed to Walter Mapes, Camden Society Publications 16 (London, 1841): 84–85.

37. "O peccatorum quia mortem nolo, redemptor / Et pugil ipsorum, cum res non debeat emptor / Emptas tam care pessundare, jamque parare / circa volui sibi purgatoria plura, / Ut se purgarent; egros sanat data cura; / Inter que majus est conjugium." Mathéolus, *Lamentationes* 3024–29; Jehan Le Fèvre, *Les Lamentations de Mathéolus* III.1673–95, ed. A.-G. Van Hamel, 2 vols. (Paris, 1892, 1905); Alcuin Blamires, ed., *Woman Defamed and Woman Defended* (Oxford, 1992): 177–97. This was the work to which Christine de Pizan took such vehement exception in the prologue to her *Livre de la Cité des Dames*.

38. *Merchant's Tale* 1669–1673; *Wife of Bath's Prologue* 489–90, from *The Riverside Chaucer*, ed. Larry Benson (Boston, 1987): 159, 111. For another case of purgatorial marriage see the *Tale of Florent* (an analogue of the *Wife of Bath's Tale*) in John Gower, *Confessio Amantis* I.1769–80, ed. Russell Peck (Toronto, 1980): 68.

39. Giovanni Boccaccio, *Decameron* III.8, trans. Mark Musa and Peter Bondanella (New York, 1982): 217–26.

40. Tertullian, *De monogamia* 10.4, ed. Paul Mattei, SC 343 (Paris, 1988): 176.

41. Guibert of Nogent, *Autobiographie* I.18, ed. E.-R. Labande (Paris, 1981); trans. C. Swinton Bland and ed. John F. Benton, *Self and Society in Medieval France* (New York, 1970): 92–97. On family issues in Guibert see Chapter 3 above, pp. 85–86.

42. Caesarius, *Dialogus miraculorum* XII.24, trans. Bland II, 313–14.

43. *Gast of Gy*, 34–35; George Keiser, "The Progress of Purgatory: Visions of the Afterlife in Later Middle English Literature," in James Hogg, ed., *Zeit, Tod und Ewigkeit in der Renaissance Literatur* (Salzburg, 1987): III, 86. The various Middle English versions are translated from a Latin work, *De spiritu Guidonis*.

44. Birgitta of Sweden, *Reuelaciones extrauagantes* 75, ed. Lennart Hollman (Uppsala, 1956): 198.

45. Ibid. 56, pp. 178–79.

46. Birgitta, *Revelations* IV.9, ed. Cumming, 51–53.

47. Hildegard, *Epistolae* 62, 99, 146 in Pitra, *Analecta Sacra*, 533, 550, 568; epistles 9 and 11 in Dronke, *Women Writers*, 262–63.

48. Birgitta, *Revelations*, ed. Cumming, 128n, cited from E. M. Fant et al., eds., *Scriptores rerum suecicarum medii aevi* 3 (Uppsala, 1876): 196–97.

49. *Book of Margery Kempe* I.19, trans. Barry Windeatt (Harmondsworth, 1985): 81–82.

50. This role could also be played by male religious. Cf. Henry Suso, *Life of the Servant* I.6, trans. Frank Tobin in *The Exemplar* (New York, 1989): 74–75: "It was quite usual that souls would appear to him when they had departed this world, telling him how things had gone for them, how they had earned their punishment, and how one might help them, or what their reward from God was like."

51. I am indebted to Rosemary Hale's unpublished paper, "Spiritism and the Cult of the Dead in Late Medieval Germany." On women in the modern spiritualist movement see Ann Braude, *Radical Spirits: Spiritualism and Women's Rights in Nineteenth-Century America* (Boston, 1989); Alex Owen, *The Darkened Room: Women, Power and Spiritualism in Late Victorian England* (Philadelphia, 1990).

52. Guibert of Nogent, *Autobiographie* I.18, Benton 95; Caesarius of Heisterbach, *Dialogus miraculorum* I.33; Thomas of Cantimpré, *Vita Lutgardis* II.1.8, AA.SS. June, tom. 4 (Paris, 1867): 197; trans. Margot King, *The Life of Lutgard of Aywières* (Saskatoon, 1987): 35; *Vita Idae Nivellensis* 10, ed. Chrysostom Henriquez, *Quinque prudentes virgines* (Antwerp, 1630): 224–25; Boccaccio, *Decameron* VII.10; Frederic C. Tubach, *Index Exemplorum: A Handbook of Medieval Religious Tales* (Helsinki, 1969), nos. 2214 and 3976 (where the promise itself is punished in purgatory).

53. Aelred of Rievaulx, *De Sanctimoniali de Wattun*, PL 195: 790; McNamara, "Need to Give," 213.

54. "Unterlinden" ch. 23, p. 398.

55. Gertrude of Helfta, *Legatus divinae pietatis* V.17, ed. Jean-Marie Clément, *Oeuvres spirituelles* V, SC 331 (Paris, 1986): 176. Gertrude in fact had no living relatives, and her family name is unknown.

56. Marie of Oignies "saw a multitude of hands before her as if in supplication," outstretched by the souls in purgatory: Jacques de Vitry, *Life of Marie d'Oignies* I.27, trans. Margot King (Toronto, 1989): 41. This vision was widely diffused through the exemplum literature; cf. Tubach, *Index Exemplorum* no. 3202.

57. Mechthild of Magdeburg, *Das fliessende Licht* III.17, V.5, V.15, VI.10; Thomas of Cantimpré, *Vita Lutgardis* II.4, II.7. II.13, II.36, III.5.

58. Margaret Ebner, *Revelations*, in *Major Works*, trans. Leonard Hindsley (New York, 1993): 129. Henry of Nördlingen, Margaret's confessor, translated Mechthild's *Flowing Light* into Alemannic for the benefit of his spiritual daughters; his version is the only surviving German text of the work.

59. *A Revelation of Purgatory by an Unknown, Fifteenth-Century Woman Visionary*, ed. Marta Harley (Lewiston, 1985): 82. This scheme of a threefold purgatory synthesizes Le Goff's "third place" with older ideas about penance and expiation. No one seemed to notice any contradiction between the idea of souls' imprisonment in purgatory and their ability to appear on earth as ghosts. On the theology of debt cf. Duffy, *Stripping of the Altars*, 356–57, 364–65.

60. Caroline Walker Bynum, *Holy Feast and Holy Fast: The Religious Significance of Food to Medieval Women* (Berkeley, 1987): 418, n.54.

61. P. F. Palmer, "Indulgences," *New Catholic Encyclopedia* (Washington, 1967): VII, 482–84; cf. Duffy, *Stripping of the Altars*, 288.

62. Charles Williams, *The Descent of the Dove: A Short History of the Holy Spirit in the Church* (London, 1939): 236 et passim. Not coincidentally, Williams was also a medievalist noted for his work on Dante, *The Figure of Beatrice* (London, 1943).

63. Charles Williams, *All Hallows' Eve* (Grand Rapids, 1981): 158–64.

64. Le Goff, *Purgatory*, 357.

65. *Vita Lutgardis* II.1.9, p. 198; *Vita Aleydis de Scarenbeka* 20, in Henriquez, *Quinque prudentes virgines*, 190; Bynum, *Holy Feast*, 121; McNamara, "Need to Give," 216–17.

66. *Vita Christinae mirabilis* I.11–12, p. 652.

67. *Vita prior Lidwinae* XI.128, AA.SS. April, tom. 2 (Paris, 1866): 296; Bynum, *Holy Feast*, 127. Ida of Nivelles suffered a fever for six weeks to liberate a soul: *Vita Idae Nivellensis* 5, in Henriquez, 213.

68. *Vida y fin de la bienabenturada virgen sancta Juana de la Cruz,* Escorial MS. K-III-13, fols. 99ᵛ–102ᵛ; Ronald Surtz, *The Guitar of God: Gender, Power, and Authority in the Visionary World of Mother Juana de la Cruz* (Philadelphia, 1990): 38–40.

69. *Vita Lutgardis* III.3.21, p. 209; Mechthild of Magdeburg, *Das fliessende Licht* III.15; *Book of Margery Kempe* I.7, p. 54.

70. The theme of religious women's illness has been much discussed in recent years. Cf. Donald Weinstein and Rudolph Bell, *Saints and Society: The Two Worlds of Western Christendom, 1000–1700* (Chicago, 1982): 234–35; Elizabeth Petroff, *Medieval Women's Visionary Literature* (Oxford, 1986): 37–44; Bynum, *Holy Feast,* 199–200 et passim.

71. McNamara, "Need to Give," 217.

72. *Vita Lutgardis* III.1.1, p. 204; *Vita Aleydis* 26, p. 197; "Unterlinden" ch. 23, 52, pp. 403, 502; *Book of Margery Kempe* I.22, p. 87.

73. *Aucassin et Nicolette,* ed. Jean Dufournet (Paris, 1984): 58.

74. J. T. Muckle, ed., "The Personal Letters Between Abelard and Heloise," *Mediaeval Studies* 15 (1953): 72–73; see Chapter 2, above, pp. 71–72.

75. "O donna . . . che soffristi per la mia salute / in inferno lasciar le tue vestige." *Paradiso* 31.80–81.

76. Mechthild of Magdeburg, *Das fliessende Licht* I.5, ed. Neumann, p. 11.

77. *The Life of Beatrice of Nazareth* III.222, ed. and trans. Roger De Ganck (Kalamazoo, 1991): 260–61. The Latin vita is based on Beatrice's mystical diary in the vernacular, which does not survive.

78. Marguerite Porete, *Le Mirouer des simples Ames,* ch. 13, 131, ed. Romana Guarnieri, CCCM 69 (Turnhout, 1986): 58, 380.

79. Johannes Tauler, Sermon 9, in *Predigten,* ed. Georg Hofmann (Freiburg, 1961): 66–67; Bynum, *Holy Feast,* 242–43.

80. *Life of Catherine of Siena,* First Prologue, p. 14, par. 15.

81. Cf. Thomas Aquinas, *Quaestiones de anima* q. 21, responsio, ed. James Robb (Toronto, 1968): 271. "Maxima igitur afflictio damnatorum erit ex eo quod a Deo separabuntur."

82. A modern version of the *demande d'amour* is presented by Nikos Kazantzakis, who imagines St. Francis offering this typically feminine prayer: "How can I enjoy heaven, Lord, when I know hell exists? Dear Lord, either take pity on the damned and put them in paradise, or let me go down to the inferno and comfort the sufferers. I'll found an order whose purpose will be to descend to the inferno and comfort the damned. And if we can't lighten their pain, we'll remain in hell ourselves and suffer along with them." *Report to Greco,* trans. P. A. Bien (New York, 1965): 309. Kazantzakis, a deeply religious man, was excommunicated by the Greek Orthodox Church.

83. Hadewijch, Poems in Couplets 16.160–68, in *Complete Works,* trans. Columba Hart (New York, 1980): 356–57.

84. Poem 10.15–18 in ibid., p. 335. Interestingly, the same sentiments were expressed by Rabi'a, the celebrated female Sufi (d. 801): "O God! if I worship Thee in fear of Hell, burn me in Hell; and if I worship Thee in hope of Paradise, ex-

clude me from Paradise; but if I worship Thee for Thine own sake, withhold not Thine everlasting beauty!" A. J. Arberry, *Sufism: An Account of the Mystics of Islam* (London, 1969): 42–43.

85. Hadewijch, Letter 22 in Hart, 98–99.

86. Hadewijch, Vision 10, ibid. 287–88; *Het Visioenenboek van Hadewijch*, ed. H. W. Vekeman (Nijmegen, 1980): 121–23.

87. Hadewijch, Vision 5, pp. 276–77; *Visioenenboek* 77.

88. According to Bernard Spaapen, Hadewijch's "Luciferian fault" was not praying for the damned per se, but believing she had a special right to this favor. "Hadewijch et la 'Cinquième Vision,'" *Ons Geestelijk Erf* 46 (1972): 197–99.

89. Cf. Dante, *Purgatorio* 10 and *Paradiso* 20.

90. Jacobus de Voragine, *The Golden Legend*, trans. William Granger Ryan (Princeton, 1993): I, 178–79. The implications of this legend, which goes back to the eighth century, are also explored in such English poems as *Piers Plowman* (B-text, passus XI) and *St. Erkenwald*. See Gordon Whatley, "The Uses of Hagiography: The Legend of Pope Gregory and the Emperor Trajan in the Middle Ages," *Viator* 15 (1984): 25–63; idem, "Heathens and Saints: *St. Erkenwald* in Its Legendary Context," *Speculum* 61 (1986): 330–63.

91. Frank Willaert, "Hadewijch und ihr Kreis in den 'Visionen,'" in Kurt Ruh, ed., *Abendländische Mystik im Mittelalter* (Stuttgart, 1986): 368–87; H. W. J. Vekeman, "Die ontrouwe maectse so diep . . . Een nieuwe interpretatie van het vijfde Visioen van Hadewijch," *De Nieuwe Taalgids* 71 (1978): 385–409. On the metaphorical use of "hell" and "purgatory," see also Franz-Josef Schweitzer, *Der Freiheitsbegriff der deutschen Mystik* (Frankfurt, 1981): 266–73.

92. Mechthild of Magdeburg, *Das fliessende Licht* VI.28, III.21, pp. 235, 102.

93. Ibid. IV.25, pp. 141–42. Cf. Birgitta of Sweden, *Liber celestis* IV.8 (Middle English text), ed. Roger Ellis, EETS 291 (Oxford, 1987): I, 261. For more legends in which the boundary is blurred see Leopold Kretzenbacher's essay, *Versöhnung in Jenseits: Zur Widerspiegelung des Apokatastasis-Denkens in Glaube, Hochdichtung und Legende* (Munich, 1971).

94. Mechthild of Magdeburg, *Das fliessende Licht* VII.21, p. 274.

95. Ibid. V.8, p. 162.

96. Ibid. II.8, p. 46.

97. Ibid. III.15, p. 95.

98. Ibid. VII.55, pp. 301–2.

99. Caroline Bynum argues that Mechthild, although technically orthodox, prays for souls in hell and is "uncomfortable with ideas of sin and damnation." "Women Mystics in the Thirteenth Century: The Case of the Nuns of Helfta," in *Jesus as Mother: Studies in the Spirituality of the High Middle Ages* (Berkeley, 1982): 231–34.

100. Marguerite Porete, *Mirouer*, ch. 117, pp. 310–14.

101. *Life of Catherine of Siena* I.10, pp. 85–95.

102. *Book of Margery Kempe* I.7, I.22, pp. 54, 88.

103. Ibid. I.84, p. 245.

104. Ibid. I.59, pp. 183–85.

105. Julian of Norwich, *Showings*, Long Text ch. 40, trans. Edmund Colledge and James Walsh (New York, 1978): 247.

106. Nicholas Watson, "'A, Good Lord, How Myte Al Ben Wele?' Julian of Norwich's Self-Invention as a Theologian" (unpublished paper, 1992).

107. *A Book of Showings to the Anchoress Julian of Norwich*, Long Text ch. 32–33, ed. Edmund Colledge and James Walsh (Toronto, 1978): II, 425–27.

108. Ibid. ch. 33, pp. 425–26.

109. Ibid. ch. 38, pp. 445–48. This famous teaching is indebted to a text from St. Anselm's *Liber de similitudinibus*, also used by Bonaventure in a sermon to the beguines of Paris (n. 18 above): "Magdalena nec Petrus habebunt pudorem in die iudicii, nec in paradiso de suis peccatis. Sed ista signa erunt eis ad magnum honorem et etiam ad honorem dei, quia in hoc glorificabitur dominus et laudabitur in eternum. Unde tuum erit gaudium de hoc quod effugisti periculum et dei erit laus et gloria, quia ipse semper de hoc laudabitur." See Alan Bernstein, "The Invocation of Hell in Thirteenth-Century Paris," in James Hankins et al., eds., *Supplementum Festivum: Studies in Honor of Paul Oskar Kristeller* (Binghamton, 1987): 48–50.

110. Nicholas Watson, "The Composition of Julian of Norwich's 'Revelation of Love,'" *Speculum* 68 (1993): 637–83; Claire Cross, "'Great Reasoners in Scripture': The Activities of Women Lollards 1380–1530," in Derek Baker, ed., *Medieval Women* (Oxford, 1978): 360–61.

111. Bernstein, "Invocation of Hell."

112. Duffy, *Stripping of the Altars*, 344–45; and see n. 93 above.

113. "[Oremus] pro illis qui sunt in purgatorio, non pro illis de inferno: de illis factum est, sed pro illis qui sunt in prisione Domini et 'crient et breient' ad nos, ut ipsos elemosinis, ieiuniis et orationibus nostris liberemus." Bériou, "La prédication au béguinage," 129.

114. Ironically, Marguerite's *Mirouer* also circulated in anonymous and pseudonymous versions. See Marilyn Doiron, ed., *The Mirrour of Simple Soules: A Middle English Translation*, Archivio italiano per la storia della pietà 5 (Rome, 1968): 241–355; Michael Sargent, "'Le Mirouer des simples âmes' and the English Mystical Tradition," in Ruh, ed., *Abendländische Mystik im Mittelalter*, 443–65.

115. Marguerite's *Pagina meditationum*, par. 79–96, includes a grisly representation of hell which emphasizes God's utter lack of compassion for the damned. *The Writings of Margaret of Oingt*, trans. Renate Blumenfeld-Kosinski (Newburyport, 1990): 37–39.

116. "Hujus igitur erroris una causa est, quae multos exagitat, atque confundit; multitudo scilicet numerosissima damnandorum, et paucitas salvandorum. Ut quid inquiunt tam paucos elegit Dei misericordia ad salutem, tam multos autem deseruit in perditione maxime cum pronior credatur ad salvandum, quam ad damnandum . . . ? Praesumptio etiam videri potest, ut pauci Christiani se solos arbitrentur salvandos, tota residua multitudine hominum, videlicet malorum Christianorum, qui longe plures sunt quam boni, et deinde Judaeorum, Saracenorum atque paganorum, sive idolatrarum in perditione relicta . . . An videtur conveniens regi regum et domino saeculorum, ut plures habaet in carcere vinctos, plures ad patibulum affixos, tormentisque traditos, quam habeat sibi famulantes et subditos?

An potest misericordia Dei, cujus nec numerus est, nec mensura, sustinere tantam carnificinam tormentorum: ut quid inquiunt tantam multitudinem damnatorum creavit Deus? . . . Movet insipientes et incredulos, quod peccatum momentaneum est et admodum brevis perpetratio ipsius. Qualiter, inquiunt, justa potest esse poena aeterna pro eo illata?" William of Auvergne, *De legibus* 21, in *Opera omnia* (Paris, 1674; repr. Frankfurt, 1963): I, 57, 60. See Alan Bernstein, "Theology Between Heresy and Folklore: William of Auvergne on Punishment After Death," *Studies in Medieval and Renaissance History* 5 (1982): 20–31.

117. "Infernus non est malus, immo valde bonus et diligendus." William of Auvergne, *De moribus* 5, in ibid., 210b; Bernstein, "Theology," 26.

118. If we take overtly heretical sources into account, skepticism about hell looms much larger. For Cathar denials of hell see Walter Wakefield and Austin Evans, eds., *Heresies of the High Middle Ages* (New York, 1969): 338, 355–56. Peter Dronke notes that in the inquisitorial records from Montaillou, where Catholics and Cathars mingled, women's depositions still express more doubts about hell than men's (*Women Writers*, 209). See also John Edwards, "Religious Faith and Doubt in Late Medieval Spain: Soria circa 1450–1500," *Past & Present* 120 (1988): 3–25.

119. "Justice moved my high Maker, divine power fashioned me, supreme wisdom and primal love." *Inferno* III.4–6.

Chapter 5

1. "Die Tochter Sion," ll. 2838–43, cited in Kurt Ruh, "Beginenmystik: Hadewijch, Mechthild von Magdeburg, Marguerite Porete," *Zeitschrift für deutsches Altertum* 106 (1977): 238.

2. Paul Mommaers, "Hadewijch: A Feminist in Conflict," *Louvain Studies* 13 (1988): 78–79.

3. In proposing a literary reading of beguine texts I follow the lead of Ursula Peters, *Religiöse Erfahrung als literarisches Faktum: Zur Vorgeschichte und Genese frauenmystischer Texte des 13. und 14. Jahrhunderts* (Tübingen, 1988), although, unlike Peters, I do believe that "beguine literature" constitutes a distinctive category.

4. Hans Neumann, "Mechthild von Magdeburg und die mittelniederländische Frauenmystik," in *Medieval German Studies Presented to Frederick Norman* (London, 1965): 235.

5. Friedrich Ohly, *Hohelied-Studien: Grundzüge einer Geschichte der Hohelied-auslegung des Abendlandes bis um 1200* (Wiesbaden, 1958); E. Ann Matter, *The Voice of My Beloved: The Song of Songs in Western Medieval Christianity* (Philadelphia, 1990).

6. I have tried to avoid translating *fine amour* and its cognate *fin amant*, since the English "courtly love" carries too much unhelpful critical baggage.

7. "Hadewijch II" is the name given *faute de mieux* to a disciple of Hadewijch, who is thought to have written the "Poems in Couplets" that appear as nos.

17–29 in the manuscripts. On their authorship, see Saskia Murk Jansen, *The Measure of Mystic Thought: A Study of Hadewijch's Mengeldichten* (Göppingen, 1991).

8. Beguines also had more conventional rules. See Joanna Ziegler, "Reality as Imitation: The Role of Religious Imagery Among the Beguines of the Low Countries," in Ulrike Wiethaus, ed., *Maps of Flesh and Light: The Religious Experience of Medieval Women Mystics* (Syracuse, 1993): 114–17.

9. "*La Règle des Fins Amans*: Eine Beginenregel aus dem Ende des XIII. Jahrhunderts," ed. Karl Christ in *Philologische Studien aus dem romanisch-germanischen Kulturkreise: Festschrift Karl Voretzsch*, ed. B. Schädel and W. Mulertt (Halle, 1927): 193, 196.

10. Sir Thomas Malory, *Le Morte Arthur*, ed. Eugène Vinaver, *Works*, 2nd ed. (Oxford, 1971): 718.

11. Andreas Capellanus, *De amore et amoris remedio*, ed. and trans. P. G. Walsh (London, 1982).

12. "Retractions," in *Riverside Chaucer*, ed. Larry Benson et al. (Boston, 1987): 328.

13. D. W. Robertson, Jr., *A Preface to Chaucer: Studies in Medieval Perspectives* (Princeton, 1962).

14. Gérard of Liège, "Quinque incitamenta amoris," ed. André Wilmart, *Revue d'ascétique et de mystique* 12 (1931): 349–430; quoted passages, 415, 421, 407. This Gérard may have been either the Cistercian abbot of Val-Saint-Lambert (d. 1206) or another abbot who ruled the same monastery from 1249 to 1254: G. Hendrix, "Les *Postillae* de Hugues de Saint-Cher et le traité *De doctrina cordis*," *Recherches de théologie ancienne et médiévale* 47 (1980): 114–30.

15. The *Règle* also proposes a unique and possibly accurate derivation for the problematic term "beguine." The author traces it to one "Jehans li beguins" of Liège, a director of holy women, whom Karl Christ has identified as Jean de Nivelles (d. 1233), a canon of Liège and a close friend of Marie of Oignies and Jacques de Vitry. *Règle*, 188–89, 197.

16. Ibid., 192–93.

17. The Sacred Heart was equally important to a contemporary monastic woman, Gertrude of Helfta, but she expressed her devotion in the language of *Brautmystik* rather than *fine amour*. Cf. her *Legatus divinae pietatis*, III.25–26; trans. Margaret Winkworth, *The Herald of Divine Love* (New York, 1993): 188–91.

18. For examples see Andreas, *De amore* II.8; Guillaume de Lorris, *Roman de la Rose*, lines 2011–2264; Chaucer, *Legend of Good Women*, Prologue.

19. The classic troubadour statement of this motif—already tinged with ambiguous religiosity—is Jaufré Rudel's canso, "Lanquan li jorn son lonc en may": "Be tenc lo Senhor per veray / Per qu'ieu veirai l'amor de lonh; / Mas per un ben que m'en eschay / N'ai dos mals, quar tan m'es de lonh. / Ai! car me fos lai pelegris . . ." "Indeed, I hold him Lord in truth / Through whom I shall see the distant love; / But for a single good that befalls me / I have two evils, for she is so far from me. / Ah, that I were a pilgrim there . . . !" R. T. Hill and T. G. Bergin, eds., *Anthology of the Provençal Troubadours*, 2nd ed. (New Haven, 1973): I, 34.

20. Kathryn Gravdal, *Ravishing Maidens: Writing Rape in Medieval French*

Literature and Law (Philadelphia, 1991): 5. Gérard of Liège actually tried to imagine God as the best rapist: "Si autem uiolentiam requirit amor noster, *cest con li face force*, nullus maiorem uiolentiam pro eo faciet quam ipse. Petit enim eum quasi gladio euaginato. Aut enim eum amabis aut eterna morte morieris. . . . Vnde hic potest dici quoddam carmen quod uulgo canitur: *Tout a force maugre uostre uorrai uostre amour auoir.*" "Quinque incitamenta," 400.

21. The key sentence in the biblical account is 1/3 Kings 10:13: "And King Solomon gave the queen of Sheba all she desired, whatever she asked." For more typological and romantic readings see Paul Watson, "The Queen of Sheba in Christian Tradition," in James Pritchard, ed., *Solomon and Sheba* (New York, 1974): 115–45.

22. *Règle*, 201.

23. The Queen of Sheba as a type of ecstasy derives from Richard of St.-Victor, *The Mystical Ark* V.12, trans. Grover Zinn (New York, 1979): 326–29. Cf. Hadewijch, Poem 26.3, in Columba Hart, trans., *Complete Works* (New York, 1980): 200.

24. Marguerite Porete, *Mirouer des simples ames*, ch. 1, ed. Romana Guarnieri, CCCM 69 (Turnhout, 1986): 10–14. Cf. Peter Dronke, *Women Writers of the Middle Ages: A Critical Study of Texts from Perpetua (†203) to Marguerite Porete (†1310)* (Cambridge, 1984): 218–19.

25. Chrétien de Troyes, *Erec et Énide*, lines 5401–6364, ed. and trans. Carleton Carroll (New York, 1987). In the "Joie de la Cort" episode the hero, having overcome the self-indulgence of his early married life, is able to free another knight who had been imprisoned in sociopathic behavior by his lady's narcissism and jealousy.

26. *Règle*, 200.

27. "He! biaus dous Jhesucris, comme je douteroie po tout le monde, s'il avoit pris guere a moi et me vosist faire del pis qu'il porroit, se je vos avoie en aide! . . . Biaux sire diex, tolés moi tout, si me donés vos tout seul, il me souffira." Ibid. 205.

28. Hans Schottmann, "Autor und Hörer in der 'Strophischen Gedichten' Hadewijchs," *Zeitschrift für deutsches Altertum* 102 (1973): 20–37; Wilhelm Breuer, "Philologische Zugänge zur Mystik Hadewijchs: Zu Form und Funktion religiöser Sprache bei Hadewijch," in Margot Schmidt and Dieter Bauer, eds., *Grundfragen christlicher Mystik* (Stuttgart, 1987): 103–21.

29. Mary Magdalene in this role became a virtual patron saint for beguines. Cf. Hadewijch, Poem 3 in Couplets, pp. 322–23; Mechthild, *Das fliessende Licht der Gottheit*, V.23 and VI.9, ed. Hans Neumann (Munich, 1990): 180–81, 216; Marguerite, *Mirouer* ch. 124, pp. 350–60. A common theme is the *noli me tangere*—Mary's need to overcome her attachment to Christ's bodily presence. As Marguerite puts it, "donc ataint Marie le cours de son estre non mie quant elle parla et que elle quist, mais quant elle se teut et elle se sist" (360). See also Michel Lauwers, "'Noli me tangere': Marie Madeleine, Marie d'Oignies et les pénitentes du XIIIe siècle," *Mélanges de l'École Française de Rome: Moyen Age* 104:1 (1992): 209–68, and Excursus 2 below.

30. "Du bist drivaltig an dir, du maht wol gottes bilde sin: Du bist ein menlich man an dinem strite, du bist ein wolgezieret juncfrowe in dem palast vor dinem

herren, du bist ein lustlichú brut in dinem minnebette gottes!" *Das fliessende Licht* II.19, p. 49.

31. Frank Willaert, "Hadewijch und ihr Kreis in den 'Visionen,'" in Kurt Ruh, ed., *Abendländische Mystik im Mittelalter* (Stuttgart, 1986): 368–87.

32. Among the best theological accounts of Hadewijch are J.-B. Porion, introduction to Hadewijch, *Lettres spirituelles* (Geneva, 1972): 7–58, and Louis Bouyer, *Figures mystiques féminines* (Paris, 1989): 13–47.

33. Hadewijch, Vision 3 in Hart, 272.

34. Vision 4, ibid. 274.

35. Vision 14, ibid. 305: "O strongest of all warriors! You have conquered everything and opened the closed totality, which never was opened by creatures who did not know, with painfully won and distressed Love, how I am God and Man! O heroine, . . . since you never yield, you are called the greatest heroine!"

36. Letter 13, ibid. 75.

37. Letter 2, ibid. 50; Letter 10, p. 66; Letter 30, p. 116.

38. Letter 12, ibid. 71.

39. Letter 21, ibid. 93.

40. Poem 9, ibid. 149–52; cf. H. van Cranenburgh, "Hadewychs zwölfte Vision und neuntes strophisches Gedicht: Versuch einer Textdeutung," in Kurt Ruh, ed., *Altdeutsche und Altniederländische Mystik* (Darmstadt, 1964): 152–74.

41. Cf. for example Bernart de Ventadorn, "Can vei la lauzeta mover," in Hill and Bergin, *Anthology*, 53–55.

42. Poem 21.6 in Hart, 184–85.

43. In the most thorough study of Hadewijch's poetry in English, Tanis Guest argues that her "pride and her strong sense of her own authority would make it very easy for her to adopt the male knightliness which would certainly come easier to her than female submissiveness. She could not play the love-lorn girl; but the disappointed and indignant suitor came naturally to her." *Some Aspects of Hadewijch's Poetic Form in the "Strofische Gedichten"* (The Hague, 1975): 218.

44. "Die brut ist trunken worden von der angesihte des edeln antlutes: In der grösten sterki kumt si von ir selber, in dem schönsten liehte ist si blint an ir selber und in der gröston blintheit sihet si allerklarost. In der grösten klarheit ist si beide tot und lebende. Ie si langer tot ist, ie si vrölicher lebt. Ie si vrölicher lebt, ie si mer ervert. Ie si minner wirt, ie ir mer züflusset. . . . Ie ir wunden tieffer werdent, ie si me sturmet. . . . Ie das minnebet enger wirt, ie die umbehalsunge naher gat. Ie das muntkussen süsser smekket, ie si sich minneclicher ansehent. Ie si sich nöter scheident, ie er ir mer gibet." Mechthild, *Das fliessende Licht* I.22, pp. 16–17.

45. "Ich bin die, die du so liep hast, und ich bin din gespile. Ich bin die heilige cristanheit, und wir haben bede einen brútgome." Ibid. IV.3, p. 116. Mechthild's allegorical vision of the Church may be indebted to Hildegard of Bingen.

46. Hadewijch, Vision 12 in Hart, 296.

47. Vision 10, ibid. 288.

48. "Do unsers vatter jubilus betrübet wart mit Adames valle, also das er müste zurnen, . . . Do erwelte mich der vatter zü einer brut, das er etwas ze minnende hette, wand sin liebu brut was tot, die edel sele; und do kos mich der sun

zü einer müter und do enpfieng mich der helig geist ze einer trutinne. Do was ich alleine brut der heligen drivaltekeit und müter der weisen." Mechthild, *Das fliessende Licht* I.22, p. 18.

49. "Ich habe din begert e der welte beginne. Ich gere din und du begerest min. Wa zwöi heisse begerunge zesamen koment, da ist die minne vollekomen." Ibid. VII.16, p. 268.

50. "Ich wil mir selben machen ein brut, dú sol mich grüssen mit irem munde und mit irem ansehen verwunden, denne erste gat es an ein minnen. . . . Ich bin got aller götten, du bist aller creaturen göttinne und ich gibe dir mine hanttrúwe, das ich dich niemer verkiese." Ibid. III.9, pp. 87–88.

51. "Ir sun ist got und si göttinne, es mag ir nieman gliche gewinnen." Ibid. III.1, p. 75. In III.4, p. 82, Mary is called "edel göttinne ob allen luteren menschen."

52. Ibid. I.44, VII.8, VII.37.

53. Ibid I.4, pp. 10–11.

54. "Da müs si fur nieman bitten noch fragen, wan er wil alleine mit ir spilen ein spil, das der lichame nut weis noch die dörper bi dem phlüge noch die ritter in dem turnei . . . Wenne das spil allerbest ist, so müs man es lassen." Ibid I.2, pp. 7–8; I.44, p. 32.

55. Ibid. III.1, II.25, III.23. "Owe herre, joch bist du mir alze lange vrömde; könde ich dich, herre, mit zovfere gewinnen, das du nit möhtest gerüwen denne an mir; eya, so gienge es an ein minnen" (106).

56. In II.26, for example, Mechthild writes of her book as image of the Trinity: the words signify God's deity, the pure parchment his humanity, and the reader's voice, his living spirit (68).

57. Ibid. IV.14, p. 129: in heaven God is host (*der wirt*) and the soul will be hostess (*die husfrowen*) at his side. "Brother Jesus and Sister Mary" appear in V.11, p. 164—one of several passages in which the roles of Jesus and Mary are strictly parallel. Cf. II.3, III.1, VI.24, VI.39.

58. "Din kintheit was ein gesellinne mines heligen geistes; din jugent was ein brut miner menscheit; din alter ist nu ein husvrovwe miner gotheit." Ibid. VII.3, p. 260.

59. For Marguerite's stages of spiritual progress see *Mirouer* ch. 59–60 (on the three deaths) and ch. 118 (on the seven degrees or states of being); discussion in Ellen Babinsky, introduction to *The Mirror of Simple Souls* (New York, 1993): 27–36.

60. The French has *dangereuse*, a term rich in connotations. *Dangier* (power or sovereignty) is in courtly literature the lady's right of refusal, which gives her dominion over her suitors. In this case the Soul is *dangereuse* because she haughtily rejects all claims on her "except the pure delight of Love."

61. "Le quart estat est que l'Ame est tiree par haultesse d'amour en delit de pensee par meditacion, et relenquie de tous labours de dehors et de obedience d'aultruy par haultesse de contemplacion; donc l'Ame est si dangereuse, noble, et delicieuse, que elle ne peut souffrir que rien la touche, sinon la touche du pur delit d'Amour, dont elle est singulierement deduisant et jolie, qui la fait orgueilleuse d'abondance d'amour, dont est maistresse du celustre, c'est a dire de la clarte de son ame." *Mirouer* ch. 118, p. 322.

62. Ibid. ch. 133, p. 392.

63. "Je suis Dieu par nature divine, et ceste Ame l'est par droicture d'amour." Ibid. ch. 21, p. 82.

64. On the importance of this claim see Kurt Ruh, "Gottesliebe bei Hadewijch, Mechthild von Magdeburg und Marguerite Porete," in *Romanische Literaturbeziehungen im 19. und 20. Jahrhundert: Festschrift für Franz Rauhut*, ed. Angel San Miguel, Richard Schwaderer, and Manfred Tietz (Tübingen, 1985): 243–54.

65. For Marguerite's influence on Eckhart, who was resident in Paris both during her lifetime (1293–94, 1302–03) and shortly after her martyrdom (1311–13), see Edmund Colledge and J. C. Marler, "'Poverty of the Will': Ruusbroec, Eckhart and *The Mirror of Simple Souls*," in Paul Mommaers and Norbert De Paepe, eds., *Jan van Ruusbroec: The Sources, Content and Sequels of His Mysticism* (Louvain, 1984): 14–47.

66. "O desrivé et habandonné amy et pour moy courtois sans mesure!" *Mirouer* ch. 38, p. 120.

67. Ibid. ch. 71, p. 198. God as *jaloux* also appears in the "Quinque incitamenta," 404: "*Quant plus me bat et destraint li ialous, tant ai ie mius en amour ma pensee.* Deus enim, ut dixit Moyses, est FORTIS ZELOTES, idest *ialous*."

68. *Mirouer* ch. 60, 118; pp. 174, 318.

69. Hildegard of Bingen, *Causae et curae*, ed. Paul Kaiser (Leipzig, 1903): 72–73, 87–88; Dronke, *Women Writers*, 223.

70. "Je di, dit l'Ame, qu'il m'esconvient pour leur rudesse taire et celer mon langage, lequel j'ay aprins es secrez de la court secrete du doulx pays, ouquel pays, courtoisie est loy, et amour mesure, et bonté pasture." *Mirouer* ch. 68, p. 192.

71. Ibid. ch. 19, 50, 74, 87, 120.

72. "Ceste Ame, dit Amour, est franche, mais plus franche, mais tres franche, mais surmontamment franche, et de plante et de stocs et de toutes ses branches, et de tous les fruiz de ses branches. Ceste Ame a son lot de franchise affinee, checun coste en a sa plaine pinte. Elle ne respont a nully, se elle ne veult, se il n'est de son lignage; car ung gentilhomme ne daigneroit respondre a ung vilain, se il l'appelloit ou requeroit de champ de bataille; et pource ne trouve telle Ame qui l'appelle; ses ennemis n'ont plus d'elle response." Ibid. ch. 85, pp. 240–42.

73. On Marguerite's trial, see Robert Lerner, *The Heresy of the Free Spirit in the Later Middle Ages* (Berkeley, 1972): 68–78, 200–08; Paul Verdeyen, "La procès d'inquisition contre Marguerite Porete et Guiard de Cressonessart," *Revue d'histoire ecclésiastique* 81 (1986): 47–94.

74. In all the extant medieval translations of the *Mirouer* (Latin, Italian, and English), Love becomes masculine or neuter, with considerable loss of nuance. On the reception history of the text see Kurt Ruh, "'Le miroir des simples âmes' der Marguerite Porete" (1975), rpt. in *Kleine Schriften* II, ed. Volker Mertens (Berlin, 1984): 212–36; Michael Sargent, "'Le Mirouer des simples âmes' and the English Mystical Tradition," in Ruh, *Abendländische Mystik*, 443–65.

75. Breuer, "Philologische Zugänge," 116–17.

76. In the sixteenth and seventeenth centuries, *amour* became masculine once again under the influence of humanistic Latin, although the plural *les amours* remains feminine in poetic usage. Walther von Wartburg, *Französisches Etymologisches Wörterbuch* 24, p. 469.

77. "Minne" is related to the verb *meinen*, "to think of (someone)," and once had a semantic range almost as wide as modern English "love." In late medieval German the term was debased to the point of obscenity, until it finally gave way to *Liebe*. Dorothea Wiercinski, *Minne: Herkunft und Anwendungsschichten eines Wortes* (Cologne, 1964).

78. Barbara Newman, *Sister of Wisdom: St. Hildegard's Theology of the Feminine* (Berkeley, 1987): 42–87.

79. Hadewijch, Vision 2 in Hart, 271.

80. The subjective reading is advanced by Norbert De Paepe in *Hadewijch Strofische Gedichten: Een Studie van de minne in het kader der 12ᵉ en 13e eeuwse mystiek en profane minnelyriek* (Ghent, 1967), while Jozef Van Mierlo and others stress theological meanings. For a good review of interpretations to date see Paul Mommaers, "Bulletin d'histoire de la spiritualité: L'École néerlandaise," *Revue d'histoire de la spiritualité* 49 (1973): 465–92.

81. Hadewijch, Letter 25 in Hart, 106.

82. Guest, *Some Aspects*, 7.

83. Elizabeth Petroff, "Gender, Knowledge, and Power in Hadewijch's *Strophische Gedichten*," in *Body and Soul: Essays on Medieval Women and Mysticism* (New York, 1994): 188.

84. Hadewijch, Vision 11 in Hart, 291, and Poem 2.5, p. 132: "Hare name *amor* es: vander doot." Hart translates "vander doot" as "delivered from death."

85. Poem 37, stanza 11, cited in Breuer, "Philologische Zugänge," 115.

86. Poem 15 in Couplets, Hart 352.

87. Mechthild, *Das fliessende Licht* I.1, I.3, III.3, IV.19 ("herzefrowe kúnegin"), VII.48.

88. Ibid. I.1, pp. 5–7.

89. Ulrike Wiethaus, "Sexuality, Gender, and the Body in Late Medieval Women's Spirituality," *Journal of Feminist Studies in Religion* 7 (1991): 45, 52.

90. "Je suis Dieu, dit Amour, car Amour est Dieu, et Dieu est amour, et ceste Ame est Dieu par condicion d'amour." *Mirouer* ch. 21, p. 82.

91. Ibid. ch. 72–74, pp. 202–6.

92. Ibid. ch. 56, p. 164.

93. Barbara Newman, "Some Mediaeval Theologians and the Sophia Tradition," *Downside Review* 108 (1990): 111–30.

94. Hadewijch, Poem 2 in Hart, 131.

95. Poem 29.5, ibid. 209.

96. Vision 13, ibid. 298. For a similar conflation of Christ with the *domna* cf. the end of Letter 6, p. 63.

97. Cf. Poem 13.8, ibid. 162, and Letter 20, p. 92: "Love will not yield to saints, men here below, Angels, heaven, or earth. She has vanquished the Divinity by her nature. She cries with a loud voice, without stay or respite, in all the hearts of those who love: 'Love ye Love!'"

98. "Swenne ich gedenke, das der himmelsche vatter da ist der seligen schenke und Jhesus der kopf, der helig geist der luter win, und wie du ganze drivaltekeit ist der volle kopf und minne du gewaltige kellerin, weis got so neme ich gerne, das mich du minne da ze huse bete." Mechthild, *Das fliessende Licht* II.24, p. 59. Cf. Mar-

got Schmidt, "*Minne dú gewaltige kellerin*: On the nature of *Minne* in Mechthild of Magdeburg's *Fliessendes Licht der Gottheit*," *Vox benedictina* 4 (1987): 100–125.

99. Hadewijch, Letter 30 in Hart, 119.

100. An exception to this stance is the recent work of John Giles Milhaven, *Hadewijch and Her Sisters: Other Ways of Loving and Knowing* (Albany, 1993). Milhaven stresses "embodied mutuality" as the keynote of Hadewijch's praxis to emphasize her distance from scholastic epistemology and ethics. His emphasis is a valuable corrective to the position I take, but in his comparatively optimistic account of the body, he tends to ignore Hadewijch's insistence on suffering and abjection.

101. Luce Irigaray, "La Mystérique," in *Speculum of the Other Woman*, trans. Gillian Gill (Ithaca, 1985): 191–202.

102. Margret Bäurle and Luzia Braun, "'Ich bin heiser in der Kehle meiner Keuschheit': Über das Schreiben der Mystikerinnen," in Hiltrud Gnüg and Renate Möhrmann, eds., *Frauen Literatur Geschichte: Schreibende Frauen vom Mittelalter bis zur Gegenwart* (Stuttgart, 1985): 1–15.

103. Wiethaus, "Sexuality," 43.

104. Elsewhere in the text the same stages are called "insuperable," "inseparable," "singular," and "insatiable." Richard of St.-Victor, *De quatuor gradibus violentae charitatis*, PL 196: 1207–24; trans. Clare Kirchberger, "Of the Four Degrees of Passionate Charity," in *Richard of Saint-Victor: Selected Writings on Contemplation* (New York, 1957): 213–33. See also Gervais Dumeige, *Richard de Saint-Victor et l'idée chrétienne de l'amour* (Paris, 1952).

105. Richard, "Four Degrees," 220.

106. This concept is summed up in one of Hadewijch's keywords, *orewoet*— the "storm" or "raging fury" of love.

107. Denis de Rougemont, *L'amour et l'Occident* (Paris, 1939); trans. Montgomery Belgion as *Love in the Western World* (New York, 1956).

108. Gottfried von Strassburg, *Tristan*, Prologue 58–66, ed. Friedrich Ranke (Stuttgart, 1981): I, 12–14.

109. Robert Pinsky, "Jesus and Isolt," in *The Want Bone* (New York, 1990): 32–40.

110. Richard, "Four Degrees," 232.

111. See Chapter 4 above, pp. 123–24.

112. For the body in Hadewijch, see Caroline Walker Bynum, *Holy Feast and Holy Fast: The Religious Significance of Food to Medieval Women* (Berkeley, 1987): 153–60; Milhaven, *Hadewijch and Her Sisters*, 108–10. For an alternative view with emphasis on Mechthild, see Wiethaus, "Sexuality, Gender, and the Body."

113. "Aber der minne nature ist, das si allererst vlússet von süssekeit, dar nach wirt si riche in der bekantnisse, zem dritten male wirt si girig in der verworfenheit." Mechthild, *Das fliessende Licht* VI.20, p. 230.

114. Ibid. IV.12, pp. 125–26; VII.65, p. 310.

115. "Si wirt an dem crutze so vaste genegelt mit dem hammer der starken minnelovffe, das si alle creaturen nit mögent wider gerüffen. Si turstet ovch vil sere an dem cruze der minne, wan si trunke vil gerne den lutern win von allen gottes kinden. So koment si al mitalle und schenkent ir die gallen. Ir licham wirt getötet

in der lebendigen minne, wenne ir geist wirt gehöhet uber alle menschliche sinne. Nach disem tode vert si zü der helle mit irer maht und tröstet die betrübeten selen mit irme gebette von gottes güti sunder irs lichamen wissenthaft. Si wirt gestochen von einem blinden durch ire siten mit eime süssen spere der unschuldiger minne; da vliessent us irem herzen manig heilig lere. Si hanget ovch hoch in dem süssen luft des heligen geistes gegen der ewigen sunnen der lebendigen gotheit an dem crutze der hohen minne, das si vollen durre wirt von allen irdenschen dingen." Ibid. III.10, p. 90.

116. "O tres bien nee, dit Amour a ceste precieuse marguerite, bien soiez vous entree ou seul franc manoir, ouquel nul ne entre, se il n'est de vostre lygnage, sans bastardise." *Mirouer* ch. 52, p. 152. Were it not for Marguerite's "entiere humilité," one might suspect a play on her own name.

117. Ibid. ch. 135, p. 396.

118. See Chapter 2 above, pp. 72–73.

119. "[Se] je savoie sans doubte que vostre vouloir le vouldroit sans vostre bonte divine amenuyser, je le vouldroie, sans jamais plus rien vouloir. Et ainsi, sire, ma voulente prent sa fin en ce dire; et pource est mon vouloir martir, et mon amour martire." *Mirouer* ch. 131, p. 388.

120. See Jan van Ruysbroeck, *The Book of the Twelve Beguines*, trans. John Francis (London, 1913); Georgette Epiney-Burgard, "L'influence des béguines sur Ruusbroec," in Mommaers and De Paepe, eds., *Jan van Ruusbroec*, 68–85.

121. Mechthild and Marguerite both spoke of their "art" in a positive, self-conscious way. Cf. *Das fliessende Licht* V.28, p. 187: "Swa dú kunst hat wisheit und minne, da bringet die erwelunge fruht"; *Mirouer* ch. 110, pp. 298–300: "art en creature est ung engin soubtil qui est en la substance de l'Ame . . . Cest art est ysnel, et pource tend par nature a ataindre le plain de son emprise. Son emprise est sans plus le droit vouloir de Dieu."

122. *Silence: A Thirteenth-Century French Romance*, ed. and trans. Sarah Roche-Mahdi (East Lansing, 1992). The otherwise unknown poet, "Master Heldris of Cornwall," might conceivably be the pseudonym of a woman.

123. Cf. Paul Mommaers: "God is and remains the Wholly Other. This being other presents itself, however, in the love experience of being-at-one as *inexhaustibility*, whereas the scholastic speculation views it as *unapproachability*." "Hadewijch," 70.

124. Lerner, *Heresy*, 71.

125. Marie de France, "Yonec," in *Lais*, trans. Robert Hanning and Joan Ferrante (New York, 1978): 137–52.

126. Hadewijch, Vision 7 in Hart, 280–82.

127. Raymond Blakney, *Meister Eckhart: A Modern Translation* (New York, 1941): 252–53. Of the nine roles that the visitor rejects, only "master" has disappeared from the second list. The absence is significantly double-edged, since of all the roles, that of teaching authority was seen as least acceptable for a woman; yet in the sequel, it is precisely the role of Meister that Eckhart ascribes to his daughter.

Excursus 1

1. Hadewijch, Vision 8, in *Complete Works*, trans. Columba Hart (New York, 1980): 282–84.
2. Nikolaus Häring, "Abelard Yesterday and Today," in René Louis and Jean Jolivet, eds., *Pierre Abélard—Pierre le Vénérable* (Paris, 1975): 341–403.
3. "Alpha and Omega, great God . . . / whose might can accomplish all, / whose intellect knows all, / whose being is the supreme good, / whose work contains all good. . . . / Within all things, yet not enclosed; / Outside of all, yet not excluded; / Above all, yet not arrogant; / Beneath all, yet not abased." Hildebert of Lavardin, *Carmina* 71, PL 171: 1411–14.
4. Letter 22 in Hart, 94–102; Notes, 370 n.93 and 382 n.79.
5. Letter 18 in Hart, 86–87; Introduction, 6; Notes, 369 n.74.
6. William of St.-Thierry, *Disputatio adversus Petrum Abaelardum* 8, PL 180: 276–80; Bernard of Clairvaux, *Capitula haeresum Petri Abaelardi* 5, PL 182: 1051a; *Letters of St. Bernard of Clairvaux*, trans. Bruno James (London, 1953), nos. 240–48, pp. 320–27.
7. Cf. Letter 12, Hart 73: "Jacob is everyone who conquers; by the power of Love, he conquered God, in order to be conquered himself."
8. Vision 8, Hart 284; cf. Vision 14, p. 305.
9. Paul Mommaers, "Hadewijch: A Feminist in Conflict," *Louvain Studies* 13 (1988): 65.
10. Letter 4, Hart 54; Mommaers, 67.

Excursus 2

1. The text has been edited by Franz-Josef Schweitzer in *Der Freiheitsbegriff der deutschen Mystik: Seine Beziehung zur Ketzerei der "Brüder und Schwestern vom Freien Geist" mit besonderer Rücksicht auf den pseudo-eckartischen Traktat "Schwester Katrei"* (Frankfurt, 1981): 322–70. There is a translation by Elvira Borgstädt in Bernard McGinn, ed., *Meister Eckhart: Teacher and Preacher* (New York, 1986): 349–87.
2. Robert Lerner, *The Heresy of the Free Spirit in the Later Middle Ages* (Berkeley, 1972): 215–21, 232.
3. F. P. Pickering, "Notes on Late Medieval German Tales in Praise of *docta ignorantia*," *Bulletin of the John Rylands Library* 24 (1940): 121–37.
4. See Chapter 5 above, p. 167.
5. Edmund Colledge and J. C. Marler, "'Poverty of the Will': Ruusbroec, Eckhart and *The Mirror of Simple Souls*," in Paul Mommaers and Norbert De Paepe, eds., *Jan van Ruusbroec: The Sources, Content and Sequels of His Mysticism* (Louvain, 1984): 14–47.
6. Pickering, "Notes," 130; Lerner, *Heresy*, 215. For the Eckhartian sources see the notes in McGinn, *Meister Eckhart*, 384–87.
7. "Sister Catherine," in McGinn, 371.
8. Ibid. 372–74, 380.

9. See Chapter 5 above, n. 29. At some points *Schwester Katrei* echoes Meister Eckhart's famous Sermon 86 on Mary and Martha (in McGinn, 338–44). But Eckhart's central point is the opposite of "Sister Catherine"'s: he sees service, performed in uninterrupted union with God, as a higher state than contemplation in solitude.

10. "Sister Catherine," 376. God's "motherhood" here denotes the exemplarist idea of the divine mind as a "womb" in which all creatures dwelt eternally "before they were created." Christ, however, is far more than a "child of God" in this generic sense.

11. Ibid. 377.

12. For gnostic and orthodox versions of this saint see Marjorie Malvern, *Venus in Sackcloth: The Magdalen's Origins and Metamorphoses* (Carbondale, 1975).

13. This conflation has been traced to Gregory the Great, *Homily 33*, PL 76: 1239. See Michel Lauwers, "'Noli me tangere': Marie Madeleine, Marie d'Oignies et les pénitentes du XIIIᵉ siècle," *Mélanges de l'École Française de Rome: Moyen Âge* 104 (1992): 221–22.

14. See Ruth Karras, "Holy Harlots: Prostitute Saints in Medieval Legend," *Journal of the History of Sexuality* 1 (1990): 17–28; Marina Warner, *Alone of All Her Sex: The Myth and the Cult of the Virgin Mary* (New York, 1976): 224–35.

15. "Sister Catherine," 380–81.

16. Lauwers, "Noli me tangere," 215, 220–21, 233–34.

17. For examples of this trend see the fourteenth-century Italian *Vita di S. Maria Maddalena*, in *Vite de alcuni santi scritte nel buon secolo della lingua toscana* (Milan, 1830), trans. Valentina Hawtrey, *The Life of Saint Mary Magdalen* (London, 1904); and the fifteenth-century Saint Antonino's claim that not corporeal but "mental virginity" (with its heavenly reward) could be restored by true penance. Bishop Antonino was responding to women's inquiries about the status of Mary Magdalene. *Lettere di Santi e Beati Fiorentini*, ed. Antommaria Biscioni (Florence, 1736): 225. I thank Ray Clemens and Katherine Jansen for the references.

18. Digby *Mary Magdalene*, lines 1900–02 and 1944–45, in David Bevington, ed., *Medieval Drama* (Boston, 1975): 745–57. See also Suzanne Craymer, "Margery Kempe's Imitation of Mary Magdalene and the 'Digby Plays,'" *Mystics Quarterly* 19 (1993): 173–81.

19. For Mary's role as gnostic spokeswoman against rival orthodox claims see Pheme Perkins, *The Gnostic Dialogue: The Early Church and the Crisis of Gnosticism* (New York, 1980): 131–41.

20. *Gospel of Philip* 63–64, 69, in James M. Robinson, ed., *The Nag Hammadi Library in English*, 3rd ed. (San Francisco, 1988): 148, 151.

21. *Gospel of Mary*, in ibid. 523–27.

22. *Dialogue of the Savior* 53, in ibid. 252.

23. *Pistis Sophia* I.19, II.87, ed. Carl Schmidt and trans. Violet MacDermot (Leiden, 1978): 28, 200.

24. *Gospel of Thomas* 114, in Robinson, 138.

25. "Sister Catherine," 351.

26. *Gospel of Philip* 73, in Robinson, 153. For this reference cf. McGinn, *Meister Eckhart*, 386 n.51.

27. *Gospel of Thomas* 11, in Robinson, 127.

28. Augustine, *De moribus Manichaeorum* 39, PL 32: 1362; Ioan Couliano, *The Tree of Gnosis: Gnostic Mythology from Early Christianity to Modern Nihilism* (San Francisco, 1992): 179.

29. "Sister Catherine," 366.

30. McGinn, *Meister Eckhart*, 13.

31. "Sister Catherine," 364–65. McGinn notes a similarity with Eriugena's *Periphyseon* on this point, but without asserting textual dependence on it: *Meister Eckhart*, 14.

32. "Sister Catherine," 361.

33. While "Sister Catherine" rejects the idea of a material place of torment and argues for hell as a "state of being" (*ein wesen*), she insists that its misery is eternal and implies that most human beings—all "people who adhere to their creatureliness"—will be damned. "Sister Catherine," 363–64.

34. Jean Duvernoy, *Le Catharisme: La religion des cathares* (Toulouse, 1976): 98–99, 265.

35. Malvern, *Venus in Sackcloth*, 72.

36. Ibid. 38; *Das Erlauer Osterspiel III*, lines 1387–89, in Eduard Hartl, ed., *Das Drama des Mittelalters*, II (Leipzig, 1937): 256.

Chapter 6

1. Gertrude Moakley, *The Tarot Cards Painted by Bonifacio Bembo for the Visconti-Sforza Family: An Iconographic and Historical Study* (New York, 1966): 72–73.

2. Felice Tocco, ed., "Il Processo dei Guglielmiti," *Rendiconti della Reale Accademia dei Lincei: Classe di Scienze Morali, Storiche e Filologiche*, ser. 5, vol. 8 (Rome, 1899): 309–42, 351–84, 407–32, 437–69.

3. Henry Charles Lea, *A History of the Inquisition of the Middle Ages* (1887; rpt. New York, 1906), III: 90–102.

4. Stephen Wessley, "The Thirteenth-Century Guglielmites: Salvation Through Women," in Derek Baker, ed., *Medieval Women* (Oxford, 1978): 289–303.

5. From the standpoints of comparative religion and of archetypal psychology, the problem that cries out for investigation is not the occasional hint of feminine deity in Judaism, Christianity, or Islam, but its nearly universal absence.

6. Tocco, 313, 360.

7. Similarly, Dorothea of Montau and Peter of Luxembourg won greater esteem for saintliness once they left their native towns: Richard Kieckhefer, *Unquiet Souls: Fourteenth-Century Saints and Their Religious Milieu* (Chicago, 1984): 42–43. Guglielma's contemporary, Mechthild, explained that she chose to live in Magdeburg precisely because she would be a stranger there.

8. Wessley, "Guglielmites," 297, 302n; Luisa Muraro, *Guglielma e Maifreda: Storia di un'eresia femminista* (Milan, 1985): 24. Among the most active families in the sect, the Malcolzati and Garbagnate were allied with the Visconti, while the Carentano family belonged to the Torriani faction.

9. Tocco, 353, 461. Most authorities give Aug. 24, 1281 as the date of Guglielma's death, although Wessley argues for 1279. "Guglielmites," 301n.

10. Tocco, 313, 377, 380, 424.

11. Ibid. 329, 371–73.

12. Ibid. 313, 319, 461.

13. For the family history see Jaroslav Polc, *Agnes von Böhmen, 1211–1282: Königstochter—Äbtissin—Heilige* (Munich, 1989): 11–18.

14. Ibid. 51. Agnes was at one time betrothed to Heinrich, the son of Emperor Frederick II, and later refused Frederick himself. For St. Clare's affectionate correspondence with Agnes, see *Francis and Clare: The Complete Works*, trans. Regis Armstrong and Ignatius Brady (New York, 1982): 189–206.

15. Polc, *Agnes von Böhmen*, 15.

16. Elizabeth's father, King Andreas II of Hungary, was the brother of Guglielma's mother, Queen Constance. On Elizabeth as a role model for her female relatives, see Gábor Klaniczay, *The Uses of Supernatural Power: The Transformation of Popular Religion in Medieval and Early-Modern Europe* (Princeton, 1990): 99–103.

17. Friedrich Prinz, *Böhmen im mittelalterlichen Europa* (Munich, 1984): 167.

18. Tocco, 323, 431.

19. Ibid. 331, 333, 374. The books, presented as evidence in the trial, were presumably burned.

20. Ibid. 317, 322, 383, 432.

21. Ibid. 334.

22. Ibid. 419, 446, 461–62.

23. Ibid. 383.

24. Ibid. 413.

25. Ibid. 415.

26. Ibid. 321, 375, 383.

27. Ibid. 334; Muraro, *Guglielma*, 28.

28. Muraro, *Guglielma*, 145–48.

29. Lea, *Inquisition* III, 102; Tocco, 461.

30. For the Guglielmite sect in relation to Joachite thought see Marjorie Reeves, *The Influence of Prophecy in the Later Middle Ages: A Study in Joachimism* (Oxford, 1969): 248–50, and M. D. Lambert, *Medieval Heresy: Popular Movements from the Gregorian Reform to the Reformation*, 2nd ed. (Cambridge, MA, 1992): 199–202.

31. Tocco, 332, 372–73.

32. Ibid. 323, 340.

33. Ibid. 336–37, 340, 368–70, 373.

34. Ibid. 320, 322, 329–30.

35. Ibid. 321, 329, 341, 355, 423, 431.

36. Ibid. 333, 353, 358, 412–14.

37. Aside from rancor against Andrea Saramita, Girardo had another reason to collaborate; he had been the sole member interrogated in 1296 and thus stood in danger of death if proven relapsed. Muraro, *Guglielma*, 53–54, 65, 70–71.

38. Tocco, 321, 411.

39. "Quelli ch'usurpa in terra il luogo mio, / il luogo mio, il luogo mio, che vaca / nella presenza del Figliuol di Dio, / fatt' ha del cimiterio mio cloaca / del sangue e della puzza." *Paradiso* 27: 22–26. Cf. *Inferno* 27:67–111.

40. Eleven men and twenty-one women were interrogated, but these numbers are misleading. Not all who testified were actually involved in the sect, and some committed members were not interrogated because they died before 1300 or were absent from Milan. Moreover, some depositions may have been contained in the lost portion of the trial records. The inquisitors did not interrogate any monks of Chiaravalle, despite their active promotion of Guglielma's cult. Members and affiliates of the sect are listed in Patrizia Costa, *Guglielma la Boema, L' "Eretica" di Chiaravalle* (Milan, 1985): 121–24.

41. Tocco, 424.

42. Two sectaries came from families with previous heretical affiliations: Bellacara Carentano's father had been signed with yellow crosses for heresy, and Allegranza Perusio's great-aunt was burnt. Tocco, 315, 327.

43. Ibid. 334, 360, 432; Muraro, *Guglielma*, 13, 23. The sons were named Paraclitolo (after the Paraclete) and Felicino (after "felice," the Italian form of Guglielma's original Slavic name, Blažena).

44. Tocco, 418, 420, 422, 426–27.

45. Ibid. 443, 446; Muraro, *Guglielma*, 162–63.

46. Carabella Toscano's husband, Amizzone, seems to have shared her faith, but he died in 1292. Except for Stefano Crimella, no spouse of a Guglielmite was implicated or sentenced.

47. Galeazzo Visconti's name is nowhere mentioned in the trial records, but later evidence suggests that he was strongly implicated and saved only through his father's intervention. Muraro, *Guglielma*, 41, 92, 200–201.

48. Tocco, 424, 431.

49. Ibid. 316, 329, 441.

50. Ibid. 320, 423, 425. The churches were Santa Maria fuori di Porta Nuova, Sant' Eufemia, the convent church of Biassono, and the abbey of Chiaravalle.

51. Muraro, *Guglielma*, 31.

52. Tocco, 320, 323, 326, 335, 339–40, 352, 356.

53. Ibid. 324, 376.

54. Ibid. 317, 320, 326, 335.

55. Costa, *Guglielma*, 92–95; Muraro, *Guglielma*, 42–43.

56. Tocco, 341, 370–71, 375, 431.

57. Ibid. 321, 329, 330, 359, 440.

58. Costa, *Guglielma*, 80, cites other cases of luxurious garb ascribed to various Free Spirit heretics.

59. Tocco, 323.

60. Ibid. 332–33.

61. Ibid. 381–83.

62. "[S]oror Mayfreda sedens super uno lecto in dicta camera reversavit sibi manicas tunice et traxit eas superius ad brachia, et cum multa alia preparatione et compositione vestium suarum et cum multo spiritu inter alia dixit omnibus suprascriptis ibi presentibus et clare audire valentibus: ego nolebam huc venire et invite veni, quia erunt hic multi Thome, idest multi increduli, et multum murmurabitis de his, que dicam; tamen feci sicut persona que vult obedire. Domina nostra, loquens de sancta Guillelma, apparuit mihi, et dixit mihi quia ego venirem ad vos, et quod

vobis omnibus dicerem quod ipsa domina nostra Guillelma est spiritus sanctus." Ibid. 422, 426.

63. Ibid. 316–17, 324.

64. Muraro, *Guglielma*, 54.

65. Tocco, 374.

66. Ibid. 329.

67. Ibid. 353, 370, 373.

68. "That torture was freely used there can be no doubt," as Lea asserts. *Inquisition* III, 100. Cf. Muraro, *Guglielma*, 63–64. Inquisitorial records do not as a rule refer to torture, but its use can be inferred from the highly incriminating confessions inquisitors were able to elicit from the accused after their initial flat denial of heretical beliefs or activities.

69. Tocco, 407–8.

70. Ibid. 315; Muraro, *Guglielma*, 86, 99. Two others interrogated in 1284, Riccadonna and Sister Meliore (the mother and sister of Andrea Saramita) died before 1300. Lea speculates that the priest Mirano was burnt, but he was not relapsed, and there is no reason to think he was treated more harshly than the others. *Inquisition* III, 101.

71. Muraro, *Guglielma*, 91–92.

72. O. Raynaldus, *Annales ecclesiastici* 5 (Lucca, 1750): 262, ad 1324.

73. "Na" is an honorific title short for *domna* ("lady"); it indicates respect and may denote Prous's status as head of a household, but does not imply aristocratic birth. Daniela Müller, "Der Prozess gegen Prous Boneta: Begine, Ketzerin, Häresiarchin (1325)," in Norbert Höhl, ed., *Ius et historia: Festgabe für Rudolf Weigand* (Würzburg, 1989): 199n.

74. On the Spiritual Franciscans, see Reeves, *Prophecy*, 191–228; Lambert, *Medieval Heresy*, 189–214.

75. In southern France the term "beguins" (or beguines) referred not to extraregular religious women, as in northern Europe, but to Franciscan tertiaries of both sexes who upheld the Spirituals' view on apostolic poverty and inclined toward a Joachite theology of history. See Robert Lerner, "Beguins," in Joseph Strayer, ed., *Dictionary of the Middle Ages* (New York, 1983), II: 162–63.

76. William H. May, ed., "The Confession of Prous Boneta, Heretic and Heresiarch," in John Mundy et al., eds., *Essays in Medieval Life and Thought Presented in Honor of Austin Evans* (New York, 1965): 3–30. There is an abridged translation of Na Prous's testimony in Elizabeth Petroff, *Medieval Women's Visionary Literature* (Oxford, 1986): 284–90.

77. The sentence of Na Prous was published by Lea, *Inquisition* III, 653–54. Louisa Burnham, in her unpublished paper "Heretic and Heresiarch: The Visionary Authority of Na Prous Boneta (1296–1328)," argues that Prous was executed in November 1328, not 1325 as commonly held, and that she continued to proselytize during her three years in prison.

78. May, "Confession," 10.

79. Ibid. 20.

80. Ibid. 29.

81. Ibid. 23, 27, 30.

82. "Item dixit et asseruit quod Christus dixit sibi quod ab illa die qua fecit votum virginitatis, computatis novem mensibus usque ad illam diem qua est festum fratris Petri Joannis, in tali die ipse dominus Deus concepit ipsam Naprous in spiritu; et quod ipsa die, eadem qua ipsa fuit in Narbona supra sepulcrum dicti fratris Petri Joannis, ipse Dominus peperit eam in spiritu." Ibid. 10. Venerating Olivi as a saint, the Spirituals paid frequent visits to his shrine.

83. Ibid. 16.

84. On Na Prous's companions see Daniela Müller, "Les Béguines," *Heresis* 13–14 (1989): 379–82. *Jean* or *Joannis* was a family name, always given in the genitive; *Olieu* (Olivi), which rarely appears in the sources, served as an identifying sobriquet. According to the testimony of Alaraxis, she and Friar Raymond were the niece and nephew of Friar Peter John: Paris, BN, Collection Doat 28, fol. 216ᵛ–219ᵛ. I thank Louisa Burnham for the reference.

85. Urschalling is a hamlet located between Prien-am-Chiemsee and Bernau in the diocese of Munich and Freising. The church, dedicated to St. James, was probably built in the late twelfth century by the Counts von Falkenstein.

86. Evamaria Ciolina, *Der Freskenzyklus von Urschalling: Geschichte und Ikonographie* (Munich, 1980): 122.

87. Ibid. 59–60.

88. See Chapter 5 above, p. 151.

89. Leopold Kretzenbacher, "Zwei eigenwillige bayerische Dreifaltigkeits-Darstellungen," *Bayerisches Jahrbuch für Volkskunde* (1992): 131.

90. See, for example, Ex. 35:31, Deut. 34:9, Isa. 11:2, Acts 6:3, as well as Irenaeus, *Contre les hérésies* IV.7.4, IV.20.1, IV.20.3, ed. Adelin Rousseau et al., SC 100 (Paris, 1965): 464, 626, 632.

91. The most important texts on personified Wisdom are Proverbs 8–9, Ecclesiasticus 24, and Wisdom of Solomon 6–10. For summaries of the tradition see Yves Congar, "The Motherhood in God and the Femininity of the Holy Spirit," in *I Believe in the Holy Spirit*, trans. David Smith (London, 1983): III, 155–64; Robert Murray, *Symbols of Church and Kingdom: A Study in Early Syriac Tradition* (Cambridge, 1975): 312–20.

92. *Odes of Solomon* 36, ed. and trans. J. H. Charlesworth (Oxford, 1973): 126–27. The lost *Gospel of the Hebrews* is cited in Origen, *Commentaire sur Saint Jean* II.87–88, ed. Cécile Blanc, SC 120 (Paris, 1966): 262–63; Jerome, *Commentariorum in Esaiam Libri* 4.11, CCSL 73 pt. 1 (Turnhout, 1963): 148; and idem, *Commentariorum in Micheam Libri* 2.7, PL 25, 1221d.

93. Cited in Hippolytus, *Refutatio omnium haeresium* IX.13, ed. Miroslav Marcovich (Berlin, 1986): 357–58.

94. *Die 50 geistlichen Homilien des Makarios* 28.4, ed. Hermann Dörries et al., *Patristische Texte und Studien* 4 (Berlin, 1964): 232–33. Cf. Homily 16.8, p. 163.

95. Aphrahat, *Demonstrationes* VI, ed. J. Parisot, *Patrologia Syriaca* I (Paris, 1894): 292–93.

96. *Didascalia apostolorum* 9, ed. Arthur Vööbus, *Corpus Scriptorum Christianorum Orientalium* 176 (Louvain, 1979): 100; *Les Constitutions apostoliques* II.26, ed. Marcel Metzger, SC 320 (Paris, 1985): 238–41.

97. *Homiliae Clementinae* 16.12, ed. Albert Schwegler (Stuttgart, 1847): 350–

51; Methodius of Olympus, *Symposium* III.8, ed. Herbert Musurillo, SC 95 (Paris, 1963): 106–10; Ephrem of Syria, *Commentaire de l'Évangile Concordant, Version arménienne* 19.15, ed. L. Leloir, *Corpus Scriptorum Christianorum Orientalium* 137 (Louvain, 1954): 277. Cf. Antonio Orbe, "La procesión del Espíritu Santo y el origen de Eva," *Gregorianum* 45 (1964): 103–18.

98. Epiphanius of Salamis, *Panarion* 48–49, ed. Karl Holl, *Griechische christliche Schriftsteller* (Berlin, 1980): II, 219–44. See also Hippolytus, *Refutatio omnium haeresium* VIII, ed. Marcovich, 338, and Eusebius, *Historia ecclesiastica* V.16, ed. Gustave Bardy, SC 41 (Paris, 1955): 46–52. The most important sources are translated in Ross Kraemer, ed., *Maenads, Martyrs, Matrons, Monastics: A Sourcebook on Women's Religions in the Greco-Roman World* (Philadelphia, 1988): 224–30.

99. This motif is characteristic of Christian Gnosticism and indicates that by the time of Epiphanius's work (ca. 374–77), there had been exchange between these two forms of sectarian Christianity. For the veneration of Eve see the tracts "The Hypostasis of the Archons" and "On the Origin of the World," in James M. Robinson et al., eds., *The Nag Hammadi Library in English*, 3rd ed. (San Francisco, 1988): 161–89.

100. Milk, transformed instantly into cheese, also figures in Perpetua's dream of paradisal communion—a vision that could conceivably have been the source of the Priscillians' ritual practice. See Ross Kraemer, *Her Share of the Blessings: Women's Religions Among Pagans, Jews, and Christians in the Greco-Roman World* (Oxford, 1992): 164–65; Elisabeth Moltmann-Wendel, *A Land Flowing with Milk and Honey: Perspectives on Feminist Theology*, trans. John Bowden (New York, 1986): 1–4.

101. Epiphanius, *Panarion* 49.1.3, trans. Kraemer, *Maenads* 230.

102. Stephen Benko, *The Virgin Goddess: Studies in the Pagan and Christian Roots of Mariology* (Leiden, 1993): 170–95.

103. Epiphanius, *Panarion* 79, ed. Holl (Berlin, 1985): III, 475–84, trans. Carolyn Osiek in Kraemer, *Maenads*, 50–58. See also *Her Share of the Blessings*, 166, and the fascinating if implausible speculation of Geoffrey Ashe, *The Virgin* (London, 1976): 149–71.

104. This is the testimony of Patriarch Eutychius of Alexandria (ca. 933–44), *Annales* 440, in J.-P. Migne, ed., *Patrologia graeca* 111: 1006b, repeated by the Arabic Christian writer Ibn Kibr (d. ca. 1363). Benko, *Virgin Goddess*, 193–94.

105. Sura 5.119: "And when God said, 'O Jesus son of Mary, didst thou say unto men, "Take me and my mother as gods, apart from God"?' he said, 'To Thee be glory! It is not mine to say what I have no right to.'" *The Koran Interpreted*, trans. A. J. Arberry (New York, 1955): 147.

106. Benko, *Virgin Goddess*, 256–57. Few historians of the Council have been able to resist a comparison with an earlier riot in the same city, when Paul was driven out of town by enraged goddess-worshippers shouting "Great is Artemis of the Ephesians!" (Acts 19:23–41).

107. Marius Victorinus, *Against Arius* IB, in *Theological Treatises on the Trinity*, trans. Mary Clark, *Fathers of the Church* 69 (Washington, 1978): 169–93.

108. Sergius Bulgakov, *The Wisdom of God: A Brief Summary of Sophiology* (London, 1937); Maura Böckeler, *Das grosse Zeichen: Die Frau als Symbol göttlicher Wirklichkeit* (Salzburg, 1941); Louis Bouyer, *Le Trône de la Sagesse: Essai sur la signification*

du culte mariale (Paris, 1957), especially ch. X; Paul Evdokimoff, *La Femme et le salut du monde* (Paris, 1958); Donald Gelpi, *The Divine Mother: A Trinitarian Theology of the Holy Spirit* (Lanham, MD, 1984); Leonardo Boff, *The Maternal Face of God: The Feminine and Its Religious Expressions*, trans. Robert Barr and John Diercksmeier (San Francisco, 1987), especially 92–103.

109. It is possible, though to my mind unlikely, that the two identical male figures represent not Father and Son but Christ in his divine and human natures. For further examples of the motif, see Caroline Walker Bynum, *Holy Feast and Holy Fast: The Religious Significance of Food to Medieval Women* (Berkeley, 1987): plates 28–29.

110. Louis Réau, *Iconographie de l'art chrétien* vol. 2, pt. 2 (Paris, 1957): 623. See also Alfred Hackel, *Die Trinität in der Kunst: Eine ikonographische Untersuchung* (Berlin, 1931): 79–85; Philippe Verdier, *Le Couronnement de la Vierge: Les origines et les premiers développements d'un thème iconographique* (Paris, 1980).

111. Further examples in Gertrud Schiller, *Ikonographie der christlichen Kunst* vol. 4, pt. 2 (Gütersloh, 1980): plates 736–50.

112. Ernst Kantorowicz, "The Quinity of Winchester," *Art Bulletin* 29 (1947): 73–85; repr. in *Selected Studies* (New York, 1965): 102, 120, and fig. 12. See also Victor Leroquais, *Un Livre d'heures de Jean sans Peur, Duc de Bourgogne* (Paris, 1939): 47–49 and plate 14.

113. Madeline Caviness has called my attention to another "Marian Trinity" depicting the Coronation of the Virgin, carved for the church of Aschara (Thuringia) circa 1500. About a century later Protestant iconoclasts cut away the figure of the Virgin, leaving only her halo and the hem of her garment, and painted a dove in her place. The vandalized altarpiece, now at the Gotha Museum, shows how easily a "Mariolatrous" reading of such images could take hold. For the reformers, too, "Our Lady" had (in their view blasphemously) become the Holy Spirit.

114. See Chapter 5 above, p. 150.

115. "[E]t postmodum ipsa vidit duas alias personas similes ipsi Deo, quae erant in ordine coniuncte una post aliam, quarum una incepit currere, et ad cursum se posuit super collum suum ipsius quae loquitur, et alia posuit se supra brachium dextrum eius, dicendo hoc modo: *ego et tu facti sumus unum, et tunc completum est illud verbum quod supra tibi dixeram, quando dedi tibi Spiritum Sanctum, et respondisti quod non erant de te tant grant causes, et ego respondi tibi que maiours les ty donneriee sol que mi fuisses fiselz, et quia modo dedi tibi alias duas personas, scilicet personam Patris et Filii; nunc completum est illud promissum quando tibi promiseram dicendo, maiores dabo tibi, quia nunc habes totam Trinitatem.*" May, "Confession," 10. This testimony is given partly in Na Prous's native Provençal dialect.

116. Cf. Jeffrey Hamburger, "The Visual and the Visionary: The Image in Late Medieval Monastic Devotions," *Viator* 20 (1989): 161–82, and Umiliana dei Cerchi's vision in which Christ "came forth from a painting" to heal her sick daughter (p. 87 above).

117. Elaine Pagels, *The Gnostic Gospels* (New York, 1979); see also Rose Arthur, *The Wisdom Goddess: Feminine Motifs in Eight Nag Hammadi Documents* (Lanham, MD, 1984).

118. See Jorunn Buckley, *Female Fault and Fulfillment in Gnosticism* (Chapel

Hill, 1986); Karen King, ed., *Images of the Feminine in Gnosticism* (Philadelphia, 1988).

119. In the gnostic Pleroma, however, these redeemers are merely the thirty-first and thirty-second Aeons, or divine emanations. Such co-optation of ecclesiastical terms no doubt contributed to the rejection of the female Holy Spirit by orthodox Christians.

120. This paragraph is indebted to Bynum, *Holy Feast and Holy Fast*, and eadem, *Fragmentation and Redemption: Essays on Gender and the Human Body in Medieval Religion* (New York, 1991).

121. "Adont si doit li peres ses mains envelopper en aucune choce, prendre les mains sa fille et dire ensi: Marie, et je vos reçoif a fille en dieu et vos aconpaigne a toz mes biens fais et a toutes mes prïeres, que vos en soiés parçonniere comme ma fille esperituel.—La fille: Sire, diex le vos mire, et je vos reçoif a pere en dieu et vos aconpaigne a mes prïeres et a tous mes biens fais, et vos otroi que vos en soiés parçonniers comme mes peres esperitueus." *"La Règle des Fins Amans*: Eine Beginenregel aus dem Ende des XIII. Jahrhunderts," ed. Karl Christ in *Philologische Studien aus dem romanisch-germanischen Kulturkreise: Festschrift Karl Voretzsch*, ed. B. Schädel and W. Mulertt (Halle, 1927): 203.

122. See John Coakley, "Gender and the Authority of Friars: The Significance of Holy Women for Thirteenth-Century Franciscans and Dominicans," *Church History* 60 (1991): 445–60; Elizabeth Petroff, "Male Confessors and Female Penitents: Possibilities for Dialogue," in *Body and Soul: Essays on Medieval Women and Mysticism* (New York, 1994): 139–60.

123. "[E]go credo quod ipsa Guillelma sit illa caro, que nata est de beata Virgine, et que crucifixa fuit in cruce in persona Christi." Tocco, 415, 426.

124. Muraro, *Guglielma*, 121–27, 132–34.

125. Tocco, 329.

126. For this formulation of eucharistic orthodoxy, which dates back to Ambrose, see Jaroslav Pelikan, *The Growth of Medieval Theology (600–1300)* (Chicago, 1978): 190–93.

127. Reeves, *Prophecy*, 249.

128. Wessley, "Guglielmites," 297–98; Costa, *Guglielma*, 24–25.

129. Tocco, 412–14.

130. *La Queste del saint Graal*, ed. Albert Pauphilet (Paris, 1967); trans. P. M. Matarasso, *The Quest of the Holy Grail* (Harmondsworth, 1969): 243–44, 273–76. Cf. Sir Thomas Malory, "The Tale of the Sankgreal," in *Works*, ed. Eugène Vinaver (Oxford, 1971): 589, 602–03.

131. *Quest of the Holy Grail*, 269.

132. Malory, *Works*, 521.

133. *Quest of the Holy Grail*, 217–18, 236–37, 247–50.

134. May, "Confession," 17.

135. Ibid. 28.

136. Ibid. 16.

137. Ibid. 17, emending *praecisiori* to *preciosiori*.

138. Ibid. 11.

139. "[D]ominus Deus dedit dicto fratri Petro Joannis complete Spiritum,

quia aliter homines et mulieres non salvarentur; quia, prout asserit sibi fuisse dictum a Deo, in corpore Jesu Christi et in corpore eius matris, scilicet virginis Mariae, non fuit aliqua mixtura, cum totum esset idem, et similiter in corpore spiritus dicti fratris Petri Joannis et in corpore spiritus eiusdem loquentis Naprous, non est aliqua mixtura, sicut dixit, quia spiritus eiusdem fratris Petri Joannis et spiritus eiusdem loquentis sunt idem, quia totum descendit a Deo, prout dixit. Item quod dixit sibi Dominus quod quemadmodum ipse Deus rexit ecclesiam per duo corpora carnis, scilicet corpora Christi et eius matris Mariae virginis, eodem modo reget de caetero ecclesiam per duo corpora spiritus dati fratri Petro Joannis praedicto et etiam spiritus dati ipsi Naprous loquenti, qui spiritus ambo sunt unum, sicut dixit. Item asseruit sibi fuisse dictum a Domino quod oportet ut quicumque voluerint se salvare, credant verbis scripturae dicti fratris Petri Joannis, cum sint scripta per virtutem Spiritus Sancti, et similiter quod verbis ipsius Naprous credant, cum sint dicta per virtutem Spiritus Sancti, sicut dixit." Ibid. 22–23.

140. Ibid. 29.

141. For biographies of Postel, see William Bouwsma, *Concordia Mundi: The Career and Thought of Guillaume Postel (1510–1581)* (Cambridge, MA, 1957); Marion Kuntz, *Guillaume Postel, Prophet of the Restitution of All Things: His Life and Thought* (The Hague, 1981).

142. The title is deliberately misleading. See M. A. Screech, "The Illusion of Postel's Feminism," *Journal of the Warburg and Courtauld Institutes* 16 (1953): 162–70.

143. Guillaume Postel, *Les très-merveilleuses victoires des femmes du Nouveau-Monde* (Turin, 1869; rpt. Geneva, 1970): 19–20.

144. Kuntz, *Postel*, 72–83.

145. "Io son el Signor per che esso habita in me, et per questo io sono in esso il Papa Santo Reformatore del mondo." London, BL, Sloane ms. 1410, fol. 51^V, cited in ibid. 79, n. 256.

146. Ibid. 84.

147. Postel, *Victoires*, 85.

148. For sensitive discussion of Postel's mental aberrations, see Bouwsma, *Concordia mundi*, 166–71, and Jacques Simonnet, "La mère du monde, miroir de la pensée de Guillaume Postel," in *Guillaume Postel, 1581–1981*, Actes du Colloque International d'Avranches (Paris, 1985): 17–21.

149. See the lucid account of François Secret, "Guillaume Postel et les courants prophétiques de la Renaissance," *Studi Francesi* 1 (1957): 375–95; Bouwsma, *Concordia Mundi*, 138–64; and Reeves, *Prophecy*, 287–89, 381–84, 479–81.

150. Guiseppe Ellero, "Postel e Venezia," in *Guillaume Postel, 1581–1981*, 25–26. My account of the Barnabites and Angeliche is taken from Ellero's article, pp. 23–28, and from Kuntz, *Postel*, 71–73.

151. According to Kuntz, the women arrived in 1539 or 1540. Ellero gives the date of 1544, following Orazio Premoli, *Storia dei Barnabiti nel Cinquecento* (Rome, 1913): 94.

152. Kuntz, *Postel*, 86. On Madre Angelica's abuse of power see Premoli, *Storia*, 92–95.

153. London, BL, Sloane ms. 1411, fols. 431–431^V, cited in Kuntz, 77 n. 246.

154. Costa, *Guglielma*, 35.

155. Tocco, 333, 430.
156. Muraro, *Guglielma*, 103–8; text in Costa, *Guglielma*, 117–19.
157. Tocco, 412–13.

Chapter 7

1. Henri Corneille Agrippa, *De nobilitate et praecellentia foeminei sexus*, ed. Charles Béné, with French translation by O. Sauvage and preface by Roland Antonioli (Geneva, 1990): 11–12.

2. Barbara Newman, "Agrippa and His Translators: The Fate of a Renaissance Feminist," *Viator*, forthcoming. On Agrippa's influence, see also Marc Angenot, *Les Champions des femmes: Examen du discours sur la superiorité des femmes, 1400–1800* (Montreal, 1977).

3. Constance Jordan, *Renaissance Feminism: Literary Texts and Political Models* (Ithaca, 1990): 122. In this chapter I use the term "feminism" very broadly to refer to any theoretical writing aimed at advancing the cause of women, with or without a call for radical social change.

4. Ian Maclean, *The Renaissance Notion of Woman* (Cambridge, 1980): 80.

5. Linda Woodbridge, *Women and the English Renaissance: Literature and the Nature of Womankind, 1540–1620* (Urbana, 1984): 42.

6. Harriett McIlquham, "Cornelius Agrippa: His Appreciation of Women," *Westminster Review* 154 (1900): 303, 313.

7. Charles Nauert, *Agrippa and the Crisis of Renaissance Thought* (Urbana, 1965): 27. For the controversy surrounding *De sacramento matrimonii* (1526), see *Epistolae* IV, letters i–iv, vii, in H. C. Agrippa, *Opera* (ca. 1600, rpt. Hildesheim, 1970): 781–89. In Ep. IV.iii, Agrippa complains that court ladies read "foedas et spurcas . . . facetias," like Ovid's *Heroides*, Boccaccio's *Novelle*, and the romances of Tristan and Lancelot, yet dare to find fault with his defense of marriage (783). Court ladies are also denounced in *De incertitudine et vanitate scientiarum*, ch. 71, "De mulieribus aulicis," although Agrippa criticizes them more qua courtiers than qua women.

8. *Apologia adversus calumnias, propter declamationem de vanitate scientiarum*, XLII, cited in Maclean, *Renaissance Notion*, 91.

9. Nauert, *Agrippa*, 216.

10. Frances Yates, *The Occult Philosophy in the Elizabethan Age* (London, 1979): 44.

11. Nauert, *Agrippa*, 93–98.

12. Yates, *Occult Philosophy*, 42.

13. "Elle s'éclaire d'une lumière lointaine, cabalisante et néoplatonicienne, qui voit dans la femme une manifestation immédiate du divin, un principe de vie originel et pur, susceptible d'effectuer des miracles qui manifestent dans son corps l'absolu pouvoir de l'esprit sur la matière." Roland Antonioli, preface, *De nobilitate*, 25.

14. "Eandem vero et masculo et foeminae, ac omnino indifferentem animae

formam tribuit [Deus], inter quas nulla prorsus sexus est distantia. Eandem ipsa mulier cum viro sortita est mentem, rationem atque sermonem, ad eundem tendit beatitudinis finem, ubi sexus nulla erit exceptio . . . Nulla itaque est ab essentia animae inter virum et mulierem, alterius super alterum nobilitatis praeeminentia: sed utriusque par dignitatis innata libertas." *De nobilitate*, 49.

15. See Rosemary Ruether, "Misogynism and Virginal Feminism in the Fathers of the Church," and Eleanor McLaughlin, "Equality of Souls, Inequality of Sexes: Woman in Medieval Theology," both in Rosemary Ruether, ed., *Religion and Sexism* (New York, 1974). On the medieval period, see Chapter 1 above.

16. "Quae autem praeter animae divinam essentiam in homine reliqua sunt, in iis muliebris inclyta stirps durum virorum genus in infinitum pene excellit." *De nobilitate*, 49.

17. Ibid. 49; punctuation altered. The critical edition, following the *editio princeps* of 1529, has a comma after "Pater" but none after "bonorum." In the undated Lyon edition of circa 1600 (rpt. Hildesheim, 1970), neither of these commas appears. Having identified the source of the quotation, I believe the erroneous comma after "Pater" misled Agrippa's translators, causing them to overlook his daring assertion here. The sole exception is Edward Fleetwood, *The Glory of Women: or, a Treatise declaring the excellency and preheminence of Women above Men* (London, 1651).

18. "[Deus] ergo, solus ut omnia, utraque sexus fecunditate plenissimus, semper voluntatis praegnans suae parit semper, quicquid voluerit procreare . . .— Utriusque sexus ergo deum dicis, O Trismegiste?—Non deum solum, Asclepi, sed omnia animalia et inanimalia . . . Procreatione enim uterque plenus est sexus et eius utriusque conexio aut, quod est verius, unitas inconprehensibilis est, quem sive Cupidinem sive Venerem sive utrumque recte poteris nuncupare . . . cui summa caritas, laetitia, hilaritas, cupiditas, amorque divinus innatus est." *Asclepius* 20–21, in A. D. Nock and A.-J. Festugière, eds., *Corpus Hermeticum*, 4th ed. (Paris, 1983): II, 321–22.

19. Conor Fahy, "Three Early Renaissance Treatises on Women," *Italian Studies* 11 (1956): 37–39.

20. Baldesar Castiglione, *Il Libro del Cortegiano*, III, ed. Vittorio Cian (Florence, 1947): 313. For the probable connections between Agrippa and Castiglione see Woodbridge, *Women and the English Renaissance*, 71–72.

21. "Saltem hoc unum mihi dicere permittant ex Cabalistarum mysticis symbolis, ipsum nomen mulieris plus affinitatis habere cum nomine ineffabili divinae omnipotentiae tetragrammaton, quam nomen viri, quod cum divino nomine nec in caracteribus, nec in figura, nec in numero convenit." *De nobilitate*, 52.

22. "Elegit eam Deus, et praeelegit eam: In tabernaculo suo habitare facit eam." Responsory for Office of the Blessed Virgin Mary. Cf. Ecclus. 24:5, 14.

23. Cf. Gregory of Nyssa's treatise *On the Making of Man*, II, in *Nicene and Post-Nicene Fathers*, 2nd series, Vol. V (New York, 1893): 390. "It was not to be looked for that the ruler should appear before the subjects of his rule; but when his dominion was prepared, the next step was that the king should be manifested. When, then, the Maker of all had prepared beforehand, as it were, a royal lodg-

ing for the future king . . . , and when all kinds of wealth had been stored in this palace . . . , he thus manifests man in the world, to be the beholder of some of the wonders therein, and the lord of others."

24. "Postremo vero creavit sibi similes homines duos, marem inquam primum, et postremo foeminam, in qua perfecti sunt coeli, et terra, et omnis ornatus eorum: ad mulieris enim creationem veniens creator, quievit in illa, ut nihil honoratius creandum prae manibus habens in ipsaque conclusa et consummata est omnis creatoris sapientia, atque potestas, ultra quam non reperitur creatura alia, nec excogitari potest. Cum itaque mulier sit ultima creaturarum ac finis, et complementum omnium operum Dei perfectissimum, ipsiusque universi perfectio, quis eam negabit super omnem creaturam praecellentia dignissimam . . . ? Sic mulier dum creatur mundus inter omnia creata tempore fuit ultima, eadem cum authoritate, tum dignitate in ipso divinae mentis conceptu omnium fuit prima, sicut de illa scriptum est per Prophetam: antequam coeli crearentur, elegit eam Deus, et praelegit eam. . . . Mulier autem fuit postremum Dei opus introducta a Deo in hunc mundum, velut ejus regina in regiam sibi jam paratam, ornatam et omnibus muneribus absolutam. Merito igitur illam omnis creatura amat, veneratur, observat, meritoque illi omnis creatura subjicitur atque obedit, quae omnium creaturarum regina est atque finis, et perfectio et gloria modis omnibus absoluta. Quamobrem de illa Sapiens inquit: generositatem mulieris glorificat, contubernium habens Dei, sed et omnium Dominus dilexit eam." *De nobilitate*, 53–54.

25. This argument, in a more modest version, recurs in several female authors' replies to the misogynist pamphlet of Joseph Swetnam, *The Araignment of Lewde, idle, froward, and unconstant women* (London, 1615). See "Ester Sowernam," *Ester Hath Hang'd Haman*, and "Constantia Munda," *The Worming of a mad Dogge: or, a Soppe for Cerberus* (both from 1617), in Katherine Henderson and Barbara McManus, *Half Humankind: Contexts and Texts of the Controversy About Women in England, 1540–1640* (Urbana, 1985): 224, 248.

26. Barbara Newman, "The Pilgrimage of Christ-Sophia," *Vox benedictina* 9, 1 (1992): 8–37. Cf. Chapter 5 above, p. 150.

27. Cf. Maurice de Gandillac: "Plus qu'une mariologie, l'auteur suggère ici (au moins entre les lignes) une référence sophilogique, d'inspiration gnostique, fort étrangère, par conséquent, au christocentrisme évangélique." "Les Secrets d'Agrippa," in *Aspects du libertinisme au XVIᵉ siècle*, Actes du Colloque International de Sommières (Paris, 1974): 129.

28. Joseph Dan, "Shekinah," *Encyclopaedia Judaica* (Jerusalem, 1971) 14: 1353–54; Moshe Idel, "The Magical and Neoplatonic Interpretations of the Kabbalah in the Renaissance," in Bernard Cooperman, ed., *Jewish Thought in the Sixteenth Century* (Cambridge, MA, 1983): 186–242; Seymour Cohen, trans., *The Holy Letter: A Study in Medieval Jewish Sexual Morality ascribed to Nahmanides* (New York, 1976): 60, 68–72.

29. See especially Henry Care, *Female Pre-eminence: or the Dignity and Excellency of that Sex, above the Male* (London, 1670).

30. Antonioli, preface, 30.

31. "Nam quum pulchritudo ipsa nihil est aliud quam divini vultus atque luminis splendor rebus insitus, per corpora formosa relucens: is certe mulieres prae

viris habitare ac replere abundantissime elegit. . . . ut nemo nisi caecus omnino non videat Deum ipsum quicquid pulchritudinis capax est mundus universus in mulierem simul congessisse, ut ob id illam omnis creatura stupescat, et multis nominibus amet ac veneretur." *De nobilitate,* 55–56. Cf. Marsilio Ficino, *Commentarii in Platonem,* cited in *De nobilitate,* 55n: "Non enim corpus hoc autem illud desiderat sed superni luminis splendorem per corpora refulgentem admiratur, affectat et stupet."

32. "Mulieres prophetae semper diviniore spiritu afflatae sunt quam viri: quod testibus Lactantio, Eusebio et Augustino de Sybillis notum est." *De nobilitate,* 75. In the fourteenth and fifteenth centuries, a disproportionate number of saints revered for prophetic gifts were in fact women. See Donald Weinstein and Rudolph Bell, *Saints and Society: The Two Worlds of Western Christendom, 1000–1700* (Chicago, 1982): 228–29; Richard Kieckhefer, *Unquiet Souls: Fourteenth-Century Saints and Their Religious Milieu* (Chicago, 1984): 161–64.

33. *De nobilitate,* 59.

34. "In menstruo, qui sanguis . . . multis id genus perniciosissimis aegritudinibus liberat, aliaque permulta, nec minus admiratu digna efficit, inter caetera miranda etiam incendia extinguit, tempestates sedat, fluctuum pericula arcet, noxia omnia pellit, maleficia solvit, ac cacodaemones fugat." Ibid. 63.

35. Pliny the Elder, *Natural History,* VII.15. In XXVIII.23 Pliny describes both noxious and beneficent powers attributed to the menses, but expresses some revulsion as well as doubts about their validity.

36. "Tanta vis eius veneficii est, ut etiam venenosis sit venenum." *De occulta philosophia* I.42 (1533); ed. Karl Nowotny (rpt. Graz, 1967): 60.

37. "Si enim matres stolidae sunt, et filii stolidi fiunt, si matres prudentes, et filii earum prudentiam redolent. . . . Nec alia ratio est cur matres plus patribus diligant filios suos nisi quia multo plus de suo sentiunt habentque in illis matres, quam patres. Ob eandem quam dixi causam, etiam arbitror nobis inditum esse, uti plus in matrem quam in patrem simus adfecti, usque adeo ut patrem diligere, matrem solam amare videamur." *De nobilitate,* 61.

38. Ibid. 63–64, 66–67.

39. "Mulier in paradiso nobilissimo loco pariter et amoenissimo formata est cum angelis, vir autem extra paradisum in agro rurali cum brutis animalibus factus est." Ibid. 54.

40. "Praecellit mulier virum materia creationis, propterea quod non ex inanimato quopiam, aut vili luto creata, quemadmodum vir, sed ex materia purificata, vivifica, et animata, anima inquam rationali mentem participante divinam. . . . Vir itaque naturae opus, mulier opificium Dei." Ibid. 55.

41. "Est etenim Aristotelis validum hoc argumentum: cuius generis optimum est nobilius optime alterius generis, hoc genus esse altero nobilius; in foemineo genere optima est virgo Maria; in masculino non surrexit maior Ioanne Baptista, atque hunc quantum excellat virgo diva . . . Iam vero scimus, quia vitiosissima ac pessima creaturarum omnium vir est, sive ille fuerit Iudas qui Christum tradidit . . . sive illo peior futurus sit antichristus aliquis." Ibid. 70–71. This is Aristotle's topos of the "double hierarchy."

42. "Etiam Christus resurgens a morte mulieribus primum apparuit, non

viris. Nec ignotum est post Christi obitum viros a fide discessisse, mulieres autem nusquam constat a fide et religione Christiana defecisse." Ibid. 67.

43. Abelard, Epistola "De auctoritate vel dignitate ordinis sanctimonialium," ed. J. T. Muckle, *Mediaeval Studies* 17 (1955): 253–81 (see especially 256–58, 268–69). The argument about Eve's creation in Paradise had first been used in an antifeminist sense by Ambrose, *De paradiso* 4:24: "Adverte quia extra paradisum vir factus est, et mulier intra paradisum. . . . In inferiori loco vir melior invenitur, et illa quae in meliore loco facta est inferior reperitur."

44. Unidentified Cambridge MS. cited in C. G. Crump and E. F. Jacob, eds., *The Legacy of the Middle Ages* (Oxford, 1926): 402.

45. This was also the proto-feminist view of Hildegard of Bingen in the twelfth century; see Barbara Newman, *Sister of Wisdom: St. Hildegard's Theology of the Feminine* (Berkeley, 1987): 112–14.

46. "Viro namque interdictus erat fructus ligni, mulieri non item, quae neque dum creata erat: illa[m] enim Deus ab initio liberam esse voluit, vir itaque comedendo peccavit, non mulier, vir mortem dedit, non mulier. Et nos omnes peccavimus in Adam, non in Eva, ipsumque originale peccatum non a matre foemina, sed a patre masculo contrahimus. Ideoque vetus lex omne masculum circumcidi jussit, foeminas autem incircumcisas manere, peccatum videlicet originis in eo sexu qui peccasset, solum modo puniendum statuens." *De nobilitate*, 65–66. Woodbridge calls this an "astonishing, thoroughly heretical, and perfectly delightful theory" but "cannot believe it was meant to be taken seriously." *Women and the English Renaissance*, 40.

47. Mary's immaculate conception, though widely believed, had not yet been defined as dogma in Agrippa's time. For Christ to be born free of original sin it was necessary only for him to be conceived by a virgin, *sine virili semine*.

48. "Non legitur prohibitum Evae, quae post praeceptum creata fuit: ratio enim posterior est fide, & fides natura prior ratione. . . . Ideo non peccavit Eva, comedendo de ligno scientiae boni & mali, . . . sed qui obtulit viro suo Adae, cui vetitum erat de illo gustare. Neque enim licet rationi turbare fidem, sed subiecta debet esse fidei." *De originali peccato*, in *Opera*, 553.

49. Cf. A. Kent Hieatt, who traces the germ of this interpretation to Augustine (*De Trinitate* 12), but characterizes Agrippa's version of it as "a typical exercise in his scandalous oscillations between the positions of the *De occulta philosophia* . . . and those of the *De vanitate scientiarum*." "Eve as Reason in a Tradition of Allegorical Interpretation of the Fall," *Journal of the Warburg and Courtauld Institutes* 43 (1980): 222.

50. "Ipsa autem opinio nostra talis est, non aliud fuisse originale peccatum, quam carnalem copulam viri & mulieris . . . hunc serpentem non alium arbitramur, quam sensibilem carnalemque affectum, imo quem recte dixerimus, ipsum carnalis concupiscentiae genitale viri membrum, membrum reptile, membrum serpens . . . Nullum itaque alium daemonem Evam tentasse arbitramur, quam illum." *De originali peccato*, in *Opera*, 554–55.

51. "Quocirca Christus natus huic mundo humillimus, quo sua humilitate superbiam expiaret peccati primi parentis, sexum assumpsit virilem, ut humiliorem,

non sexum foemineum, sublimiorem et nobiliorem." *De nobilitate*, 66. A modern feminist theologian, Donald Gelpi, argues likewise that Christ had to be male "because in the patriarchal world in which we live, males spontaneously tend to align themselves with anti-Christ." *The Divine Mother: A Trinitarian Theology of the Holy Spirit* (Lanham, 1984): 230.

52. As early as the twelfth century, Peter Lombard mentioned the question whether Christ could have been a woman as a minor disputed issue. Citing Augustine, he concluded that God could indeed have assumed the female sex, but it was "more appropriate and fitting" for the Word to be incarnate as a man born of a woman, so that both sexes might thereby be liberated. Petrus Lombardus, *Sententiae in IV libris distinctae*, III.12.4, 3rd ed. (Rome, 1981): vol. II, p. 83. Cf. Joan Gibson, "Could Christ have been born a woman? A medieval debate," *Journal of Feminist Studies in Religion* 8 (1992): 65–82.

53. *De nobilitate*, 78.

54. Ibid. 70, trans. Fleetwood, *The Glory of Women*, 17–18.

55. For examples see Newman, *Sister of Wisdom*, 255–57.

56. "Quis patientior Iob? quem diabolus fortunis omnibus exuit, familiam et filios occidit, . . . tamen a pristina animi simplicitate patientiaque ad iracundiam provocare non potuit, provocavit autem mulier, in hoc diabolo superior confidentiorque, quem ad maledicendum irritavit." *De nobilitate*, 68.

57. "Quod si modo fas est vel Christum ipsum in hanc comparationem vocare, quo nihil potentius, nihil sapientius, cum sit aeterna Dei sapientia atque potestas, nonne a Chananaea illa muliercula sese superari passus est . . . ? cumque iam vidisset Christus, quia illam hoc argumento superare non posset, benedixit illi dicens: Fiat tibi sicut vis. Quis Petro Apostolorum primo in fide ferventior? mulier illum non minimum Ecclesiae pastorem ad negandum Christum seduxit." Ibid. 68–69.

58. See Maclean, *Renaissance Notion*, 68–81.

59. On women in the New Prophecy (Montanist) movement see Ross Kraemer, *Her Share of the Blessings: Women's Religions Among Pagans, Jews, and Christians in the Greco-Roman World* (New York, 1992): ch. 11–12. For contemporary exegesis see Elisabeth Schüssler Fiorenza, *In Memory of Her: A Feminist Theological Reconstruction of Christian Origins* (New York, 1983); Letty Russell, ed., *Feminist Interpretation of the Bible* (Philadelphia, 1985).

60. "Quid rursus de Priscilla illa sanctissima foemina, quae Apollo virum apostolicum, et in lege doctissimum Corinthiorum episcopum erudivit? Nec turpe fuit apostolo discere a muliere quae doceret in ecclesia." *De nobilitate*, 77. Most of the translators choose a weaker reading of this passage by taking the final "quae" as a neuter plural, so that Apollos and not Priscilla becomes a teacher in the Church. Cf. the anonymous *Traité agréable & Curieux de la Noblesse & Excellence du Sexe de la Femme, Par dessus celui de l'Homme* (The Hague, 1686): 46–47: "Oui un Apôtre n'eût point de honte d'apprendre d'une femme, les verités celestes, qu'il devoit enseigner à toute l'Eglise."

61. "In nostra autem religione, licet mulieribus sacerdotii functione interdictum sit, scimus tamen historiis proditum, mulierem aliquando mentito sexu, ad

summi pontificatus apicem conscendisse. Nec obscurae sunt ex nostris tot sanctissimae abbates [*sic*] et moniales, quas antiquitas non dedignatur vocare sacerdotes." *De nobilitate*, 78.

62. On this theme see Caroline Walker Bynum, *Holy Feast and Holy Fast: The Religious Significance of Food to Medieval Women* (Berkeley, 1987): 227–44.

63. Harald Zimmermann, *Das Papsttum im Mittelalter* (Stuttgart, 1981): 194–95. Cf. *De nobilitate*, 68–69: "Dicant quicquid velint canonistae, Ecclesiam suam non posse errare; Papa mulier illam egregia impostura delusit."

64. Clarissa Atkinson, *The Oldest Vocation: Christian Motherhood in the Middle Ages* (Ithaca, 1991): 1–3.

65. Jean Wirth, "'Libertins' et 'Epicuriens': Aspects de l'irreligion au XVIe siècle," *Bibliothèque d'humanisme et renaissance* 39 (1977): 612.

66. "Item repulluntur in verbi Dei praedicatione, contra expressam scripturam, qua promisit illis Spiritus Sanctus per Ioëlem, inquiens: Et prophetabunt filiae vestrae. Quemadmodum et Apostolorum aetate publice docebant, sicut de Anna Simeonis et filiabus Philippi, atque Priscilla Aquilae notum est. . . . Sunt praeterea qui ex religione autoritatem sibi arrogant in mulieres, et ex sacris litteris suam probant tyrannidem, quibus illud Evae maledictum continuo in ore est: Sub potestate viri eris, et ipse dominabitur tui. Quod si illis respondeatur Christum abstulisse maledictum, obicient rursus idem ex dictis Petri, cui accedit et Paulus: Mulieres viris subditae sint. Mulieres in Ecclesia taceant. Sed qui noverit varios scripturae tropos, eiusdemque affectus, facile cernet haec non nisi in cortice repugnare. Est enim is ordo in ecclesia, ut viri praeponantur in ministerio mulieribus sicuti Iudaei Graecis in promissione; non tamen est acceptor personarum Deus: in Christo enim nec mas, nec foemina, sed nova creatura. Quin et pleraque viris propter duritiem cordis eorum in mulieres permissa sunt, sicut Iudaeis quondam concessa repudia, quae tamen mulierum dignitati nihil officiunt, quin et deficientibus errantibusque viris, mulieres in virorum opprobrium potestatem habent iudicii. Et ipsa regina Saba iudicatura est viros Hierusalem. Qui ergo iustificati per fidem effecti sunt filii Abrahae, filii, inquam, promissionis, subiciuntur mulieri, et obnoxii sunt praecepto Dei ad Abraham inquientis: Omnia quaecumque dicit tibi Sara, audi vocem eius." *De nobilitate*, 87–89.

67. Sarah also plays a role in "kabbalistic mysteries," where the transfer of the letter H from Sara[h]'s name to Abra[h]am's (Gen. 17:5,15) signifes the fulfillment of God's promise and is said to prove that man receives divine blessing only through woman. Cf. *De nobilitate*, 65.

68. "Sed virorum nimia tyrannide contra divinum ius naturaeque leges praevalente, data mulieribus libertas iam iniquis legibus interdicitur, consuetudine usuque aboletur, educatione extinguitur. Mulier namque mox ut nata est, a primis annis domi detinetur in desidia, ac velut altioris provinciae incapax, nihil praeter acus et filum concipere permittitur. Ubi exinde pubertatis annos attigerit, in mariti traditur zelotypum imperium, aut vestalium ergastulo perpetuo recluditur. Publica quaeque officia legibus sibi interdicta sunt. Postulare in iudicio licet prudentissimae non permittitur. Repelluntur praeterea in iurisdictione, in arbitrio, in adoptione, in intercessione, in procuratione, in tutela, in cura, in testamentaria et criminali causa. . . . Sed tanta est recentium legislatorum improbitas, qui irritum

fecerunt mandatum Dei, propter traditiones suas quod mulieres alias naturae eminentia et dignitate nobilissimas pronuntiarunt cunctis viris conditione viliores. His itaque legibus mulieres viris tanquam bello victae victoribus cedere coguntur, non naturali, non divina aliqua necessitate aut ratione, sed consuetudine, educatione, fortuna et tyrannica quadam occasione id agente." Ibid. 87–88.

69. Maclean, *Renaissance Notion*, 12–13. A scholar named Valens Acidalius hotly denied authorship of this tract.

70. Johannes Bellin, *Abigail, das ist des löb-würdigen Frauen-Zimmers Adel und Fôrträfligkeit* (Lübeck, 1650).

71. See Chapter 6 above, pp. 218–20, and Guillaume Postel, *Les très-merveilleuses victoires des femmes du Nouveau-Monde* (1553); Turin, 1869, rpt. Geneva 1970 (ch. 7 and 8 on "Jehanne la Pucelle").

72. Nils Thune, *The Behmenists and the Philadelphians: A Contribution to the Study of English Mysticism in the Seventeenth and Eighteenth Centuries* (Uppsala, 1948); Desirée Hirst, *Hidden Riches: Traditional Symbolism from the Renaissance to Blake* (London, 1964).

73. See Rosemary Ruether, "Prophets and Humanists: Types of Religious Feminism in Stuart England," *Journal of Religion* 70 (1990): 1–18; Margaret Thickstun, "'This was a Woman that taught': Feminist Scriptural Exegesis in the Seventeenth Century," *Studies in Eighteenth-Century Culture* 21, ed. Patricia Craddock and Carla Hay (East Lansing, 1991): 149–58.

Epilogue

1. *Speculum uirginum* VI, ed. Jutta Seyfarth, CCCM 5 (Turnhout, 1990): 173. See Chapter 1 above, p. 23 and n. 16.

2. Henri Corneille Agrippa, *De nobilitate et praecellentia foeminei sexus*, ed. Charles Béné (Geneva, 1990): 66. See Chapter 7 above, p. 235 and n. 51.

3. In the translation by H. C. [Hugh Crompton], *The Glory of Women: or a Looking-Glasse for Ladies* (London, 1652), this passage is omitted. J. d'Arnaudin, one of Agrippa's more serious translators, nervously annotated the text: "J'ai déja fort adouci le sentiment d'Agrippa touchant le peché originel; mais si ce qui se lit dans ma traduction, & ce qui se trouve dans le reste de cet article, ne paroît pas tout à fait conforme à la maniere ordinaire, avec laquelle les Theologiens parlent de ces choses; je prie qu'on se souvienne que je suis ici traducteur, & non Auteur original." *De la Grandeur et de l'excellence des femmes, audessus des hommes* (Paris, 1713): 55. In the translation of "Roétitg" [François Péyrard], the passage supplies the occasion for a bawdy joke: "Si j'avois eu l'honneur d'être Dieu, je me serois fait fenme, et non pas homme, malgré tous les beaux raisonnemens d'Agrippa"—in order to see if Tiresias was right when he judged Jupiter's quarrel with Juno about which had more pleasure in sex. *De l'Excellence et de la Supériorité de la Femme* (Paris, 1801): 120.

4. *The Letters of Osbert of Clare* 40, ed. E. W. Williamson (London, 1929): 139. See Chapter 1 above, p. 23 and n. 17.

5. *Het Visioenenboek van Hadewijch*, Vision 14, ed. H. W. Vekeman (Nijmegen, 1980): 191 (translation mine).

Appendix A: Religious Literature of Formation, 1075–1225

Texts are listed alphabetically according to author (if known) or title. Information is given in the following order: author's name; title of work; genre; audience; date; diffusion, if available; edition.

Abelard, Peter. Epistles 7 and 9: *De auctoritate vel dignitate ordinis sanctimonialium* and *De studio litterarum*. Letters of vocation; Heloise and nuns of the Paraclete. Circa 1132–1135. Nine MSS. J. T. Muckle, ed., *Mediaeval Studies* 17 (1955): 240–81; PL 178: 332–33.

———. Epistle 8: *Institutio seu regula sanctimonialium*. Rule for nuns; Heloise and nuns of the Paraclete. Circa 1132–1135. One complete MS and six fragments. T. P. McLaughlin, ed., *Mediaeval Studies* 18 (1956): 242–82.

Adam of Perseigne. Epistle 5: *De institutione novitiorum*. Instruction for novices; Osmund, monk and novice master. Circa 1190–1196. Two MSS. Jean Bouvet, ed., SC 66 (Paris: Éditions du Cerf, 1960): 110–29.

Aelred of Rievaulx. *De institutione inclusarum*, alias *De vita eremitica ad sororem reclusam*. Rule for a recluse and treatise on spiritual life; Aelred's sister. Circa 1160–1162. Wide diffusion; many abridgments and translations. C. H. Talbot, ed., CCCM 1 (Turnhout: Brepols, 1971): 653–82.

———. *De spiritali amicitia*. Dialogue on monastic friendship; monks of Rievaulx. Part 1 circa 1147; Part 2 circa 1166. Wide diffusion; four abridgements. Anselm Hoste, ed., CCCM 1 (Turnhout: Brepols, 1971).

———. *Speculum caritatis* 2.17–20. Instruction for novices in dialogue form; Cistercian novices. 1142–1143. Wide diffusion. C. H. Talbot, ed., CCCM 1 (Turnhout: Brepols, 1971): 86–96.

Alan of Lille. *Summa de arte praedicatoria*, chs. 43, 45, 46, 47. Model sermons; *claustrales*, married folk, widows, virgins. Late twelfth century. PL 210: 189–95.

Anselm of Canterbury. Epistle 22. Letter of vocation; Hugh, a recluse. Circa 1078–1093. PL 158: 1171–73.

———. Epistles 230 and 414. Letters of instruction; Robert, a spiritual father, and his six spiritual daughters. Circa 1102–1107. Franciscus Schmitt, ed., *Opera omnia* (Edinburgh: T. Nelson, 1946–61): IV, 134–35 and V, 359–62.

Arnulf of Bohéries. *Speculum monachorum*. Instruction for novices; Cistercian novices. Circa 1200. PL 184: 1175–78.

Bernard of Clairvaux. Epistles 113, 114, 115. Letters of vocation on virginity; three nuns. Before 1153. PL 182: 256–62.

————. *De gradibus humilitatis et superbiae.* Treatise on spiritual life; Cistercians. Circa 1120–1124. Wide diffusion. Jean Leclercq, Henri Rochais, and C. H. Talbot, eds., *Sancti Bernardi Opera* (Rome: Editiones cistercienses, 1957–77): III, 12–59.

Brian of Lingen (?), *Ancrene Wisse,* alias *Ancrene Riwle.* Rule for anchoresses and treatise on spiritual life; anchoresses of Limebrook. Circa 1215–1221. Wide diffusion; Latin and French translations. EETS vols. 225, 229, 232, 249, 252, 267 (Middle English); 216 (Latin); 219, 240 (French).

De doctrina vitae agendae, alias *De regimine cordis, oris et operis.* Letter of vocation; unnamed spiritual son. Probably twelfth century. PL 184: 1185–90.

Geoffrey of Vendôme. Epistle 48. Letter of vocation; Hervé and Eve, recluses. Circa 1102. PL 157: 184–86.

Goscelin of St.-Bertin. *Liber confortatorius.* Rule for solitaries; Eve of Angers, anchoress. Circa 1082. One MS. C. H. Talbot, ed., *Analecta Monastica* ser. 3, *Studia Anselmiana* 38 (1955): 1–117.

Goswin of Anchin. *De novitiis instruendis.* Instruction for novices; novices of Anchin. Second half of twelfth century. One MS. Jean Leclercq, ed., "Deux opuscules sur la formation des jeunes moines," *Revue d'ascétique et de mystique* 33 (1957): 387–99.

Guibert of Nogent. *De virginitate.* Treatise on virginity; addressed to "Solomon." Circa 1080–1084. PL 156: 579–608.

Guigo II, the Carthusian. *Scala claustralium,* alias *Epistola de vita contemplativa.* Treatise on spiritual life; Brother Gervase, Guigo's teacher. Circa 1173–1188. Wide pseudonymous diffusion. Edmund Colledge and James Walsh, eds., SC 163 (Paris: Éditions du Cerf, 1970).

Hali Meidhad. Treatise on virginity; virgins, possibly recluses or canonesses. Circa 1190–1220. Two MSS. Bella Millett, ed., EETS o.s. 284 (London: Oxford University Press, 1982).

Heloise. Epistle 3. Letter of instruction and inquiry and treatise on the cloistered life; Abelard. Circa 1132–1135. Nine MSS. J. T. Muckle, ed., *Mediaeval Studies* 17 (1955): 240–81.

Hildebert of Lavardin. Epistle 21. Letter of vocation on virginity; Athalisa, a recluse. Before 1133. At least ten MSS. PL 171: 193–97.

Hildegard of Bingen. Epistle 52r. Letter on cloistered life and virginity; Tenxwind of Andernach, an Augustinian nun. Circa 1148–1150. Five MSS. Lieven Van Acker, ed., *Epistolarium* I, CCCM 91 (Turnhout: Brepols, 1991): 127–30.

Honorius of Regensburg. *De vita claustrali.* Treatise on cloistered life; monks. First half of twelfth century. PL 172: 1247–48.

Hugh of Fouilloy. *De claustro animae.* Treatise on cloistered life; monks and canons. Before 1174. Wide diffusion. PL 176: 1017–1182.

Hugh of St.-Victor. *De institutione novitiorum.* Instruction for novices; canons of St.-Victor. Before 1141. PL 176: 925–52.

Idung of Prüfening. *Argumentum de quattuor quaestionibus.* Epistolary argument; quaestio 3 on virginity; Master Herbord, a *scholasticus* of Bamberg. Before 1153. Bernhard Pez, ed., *Thesaurus anecdotorum novissimus* II.2 (Augsburg, 1721).

Instructio noviciorum secundum consuetudinem ecclesiae Cantuariensis. Instruction for novices and monastic rule; novices of Christ Church, Canterbury. Uncertain date. One MS. David Knowles, ed., *The Monastic Constitutions of Lanfranc* (London: Oxford University Press, 1951): 133–49.

Ivo of Chartres. Epistle 10. Letter of vocation on virginity; nuns of St.-Avit. Circa 1092. PL 162: 22–24.

John of Fruttuaria (Johannes Homo Dei). *Tractatus de ordine vitae et morum institutione,* alias *De correctione ac doctrina puerorum* and *De moribus adolescentum.* Instruction for novices; novices of Fruttuaria. Circa 1030–1049. Wide pseudonymous diffusion. PL 184: 559–84.

Libellus de diversis ordinibus et professionibus. Treatise on cloistered life; an unnamed monk. Mid-twelfth century. One MS. Giles Constable and B. Smith, eds. (Oxford: Clarendon, 1972).

Monachelus, alias *Tractatus de constructione tropologici orti.* Instruction for novices; an unnamed youth. No later than thirteenth century. One MS. Jean Leclercq, "Deux opuscules sur la formation des jeunes moines," *Revue d'ascétique et de mystique* 33 (1957): 387–99.

Octo puncta perfectionis assequendae. Instruction for novices; unnamed spiritual son. Probably twelfth century. PL 184: 1181–86.

Odo of St.-Victor. *Epistolae de observantia canonicae professionis recte praestanda.* Letters of vocation and direction; three or more *fratres.* Circa 1133–1148. PL 196: 1399–1418.

Osbert of Clare. Epistles 21, 22, 40, 41, 42. Letters of vocation on virginity; five nuns. Circa 1139–1163. One MS. E. W. Williamson, ed., *The Letters of Osbert of Clare* (London: Oxford University Press, 1929).

Peter of Blois. Epistles 35, 36, 55. Letters of vocation on virginity; three nuns. 1184. Wide diffusion. PL 207: 113–16, 166–68.

———. Sermons 62, 63, 64. Model sermons; *claustrales* and nuns. Circa 1184–1212. PL 207: 741–50.

Peter of Celle. *De disciplina claustrali.* Treatise on cloistered life; Richard of Salisbury, canon of Merton Priory. 1179. Two MSS. Gérard de Martel, ed., SC 240 (Paris: Éditions du Cerf, 1977).

Peter of Porto (Petrus Peccator). *Regula clericorum.* Rule for canons; canons of Porto. Circa 1110–1116. PL 163: 703–48.

Peter the Venerable. Epistle 1.20: *De conversationis eremiticae laudibus.* Letter of vocation; Gilbert, a recluse. Mid-twelfth century. Wide diffusion. PL 189: 89–100.

Philip of Harvengt. *De institutione clericorum.* Six treatises on cloistered life; regular canons. Circa 1140–1150. PL 203: 665–1206.

Speculum virginum. Dialogue on virginity and cloistered life; nuns. Early twelfth century. Wide diffusion; German translation. Jutta Seyfarth, ed., CCCM 5 (Turnhout: Brepols, 1990).

Stephen of Sawley. *Speculum novitii.* Instruction for novices; Cistercian novices. Circa 1223–1252. Edmond Mikkers, ed., *Collectanea ordinis Cisterciensium Reformatorum* 8 (1946): 17–68.

Thomas of Froidmont. *Liber de modo bene vivendi ad sororem*. Treatise on cloistered life and virginity; Thomas's sister. Late twelfth century. Pseudonymous
diffusion. PL 184: 1199–1306.

William of St.-Thierry. *Epistola ad fratres de Monte Dei de caritate*, alias *Golden Epistle*.
Treatise on spiritual life; Carthusians of Mont-Dieu. Circa 1144. Wide pseudonymous diffusion. Jean Déchanet, ed., SC 223 (Paris: Éditions du Cerf, 1975):
131–84.

Appendix B: Glossary of Religious Women

This list includes all the religious women discussed in this book, but is not intended to be exhaustive. The subjects are identified by date, religious house or region, order or status, and texts composed by or about them. All titles are given in English.

Adelheid of Frauenberg (14th c.), Dominican nun at Töss. Vita by Elsbeth Stagel, *Life of the Sisters of Töss*, ch. 22.

Adelheid of Rheinfelden (13th c.), fugitive wife; Dominican prioress at Unterlinden, ca. 1255–1264. Vita by Catherine of Gueberschwihr, *Unterlinden* ch. 23.

Agnes of Bohemia (ca. 1211–1282), royal foundress and abbess of Poor Clares in Prague; sister of Guglielma of Milan. Canonized 1989.

Agnes of Herenkeim (13th c.), noble widow; Dominican foundress of Unterlinden in Colmar, Alsace (1232). *Unterlinden* ch. 21.

Aldobrandesca of Siena (1245–1310), widow and tertiary, order of Umiliati. Vita by Gregory Lombardelli (16th c.).

Alice of Schaerbeke (d. 1250), Cistercian nun of La Cambre, then leper and recluse. Anonymous vita.

Angela of Foligno (c. 1248–1309), Italian widow; Franciscan tertiary and mystic. Author, *Memorial* and *Instructions* (Latin), dictated to "Brother A."

Anna of Wineck (13th c.), Dominican nun. *Unterlinden* ch. 31.

Beatrice of Nazareth (1200–1268), Flemish Cistercian nun and mystic. Author, *Seven Manners of Love* (Dutch). Anonymous vita based on lost vernacular autobiography.

Birgitta of Sweden (1303–1373), noblewoman and mother of eight; visionary, prophet, and activist; foundress of Brigittine Order. Author, *Revelations*, dictated to Peter of Skenninge and Peter of Alvastra (Swedish and Latin). Canonized 1391.

Catherine of Genoa (1447–1510), mystic, spiritual teacher, and hospital sister. Author, *Treatise on Purgatory* and *Spiritual Dialogue* (Italian), recorded posthumously by her disciples. Vita by Don Cattaneo Marabotto and Ettore Vernazza. Canonized 1737.

Catherine of Gueberschwihr (late 13th-early 14th c.), Dominican nun. Author, *Lives of the Sisters of Unterlinden*.

Catherine of Siena (1347–1380), Dominican tertiary, activist, and mystic. Author, *Dialogue* and *Letters* (Italian). Vita by Raymond of Capua. Canonized 1461.

Christina Mirabilis of St.-Trond (1150–1224), Flemish peasant, freelance miracleworker and "holy fool." Vita by Thomas of Cantimpré.

Christina of Markyate (c. 1096–1160), also called Theodora; English recluse, later Benedictine nun at St. Albans and prioress of Markyate. Anonymous vita.

Christine de Pizan (1364–c. 1430), Franco-Italian courtier, poet, humanist, and feminist; retired to Dominican abbey of Poissy. Author, *Book of the City of Ladies, Book of the Three Virtues, Epistle to the God of Love, Quarrel over the Rose, Vision of Christine, Tale of Joan of Arc,* and other works (French).

Christine of Stommeln (1242–1312), beguine and mystic in the region of Cologne. Vita by Peter of Dacia.

Clare of Assisi (1194–1253), companion of St. Francis and leader of Franciscan sisters at San Damiano; foundress of the Poor Clares. Author, *Testament* and letters (Latin). Vita by Thomas of Celano. Canonized 1255.

Columba of Rieti (1467–1501), Dominican tertiary and ascetic. Vita by Sebastian of Perugia.

Dorothea of Montau (1347–1394), Prussian mystic and mother of eight, later recluse. Vita by John Marienwerder.

Eligenta of Sulzmatt (13th c.), widow; Dominican nun. *Unterlinden* ch. 38.

Elisabeth of Schönau (c. 1129–1165), Benedictine nun and visionary. Co-author, with her brother Ekbert, of three *Books of Visions, Book of the Ways of God, Letters,* and *Revelation concerning [St. Ursula and] the Virgins of Cologne* (Latin).

Elizabeth of Hungary (or Thuringia, 1207–1231), widowed princess and Franciscan tertiary; benefactor of the poor. Vitae by Conrad of Marburg and Jacobus de Voragine, *Golden Legend.* Canonized 1235.

Elsbeth Stagel (d. circa 1360), Dominican nun and associate of Henry Suso. Author, *Life of the Sisters of Töss;* co-author of Suso's *Life of the Servant* (German).

Felicitas (d. 203), slave and martyr at Carthage; companion of Perpetua and Saturus.

Gertrude "the Great" of Helfta (1256–c. 1302), Benedictine nun and mystic. Author, *Herald of Divine Love* and *Spiritual Exercises* (Latin). Vita by an anonymous nun.

Gertrude of Saxony (13th c.), fugitive wife; Dominican nun. *Unterlinden* ch. 49.

Gherardesca of Pisa (c. 1207–c. 1267), widow and tertiary, Camaldolese order. Anonymous vita.

Guglielma of Milan (1210–1281), Bohemian princess who traveled incognita to Italy and became a Cistercian oblate. Venerated locally as a saint and identified by heretical Guglielmites as the Holy Spirit incarnate. Exhumed and burnt by inquisitors in 1300.

Hadewijch (fl. ca. 1220–1240), Flemish beguine and mystic. Author of 14 *Visions,* 31 *Letters,* 45 *Stanzaic Poems,* and 16 *Poems in Couplets* (Dutch).

Hadewijch II (13th c.), name given to protégée or disciple of the beguine; probable author of *Poems in Couplets* nos. 17–29, formerly ascribed to Hadewijch (Dutch).

Heloise (ca. 1100–1163), student, lover and wife of Peter Abelard; became Benedictine nun and prioress at Argenteuil, then founder and abbess of the Paraclete. Author of three extant letters to Abelard; co-author with him of *Problems of Heloise* (Latin).

Herrad of Hohenbourg (or Landsberg, d. 1195), Benedictine abbess of St.-Odile. Compiler of illustrated encyclopedia, *The Garden of Delights* (Latin).

Hildegard of Bingen (1098–1179), Benedictine abbess and founder of St.-Rupert; visionary, prophet, theologian, preacher, composer. Author of *Scivias*, *Book of Life's Merits*, *Book of Divine Works*, *Symphonia* (liturgical song cycle), *Play of Virtues*, *Letters*, *Book of Simple Medicine*, *Causes and Cures*, and other works (Latin). Vita by Gottfried of St.-Disibod and Theoderich of Echternach.

Hrotswitha (Hrotsvit) of Gandersheim (c. 932–c. 1000), German canoness and poet. Author of six plays and eight verse legends on saints' lives, *Origins of Gandersheim*, and *Epic on the Deeds of the Emperor Otto* (Latin).

Ida of Barking (12th c.), English Benedictine nun; correspondent of Osbert of Clare.

Ida of Nivelles (1199–1231), Flemish beguine and mystic, later Cistercian nun of La Ramée; friend of Beatrice of Nazareth. Vita possibly by Goswin of Bossut.

Joan of Arc (1412–1431), French peasant, prophet, and military leader; captured and burned by her English and Burgundian enemies as a heretic. Canonized 1920.

Juana de la Cruz (1491–1534), Franciscan abbess, visionary, and mystic. Author of unpublished *Book of Consolation* (Spanish). Anonymous vita.

Juette (Yvette) of Huy (1158–1228), Flemish widow; caretaker of lepers, then recluse. Vita by Hugh of Floreffe.

Julian of Norwich (1343–c. 1416), anchoress, visionary, and theologian. Author, *Showings of Divine Love* (English).

Lidwina of Schiedam (1380–1433), Dutch invalid and mystic. Vitae by Jan Gerlac, Jan Brugman, and Thomas à Kempis.

Lutgard of Aywières (c. 1182–1246), Flemish Cistercian nun and mystic. Vita by Thomas of Cantimpré.

Maifreda da Pirovano (d. 1300), Umiliati sister in Milan and leader of Guglielmite sect; accepted the role of Pope-elect and celebrated Easter Mass in 1300. Burnt as a heretic. Author of lost hymns and litanies to the Holy Spirit.

Margaret Ebner (1291–1351), Dominican nun of Maria Medingen near Nuremberg; sister of the mystic Christine Ebner. Author, *Revelations* (German).

Margaret of Brisach (13th c.), Dominican nun. *Unterlinden* ch. 52.

Margaret of Cortona (c. 1247–1297), peasant, mother of an illegitimate son, then Franciscan tertiary and mystic. Vita by Giunta Bevignati.

Margery Kempe (c. 1373–c. 1439), mother of fourteen, free-lance mystic and pilgrim. Author, *Book of Margery Kempe*, dictated to two scribes (English).

Marguerite of Oingt (c. 1240–1310), Carthusian prioress and mystic; author, *A Page of Meditations* (Latin), *Mirror* (French), and *Life of St. Beatrice of Ornacieux* (Francoprovençal).

Marguerite Porete (d. 1310), beguine and mystical theologian; author, *Mirror of Simple Souls* (French). Condemned for heresy and burned by William Humbert at Paris.

Marie of Oignies (c. 1177–1213), married Flemish beguine and caretaker of lepers. Vita by Jacques de Vitry; supplement by Thomas of Cantimpré.

Marie of the Incarnation (1599–1673), French Canadian nun and mystic.

Mechthild of Hackeborn (1241–1298), Benedictine nun and chantress at Helfta; sister of Abbess Gertrude of Hackeborn. Author, *Book of Special Grace* (Latin), dictated to Gertrude the Great and another nun.

Mechthild of Magdeburg (c. 1207–1282), beguine and mystic; later nun of Helfta. Author, *Flowing Light of the Godhead* (German).

Mechthild of Winzenheim (13th c.), Dominican nun. *Unterlinden* ch. 15.

Michelina of Pesaro (c. 1300–1356), widow; Franciscan tertiary. Vita by Mariano Florentino.

Paula (4th c.), Roman aristocrat, ascetic, biblical scholar, and patroness of monasteries in the Holy Land. Vita by St. Jerome.

Perpetua (d. 203), visionary and martyr at Carthage. Author, autobiographical section of *The Passion of Saints Perpetua and Felicitas* (Latin).

Prous Boneta (1296–1328), Franciscan tertiary, follower of Peter John Olivi, and visionary sectarian leader; claimed to be an incarnation of the Holy Spirit. Burned as a heretic and heresiarch at Carcassonne.

Rilindis of Bissegg (13th c.), fugitive wife and mother of eight; Dominican nun. *Unterlinden* ch. 40.

Tenxwind of Andernach (12th c.), mistress of a house of Augustinian nuns. Sister of Richard of Springiersbach; correspondent of Hildegard of Bingen.

Thecla (1st c.), legendary preacher and evangelist; said to have been converted to Christianity and virginity by St. Paul. Heroine of anonymous *Acts of Paul and Thecla*.

Tuoda of Colmar (13th c.), Dominican nun. *Unterlinden* ch. 32.

Umiliana dei Cerchi (1219–1246), Florentine widow and Franciscan recluse. Vitae by Vito of Cortona and Raffaelo da Volterra.

Zuana (Johanna) of Venice (d. 1550), foundress and director of the Hospital of San Giovanni and San Paolo; allegedly claimed to be the Angelic Pope. Celebrated as "Mother of the World" in Guillaume Postel, *The Astonishing Victories of Women of the New World*.

Works Cited

PRIMARY SOURCES

Names of medieval authors are given in anglicized form. Editions are cited before translations, which are listed when available. This bibliography excludes the sources listed in Appendix A.

Abelard, Peter. *Historia calamitatum*, ed. Jacques Monfrin. Paris: J. Vrin, 1959. Trans. Betty Radice, *The Letters of Abelard and Heloise*. Harmondsworth: Penguin, 1974.
———. *Letters IX–XIV*, ed. E. R. Smits. Groningen: Bouma, 1983.
Aelred of Rievaulx. *De Sanctimoniali de Wattun*. PL 195.
Agrippa von Nettesheim, Heinrich Cornelius (Henri Corneille Agrippa). *De nobilitate et praecellentia foeminei sexus*, ed. Charles Béné. Geneva: Droz, 1990. Trans. Johannes Bellin, *Abigail, das ist des löb-würdigen Frauen-Zimmers Adel und Fôrträfligkeit*. Lübeck: H. Schernwebel, 1650. Trans. Edward Fleetwood, *The Glory of Women: or, a Treatise declaring the excellency and preheminence of Women above Men*. London: R. Ibbitson, 1651. Trans. Hugh Crompton, *The Glory of Women: or a Looking-Glasse for Ladies*. London, 1652. Trans. Henry Care, *Female Pre-eminence: or the Dignity and Excellency of that Sex, above the Male*. London, 1670. Anon. trans., *Traité Agréable & Curieux de La Noblesse & Excellence du Sexe de la Femme, Par dessus celui de l'Homme*. The Hague: P. Perier, 1686. Trans. J. d'Arnaudin, *De la Grandeur et de l'excellence des femmes, au dessus des hommes*. Paris, 1713. Trans. François Péyrard ["Roétitg"], *De l'Excellence et de la Supériorité de la Femme*. Paris, 1801.
———. *De occulta philosophia*, ed. Karl Nowotny. Graz: Akademische Druck, 1967.
———. *De originali peccato, De sacramenti matrimonii*, and *Epistolae*, in *Opera*, 1600. Rpt. Hildesheim: G. Olms, 1970.
Albert the Great. *Commentarii in IV sententiarum*, in *Opera omnia* 29. Paris, 1894.
Alcuin. *Interrogationes et Responsiones in Genesin*. PL 100.
Amis and Amiloun, ed. MacEdward Leach, EETS o.s. 203. London, 1937.
Andreas Capellanus. *De amore et amoris remedio*, ed. and trans. P. G. Walsh. London: Duckworth, 1982.
Angela of Foligno. *Il libro della Beata Angela da Foligno*, ed. Ludger Thier and Abele Calufetti. Rome: Editiones Collegii S. Bonaventurae, 1985. Trans. Paul Lachance, *Complete Works*. New York: Paulist, 1993.
Antoine de la Sale. *Le Réconfort de Madame de Fresne*, ed. Ian Hill. Exeter: University of Exeter Press, 1979.

Aphrahat of Syria. *Demonstrationes*, ed. J. Parisot, *Patrologia Syriaca* I. Paris, 1894.

Apostolic Constitutions, ed. Marcel Metzger, SC 320. Paris: Éditions du Cerf, 1985.

Aucassin et Nicolette, ed. Jean Dufournet. Paris: Garnier-Flammarion, 1984. Trans. Eugene Mason. New York, 1958.

Augustine of Hippo. *De civitate Dei*, CCSL 48. Turnhout: Brepols, 1955. Trans. Henry Bettenson, *The City of God*. Harmondsworth: Penguin, 1972.

———. *De moribus Manichaeorum*. PL 39.

Beggiato, Fabrizio, ed. *Le lettere de Abelardo ed Eloisa nella traduzione di Jean de Meun*, 2 vols. Modena: S.T.E.M.-Mucchi, 1977.

Bernard of Clairvaux. *Capitula haeresum Petri Abaelardi*. PL 182.

———. *Epistolae*, ed. Jean Leclercq, Henri Rochais, and C. H. Talbot, *Sancti Bernardi Opera*, 7–8. Rome: Editiones cistercienses, 1957–1977. Trans. Bruno James, *The Letters of St. Bernard of Clairvaux*. London: Burns & Oates, 1953.

Bevignati, Giunta. *Vita Margaritae de Cortona*, AA.SS. February, tom. 3, 304–62. Paris: Palmé, 1864.

Birgitta of Sweden. *Liber celestis* (Middle English), ed. Roger Ellis, EETS 291. Oxford, 1987.

———. *Reuelaciones extrauagantes*, ed. Lennart Hollman. Uppsala: Almqvist & Wiksell, 1956.

———. *Revelations* (Middle English), ed. William Cumming, EETS o.s. 178. London, 1929. Trans. Albert Kezel, *Birgitta of Sweden: Life and Selected Revelations*. New York: Paulist, 1990.

Boccaccio, Giovanni. *De mulieribus claris*, ed. Vittorio Zaccaria. Milan, 1967. Trans. Guido Guarino, *Concerning Famous Women*. New Brunswick: Rutgers University Press, 1963.

———. *Decameron*, ed. Vittore Branca. Turin: Einaudi, 1980. Trans. Mark Musa and Peter Bondanella. Harmondsworth: Penguin, 1982.

Bokenham, Osbern. *Legendys of Hooly Wummen*, ed. Mary Serjeantson, EETS o.s. 206. London, 1938. Trans. Sheila Delany, *A Legend of Holy Women*. Notre Dame: Notre Dame University Press, 1992.

Brown, Carleton, ed. *Religious Lyrics of the XIVth Century*, 2nd ed. Oxford: Oxford University Press, 1952.

Caesarius of Heisterbach. *Dialogus miraculorum*, ed. Joseph Strange, 2 vols. Cologne: J. M. Heberle, 1851. Trans. C. Swinton Bland, *Dialogue on Miracles*, 2 vols. London: Routledge, 1929.

Cartulaire de l'abbaye du Paraclet, ed. Charles Lalore. Paris: E. Thorin, 1878.

Castiglione, Baldesar. *Il Libro del Cortegiano*, ed. Vittorio Cian. Florence: Sansoni, 1947. Trans. Charles Singleton, *The Book of the Courtier*. Garden City, NY: Doubleday, 1959.

Catherine of Gueberschwihr. "Les '*Vitae Sororum*' d'Unterlinden." Ed. Jeanne Ancelet-Hustache, *Archives d'histoire doctrinale et littéraire du moyen âge* 5 (1930): 317–509.

Chaucer, Geoffrey. *Canterbury Tales* and *Legend of Good Women*, in *The Riverside Chaucer*, ed. Larry Benson et al. Boston: Houghton Mifflin, 1987.

Chester Plays, part I, ed. Hermann Deimling, EETS e.s. 62. London, 1893.

Chrétien de Troyes. *Erec et Énide*, ed. and trans. Carleton Carroll. New York: Garland, 1987.

Christine de Pizan. *Le Livre de la Cité des Dames*. Trans. Earl Jeffrey Richards, *The Book of the City of Ladies*. New York: Persea, 1982.

Corpus Hermeticum, ed. A. D. Nock and A.-J. Festugière, 4th ed. Paris: Les Belles Lettres, 1983.

Damian, Peter. *De variis apparitionibus et miraculis*. PL 145.

Daniel, Walter. *Life of Ailred of Rievaulx*, ed. and trans. F. M. Powicke. London: T. Nelson, 1950.

Dante Alighieri. *Commedia*, ed. and trans. John Sinclair, 3 vols: *Inferno, Purgatorio, Paradiso*. New York: Oxford University Press, 1961.

Didascalia apostolorum, ed. Arthur Vööbus, *Corpus Scriptorum Christianorum Orientalium* 176. Louvain: E. Peeters, 1979.

Digby *Mary Magdalene*. In David Bevington, ed., *Medieval Drama*, 689–753. Boston: Houghton Mifflin, 1975.

Ebner, Margaret. *Revelations*, trans. Leonard Hindsley, *Complete Works*. New York: Paulist, 1993.

Ephrem of Syria. *Commentaire de l'Évangile Concordant, Version arménienne*, ed. L. Leloir, *Corpus Scriptorum Christianorum Orientalium* 137. Louvain: E. Peeters, 1954.

Epiphanius of Salamis. *Panarion*, ed. Karl Holl, *Griechische christliche Schriftsteller*, 3 vols. Berlin: Akademie Verlag, 1980–1985. Trans. Philip Amidon, *Selections*. New York: Oxford University Press, 1990.

Epistolae duorum amantium, ed. Ewald Könsgen. Leiden: Brill, 1974.

Euripides. *Iphigenia in Aulis* and *Iphigenia in Tauris*, in David Grene and Richmond Lattimore, eds., *The Complete Greek Tragedies*: III, IV. Chicago: University of Chicago Press, 1969.

Eusebius of Caesaria. *Historia ecclesiastica*, ed. Gustave Bardy, SC 41. Paris: Éditions du Cerf, 1955. Trans. Roy Deferrari, *Ecclesiastical History*, 2 vols. New York: Fathers of the Church, 1953, 1955.

Eutychius of Alexandria. *Annales*, ed. J.-P. Migne, *Patrologia graeca*, vol. 111. Paris: Migne, 1857–1866.

Florentino, Mariano. *Vita Michelinae Pisauri*, AA.SS. June, tom. 4, 777–84. Paris: Palmé, 1867.

Francis and Clare of Assisi. *Complete Works*, trans. Regis Armstrong and Ignatius Brady. New York: Paulist, 1982.

The Gast of Gy: A Middle-English Religious Prose Tract. Ed. R. H. Bowers, *Beiträge zur englischen Philologie* 32. Leipzig: B. Tauchnitz, 1938.

Gérard of Liège. "Quinque incitamenta amoris." Ed. André Wilmart, *Revue d'ascétique et de mystique* 12 (1931): 349–430.

Gerson, Jean. "Consolation sur la mort des amis." In *Oeuvres complètes*, VII, ed. P. Glorieux. Paris: Desclee, 1966.

Gertrude of Helfta. *Legatus divinae pietatis*, ed. Jean-Marie Clément, *Oeuvres spirituelles* V, SC 331. Paris: Éditions du Cerf, 1986. Trans. Margaret Winkworth, *The Herald of Divine Love*. New York: Paulist, 1993.

"Golias de conjuge non ducenda." Ed. Thomas Wright, *Latin Poems Commonly Attributed to Walter Mapes*. Camden Society Publications 16. London, 1841.

Gottfried of Strassburg. *Tristan*, ed. Friedrich Ranke. Stuttgart: Reclam, 1981. Trans. A. T. Hatto. Harmondsworth: Penguin, 1960.

Gower, John. *Confessio amantis*, ed. Russell Peck. Toronto: University of Toronto Press, 1980. Trans. Terence Tiller. Harmondsworth: Penguin, 1963.

Gregory of Nyssa. *On the Making of Man*, in *Nicene and Post-Nicene Fathers*, 2nd series, Vol. V. New York, 1893.

Gregory the Great. *Homily 33* on Mary Magdalene. PL 76.

Guibert of Nogent. *Autobiographie*, ed. E.-R. Labande. Paris: Les Belles Lettres, 1981. Trans. C. Swinton Bland and ed. John F. Benton, *Self and Society in Medieval France*. New York: Harper & Row, 1970.

Guillaume de Lorris and Jean de Meun. *Le Roman de la Rose*, ed. Daniel Poirion. Paris: Garnier-Flammarion, 1974. Trans. Harry Robbins, *The Romance of the Rose*. New York: E. P. Dutton, 1962.

Hadewijch. *Lettres spirituelles*, trans. J.-B. Porion. Geneva: C. Martingay, 1972.

———. *Strophische Gedichten, Brieven*, and *Mengeldichten*, ed. Jozef Van Mierlo, 5 vols. Antwerp: Standaard-Boekhandel, 1942–1952. Trans. Columba Hart, *Complete Works*. New York: Paulist, 1980.

———. *Het Visioenenboek van Hadewijch*, ed. H. W. Vekeman. Nijmegen: Dekker & Van de Vegt, 1980.

Harley Lyrics, ed. G. L. Brook. Manchester: Manchester University Press, 1956.

Heloise. *Letters*, ed. J. T. Muckle, "The Personal Letters Between Abelard and Heloise." *Mediaeval Studies* 15 (1953). Trans. Betty Radice, *The Letters of Abelard and Heloise*. Harmondsworth: Penguin, 1974.

Herrad of Hohenbourg. *Hortus deliciarum*, reconstructed by Rosalie Green, Michael Evans, et al., 2 vols. London: Warburg Institute, 1979.

Hildebert of Lavardin. *Carmina*. PL 171.

Hildegard of Bingen. *Causae et curae*, ed. Paul Kaiser. Leipzig: Teubner, 1903.

———. *Epistolarium*, ed. Lieven van Acker, CCCM 91–91A. Turnhout: Brepols, 1991, 1993.

———. *Liber divinorum operum*, ed. Albert Derolez and Peter Dronke, CCCM 92. Turnhout: Brepols, 199 .

———. *Liber vitae meritorum*, ed. J.-B. Pitra, *Analecta sacra* 8. Monte Cassino: Spicilegium Solesmensis, 1882. Trans. Bruce Hozeski, *The Book of the Rewards of Life*. New York: Garland, 1993.

———. *Scivias*, ed. Adelgundis Führkötter, CCCM 43–43A. Turnhout: Brepols, 1978. Trans. Columba Hart and Jane Bishop. New York: Paulist, 1990.

Hill, R. T., and T. G. Bergin, eds. *Anthology of the Provençal Troubadours*, 2 vols. New Haven, CT: Yale University Press, 1973.

Hippolytus. *Refutatio omnium haeresium*, ed. Miroslav Marcovich. Berlin: W. De Gruyter, 1986.

Homiliae Clementinae, ed. Albert Schwegler. Stuttgart, 1847.

Hugh of Floreffe. *Vita Ivettae Reclusae*, AA.SS. January, tom. 2, 145–69. Paris: Palmé, 1867.

Hugh of St.-Victor. *De sacramentis christianae fidei*. PL 176. Trans. Roy Deferrari,

On the Sacraments of the Christian Faith. Cambridge, MA: Medieval Academy of America, 1951.

Irenaeus of Lyon. *Contre les hérésies* IV, ed. Adelin Rousseau et al., SC 100. Paris: Éditions du Cerf, 1965.

Isidore of Seville. *Quaestiones in Librum Iudicum*. PL 83.

Jacobus de Voragine. *Legenda aurea*. Trans. William Granger Ryan, *The Golden Legend: Readings on the Saints*. Princeton, NJ: Princeton University Press, 1993.

Jacques de Vitry. *Vita Mariae Oigniacensis*, AA.SS. June, tom. 5, 547–72. Paris: Palmé, 1867. Trans. Margot King, *The Life of Marie d'Oignies*, 2nd ed. Toronto: Peregrina, 1993.

Jehan Le Fèvre. *Les Lamentations de Mathéolus*, ed. A.-G. Van Hamel, 2 vols. Paris: E. Bouillon, 1892, 1905.

Jerome. *Commentariorum in Esaiam Libri*. CCSL 73, part 1. Turnhout: Brepols, 1963.

———. *Commentariorum in Micheam Libri*. PL 25.

———. *Letters*, ed. Jérôme Labourt, 7 vols. Paris: Les Belles Lettres, 1949–1961.

Jourdain de Blaye, ed. Peter Dembowski. Paris: H. Champion, 1991.

Julian of Norwich. *A Book of Showings to the Anchoress Julian of Norwich*, ed. Edmund Colledge and James Walsh, 2 vols. Toronto: Pontifical Institute, 1978. Trans. Colledge and Walsh, *Showings*. New York: Paulist, 1978.

Kempe, Margery. *Book of Margery Kempe*, ed. Sanford Meech and Hope Emily Allen, EETS o.s. 212. London, 1940. Trans. Barry Windeatt. Harmondsworth: Penguin, 1985.

The Koran Interpreted, trans. A. J. Arberry. New York: Macmillan, 1955.

"Legends of Meister Eckhart." In Raymond Blakney, *Meister Eckhart: A Modern Translation*. New York: Harper & Row, 1941.

Lettere di Santi e Beati Fiorentini, ed. Antommaria Biscioni. Florence: Francesco Moucke, 1736.

Liber de ordine creaturarum, ed. Manuel Diaz y Diaz. Santiago de Compostela: Universidad de Santiago, 1972.

Life of Beatrice of Nazareth, ed. and trans. Roger De Ganck. Kalamazoo, MI: Cistercian Publications, 1991.

Life of Christina of Markyate, ed. and trans. C. H. Talbot. Oxford: Clarendon, 1959.

Lombard, Peter. *Sententiae in IV libris distinctae*, 3rd. ed. Grottaferrata: Editiones Collegii S. Bonaventurae, 1981.

Ludolf of Saxony. *The Hours of the Passion, Taken from the Life of Christ*, trans. H. J. Coleridge. London: Burns & Oates, 1887.

Makarios of Egypt. *Die 50 geistlichen Homilien des Makarios*, ed. Hermann Dörries et al., *Patristische Texte und Studien* 4. Berlin: De Gruyter, 1964.

Malory, Sir Thomas. *Works*, ed. Eugène Vinaver, 2nd ed. Oxford: Oxford University Press, 1971. Caxton's version ed. Janet Cowen, *Le Morte d'Arthur*, 2 vols. Harmondsworth: Penguin, 1969.

Marguerite of Oingt. *Oeuvres*, ed. Antonin Duraffour et al. Paris: Les Belles Lettres, 1965. Trans. Renate Blumenfeld-Kosinski, *Writings*. Newburyport, MA: Focus Library of Medieval Women, 1990.

Marguerite Porete. *Le Mirouer des simples ames*, ed. Romana Guarnieri and Paul Verdeyen, CCCM 69. Turnhout: Brepols, 1986. *The Mirrour of Simple Soules:*

A Middle English Translation, ed. Marilyn Doiron, *Archivio italiano per la storia della pietà* 5. Rome, 1968, 241–355. Trans. Ellen Babinsky, *The Mirror of Simple Souls*. New York: Paulist, 1993.

Marie de France. *Lais*, ed. Jean Rychner. Paris: H. Champion, 1973. Trans. Robert Hanning and Joan Ferrante, *The Lais of Marie de France*. New York: Dutton, 1978.

———. *Saint Patrick's Purgatory*, ed. and trans. Michael Curley. Binghamton, NY: Medieval and Renaissance Texts and Studies, 1993.

Marius Victorinus. *Theological Treatises on the Trinity*, trans. Mary Clark, *Fathers of the Church* 69. Washington: Catholic University of America Press, 1978.

May, William, ed. "The Confession of Prous Boneta, Heretic and Heresiarch." In John Mundy et al., eds., *Essays in Medieval Life and Thought Presented in Honor of Austin Evans*. New York: Biblo & Tanner, 1965, 3–30. Trans. Elizabeth Petroff, *Medieval Women's Visionary Literature*. Oxford: Oxford University Press, 1986, 284–90.

Mechthild of Magdeburg. *Das fliessende Licht der Gottheit*, ed. Hans Neumann. Munich: Artemis Verlag, 1990. Trans. Christiane Mesch Galvani, *Flowing Light of the Divinity*. New York: Garland, 1991.

Methodius of Olympus. *Symposium*, ed. Herbert Musurillo, SC 95. Paris: Éditions du Cerf, 1963.

N-Town Play, ed. Stephen Spector. Oxford: Oxford University Press, 1991.

Odes of Solomon, ed. and trans. J. H. Charlesworth. Oxford: Clarendon, 1973.

Origen. *Commentaire sur Saint Jean*, ed. Cécile Blanc, SC 120. Paris: Éditions du Cerf, 1966.

Passio SS. Perpetuae et Felicitatis, ed. and trans. Herbert Musurillo, *The Acts of the Christian Martyrs*. Oxford: Clarendon, 1972.

Pistis Sophia, ed. Carl Schmidt and trans. Violet MacDermot. Leiden: Brill, 1978.

Pliny the Elder. *Naturalis historia*, 6 vols. Stuttgart: Teubner, 1967–1970.

Plutarch. *Moralia*, in *Oeuvres morales*, tom. II, ed. Jean Dumortier and Jean Defradas. Paris: Les Belles Lettres, 1985.

Postel, Guillaume. *Les très-merveilleuses victoires des femmes du Nouveau-Monde*. Turin, 1869; rpt. Geneva: Slatkine Reprints, 1970.

La Queste del saint Graal, ed. Albert Pauphilet. Paris: E. Champion, 1923. Trans. P. M. Matarasso, *The Quest of the Holy Grail*. Harmondsworth: Penguin, 1969.

Raymond of Capua. *Vita de S. Catharina (Legenda major)*, AA.SS. April, tom. 3, 861–967. Paris: Palmé, 1866. Trans. Conleth Kearns, *Life of Catherine of Siena*. Wilmington, DE: Michael Glazier, 1980.

"*La Règle des Fins Amans*: Eine Beginenregel aus dem Ende des XIII. Jahrhunderts." Ed. Karl Christ, in B. Schädel and W. Mulertt, eds., *Philologische Studien aus dem romanisch-germanischen Kulturkreise: Festgabe Karl Voretzsch*. Halle: Max Niemeyer, 1927.

A Revelation of Purgatory by an Unknown, Fifteenth-Century Woman Visionary, ed. Marta Harley. Lewiston, NY: Edwin Mellen, 1985.

Richard of St.-Victor. *Benjamin major* and *Benjamin minor*. PL 196. Trans. Grover Zinn as *The Mystical Ark* and *The Twelve Patriarchs*. New York: Paulist, 1979.

———. *De quatuor gradibus violentae charitatis*. PL 196. Trans. Clare Kirchberger,

"Of the Four Degrees of Passionate Charity." In *Richard of Saint-Victor: Selected Writings on Contemplation.* New York: Harper & Brothers, 1957.

Robinson, James, ed. *The Nag Hammadi Library in English*, 3rd ed. San Francisco: Harper & Row, 1988.

Rupert of Deutz. *De sancta Trinitate et operibus eius*, ed. Hraban Haacke, CCCM 22. Turnhout: Brepols, 1972.

Ruysbroeck, Jan van. *The Book of the Twelve Beguines*, trans. John Francis. London, 1913.

Schwester Katrei, ed. Franz-Josef Schweitzer, *Der Freiheitsbegriff der deutschen Mystik.* Frankfurt: Peter Lang, 1981, 322–70. Trans. Elvira Borgstädt, "Sister Catherine." In Bernard McGinn, ed., *Meister Eckhart: Teacher and Preacher.* New York: Paulist, 1986, 349–84.

Silence: A Thirteenth-Century French Romance, ed. and trans. Sarah Roche-Mahdi. East Lansing: Colleagues Press, 1992.

Sir Amadace and The Avowing of Arthur, ed. Christopher Brookhouse. Copenhagen: Rosenkilde & Bagger, 1968.

Sisam, Celia and Kenneth, eds. *The Oxford Book of Medieval English Verse.* Oxford: Oxford University Press, 1970.

Sprenger, Jacobus, and Henricus Institoris. *Malleus maleficarum.* Lyon, 1669. Trans. Montague Summers, 2nd ed. London: J. Rodker, 1948.

Stagel, Elsbet. *Das Leben der Schwestern zu Töss*, ed. Ferdinand Vetter. Deutsche Texte des Mittelalters, Bd. 6. Berlin, 1906.

Suso, Henry. *Vita*, ed. Karl Bihlmeyer, *Deutsche Schriften.* Stuttgart: W. Kohlhammer, 1907. Trans. Frank Tobin in *The Exemplar.* New York: Paulist, 1989.

Tauler, Johannes. *Predigten*, ed. Georg Hofmann. Freiburg: Herder, 1961. Trans. Maria Shrady, *Sermons.* New York: Paulist, 1985.

Tertullian. *De monogamia*, ed. Paul Mattei, SC 343. Paris: Éditions du Cerf, 1988.

Thomas Aquinas. *Quaestiones de anima*, ed. James Robb. Toronto: Pontifical Institute, 1968.

Thomas of Cantimpré. *Vita Christinae mirabilis*, AA.SS. July, tom. 5, 650–60. Paris: Palmé, 1868. Trans. Margot King, *The Life of Christina of Saint Trond.* Saskatoon: Peregrina, 1986.

———. *Vita Lutgardis*, AA.SS. June, tom. 4, 189–209. Paris: Palmé, 1867. Trans. Margot King, *The Life of Lutgard of Aywières.* Saskatoon: Peregrina, 1987.

Thomas of Chobham. *Summa confessorum*, ed. F. Broomfield, *Analecta mediaevalia Namurcensia* 25. Louvain, 1968.

Tocco, Felice, ed. "Il Processo dei Guglielmiti." *Rendiconti della Reale Accademia dei Lincei: Classe di Scienze Morali, Storiche e Filologiche*, ser. 5, vol. 8. Rome, 1899, 309–42, 351–84, 407–32, 437–69.

Tubach, Frederic C. *Index exemplorum: A Handbook of Medieval Religious Tales.* Helsinki: Suomalainen Tiedeakatemia, 1969.

Vie et miracles de sainte Thècle, ed. and trans. Gilbert Dagron and Marie Dupré La Tour. Subsidia hagiographica 62. Brussels: Société des bollandistes, 1978.

Vita Aleydis de Scarenbeka, ed. Chrysostom Henriquez, *Quinque prudentes virgines.* Antwerp, 1630, 168–98. Trans. Martinus Cawley, *Lives of Ida of Nivelles, Lutgard and Alice the Leper.* Lafayette, OR: Guadalupe Translations, 1987.

Vita di S. Maria Maddalena, in *Vite de alcuni santi scritte nel buon secolo della lingua toscana*. Milan, 1830. Trans. Valentina Hawtrey, *The Life of Saint Mary Magdalene*. London: John Lane, 1904.

Vita Idae Nivellensis, ed. Chrysostom Henriquez, *Quinque prudentes virgines*. Antwerp, 1630. 199–293. Trans. Martinus Cawley, *Lives of Ida of Nivelles, Lutgard and Alice the Leper*. Lafayette, OR: Guadalupe Translations, 1987.

Vita Odiliae Abbatissae Hohenburgensis, ed. Bruno Krusch and W. Levison, *MGH Scriptorum rerum merovingicarum* 6. Hannover: Hahnsche Buchhandlung, 1913.

Vita prior Lidwinae, AA.SS. April, tom. 2, 270–300. Paris: Palmé, 1866.

Vito of Cortona. *Vita Umilianae*, AA.SS. May, tom. 4, 385–400. Paris: Palmé, 1866.

Waddell, Chrysogonus, ed. *The Paraclete Statutes Institutiones Nostrae: Introduction, Edition, Commentary*. Trappist, KY: Gethsemani Abbey, 1987.

William of Auvergne. *De legibus* and *De moribus*, in *Opera omnia* I. Paris, 1674; rpt. Frankfurt: Minerva, 1963.

William of St.-Thierry. *Disputatio adversus Petrum Abaelardum*. PL 180.

SECONDARY SOURCES

Ahldén, Tage. *Nonnenspiegel und Mönchsvorschriften*. Goteborg: Elanders, 1952.

Amore, Roy and Larry Shinn, eds. *Lustful Maidens and Ascetic Kings: Buddhist and Hindu Stories of Life*. New York: Oxford University Press, 1981.

Angenot, Marc. *Les Champions des femmes: Examen du discours sur la superiorité des femmes, 1400–1800*. Montréal: Presses de l'Université du Québec, 1977.

Arberry, A. J. *Sufism: An Account of the Mystics of Islam*. London: Allen & Unwin, 1969.

Arduini, M. L. "Il tema 'vir' e 'mulier' nell' esegesi patristica e medioeuale di Eccli. XLII.14." *Aevum* 55 (1981): 246–61.

Arthur, Rose. *The Wisdom Goddess: Feminine Motifs in Eight Nag Hammadi Documents*. Lanham, MD: University Press of America, 1984.

Ashe, Geoffrey. *The Virgin*. London: Routledge & Kegan Paul, 1976.

Ashley, Kathleen and Pamela Sheingorn, eds. *Interpreting Cultural Symbols: Saint Anne in Late Medieval Society*. Athens: University of Georgia Press, 1990.

Aspegren, Kerstin. *The Male Woman: A Feminine Ideal in the Early Church*. Uppsala: Almqvist & Wiksell, 1990.

Atkinson, Clarissa. *The Oldest Vocation: Christian Motherhood in the Middle Ages*. Ithaca, NY: Cornell University Press, 1991.

———. "'Precious Balsam in a Fragile Glass': The Ideology of Virginity in the Later Middle Ages." *Journal of Family History* 8 (1983): 131–43.

Auerbach, Erich. *Mimesis: The Representation of Reality in Western Literature*, trans. Willard Trask. Princeton, NJ: Princeton University Press, 1953.

Baker, Derek, ed. *Medieval Women*. Oxford: Blackwell, 1978.

Banker, James. "Mourning a Son: Childhood and Paternal Love in the *Consolateria* of Giannozzo Manetti." *History of Childhood Quarterly* 3 (1976): 351–62.

Baron, F. X. "Children and Violence in Chaucer's *Canterbury Tales*." *Journal of Psychohistory* 7 (1979): 77–103.

Barron, W. R. J. *English Medieval Romance*. London: Longman, 1987.

Baumgartner, Emmanuèle. "De Lucrèce à Héloïse: Remarques sur deux *exemples* du *Roman de la Rose* de Jean de Meun." *Romania* 95 (1974): 433–42.

Bäurle, Margret and Luzia Braun. "'Ich bin heiser in der Kehle meiner Keuschheit': Über das Schreiben der Mystikerinnen." In Hiltrud Gnüg and Renate Möhrmann, eds., *Frauen Literatur Geschichte: Schreibende Frauen vom Mittelalter bis zur Gegenwart*. Stuttgart: J. B. Metzler, 1985, 1–15.

Benko, Stephen. *The Virgin Goddess: Studies in the Pagan and Christian Roots of Mariology*. Leiden: Brill, 1993.

Benton, John F. "The Court of Champagne as a Literary Center." *Speculum* 36 (1961): 551–91.

———. "Fraud, Fiction and Borrowing in the Correspondence of Abelard and Heloise." In René Louis and Jean Jolivet, eds., *Pierre Abélard—Pierre le Vénérable*, 469–506.

———. "Philology's Search for Abelard in the *Metamorphosis Goliae*." *Speculum* 50 (1975): 199–217.

———. "A Reconsideration of the Authenticity of the Correspondence of Abelard and Heloise." In Rudolf Thomas, ed., *Petrus Abaelardus*, 41–52.

———. "Trotula, Women's Problems, and the Professionalization of Medicine in the Middle Ages." *Bulletin of the History of Medicine* 59 (1985): 30–53.

Benton, John F. and F. P. Ercoli. "The Style of the *Historia Calamitatum*." *Viator* 6 (1975): 59–86.

Bériou, Nicole. "La prédication au béguinage de Paris pendant l'année liturgique 1272–1273." *Recherches augustiniennes* 13 (1978): 105–229.

Bernards, Matthäus. "Die mittelrheinischen Handschriften des Jungfrauenspiegels." *Archiv für mittelrheinische Kirchengeschichte* 3 (1951): 357–64.

———. *Speculum virginum: Geistigkeit und Seelenleben der Frau im Hochmittelalter*. Cologne: Böhlau, 1955.

Bernstein, Alan. "The Invocation of Hell in Thirteenth-Century Paris." In James Hankins et al., eds., *Supplementum Festivum: Studies in Honor of Paul Oskar Kristeller*. Binghamton, NY: Medieval and Renaissance Texts and Studies, 1987, 13–54.

———. "Theology Between Heresy and Folklore: William of Auvergne on Punishment after Death." *Studies in Medieval and Renaissance History* 5 (1982): 20–31.

Blamires, Alcuin, ed. *Woman Defamed and Woman Defended*. Oxford: Clarendon Press, 1992.

Bloch, R. Howard. "Medieval Misogyny." *Representations* 20 (1987): 1–24.

———. *Medieval Misogyny and the Invention of Western Romantic Love*. Chicago: University of Chicago Press, 1991.

Blumenfeld-Kosinski, Renate and Timea Szell, eds. *Images of Sainthood in Medieval Europe*. Ithaca, NY: Cornell University Press, 1991.

Böckeler, Maura. *Das grosse Zeichen: Die Frau als Symbol göttlicher Wirklichkeit*. Salzburg: Otto Müller-Verlag, 1941.

Boff, Leonardo. *The Maternal Face of God: The Feminine and Its Religious Expressions*, trans. Robert Barr and John Diercksmeier. San Francisco: Harper & Row, 1987.

Bolton, Brenda. "Mulieres sanctae." In Susan M. Stuard, ed., *Women in Medieval Society.* Philadelphia: University of Pennsylvania Press, 1976, 141–58.

———. "Vitae Matrum: A Further Aspect of the *Frauenfrage*." In Derek Baker, ed., *Medieval Women*, 253–73.

Bonney, Françoise. "Jean Gerson: Un nouveau regard sur l'enfance." *Annales de démographie historique* (1973): 137–42.

Bornstein, Daniel. "The Uses of the Body: The Church and the Cult of Santa Margherita da Cortona." *Church History* 62 (1993): 163–77.

Bossy, John. *Christianity in the West, 1400–1700*. Oxford: Oxford University Press, 1985.

Boswell, John. *Christianity, Social Tolerance, and Homosexuality: Gay People in Western Europe from the Beginning of the Christian Era to the Fourteenth Century*. Chicago: University of Chicago Press, 1980.

———. *The Kindness of Strangers: The Abandonment of Children in Western Europe from Late Antiquity to the Renaissance*. New York: Pantheon Books, 1988.

Bourgain, Pascale. "Héloïse." In *Abélard en son temps*, Actes du Colloque International, 1979. Paris: Les Belles Lettres, 1981, 211–37.

Bouwsma, William. *Concordia Mundi: The Career and Thought of Guillaume Postel (1510–1581)*. Cambridge, MA: Harvard University Press, 1957.

Bouyer, Louis. *Figures mystiques féminines*. Paris: Éditions du Cerf, 1989.

———. *Le Trône de la Sagesse: Essai sur la signification du culte mariale*. Paris: Éditions du Cerf, 1957.

Bozzolo, Carla. "L'humaniste Gontier Col et la traduction française des Lettres d'Abélard et Héloïse." *Romania* 95 (1974): 199–215.

Braude, Ann. *Radical Spirits: Spiritualism and Women's Rights in Nineteenth-Century America*. Boston: Beacon Press, 1989.

Bredero, Adriaan. "Le Moyen Âge et le Purgatoire." *Revue d'histoire ecclésiastique* 78 (1983): 429–52.

Breuer, Wilhelm. "Philologische Zugänge zur Mystik Hadewijchs: Zu Form und Funktion religiöser Sprache bei Hadewijch." In Margot Schmidt and Dieter Bauer, eds., *Grundfragen christlicher Mystik*, 103–21.

Brissaud, Yves. "L'infanticide à la fin du moyen âge, ses motivations psychologiques et sa repression." *Revue historique de droit français et étranger* 50 (1972): 229–56.

Brook, Leslie. "Christine de Pisan, Heloise, and Abelard's Holy Women." *Zeitschrift für romanische Philologie* 109 (1993): 556–63.

Brooke, Christopher. *The Medieval Idea of Marriage*. Oxford: Oxford University Press, 1991.

Brown, Joanne Carlson and Carole Bohn, eds. *Christianity, Patriarchy, and Abuse: A Feminist Critique*. New York: Pilgrim Press, 1989.

Brown, Peter. *The Body and Society: Men, Women and Sexual Renunciation in Early Christianity*. New York: Columbia University Press, 1988.

Brundage, James. *Law, Sex, and Christian Society in Medieval Europe*. Chicago: University of Chicago Press, 1987.

Buckley, Jorunn. *Female Fault and Fulfillment in Gnosticism*. Chapel Hill: University of North Carolina Press, 1986.

Bulgakov, Sergius. *The Wisdom of God: A Brief Summary of Sophiology*, trans. Patrick Thompson et al. London: Williams & Norgate, 1937.

Bynum, Caroline Walker. *Docere verbo et exemplo: An Aspect of Twelfth-Century Spirituality*. Missoula, MT: Scholars Press, 1979.

———. *Fragmentation and Redemption: Essays on Gender and the Human Body in Medieval Religion*. New York: Zone Books, 1991.

———. *Holy Feast and Holy Fast: The Religious Significance of Food to Medieval Women*. Berkeley: University of California Press, 1987.

———. *Jesus as Mother: Studies in the Spirituality of the High Middle Ages*. Berkeley: University of California Press, 1982.

Cameron, Averil. "Virginity as Metaphor: Women and the Rhetoric of Early Christianity." In *History as Text: The Writing of Ancient History*. London: Duckworth, 1989, 181–205.

Carpenter, Jennifer. "Juette of Huy, Recluse and Mother (1158–1228): Children and Mothering in the Saintly Life." In Jennifer Carpenter and Sally-Beth MacLean, eds., *Power of the Weak: Studies on Medieval Women*. Urbana: University of Illinois Press, 1995.

Cazelles, Brigitte. *The Lady as Saint: A Collection of French Hagiographic Romances of the Thirteenth Century*. Philadelphia: University of Pennsylvania Press, 1991.

Charrier, Charlotte. *Héloïse dans l'histoire et dans la légende*. Paris: H. Champion, 1933.

Chenu, Marie-Dominique. *Nature, Man, and Society in the Twelfth Century: Essays on New Theological Perspectives in the Latin West*, trans. Jerome Taylor and Lester K. Little. Chicago: University of Chicago Press, 1968.

Cherewatuk, Karen and Ulrike Wiethaus, eds. *Dear Sister: Medieval Women and the Epistolary Genre*. Philadelphia: University of Pennsylvania Press, 1993.

Childress, Diana. "Between Romance and Legend: 'Secular Hagiography' in Middle English Literature." *Philological Quarterly* 57 (1978): 311–22.

Ciolina, Evamaria. *Der Freskenzyklus von Urschalling: Geschichte und Ikonographie*. Munich: Kommissionsbuchhandlung R. Wolfle, 1980.

Clark, Anne. *Elisabeth of Schönau: A Twelfth-Century Visionary*. Philadelphia: University of Pennsylvania Press, 1992.

Coakley, John. "Gender and the Authority of Friars: The Significance of Holy Women for Thirteenth-Century Franciscans and Dominicans." *Church History* 60 (1991): 445–60.

Cochelin, Isabelle. "Sainteté laïque: l'exemple de Juette de Huy." *Le Moyen Âge* 95 (1989): 397–417.

Cohen, Jeremy. "Philosophical Exegesis in Historical Perspective: The Case of the Binding of Isaac." In Tamar Rudavsky, ed., *Divine Omniscience and Omnipotence in Medieval Philosophy*. Boston: D. Reidel, 1985, 135–42.

Cohen, Seymour, trans. *The Holy Letter: A Study in Medieval Jewish Sexual Morality Ascribed to Nahmanides*. New York: Ktav, 1976.

Colledge, Edmund and J. C. Marler. "'Poverty of the Will': Ruusbroec, Eckhart and *The Mirror of Simple Souls.*" In Paul Mommaers and Norbert De Paepe, eds., *Jan van Ruusbroec*, 14–47.

Congar, Yves. "The Motherhood in God and the Femininity of the Holy Spirit." In *I Believe in the Holy Spirit*, trans. David Smith. London: G. Chapman, 1983, III, 155–64.

Constable, Giles. *Letters and Letter-Collections*, Typologie des sources du moyen âge occidental, fasc. 17. Turnhout: Brepols, 1976.

———. "The Popularity of Twelfth-Century Spiritual Authors in the Late Middle Ages." In Anthony Molho and John Tedeschi, eds., *Renaissance Studies in Honor of Hans Baron*. DeKalb: Northern Illinois University Press, 1971, 5–28.

Costa, Patrizia. *Guglielma la Boema, L' "Eretica" di Chiaravalle*. Milan: NED, 1985.

Couliano, Ioan. *The Tree of Gnosis: Gnostic Mythology from Early Christianity to Modern Nihilism*. San Francisco: HarperCollins, 1992.

Craymer, Suzanne. "Margery Kempe's Imitation of Mary Magdalene and the 'Digby Plays.'" *Mystics Quarterly* 19 (1993): 173–81.

Crump, C. G. and E. F. Jacob, eds. *The Legacy of the Middle Ages*. Oxford: Clarendon, 1926.

Dan, Joseph. "Shekinah." *Encyclopaedia Judaica*. Jerusalem, 1971, vol. 14, 1353–54.

Davies, Stevan. *The Revolt of the Widows: The Social World of the Apocryphal Acts*. Carbondale: Southern Illinois University Press, 1980.

De Gandillac, Maurice. "Les Secrets d'Agrippa." In *Aspects du libertinisme au XVI*e *siècle*, Actes du Colloque International de Sommières. Paris: J. Vrin, 1974, 123–36.

DeMause, Lloyd, ed. *The History of Childhood*. New York: Psychohistory Press, 1974.

De Paepe, Norbert. *Hadewijch Strofische Gedichten: Een Studie van de minne in het kader der 12*e *en 13*e *eeuwse mystiek en profane minnelyriek*. Ghent: Secretariaat van de Koninlijke Vlaamse Academie, 1967.

De Rougemont, Denis. *Love in the Western World*, trans. Montgomery Belgion, rev. ed. New York: Harper & Row, 1974.

Dinzelbacher, Peter and Dieter Bauer, eds. *Frauenmystik im Mittelalter*. Ostfildern: Schwabenverlag, 1985.

Dobson, E. J. *The Origins of Ancrene Wisse*. Oxford: Oxford University Press, 1976.

Dronke, Peter. *Abelard and Heloise in Medieval Testimonies*. Glasgow: University of Glasgow Press, 1976.

———. "Francesca and Héloïse." *Comparative Literature* 27 (1975): 113–35.

———. "Heloise, Abelard, and Some Recent Discussions." In *Intellectuals and Poets in Medieval Europe*. Rome: Edizioni di storia e letteratura, 1992, 323–42.

———. "Heloise's *Problemata* and *Letters*: Some Questions of Form and Content." In Rudolf Thomas, ed., *Petrus Abaelardus*, 53–73.

———. *Women Writers of the Middle Ages: A Critical Study of Texts from Perpetua (†203) to Marguerite Porete (†1310)*. Cambridge: Cambridge University Press, 1984.

Duby, Georges. *The Knight, the Lady and the Priest: The Making of Modern Marriage in Medieval France*, trans. Barbara Bray. New York: Pantheon Books, 1983.

Dudbridge, Glen. *The Legend of Miao-shan*. London: Ithaca Press, 1978.

Duffy, Eamon. *The Stripping of the Altars: Traditional Religion in England c. 1400– c. 1580.* New Haven, CT: Yale University Press, 1992.

Dumeige, Gervais. *Richard de Saint-Victor et l'idée chrétienne de l'amour.* Paris: Presses universitaires de France, 1952.

Dutton-Stuckey, Marsha. "A Prodigal Writes Home: Aelred of Rievaulx' *De institutione inclusarum*." In E. Rozanne Elder, ed., *Heaven on Earth*. Kalamazoo, MI: Cistercian Publications, 1983, 35–42.

Duvernoy, Jean. *Le Catharisme: La religion des cathares.* Toulouse: Privat, 1976.

Edwards, Graham. "Purgatory: Birth or Evolution?" *Journal of Ecclesiastical History* 36 (1985): 634–46.

Edwards, John. "Religious Faith and Doubt in Late Medieval Spain: Soria circa 1450–1500." *Past & Present* 120 (1988): 3–25.

Elkins, Sharon. *Holy Women of Twelfth-Century England.* Chapel Hill: University of North Carolina Press, 1988.

Ellero, Giuseppe. "Postel e Venezia." In *Guillaume Postel, 1581–1981*, 23–28.

Elliott, Dyan. *Spiritual Marriage: Sexual Abstinence in Medieval Wedlock.* Princeton, NJ: Princeton University Press, 1993.

Elliott, John R., Jr. "The Sacrifice of Isaac as Comedy and Tragedy." In Jerome Taylor and Alan Nelson, eds., *Medieval English Drama*. Chicago: University of Chicago Press, 1972, 157–76.

Elm, Kaspar. "Die Stellung der Frau in Ordenwesen, Semireligiösentum und Häresie zur Zeit der heiligen Elisabeth." In *Sankt Elisabeth*, 7–28.

Epiney-Burgard, Georgette. "L'influence des béguines sur Ruusbroec." In Paul Mommaers and Norbert De Paepe, eds., *Jan van Ruusbroec*, 68–85.

Evdokimoff, Paul. *La Femme et le salut du monde: Étude d'anthropologie chrétienne sur les charismes de la femme.* Tournai: Casterman, 1958.

Fahy, Conor. "Three Early Renaissance Treatises on Women." *Italian Studies* 11 (1956): 30–55.

Fälschungen im Mittelalter, Internationaler Kongress der Monumenta Germaniae Historica, Munich, 1986, Teil V: *Fingierte Briefe, Frömmigkeit und Fälschung, Realienfälschungen*, MGH.SS Bd. 33, V. Hannover: Hahnsche Buchhandlung, 1988.

Farmer, Sharon. "Persuasive Voices: Clerical Images of Medieval Wives." *Speculum* 61 (1986): 517–43.

Finnegan, Mary Jeremy. *The Women of Helfta: Scholars and Mystics.* Athens: University of Georgia Press, 1991.

Fiorenza, Elisabeth Schüssler. *In Memory of Her: A Feminist Theological Reconstruction of Christian Origins.* New York: Crossroad, 1983.

Flanagan, Sabina. *Hildegard of Bingen, 1098–1179: A Visionary Life.* London: Routledge, 1989.

Fox, J. C. "Mary Abbess of Shaftesbury." *English Historical Review* 26 (1911): 317–26.

Fraioli, Deborah. "The Importance of Satire in Jerome's *Adversus Jovinianum* as an Argument Against the Authenticity of the *Historia calamitatum*." In *Fälschungen im Mittelalter*, Teil V, 167–200.

Freed, John. "Urban Development and the 'Cura Monialium' in Thirteenth-Century Germany." *Viator* 3 (1972): 311–27.

Garnier, Annette. "Autour de la mort: Temps de la dilation et Purgatoire dans les *Miracles de Notre Dame* de Gautier de Coinci." *Le Moyen Âge* 94 (1988): 183–202.

Gelpi, Donald. *The Divine Mother: A Trinitarian Theology of the Holy Spirit.* Lanham, MD: University Press of America, 1984.

Georgianna, Linda. "Any Corner of Heaven: Heloise's Critique of Monasticism." *Mediaeval Studies* 49 (1987): 221–53.

Gibson, Joan. "Could Christ have been born a woman? A medieval debate." *Journal of Feminist Studies in Religion* 8 (1992): 65–82.

Gilson, Étienne. *Héloïse et Abélard.* Paris: J. Vrin, 1938.

Ginzberg, Louis. *The Legends of the Jews*, trans. Henrietta Szold. Philadelphia: Jewish Publication Society of America, 1913.

Gold, Penny Schine. "Male/Female Cooperation: The Example of Fontevrault." In John Nichols and Lillian T. Shank, eds., *Distant Echoes*, 151–68.

———. "The Marriage of Mary and Joseph in the Twelfth-Century Ideology of Marriage." In Vern Bullough and James Brundage, eds., *Sexual Practices and the Medieval Church.* Buffalo: Prometheus Books, 1982, 102–17, 249–51.

Gravdal, Kathryn. *Ravishing Maidens: Writing Rape in Medieval French Literature and Law.* Philadelphia: University of Pennsylvania Press, 1991.

Guest, Tanis. *Some Aspects of Hadewijch's Poetic Form in the "Strofische Gedichten."* The Hague: Martinus Nijhoff, 1975.

Guillaume Postel, 1581–1981. Actes du Colloque International d'Avranches. Paris: Éditions de la Maisnie, 1985.

Gurevich, Aron. "Popular and Scholarly Medieval Cultural Traditions: Notes in the Margin of Jacques Le Goff's Book." *Journal of Medieval History* 9 (1983): 71–90.

Hackel, Alfred. *Die Trinität in der Kunst: Eine ikonographische Untersuchung.* Berlin: Reuther & Reichard, 1931.

Hale, Rosemary. *Imitatio Mariae: Motherhood Motifs in Late Medieval German Spirituality.* Diss. Harvard, 1992.

Hamburger, Jeffrey. "The Visual and the Visionary: The Image in Late Medieval Monastic Devotions." *Viator* 20 (1989): 161–82.

Häring, Nikolaus. "Abelard Yesterday and Today." In René Louis and Jean Jolivet, eds., *Pierre Abélard—Pierre le Vénérable*, 341–403.

Hartl, Eduard, ed. *Das Drama des Mittelalters.* Leipzig: P. Reclam, 1937.

Haverkamp, Alfred. "Tenxwind von Andernach und Hildegard von Bingen: Zwei 'Weltanschauungen' in der Mitte des 12. Jahrhunderts." In Lutz Fenske, Werner Rösener, and Thomas Zotz, eds., *Institutionen, Kultur und Gesellschaft im Mittelalter.* Sigmaringen: Jan Thorbecke Verlag, 1984, 515–48.

Henderson, Katherine and Barbara McManus. *Half Humankind: Contexts and Texts of the Controversy about Women in England, 1540–1640.* Urbana: University of Illinois Press, 1985.

Hendrix, G. "Les *Postillae* de Hugues de Saint-Cher et le traité *De doctrina cordis.*" *Recherches de théologie ancienne et médiévale* 47 (1980): 114–30.

Herlihy, David. "Medieval Children." In Bede Lackner and Kenneth Philp, eds., *Essays on Medieval Civilization.* Austin: University of Texas Press, 1978, 109–41.

———. *Medieval Households.* Cambridge, MA: Harvard University Press, 1985.

Hexter, Ralph. *Equivocal Oaths and Ordeals in Medieval Literature*. Cambridge, MA: Harvard University Press, 1975.

Hieatt, A. Kent. "Eve as Reason in a Tradition of Allegorical Interpretation of the Fall." *Journal of the Warburg and Courtauld Institutes* 43 (1980): 221–26.

Hirst, Desirée. *Hidden Riches: Traditional Symbolism from the Renaissance to Blake*. London: Eyre & Spottiswoode, 1964.

Hoffman, Richard. "Jephthah's Daughter and Chaucer's Virginia." *Chaucer Review* 2 (1967): 20–31.

Honemann, Volker. *Die Epistola ad fratres de Monte Dei des Wilhelm von Saint-Thierry*. Munich: Artemis Verlag, 1978.

Howes, Laura. "On the Birth of Margery Kempe's Last Child." *Modern Philology* 90 (1992): 220–25.

Huchet, Jean-Charles. "La Voix d'Héloïse." *Romance Notes* 25 (1985): 271–87.

Idel, Moshe. "The Magical and Neoplatonic Interpretations of the Kabbalah in the Renaissance." In Bernard Cooperman, ed., *Jewish Thought in the Sixteenth Century*. Cambridge, MA: Harvard University Press, 1983, 186–242.

Irigaray, Luce. "La Mystérique." In *Speculum of the Other Woman*, trans. Gillian Gill. Ithaca, NY: Cornell University Press, 1985, 191–202.

Jansen, Saskia Murk. *The Measure of Mystic Thought: A Study of Hadewijch's Mengeldichten*. Göppingen: Kummerle, 1991.

Johnson, Penelope. *Equal in Monastic Profession: Religious Women in Medieval France*. Chicago: University of Chicago Press, 1991.

Jolivet, Jean. "Abélard entre chien et loup." *Cahiers de civilisation médiévale* 20 (1977): 307–22.

Jordan, Constance. *Renaissance Feminism: Literary Texts and Political Models*. Ithaca, NY: Cornell University Press, 1990.

Kamuf, Peggy. *Fictions of Feminine Desire: Disclosures of Heloise*. Lincoln: University of Nebraska Press, 1982.

Kantorowicz, Ernst. "The Quinity of Winchester." In *Selected Studies*. Locust Valley, NY: J. J. Augustin, 1965, 100–120.

Karras, Ruth. "Holy Harlots: Prostitute Saints in Medieval Legend." *Journal of the History of Sexuality* 1 (1990): 3–32.

Kaufmann, Linda. *Discourses of Desire: Gender, Genre, and Epistolary Fictions*. Ithaca, NY: Cornell University Press, 1986.

Kazantzakis, Nikos. *Report to Greco*, trans. P. A. Bien. New York: Simon & Schuster, 1965.

Keiser, George. "The Progress of Purgatory: Visions of the Afterlife in Later Middle English Literature." In James Hogg, ed., *Zeit, Tod und Ewigkeit in der Renaissance Literatur*. Salzburg: Institut für Anglistik und Amerikanistik, 1987, III, 72–100.

Kellum, Barbara. "Infanticide in England in the Later Middle Ages." *History of Childhood Quarterly* 1 (1974): 367–88.

Kieckhefer, Richard. *Unquiet Souls: Fourteenth-Century Saints and Their Religious Milieu*. Chicago: University of Chicago Press, 1984.

Kierkegaard, Søren. *Fear and Trembling*, trans. Walter Lowrie. Princeton, NJ: Princeton University Press, 1941.

King, Karen, ed. *Images of the Feminine in Gnosticism*. Philadelphia: Fortress Press, 1988.

Klaniczay, Gábor. *The Uses of Supernatural Power: The Transformation of Popular Religion in Medieval and Early-Modern Europe*. Princeton, NJ: Princeton University Press, 1990.

Klapisch-Zuber, Christiane. "La 'Mère cruelle': Maternité, veuvage et dot dans la Florence des XIV^c–XV^c siècles." *Annales* 38 (1983): 1097–1109.

Kraemer, Ross. *Her Share of the Blessings: Women's Religions Among Pagans, Jews, and Christians in the Greco-Roman World*. New York: Oxford University Press, 1992.

———, ed. *Maenads, Martyrs, Matrons, Monastics: A Sourcebook on Women's Religions in the Greco-Roman World*. Philadelphia: Fortress Press, 1988.

Kretzenbacher, Leopold. *Versöhnung in Jenseits: Zur Widerspiegelung des Apokatastasis-Denkens in Glaube, Hochdichtung und Legende*. Munich: Verlag der Bayerischen Akademie der Wissenschaften, 1971.

———. "Zwei eigenwillige bayerische Dreifaltigkeits-Darstellungen." *Bayerisches Jahrbuch für Volkskunde* (1992): 129–40.

Kuntz, Marion. *Guillaume Postel, Prophet of the Restitution of All Things: His Life and Thought*. The Hague: Nijhoff, 1981.

Lambert, M. D. *Medieval Heresy: Popular Movements from the Gregorian Reform to the Reformation*, 2nd ed. Cambridge, MA: Blackwell, 1992.

Lauwers, Michel. "'Noli me tangere': Marie Madeleine, Marie d'Oignies et les pénitentes du XIII^c siècle." *Mélanges de l'École Française de Rome: Moyen Âge* 104 (1992): 209–68.

Lea, Henry Charles. *A History of the Inquisition of the Middle Ages*. New York: Russell & Russell, 1906.

Leclercq, Jean. "Modern Psychology and the Interpretation of Medieval Texts." *Speculum* 48 (1973): 476–90.

Le Goff, Jacques. *The Birth of Purgatory*, trans. Arthur Goldhammer. Chicago: University of Chicago Press, 1984.

Lerner, Robert. "Beguins." In Joseph Strayer, ed., *Dictionary of the Middle Ages*. New York: Scribner, 1983, II: 162–63.

———. *The Heresy of the Free Spirit in the Later Middle Ages*. Berkeley: University of California Press, 1972.

Leroquais, Victor. *Un Livre d'heures de Jean sans Peur, Duc de Bourgogne (1404–1419)*. Paris: G. Andrieux, 1939.

Lewis, Gertrud Jaron. *Bibliographie zur deutschen Frauenmystik des Mittelalters*. Berlin: E. Schmidt, 1989.

Louis, René and Jean Jolivet, eds. *Pierre Abélard—Pierre le Vénérable: Les Courants philosophiques, littéraires et artistiques en Occident au milieu du XIIe siècle*. Colloques internationaux du Centre nationale de la recherche scientifique, Abbaye du Cluny, 1972. Paris: Éditions du Centre nationale de la recherche scientifique, 1975.

Luscombe, D. E. "From Paris to the Paraclete: The Correspondence of Abelard and Heloise." *Proceedings of the British Academy* 74 (1988): 247–83.

———. "The *Letters* of Heloise and Abelard since 'Cluny 1972.'" In Rudolf Thomas, ed., *Petrus Abaelardus*, 19–39.

Malvern, Marjorie. *Venus in Sackcloth: The Magdalen's Origins and Metamorphoses.* Carbondale: Southern Illinois University Press, 1975.

Matter, E. Ann. *The Voice of My Beloved: The Song of Songs in Western Medieval Christianity.* Philadelphia: University of Pennsylvania Press, 1990.

MacDonald, Dennis. "The Role of Women in the Production of the Apocryphal Acts of the Apostles." *Iliff Review* 41 (1984): 21–38.

McGuire, Brian. *Friendship and Community: The Monastic Experience, 350–1250.* Kalamazoo, MI: Cistercian Publications, 1988.

———. "Purgatory, the Communion of Saints, and Medieval Change." *Viator* 20 (1989): 61–84.

McIlquham, Harriett. "Cornelius Agrippa: His Appreciation of Women." *Westminster Review* 154 (1900): 303–13.

McLaughlin, Eleanor. "Equality of Souls, Inequality of Sexes: Woman in Medieval Theology." In Rosemary Ruether, ed., *Religion and Sexism: Images of Woman in the Jewish and Christian Traditions.* New York: Simon & Schuster, 1974, 213–66.

McLaughlin, Mary. "Abelard as Autobiographer: The Motives and Meaning of His *Story of Calamities.*" *Speculum* 42 (1967): 463–88.

———. "Peter Abelard and the Dignity of Women: Twelfth Century 'Feminism' in Theory and Practice." In René Louis and Jean Jolivet, eds., *Pierre Abélard—Pierre le Vénérable,* 287–333.

———. "Survivors and Surrogates: Children and Parents from the Ninth to the Thirteenth Centuries." In Lloyd deMause, ed., *The History of Childhood,* 101–81.

Maclean, Ian. *The Renaissance Notion of Woman.* Cambridge: Cambridge University Press, 1980.

McLeod, Enid. *Héloïse: A Biography.* London: Chatto & Windus, 1938.

McLeod, Glenda. " 'Wholly Guilty, Wholly Innocent': Self-Definition in Héloïse's Letters to Abélard." In Karen Cherewatuk and Ulrike Wiethaus, eds., *Dear Sister,* 64–86.

McNamara, Jo Ann. "The Need to Give: Suffering and Female Sanctity in the Middle Ages." In Renate Blumenfeld-Kosinski and Timea Szell, eds., *Images of Sainthood in Medieval Europe,* 199–221.

———. *A New Song: Celibate Women in the First Three Christian Centuries.* New York: Haworth Press, 1983.

Milhaven, John Giles. *Hadewijch and Her Sisters: Other Ways of Loving and Knowing.* Albany, NY: SUNY Press, 1993.

Mirrer, Louise, ed. *Upon My Husband's Death: Widows in the Literature and Histories of Medieval Europe.* Ann Arbor: University of Michigan Press, 1992.

Moakley, Gertrude. *The Tarot Cards Painted by Bonifacio Bembo for the Visconti-Sforza Family: An Iconographic and Historical Study.* New York: New York Public Library, 1966.

Mohr, Rudolf. "Der Gedankenaustausch zwischen Heloisa und Abaelard über eine Modifizierung der *Regula Benedicti* für Frauen." *Regulae Benedicti Studia* 5 (1976): 307–33.

Moltmann-Wendel, Elisabeth. *A Land Flowing with Milk and Honey: Perspectives on Feminist Theology*, trans. John Bowden. New York: Crossroad, 1986.

Mommaers, Paul. "Bulletin d'histoire de la spiritualité: L'École néerlandaise." *Revue d'histoire de la spiritualité* 49 (1973): 465–92.

———. "Hadewijch: A Feminist in Conflict." *Louvain Studies* 13 (1988): 55–81.

Mommaers, Paul and Norbert De Paepe, eds. *Jan van Ruusbroec: The Sources, Content and Sequels of His Mysticism*. Leuven: Leuven University Press, 1984.

Monfrin, Jacques. "Le problème de l'authenticité de la correspondance d'Abélard et d'Héloïse." In René Louis and Jean Jolivet, eds., *Pierre Abélard—Pierre le Vénérable*, 409–24.

Müller, Daniela. "Les Béguines." *Heresis* 13–14 (1989): 351–89.

———. "Der Prozess gegen Prous Boneta: Begine, Ketzerin, Häresiarchin (1325)." In Norbert Höhl, ed., *Ius et historia: Festgabe für Rudolf Weigand*. Würzburg: Echter, 1989, 199–221.

Muraro, Luisa. *Guglielma e Maifreda: Storia di un'eresia femminista*. Milan: La Tartaruga, 1985.

Murray, Robert. *Symbols of Church and Kingdom: A Study in Early Syriac Tradition*. London: Cambridge University Press, 1975.

Nauert, Charles. *Agrippa and the Crisis of Renaissance Thought*. Urbana: University of Illinois Press, 1965.

Neumann, Hans. "Mechthild von Magdeburg und die mittelniederländische Frauenmystik." In *Medieval German Studies Presented to Frederick Norman*. London: Institute of Germanic Studies, 1965, 231–46.

Newman, Barbara. "Divine Power Made Perfect in Weakness: St. Hildegard on the Frail Sex." In John Nichols and Lillian T. Shank, eds., *Peaceweavers*, 103–22.

———. "Hildegard of Bingen and the 'Birth of Purgatory.'" *Mystics Quarterly* 19 (1993): 90–97.

———. "The Pilgrimage of Christ-Sophia." *Vox benedictina* 9 (1992): 8–37.

———. *Sister of Wisdom: St. Hildegard's Theology of the Feminine*. Berkeley: University of California Press, 1987.

———. "Some Mediaeval Theologians and the Sophia Tradition." *Downside Review* 108 (1990): 111–30.

Nichols, John and Lillian T. Shank, eds. *Medieval Religious Women*, vol. 1, *Distant Echoes*. Kalamazoo, MI: Cistercian Publications, 1984.

———. *Medieval Religious Women*, vol. 2, *Peaceweavers*. Kalamazoo, MI: Cistercian Publications, 1987.

Ohly, Friedrich. *Hohelied-Studien: Grundzüge einer Geschichte der Hoheliedauslegung des Abendlandes bis um 1200*. Wiesbaden: F. Steiner, 1958.

Orbe, Antonio. "La procesión del Espíritu Santo y el origen de Eva." *Gregorianum* 45 (1964): 103–18.

Owen, Alex. *The Darkened Room: Women, Power and Spiritualism in Late Victorian England*. Philadelphia: University of Pennsylvania Press, 1990.

Pagels, Elaine. *The Gnostic Gospels*. New York: Random House, 1979.

Paris, Ginette. *The Sacrament of Abortion*. Dallas: Spring Publications, 1992.

Partner, Nancy. "No Sex, No Gender." *Speculum* 68 (1993): 419–43.

———. "Reading *The Book of Margery Kempe*." *Exemplaria* 3 (1991): 29–66.

Pelikan, Jaroslav. *The Growth of Medieval Theology (600–1300)*. Chicago: University of Chicago Press, 1978.

Perkins, Pheme. *The Gnostic Dialogue: The Early Church and the Crisis of Gnosticism*. New York: Paulist, 1980.

Peters, Ursula. *Religiöse Erfahrung als literarisches Faktum: Zur Vorgeschichte und Genese frauenmystischer Texte des 13. und 14. Jahrhunderts*. Tübingen: Niemeyer, 1988.

Petroff, Elizabeth. *Body and Soul: Essays on Medieval Women and Mysticism*. New York: Oxford University Press, 1994.

———. *Consolation of the Blessed*. New York: Alta Gaia Society, 1979.

———. *Medieval Women's Visionary Literature*. Oxford: Oxford University Press, 1986.

Pickering, F. P. "Notes on Late Medieval German Tales in Praise of *docta ignorantia*." *Bulletin of the John Rylands Library* 24 (1940): 121–37.

Pinsky, Robert. "Jesus and Isolt." In *The Want Bone*. New York: Ecco Press, 1990, 32–40.

Plaskow, Judith and Carol Christ, eds. *Weaving the Visions: New Patterns in Feminist Spirituality*. San Francisco: Harper & Row, 1989.

Polc, Jaroslav. *Agnes von Böhmen, 1211–1282: Königstochter—Äbtissin—Heilige*. Munich: R. Oldenbourg, 1989.

Premoli, Orazio. *Storia dei Barnabiti nel Cinquecento*. Rome, 1913.

Prinz, Friedrich. *Böhmen im mittelalterlichen Europa*. Munich: C. H. Beck, 1984.

Réau, Louis. *Iconographie de l'art chrétien*. Paris: Presses universitaires de France, 1957.

Reeves, Marjorie. *The Influence of Prophecy in the Later Middle Ages: A Study in Joachimism*. Oxford: Clarendon, 1969.

Richards, Earl Jeffrey. " '*Seulette a part*'—The 'Little Woman on the Sidelines' Takes Up Her Pen: The Letters of Christine de Pizan." In Karen Cherewatuk and Ulrike Wiethaus, eds., *Dear Sister*, 139–70.

Robertson, D. W. Jr. *Abelard and Heloise*. New York: Dial Press, 1972.

———. *A Preface to Chaucer: Studies in Medieval Perspectives*. Princeton, NJ: Princeton University Press, 1962.

Ross, James. "The Middle-Class Child in Urban Italy, Fourteenth to Early Sixteenth Century." In Lloyd deMause, ed., *History of Childhood*, 183–228.

Ruether, Rosemary. "Misogynism and Virginal Feminism in the Fathers of the Church." In *Religion and Sexism: Images of Woman in the Jewish and Christian Traditions*. New York: Simon & Schuster, 1974, 150–83.

———. "Prophets and Humanists: Types of Religious Feminism in Stuart England." *Journal of Religion* 70 (1990): 1–18.

Ruh, Kurt, ed. *Abendländische Mystik im Mittelalter*. Stuttgart: J. B. Metzler, 1986.

———, ed. *Altdeutsche und altniederländische Mystik*. Darmstadt: Wissenschaftliche Buchgesellschaft, 1964.

———. "Beginenmystik: Hadewijch, Mechthild von Magdeburg, Marguerite Porete." *Zeitschrift für deutsches Altertum* 106 (1977): 265–77.

———. "Gottesliebe bei Hadewijch, Mechthild von Magdeburg und Marguerite Porete." In *Romanische Literaturbeziehungen im 19. und 20. Jahrhundert: Fest-*

schrift für Franz Rauhut, ed. Angel San Miguel, Richard Schwaderer, and Manfred Tietz. Tübingen: Narr, 1985, 243–54.

——. " 'Le miroir des simples âmes' der Marguerite Porete." In *Kleine Schriften*, II, ed. Volker Mertens. Berlin: De Gruyter, 1984, 212–36.

Russell, Letty, ed. *Feminist Interpretation of the Bible*. Philadelphia: Westminster, 1985.

Sankt Elisabeth: Fürstin, Dienerin, Heilige. Sigmaringen: Thorbecke, 1981.

Sargent, Michael. " 'Le Mirouer des simples âmes' and the English Mystical Tradition." In Kurt Ruh, ed., *Abendländische Mystik im Mittelalter*, 443–65.

Schiller, Gertrud. *Ikonographie der christlichen Kunst*. Gütersloh: G. Mohn, 1980.

Schmeidler, Bernhard. "Der Briefwechsel zwischen Abaelard und Heloise dennoch eine literarische Fiction Abaelards." *Revue bénédictine* 52 (1940): 85–95.

Schmidt, Margot. *"Minne dú gewaltige kellerin*: On the nature of *Minne* in Mechthild of Magdeburg's *Fliessendes Licht der Gottheit.*" *Vox benedictina* 4 (1987): 100–25.

Schmidt, Margot and Dieter Bauer, eds. *Grundfragen christlicher Mystik*. Stuttgart: Frommann-Holzboog, 1987.

Schottmann, Hans. "Autor und Hörer in der 'Strophischen Gedichten' Hadewijchs." *Zeitschrift für deutsches Altertum* 102 (1973): 20–37.

Schulenburg, Jane. "Sexism and the Celestial Gynaeceum—from 500 to 1200." *Journal of Medieval History* 4 (1978): 117–33.

——. "Strict Active Enclosure and its Effects on the Female Monastic Experience (500–1100)." In John Nichols and Lillian T. Shank, eds., *Distant Echoes*, 51–86.

Schulte, Aloys. *Der Adel und die deutsche Kirche im Mittelalter*, 3rd ed. Darmstadt: Hermann Gentner, 1958.

Schweitzer, Franz-Josef. *Der Freiheitsbegriff der deutschen Mystik: Seine Beziehung zur Ketzerei der "Brüder und Schwestern vom Freien Geist" mit besonderer Rücksicht auf den pseudo-eckartischen Traktat "Schwester Katrei."* Frankfurt: Peter Lang, 1981.

Screech, M. A. "The Illusion of Postel's Feminism." *Journal of the Warburg and Courtauld Institutes* 16 (1953): 162–70.

Secret, François. "Guillaume Postel et les courants prophétiques de la Renaissance." *Studi Francesi* 1 (1957): 375–95.

Shaffern, Robert. "Learned Discussion of Indulgences for the Dead in the Middle Ages." *Church History* 61 (1992): 367–81.

Shahar, Shulamith. *Childhood in the Middle Ages*. London: Routledge, 1990.

——. *The Fourth Estate: A History of Women in the Middle Ages*, trans. Chaya Galai. London: Methuen, 1983.

Shaw, Brent. "The Passion of Perpetua." *Past & Present* 139 (1993): 3–45.

Silvestre, Hubert. "Die Liebesgeschichte zwischen Abaelard und Heloise: der Anteil des Romans." In *Fälschungen im Mittelalter*, Teil V (1986): 121–65.

——. "Reflexions sur la thèse de J. F. Benton relative au dossier 'Abélard-Héloïse'." *Recherches de théologie ancienne et médiévale* 44 (1977): 211–16.

Simonnet, Jacques. "La mère du monde, miroir de la pensée de Guillaume Postel." In *Guillaume Postel, 1581–1981*, 17–21.

Sinanoglou, Leah. "The Christ Child as Sacrifice: A Medieval Tradition and the Corpus Christi Plays." *Speculum* 48 (1973): 491–509.

Smith, Jacqueline. "Robert of Arbrissel: *Procurator mulierum*." In Derek Baker, ed., *Medieval Women*, 175–84.

Soelle, Dorothee. *Suffering*, trans. Everett Kalin. Philadelphia: Fortress Press, 1975.

Southern, R. W. *Medieval Humanism*. Oxford: Blackwell, 1970.

Spaapen, Bernard. "Hadewijch et la 'Cinquième Vision.'" *Ons Geestelijk Erf* 46 (1972): 197–99.

Sticca, Sandro. *The Planctus Mariae in the Dramatic Tradition of the Middle Ages*, trans. Joseph Berrigan. Athens: University of Georgia Press, 1988.

Stiller, Nikki. *Eve's Orphans: Mothers and Daughters in Medieval English Literature*. Westport, CT: Greenwood Press, 1980.

Sullerot, Evelyne. *Women on Love: Eight Centuries of Feminine Writing*, trans. Helen Lane. Garden City, NY: Doubleday, 1979.

Surtz, Ronald. *The Guitar of God: Gender, Power, and Authority in the Visionary World of Mother Juana de la Cruz*. Philadelphia: University of Pennsylvania Press, 1990.

Sweetman, Robert. "Christine of Saint-Trond's Preaching Apostolate: Thomas of Cantimpré's Hagiographical Method Revisited." *Vox benedictina* 9 (1992): 67–97.

Thickstun, Margaret. "'This was a Woman that taught': Feminist Scriptural Exegesis in the Seventeenth Century." *Studies in Eighteenth-Century Culture* 21, ed. Patricia Craddock and Carla Hay. East Lansing, MI: Colleagues Press, 1991, 149–58.

Thiébaux, Marcelle, ed. and trans. *The Writings of Medieval Women*. New York: Garland, 1987.

Thomas, Rudolf, ed. *Petrus Abaelardus*. Trierer Theologische Studien, Bd. 38. Trier: Paulinus-Verlag, 1980.

Thompson, Sally. "The Problem of the Cistercian Nuns in the Twelfth and Early Thirteenth Centuries." In Derek Baker, ed., *Medieval Women*, 227–52.

Thune, Nils. *The Behmenists and the Philadelphians: A Contribution to the Study of English Mysticism in the Seventeenth and Eighteenth Centuries*. Uppsala: Almqvist & Wiksells, 1948.

Van Cranenburgh, H. "Hadewychs zwölfte Vision und neuntes strophisches Gedicht: Versuch einer Textdeutung." In Kurt Ruh, ed., *Altdeutsche und Altniederländische Mystik*, 152–74.

Van den Eynde, Damien. "Chronologie des écrits d'Abélard à Héloïse." *Antonianum* 37 (1962): 337–49.

Vekeman, H. W. J. "Die ontrouwe maectse so diep . . . Een nieuwe interpretatie van het vijfde Visioen van Hadewijch." *De Nieuwe Taalgids* 71 (1978): 385–409.

Verdeyen, Paul. "La procès d'inquisition contre Marguerite Porete et Guiard de Cressonessart." *Revue d'histoire ecclésiastique* 81 (1986): 47–94.

Verdier, Philippe. *Le Couronnement de la Vierge: Les origines et les premiers développements d'un thème iconographique*. Paris: J. Vrin, 1980.

Von Moos, Peter. *Mittelalterforschung und Ideologiekritik: Der Gelehrtenstreit um Heloise*. Munich: W. Fink, 1974.

————. "*Post festum*—Was kommt nach der Authentizitätsdebatte über die Briefe Abaelards und Heloises?" In Rudolf Thomas, ed., *Petrus Abaelardus*, 75–100.

————. "Le Silence d'Héloïse et les idéologies modernes." In René Louis and Jean Jolivet, eds., *Pierre Abélard—Pierre le Vénérable*, 425–68.

Wakefield, Walter and Austin Evans, eds. *Heresies of the High Middle Ages*. New York: Columbia University Press, 1969.

Warner, Marina. *Alone of All Her Sex: The Myth and the Cult of the Virgin Mary*. New York: Vintage Books, 1976.

Wathen, Ambrose. *Silence: The Meaning of Silence in the Rule of St. Benedict*. Washington: Catholic University of America Press, 1973.

Watson, Nicholas. "The Composition of Julian of Norwich's *Revelation of Love*." *Speculum* 68 (1993): 637–83.

Watson, Paul. "The Queen of Sheba in Christian Tradition." In James Pritchard, ed., *Solomon and Sheba*. New York: Praeger, 1974, 115–45.

Weber, Christin Lore. *WomanChrist: A New Vision of Feminist Spirituality*. San Francisco: Harper & Row, 1987.

Weinstein, Donald and Rudolph Bell. *Saints and Society: The Two Worlds of Western Christendom, 1000–1700*. Chicago: University of Chicago Press, 1982.

Wessley, Stephen. "The Thirteenth-Century Guglielmites: Salvation Through Women." In Derek Baker, ed., *Medieval Women*, 289–303.

Whatley, Gordon. "The Uses of Hagiography: The Legend of Pope Gregory and the Emperor Trajan in the Middle Ages." *Viator* 15 (1984): 25–63.

Wiercinski, Dorothea. *Minne: Herkunft und Anwendungsschichten eines Wortes*. Cologne: Böhlau, 1964.

Wiethaus, Ulrike, ed. *Maps of Flesh and Light: The Religious Experience of Medieval Women Mystics*. Syracuse, NY: Syracuse University Press, 1993.

————. "Sexuality, Gender, and the Body in Late Medieval Women's Spirituality." *Journal of Feminist Studies in Religion* 7 (1991): 35–52.

Willaert, Frank. "Hadewijch und ihr Kreis in den 'Visionen.'" In Kurt Ruh, ed., *Abendländische Mystik im Mittelalter*, 368–87.

Willard, Charity Cannon. *Christine de Pizan: Her Life and Works*. New York: Persea, 1984.

Williams, Charles. *All Hallows' Eve*. Grand Rapids, MI: Eerdmans, 1981.

————. *The Descent of the Dove: A Short History of the Holy Spirit in the Church*. London: Faber & Faber, 1939.

Wilner, Eleanor. *Sarah's Choice*. Chicago: University of Chicago Press, 1989.

Wilson, Katharina, ed. *Medieval Women Writers*. Athens: University of Georgia Press, 1984.

————. *Wykked Wyves and the Woes of Marriage: Misogamous Literature from Juvenal to Chaucer*. Albany, NY: SUNY Press, 1990.

Wilt, Judith. *Abortion, Choice, and Contemporary Fiction: The Armageddon of the Maternal Instinct*. Chicago: University of Chicago Press, 1990.

Wirth, Jean. "'Libertins' et 'Epicuriens': Aspects de l'irreligion au XVIe siècle." *Bibliothèque d'humanisme et renaissance* 39 (1977): 601–27.

Woodbridge, Linda. *Women and the English Renaissance: Literature and the Nature of Womankind, 1540–1620*. Urbana: University of Illinois Press, 1984.

Yates, Frances. *The Occult Philosophy in the Elizabethan Age*. London: Routledge & Kegan Paul, 1979.

Ziegler, Joanna. "Reality as Imitation: The Role of Religious Imagery Among the Beguines of the Low Countries." In Ulrike Wiethaus, ed., *Maps of Flesh and Light*, 112–26.

Zimmermann, Harald. *Das Papsttum im Mittelalter*. Stuttgart: Ulmer, 1981.

Zumthor, Paul, trans. *Abélard et Héloïse, Correspondance*. Paris: Union générale d'éditions, 1979.

Index

University of Pennsylvania Press
MIDDLE AGES SERIES
Edward Peters, General Editor

F. R. P. Akehurst, trans. *The* Coutumes de Beauvaisis *of Philippe de Beaumanoir.* 1992

Peter L. Allen. *The Art of Love: Amatory Fiction from Ovid to the* Romance of the Rose. 1992

David Anderson. *Before the Knight's Tale: Imitation of Classical Epic in Boccaccio's* Teseida. 1988

Benjamin Arnold. *Count and Bishop in Medieval Germany: A Study of Regional Power, 1100–1350.* 1991

Mark C. Bartusis. *The Late Byzantine Army: Arms and Society, 1204–1453.* 1992

J. M. W. Bean. *From Lord to Patron: Lordship in Late Medieval England.* 1990

Thomas N. Bisson, ed. *Cultures of Power: Lordship, Status, and Process in Twelfth-Century Europe.* 1995

Uta-Renate Blumenthal. *The Investiture Controversy: Church and Monarchy from the Ninth to the Twelfth Century.* 1988

Daniel Bornstein, trans. *Dino Compagni's* Chronicle *of Florence.* 1986

Maureen Boulton. *The Song in the Story: Lyric Insertions in French Narrative Fiction, 1200–1400.* 1993

Betsy Bowden. *Chaucer Aloud: The Varieties of Textual Interpretation.* 1987

Charles R. Bowlus. *Franks, Moravians, and Magyars: The Struggle for the Middle Danube, 788–907.* 1995

James William Brodman. *Ransoming Captives in Crusader Spain: The Order of Merced on the Christian-Islamic Frontier.* 1986

Kevin Brownlee and Sylvia Huot, eds. *Rethinking the* Romance of the Rose: *Text, Image, Reception.* 1992

Matilda Tomaryn Bruckner. *Shaping Romance: Interpretation, Truth, and Closure in Twelfth-Century French Fictions.* 1993

Otto Brunner (Howard Kaminsky and James Van Horn Melton, eds. and trans.). *Land and Lordship: Structures of Governance in Medieval Austria.* 1992

Robert I. Burns, S.J., ed. *Emperor of Culture: Alfonso X the Learned of Castile and His Thirteenth-Century Renaissance.* 1990

David Burr. *Olivi and Franciscan Poverty: The Origins of the* Usus Pauper *Controversy.* 1989

David Burr. *Olivi's Peaceable Kingdom: A Reading of the Apocalypse Commentary.* 1993

Thomas Cable. *The English Alliterative Tradition.* 1991

Anthony K. Cassell and Victoria Kirkham, eds. and trans. *Diana's Hunt/Caccia di Diana: Boccaccio's First Fiction.* 1991

John C. Cavadini. *The Last Christology of the West: Adoptionism in Spain and Gaul, 785–820.* 1993

Brigitte Cazelles. *The Lady as Saint: A Collection of French Hagiographic Romances of the Thirteenth Century.* 1991

Karen Cherewatuk and Ulrike Wiethaus, eds. *Dear Sister: Medieval Women and the Epistolary Genre.* 1993

Anne L. Clark. *Elisabeth of Schönau: A Twelfth-Century Visionary.* 1992

Willene B. Clark and Meradith T. McMunn, eds. *Beasts and Birds of the Middle Ages: The Bestiary and Its Legacy.* 1989

Richard C. Dales. *The Scientific Achievement of the Middle Ages.* 1973

Charles T. Davis. *Dante's Italy and Other Essays.* 1984

William J. Dohar. *The Black Death and Pastoral Leadership: The Diocese of Hereford in the Fourteenth Century.* 1994

Katherine Fischer Drew, trans. *The Burgundian Code.* 1972

Katherine Fischer Drew, trans. *The Laws of the Salian Franks.* 1991

Katherine Fischer Drew, trans. *The Lombard Laws.* 1973

Nancy Edwards. *The Archaeology of Early Medieval Ireland.* 1990

Richard K. Emmerson and Ronald B. Herzman. *The Apocalyptic Imagination in Medieval Literature.* 1992

Theodore Evergates. *Feudal Society in Medieval France: Documents from the County of Champagne.* 1993

Felipe Fernández-Armesto. *Before Columbus: Exploration and Colonization from the Mediterranean to the Atlantic, 1229–1492.* 1987

Jerold C. Frakes. *Brides and Doom: Gender, Property, and Power in Medieval Women's Epic.* 1994

R. D. Fulk. *A History of Old English Meter.* 1992

Patrick J. Geary. *Aristocracy in Provence: The Rhône Basin at the Dawn of the Carolingian Age.* 1985

Peter Heath. *Allegory and Philosophy in Avicenna (Ibn Sînâ), with a Translation of the Book of the Prophet Muḥammad's Ascent to Heaven.* 1992

J. N. Hillgarth, ed. *Christianity and Paganism, 350–750: The Conversion of Western Europe.* 1986

Richard C. Hoffmann. *Land, Liberties, and Lordship in a Late Medieval Countryside: Agrarian Structures and Change in the Duchy of Wrocław.* 1990

Robert Hollander. *Boccaccio's Last Fiction: Il Corbaccio.* 1988

John Y. B. Hood. *Aquinas and the Jews.* 1995

Edward B. Irving, Jr. *Rereading* Beowulf. 1989

Richard A. Jackson, ed. Ordines Coronationis Franciae: *Texts and Ordines for the Coronation of Frankish and French Kings and Queens in the Middle Ages, Vol. I.* 1995

C. Stephen Jaeger. *The Envy of Angels: Cathedral Schools and Social Ideals in Medieval Europe, 950–1200.* 1994

C. Stephen Jaeger. *The Origins of Courtliness: Civilizing Trends and the Formation of Courtly Ideals, 939–1210.* 1985

Donald J. Kagay, trans. *The Usatges of Barcelona: The Fundamental Law of Catalonia.* 1994

Richard Kay. *Dante's Christian Astrology*. 1994

Ellen E. Kittell. *From* Ad Hoc *to Routine: A Case Study in Medieval Bureaucracy*. 1991

Alan C. Kors and Edward Peters, eds. *Witchcraft in Europe, 1100–1700: A Documentary History*. 1972

Barbara M. Kreutz. *Before the Normans: Southern Italy in the Ninth and Tenth Centuries*. 1992

Michael P. Kuczynski. *Prophetic Song: The Psalms as Moral Discourse in Late Medieval England*. 1995

E. Ann Matter. *The Voice of My Beloved: The Song of Songs in Western Medieval Christianity*. 1990

A. J. Minnis. *Medieval Theory of Authorship*. 1988

Lawrence Nees. *A Tainted Mantle: Hercules and the Classical Tradition at the Carolingian Court*. 1991

Lynn H. Nelson, trans. *The Chronicle of San Juan de la Peña: A Fourteenth-Century Official History of the Crown of Aragon*. 1991

Barbara Newman. *From Virile Woman to WomanChrist: Studies in Medieval Religion and Literature*. 1995

Joseph F. O'Callaghan. *The Cortes of Castile-León, 1188–1350*. 1989

Joseph F. O'Callaghan. *The Learned King: The Reign of Alfonso X of Castile*. 1993

Odo of Tournai (Irven M. Resnick, trans.). *Two Theological Treatises*: On Original Sin *and* A Disputation with the Jew, Leo, Concerning the Advent of Christ, the Son of God. 1994

David M. Olster. *Roman Defeat, Christian Response, and the Literary Construction of the Jew*. 1994

William D. Paden, ed. *The Voice of the Trobairitz: Perspectives on the Women Troubadours*. 1989

Edward Peters. *The Magician, the Witch, and the Law*. 1982

Edward Peters, ed. *Christian Society and the Crusades, 1198–1229: Sources in Translation, including* The Capture of Damietta *by Oliver of Paderborn*. 1971

Edward Peters, ed. *The First Crusade: The* Chronicle of Fulcher of Chartres *and Other Source Materials*. 1971

Edward Peters, ed. *Heresy and Authority in Medieval Europe*. 1980

James M. Powell. *Albertanus of Brescia: The Pursuit of Happiness in the Early Thirteenth Century*. 1992

James M. Powell. *Anatomy of a Crusade, 1213–1221*. 1986

Susan A. Rabe. *Faith, Art, and Politics at Saint-Riquier: The Symbolic Vision of Angilbert*. 1994

Jean Renart (Patricia Terry and Nancy Vine Durling, trans.). *The Romance of the Rose or Guillaume de Dole*. 1993

Michael Resler, trans. Erec *by Hartmann von Aue*. 1987

Pierre Riché (Michael Idomir Allen, trans.). *The Carolingians: A Family Who Forged Europe*. 1993

Pierre Riché (Jo Ann McNamara, trans.). *Daily Life in the World of Charlemagne*. 1978

Jonathan Riley-Smith. *The First Crusade and the Idea of Crusading*. 1986

Joel T. Rosenthal. *Patriarchy and Families of Privilege in Fifteenth-Century England.* 1991

Teofilo F. Ruiz. *Crisis and Continuity: Land and Town in Late Medieval Castile.* 1994

James A. Rushing, Jr. *Images of Adventure: Ywain in the Visual Arts.* 1995

Steven D. Sargent, ed. and trans. *On the Threshold of Exact Science: Selected Writings of Anneliese Maier on Late Medieval Natural Philosophy.* 1982

Pamela Sheingorn, ed. and trans. *The Book of Sainte Foy's Miracles.* 1995

Robin Chapman Stacey. *The Road to Judgment: From Custom to Court in Medieval Ireland and Wales.* 1994

Sarah Stanbury. *Seeing the* Gawain-*Poet: Description and the Act of Perception.* 1992

Robert D. Stevick. *The Earliest Irish and English Bookart: Visual and Poetic Forms Before A.D. 1000.* 1994

Thomas C. Stillinger. *The Song of Troilus: Lyric Authority in the Medieval Book.* 1992

Susan Mosher Stuard. *A State of Deference: Ragusa/Dubrovnik in the Medieval Centuries.* 1992

Susan Mosher Stuard, ed. *Women in Medieval History and Historiography.* 1987

Susan Mosher Stuard, ed. *Women in Medieval Society.* 1976

Jonathan Sumption. *The Hundred Years War: Trial by Battle.* 1992

Ronald E. Surtz. *The Guitar of God: Gender, Power, and Authority in the Visionary World of Mother Juana de la Cruz (1481–1534).* 1990

William H. TeBrake. *A Plague of Insurrection: Popular Politics and Peasant Revolt in Flanders, 1323–1328.* 1993

Patricia Terry, trans. *Poems of the Elder Edda.* 1990

Hugh M. Thomas. *Vassals, Heiresses, Crusaders, and Thugs: The Gentry of Angevin Yorkshire, 1154–1216.* 1993

Ralph V. Turner. *Men Raised from the Dust: Administrative Service and Upward Mobility in Angevin England.* 1988

Mary F. Wack. *Lovesickness in the Middle Ages: The* Viaticum *and Its Commentaries.* 1990

Benedicta Ward. *Miracles and the Medieval Mind: Theory, Record, and Event, 1000–1215.* 1982

Suzanne Fonay Wemple. *Women in Frankish Society: Marriage and the Cloister, 500–900.* 1981

Kenneth Baxter Wolf. *Making History: The Normans and Their Historians in Eleventh-Century Italy.* 1995

Jan M. Ziolkowski. *Talking Animals: Medieval Latin Beast Poetry, 750–1150.* 1993

This book has been set in Linotron Galliard. Galliard was designed for Mergenthaler in 1978 by Matthew Carter. Galliard retains many of the features of a sixteenth-century typeface cut by Robert Granjon but has some modifications that give it a more contemporary look.

Printed on acid-free paper.